CHILDREN'S JUSTICE

How to Improve Legal Representation of Children in the Child Welfare System

DONALD N. DUQUETTE

WITH BRITANY ORLEBEKE, ANDREW ZINN, ROBBIN POTT,
ADA SKYLES, AND XIAOMENG ZHOU

Cover design by Amanda Fry/ABA Design

The materials contained herein represent the opinions of the authors and/or the editors, and should not be construed to be the views or opinions of the law firms, companies or law schools with whom such persons are in partnership with, associated with, or employed by, nor of the American Bar Association unless adopted pursuant to the bylaws of the Association.

Nothing contained in this book is to be considered as the rendering of legal advice for specific cases, and readers are responsible for obtaining such advice from their own legal counsel. This book is intended for educational and informational purposes only.

© 2016 American Bar Association. All rights reserved.

This product was created by the National Quality Improvement Center on the Representation of Children in the Child Welfare System, Cooperative Agreement No. 90CO1047, funded by the Children's Bureau, Administration for Children and Families, U.S. Department of Health and Human Services. The views expressed in this document do not necessarily reflect the position of the Children's Bureau.

The American Bar Association holds the following licenses to the Work in any and all media or form of communication whether now existing or hereafter developed: (1) an exclusive license of first publication of the Work worldwide as part of the Publication; (2) a non-exclusive worldwide license to reproduce, distribute, sell, display, and license the Work, or any part thereof, as published in the Publication, alone or in conjunction with other materials; (3) a non-exclusive worldwide license to use the Work, or any part thereof, in any other publication produced by the ABA (with appropriate attribution); (4) a non-exclusive worldwide license to use the Work to promote and publicize the ABA or its publications; and (5) a non-exclusive license to use Author's name, likeness and biography in connection with the advertising, publicity and promotion of the Work.

Printed in the United States of America

20 19 18 17 16   5 4 3 2 1

ISBN 978-1-63425-756-5
e-ISBN 978-1-63425-757-2

Library of Congress Cataloging-in-Publication Data
Names: Duquette, Donald N., author.
Title: Children's justice : how to improve legal representation of children in the child welfare system / Donald N. Duquette ; With Britany Orlebeke, Andrew Zinn, Robbin Pott, Ada Skyles, and Xiaomeng Zhou.
Description: Chicago : American Bar Association, 2016. | Includes index.
Identifiers: LCCN 2016049814 (print) | LCCN 2016050130 (ebook) | ISBN 9781634257565 (pbk. : alk. paper) | ISBN 9781634257572 ( )
Subjects: LCSH: Children—Legal status, laws, etc.—United States. | Legal assistance to children—United States.
Classification: LCC KF3735 .D87 2016 (print) | LCC KF3735 (ebook) | DDC 362.71/6—dc23
LC record available at https://lccn.loc.gov/2016049814

Discounts are available for books ordered in bulk. Special consideration is given to state bars, CLE programs, and other bar-related organizations. Inquire at Book Publishing, ABA Publishing, American Bar Association, 321 N. Clark Street, Chicago, Illinois 60654-7598.

www.ShopABA.org

Lawyers, I suppose, were children once.
—Charles Lamb

In recognition of Harper Lee (1926–2016) who chose this quote as the epigraph for *To Kill a Mockingbird*, a book that has inspired many a child to become a lawyer.

To the dedicated lawyers who work day in and day out representing children, parents, and child welfare agencies in America's still-inadequate child protection system. Struggle on!

CONTENTS

Introduction vii

Chapter 1: Challenge: Improve Child Representation
in America. 1

Chapter 2: Evolution of Child Representation. 7

Chapter 3: National Needs Assessment. 35

Chapter 4: Emerging Consensus and the QIC Best
Practice Model. 49

Chapter 5: Six Core Skills and the QIC Best Practice Training 65

Chapter 6: What the Lawyers Say About Implementing
the Six Core Skills 95

Chapter 7: Sample Selection and Research Methods 109
Britany Orlebeke, Andrew Zinn, Xiaomeng Zhou, Ada Skyles

Chapter 8: Profile of Lawyers Representing Children 123
Britany Orlebeke, Andrew Zinn

Chapter 9: Lawyer Activities and Their Impact. 145
Andrew Zinn and Britany Orlebeke

Chapter 10: Findings of the Evaluation of the QIC-ChildRep Best
Practices Model Training for Attorneys 163
Britany Orlebeke, Xiaomeng Zhou, Ada Skyles and Andrew Zinn

Chapter 11: Reflections on QIC Empirical Findings 179

Chapter 12: The Flint MDT Study: A Description and Evaluation of a Multidisciplinary Team Representing Children in Child Welfare Cases 189
Robbin Pott

Chapter 13: How to Improve Legal Representation of Children in America's Child Welfare System 213

Acknowledgments 229

Appendix A: QIC Best Practice Model of Child Representation in the Child Welfare System 235

Appendix B: 1996 American Bar Association Standards of Practice for Lawyers Who Represent Children in Abuse and Neglect Cases 243

Appendix C: 2011 ABA Model Act Governing Representation of Children in Abuse, Neglect and Dependency Proceedings 269

Index 293

INTRODUCTION

The U.S. Children's Bureau says one of the barriers to successful outcomes for children who come to the attention of the court in child welfare cases is a *lack of a trained and effective representatives*; someone to advocate for timeliness in agency and court handling of the child's case. Despite a widespread conviction that children ought to be independently represented in child abuse and neglect court proceedings, a national consensus has eluded us as to:

- *who* should represent the child,
- *what* should be the duties of that advocate, and
- *how* should effective child advocacy be organized and delivered.

Assessments of America's child welfare system regularly identify inadequate representation of children as a chief obstacle to achieving a well-functioning child welfare system. .

Since 1974 Federal law has required states to appoint a representative for the child in all child protection court proceedings. Legal scholars have written and debated about the role of the child advocate for several decades. National advocacy groups have pushed to improve child representation. There is even a national membership organization of mostly lawyers devoted to the professionalization of this child advocate role—the National Association of Counsel for Children. There are an estimated 50,000 to 75,000 lawyers engaged in child welfare legal cases in the U.S. Yet a consensus as to *who*, *what* and *how*, has eluded us—until now.

The central argument of this book is that using the National Quality Improvement Center on the Representation of Children in the Child Welfare System (QIC-ChildRep) Best Practice Model of Child Representation improves lawyers' approach to representing children and results in measurable improvements in case outcomes for some children.

This book discusses a challenge put forth by the U.S. Children's Bureau and duly accepted by the Child Advocacy Law Clinic at the University of Michigan Law School. In October 2009, the **U.S. Children's Bureau** named the **University of Michigan Law School** the National Quality Improvement Center on the Representation of Children in the Child Welfare System (QIC-ChildRep). The QIC-ChildRep was charged with gathering, developing and communicating knowledge on child representation and also with promoting consensus on the role of the child's legal representative. The Children's Bureau charged the QIC-ChildRep with improving the quality and quantity of competent representation for children and youth in child welfare cases to help the States and Tribes achieve the best safety, permanency and well-being outcomes for them.

Legal representation of a child in child protection and foster care cases is a unique role in American jurisprudence and has lacked clear definition. The close interface between the social services agencies and the court, the mix of fundamental constitutional rights and the extremely complex intersecting problems of poverty, social service delivery, and family dynamics has no parallel among American institutions or systems. The unusual nature of child welfare in the panoply of American institutions has significant implications for the child's legal advocate. It is no wonder that the struggle for clear role definition has been so challenging.

In its first phase (2010) the QIC-ChildRep conducted a nation-wide needs assessment of the condition of child representation in the United States. Information on academic literature, empirical research, policy proscriptions, and actual daily practice was integrated from many sources. We examined state laws, journal articles, government and foundation issued reports, annual reports submitted by States, and conducted structured in-person and phone discussions with a wide range of policy makers and practitioners. The national needs assessment synthesized the current state of academic discussion, federal and state laws, law in practice and intense activism and reform efforts by the child advocacy community.

This synthesis led to a QIC Best Practice Model of Child Representation that reflects an emerging national consensus on nearly all aspects of the role. The QIC Best Practice Model is based on the 1996 American Bar Association Standards of Practice for Lawyers Who Represent Children in Abuse and Neglect Cases but updated by the current thinking about how best to represent children in the child welfare system. The QIC Best Practice Model represents the general agreement by practitioners, academics, and child welfare policy makers across the country as to what the role and duties of the child's legal representative ought to be. The QIC Best Practice Model innovation is carefully extracted from decades of scholarship, experience and national debate. It rests solidly on the shoulders of many others wrestling with these same issues.

But what will happen if lawyers practice according to this updated Best Practice Model? Will it make any difference to the children and their families facing the problematic American child welfare system? Effectiveness in the field is the real test.

In fall of 2010 the QIC-ChildRep and its independent evaluator Chapin Hall at the University of Chicago recommended a random assignment research design to the Children's Bureau. It would test the hypothesis that attorneys practicing according to the QIC Best Practice Model would change their approach to cases—and consequently improve safety, permanency and well-being outcomes for children involved with the child

INTRODUCTION

welfare system, relative to attorneys whose practice was not influenced by the model. The goal was to implement an intervention that, if successful, could be replicated in other jurisdictions around the country. The U.S. Children's Bureau agreed to this ambitious research proposal.

QIC-ChildRep solicited state partners for the research, which resulted in collaborations with Georgia and Washington State. Attorneys in both states who represented children in child welfare cases were randomly assigned to either a QIC treatment group or a control group of lawyers. The QIC lawyers were given two days of training in the QIC Best Practice Model and received regular follow up through coaching and pod meetings meant to reinforce the principles of the Best Practice Model. The training was organized around Six Core Skills intended to capture the essence of the QIC Best Practice Model. Over three years Chapin Hall gathered data from multiple sources and we now have an unprecedented data set covering 250 lawyers representing about 4,500 children. Chapin Hall's evaluation shows that QIC lawyers changed their behavior, that is, they changed their approach in the direction sought by the intervention. And their change in behavior resulted in measurable improvement in case outcomes for some children.

This book also brings together new knowledge about the *who*, *what* and *how* of child representation using information collected as part of the evaluation. Legal representation of children has not been carefully studied and there are many outstanding questions looking for some empirical light. As to *who* should represent the child, this book contains a profile of the characteristics of lawyers representing children. As to *how* children are represented, we provide a profile of the child advocates and how they are organized and discuss implications for developing and sustaining a state's child representation workforce. As to *who* should represent the child, we provide empirical evidence that multidisciplinary team (MDT) representation of children, by a lawyer and a social worker, significantly improves case outcomes and the experience of children facing foster care. The Flint MDT study found that children represented by the MDT had fewer removals after the intervention was assigned, fewer adjudications of jurisdiction, and fewer petitions to terminate the rights of parents. When children were removed, they were more likely to be placed with relatives and less likely to be placed in stranger foster care. Despite the challenges of merging two different professions with quite different cultures, children benefitted from the collaboration.

As to *what duties* the child advocate should embrace, the chapter on attorney activity uses data collected for the evaluation to show that different lawyers use their time differently; they engage in and prioritize different tasks in their representation of children. Among other things, attorney effort is correlated with a personal belief that their role as children's lawyers is important.

Finally, the book offers a vision for the future of child representation in America based on what we have learned through this QIC experience. There are implications for the statutory structure of child welfare proceedings, the role of the child's lawyer, how legal services for children should be organized and delivered, the benefits of multidisciplinary representation of children, and how lawyers for children can best be recruited, trained and sustained in doing this important work.

This is the QIC-ChildRep story. All of us associated with this long but exciting project hope that our experiences and these findings will enhance the way child welfare cases are handled. Ultimately we hope to realize an efficient—and just and fair—experience for children and their families requiring the protection and rehabilitation of the child welfare system. May we realize *Children's Justice*! On we go!

CHAPTER 1

U.S. Children's Bureau Challenge: Improve Child Representation in America

Abstract
This chapter reviews the legal representation of the child in the United States child welfare system, including:

- The central importance of an effective legal advocate for the child
- Lack of effective national standards to guide child representation
- Insufficient number of attorneys trained in child welfare law
- Inadequate compensation for attorneys in dependency cases

To address these weaknesses, the U.S. Children's Bureau launched QIC-ChildRep: "to gather, develop and communicate knowledge on child representation, promote consensus on the role of the child's legal representative, and provide empirically-based analysis of how legal representation for the child might best be delivered."

1.1 The Problem to Be Addressed
In America's child welfare system, when a child alleged to be abused or neglected is brought before a court for protective proceedings, State and Federal law generally provide that the child is entitled to an independent representative to safeguard their interests. The child's representative may be a lawyer or a lay volunteer or both. A large number of American children are affected by these child protection proceedings. The U.S. Children's Bureau estimates that there are more than 400,000 children in foster

care at any given time[1]. There are approximately 50,000 lawyers involved in these cases, serving as judges and as counsel for the children, parents and state agencies.

The modern era of legal representation of children in child welfare cases began in 1974 with the Federal Child Abuse Prevention and Treatment Act (CAPTA).[2] In CAPTA, Congress attempted the first comprehensive legislation on child abuse and neglect. It is the touchstone and source point for the evolution of representation of children by lawyers and nonlawyer guardians ad litem alike. It required states to provide a guardian ad litem for children in child protection court proceedings, but did not describe qualifications, training, or responsibilities of the representative. Congress has regularly reauthorized CAPTA with various amendments. The 2003 amendments included as a purpose: "to ensure higher quality representation and to bar appointment of untrained or poorly trained court-appointed representatives for children."[3] CAPTA now requires appointment of "a guardian ad litem, who has received training appropriate to the role, and who may be an attorney or a court appointed special advocate who has received training appropriate to that role (or both), "to obtain first-hand a clear understanding of the situation and needs of the child, and . . . to make recommendations to the court concerning the best interests of the child."[4] Congress reauthorized CAPTA again in 2010.[5]

CAPTA began the modern development of legal representation of children, but left many questions unresolved. Evaluations of America's child welfare system consistently register disappointment in the quality of representation of children.[6] The U.S. Children's Bureau highlights the importance of the child's legal advocate:

> A key component of court processes for handling child abuse and neglect cases is the appointment of quality legal representation. The American legal system is based on the premise that parties have a due process right to be heard and that

---

1. U.S. DEP'T OF HEALTH AND HUMAN SERVS., ADMIN. FOR CHILDREN AND FAMILIES, ADMIN. ON CHILDREN, YOUTH, AND FAMILIES, CHILDREN'S BUREAU, THE AFCARS REPORT (No. 22), (2014).

2. Child Abuse Prevention and Treatment Act, Pub. L. No. 93-247 (1974) (codified as amended in scattered sections of 42 U.S.C.). The complete text of U.S. Code title 42, chapter 67 is available at www4.law.cornell.edu/uscode/42/ch67.html. *See also* CHILD WELFARE INFORMATION GATEWAY, ABOUT CAPTA: A LEGISLATIVE HISTORY (2011), http://www.childwelfare.gov/pubs/factsheets/about.cfm; JEAN KOH PETERS, REPRESENTING CHILDREN IN CHILD PROTECTIVE PROCEEDINGS: ETHICAL AND PRACTICAL DIMENSIONS § 2-A (3d ed. 2007) M. Carmela Welte , *Gal Training Mandated in CAPTA: HHS Issue Guidelines, National CASA Volunteer Curriculum Cited as Model for Volunteer Training*, July 2004.

3. *Id.*

4. 42 U.S.C. § 5106a(b)(2)(A)(xiii) (2015).

5. For additional information on the history of federal child-welfare statutes, see Howard Davidson, *Federal Law and State Intervention When Parents Fail: Has National Guidance of Our Child Welfare System Been Successful?* 42 FAM. L.Q. 481, 485–90 (2008).

6. SHIRLEY A. DOBBIN ET.AL, NAT'L COUNCIL OF JUVENILE AND FAMILY COURT JUDGES, CHILD ABUSE AND NEGLECT CASES: REPRESENTATION AS A CRITICAL COMPONENT OF EFFECTIVE PRACTICE (1998); PEW COMMISSION ON CHILDREN IN FOSTER CARE, FOSTERING THE FUTURE: SAFETY, PERMANENCE AND WELL-BEING FOR CHILDREN IN FOSTER CARE (2004).

competing independent advocacy produces just results in each case. Competent representation is important for the agency and the parents in child welfare cases, but *it is crucial for the child*, as a court reviews agency decisions about the family and the need for removal, the suitability of the child's temporary placement, and the permanency decision that will result in either reunification or adoption. Numerous studies and reports have pointed out the importance of competent representation of children so that judges can make informed decisions about their future.[7] (Emphasis added.)

Children's Bureau goes on to say that although CAPTA mandates a trained guardian ad litem for a child "... it is clear that practice and policy in the States have not kept pace."[8] The American Bar Association adopted Standards of Practice for Lawyers Representing Children[9] but the ABA Standards are merely advisory and have no legal authority in individual states.

In spite of the enactment of State laws mandating representation for children and dissemination of these national standards, funding for GALs has been inconsistent and inadequate, and the quality of representation of children in dependency court remains poor in many cases.[10]

There is an extraordinary range in the quality of counsel for children, from a high degree of dedication and professionalism to inactivity and incompetence. The PEW Commission on Children in Foster Care found that "the availability and competence of legal representation for children and their parents in dependency proceedings is wildly inconsistent across the country, for many reasons."[11] The Commission called for an informed and effective voice for children of all ages and capabilities in court through representation by better-trained attorneys and volunteer advocates.[12]

The Federal Court Improvement Program (CIP) requires State courts to conduct assessments of the state's effectiveness in carrying out the Federal laws related to dependency court proceedings, including legal representation.[13] But despite some improvements in child representation, many barriers remain. For example:

---

7. Department of Health and Human s Services, ACYF Funding Opportunity #HHS-2009-ACF-ACYF-CO-0077 4, National Quality Improvement Center on the Representation of Children in the Child Welfare System, 2 (April 2009), may be found in the internet archives at http://www.acf.hhs.gov/grants/open/HHS-2009-ACF-ACYF-CO-0077.html. [Hereinafter *ACYF Funding Announcement*]

8. *Id.* at 3.

9. A.B.A, STANDARDS FOR LAWYERS WHO REPRESENT CHILDREN IN ABUSE AND NEGLECT CASES (1996). [Hereinafter *1996 ABA Standards*]

10. *ACYF Funding Announcement, supra* note 7, at 3.

11. *Id.*

12. PEW COMMISSION ON CHILDREN IN FOSTER CARE, *supra* note 6.

13. Social Security Act, 42 U.S.C. 629h (2015).

- Very commonly the States that report on training, experience, and standards for attorneys are reporting a lack of or inconsistent training, lack of experience, and confusion regarding standards.
- Several reassessments expressly note that attorneys who represent parents and children are often quite inexperienced.
- States report that even enacting standards of practice for the representation of parents or children is not a guarantee of adequate representation.

* * *

- When the reassessments deal with the amount and timing of attorney-client contact, the resulting conclusions nearly always emphasize the need for more and earlier contact.
- Most reassessments do not address caseloads for attorneys but those that do typically report higher than desirable caseloads for GALs.
- Attorney compensation is addressed by less than a third of the reassessments, but those that address the issue were uniform in their conclusion that compensation levels, especially for defense and children's attorneys, are too low. These reassessments note that poor compensation complicates the recruitment and retention of skilled, committed attorneys.[14]

The Child and Family Service Reviews (CFSR)[15] support the conclusions about the poor quality of child representation in dependency courts. In some States and localities there are an insufficient number of attorneys trained in child welfare, which results in delays in adoption and other forms of permanency. CSFR stakeholders report that attorney representation of children is not guaranteed in all courts, particularly in some rural areas, leading to inconsistent child representation across these states.[16]

Among the positive developments in the field, the Children's Bureau identified the recent movement toward consensus on a national model of best practices for child welfare attorneys based on Federal law and national standards.[17] An important step in

---

14. Evaluation of the CIPs conducted by Planning and Learning Technologies analyzing state assessments of child representation, *ACYF Funding Announcement, supra* note 7, at 4.

15. The Children's Bureau conducts the Child and Family Service Reviews (CFSRs), which are periodic reviews of state child welfare systems, to achieve three goals: 1) Ensure conformity with federal child welfare requirements; 2) Determine what is actually happening to children and families as they are engaged in child welfare services: and 3) Assist states in helping children and families achieve positive outcomes. After a CFSR is completed, states develop a Program Improvement Plan (PIP) to address areas in their child welfare services that need improvement. *Child & Family Services Reviews (CFSR)*, CHILD'S BUREAU, http://www.acf.hhs.gov/programs/cb/monitoring/child-family-services-reviews (last visited Apr. 4, 2016).

16. *ACYF Funding Announcement, supra* note 7, at 4.

17. For a framing of the national model of best practice, see generally CHILD WELFARE LAW AND PRACTICE: REPRESENTING CHILDREN, PARENTS AND STATE AGENCIES IN ABUSE, NEGLECT AND

improving child welfare lawyer practice was the definition and creation of a new legal specialty in child welfare law, recognized by the American Bar Association, which accredited the National Association of Counsel for Children to certify lawyers as "child welfare law specialists" once they met rigorous experience and qualification standards, including passing a national certifying examination.[18]

Children's Bureau addressed the weaknesses in child representation by establishing a National Quality Improvement Center on Child Representation in the Child Welfare System at the University of Michigan Law School. (QIC-ChildRep) The project is completed and this is our report.

1.2 Child Representation—A Unique Legal Role

The legal representative of the child in the child welfare field is unique in American jurisprudence. The close interface between social services agencies and the court has few parallels among American institutions or systems. Fundamental constitutional rights of both parents and children are implicated so that any non-voluntary interference with the parent-child relationship requires court review. If the court enters an order suspending the parental rights and interfering with the constitutionally protected parent-child relationship, the court itself becomes the ultimate monitor of the government action and thus the *de-facto* supervisor of the agencies providing services to the family. There is a strong governmental interest in protecting children and enhancing the welfare of the parents and the family.[19]

When the court enters orders to protect a child in the home or remove a child from the custody of a parent, the interference with parental rights is justified in part because of the rehabilitative benefit received by the parent and child.[20] State and federal law put the family court in a position of reviewing and authorizing the interference with personal liberty imposed by the child's removal and the rehabilitative services required of the child and family. The court is the gatekeeper for the American foster care system. Except in the most serious emergencies, no child enters foster care or remains in foster care without an authorization by a court.

From the perspective of delivering social services, having a court be the ultimate supervisor and authority in delivering executive branch child welfare services is a most unique arrangement. The working parts of the system, including the public agencies,

---

DEPENDENCY CASES (Donald N. Duquette, Ann M. Haralambie, & Vivek Sankaran eds., Bradford 3d ed. 2016).

18. NACC Certification is available to attorneys serving in the role of Child's Attorney, Parent's Attorney, or Agency Attorney. There are about 600 NACC Certified Child Welfare Law Specialists located in 43 jurisdictions. *NACC Child Welfare Law Certification*, Nat'l Ass'n of Counsel for Children, http://www.naccchildlaw.org/?page=Certification (last visited June 27, 2016).

19. Prince v. Massachusetts, 321 U.S. 158 (1944).

20. Youngberg v. Romeo, 457 U.S. 307 (1982).

private child caring agencies and contract service providers—all supervised or monitored by the court—create an extremely complex social service delivery system. Moreover, this "system" is charged with addressing and resolving the extremely complicated intersecting problems of family dynamics and dysfunction, poverty, and social agency bureaucracy.

From the legal perspective, child welfare is similarly unusual. With the exception of private child custody cases and certain equitable remedies, a legal dispute is generally presented to a court, a resolution is reached, and the matter is dismissed. Generally a court does not retain ongoing authority and detailed supervision of a matter. Even in a mental health civil commitment case the court tends to grant an order of hospitalization or guardianship, but delegates the administrative details to the hospital or guardian. In child welfare, however, there is very close scrutiny of the case plan and its implementation. In child welfare the court not only adjudicates as to whether there is a legal basis to suspend parental rights, but also closely monitors the specific details surrounding delivery of rehabilitative services to the family.

The unusual nature of child welfare in the panoply of American institutions has significant implications for the child's legal advocate. Typically, a child who is the subject of a large but well-meaning bureaucracy has a parent to look out for his or her interests. Any person who has ever had a child in the hospital or with special needs in a school system knows that the bureaucracies and the individuals involved may be well meaning, but they can also be clumsy and, despite the best intentions, occasionally fail to provide the needed services. Without an advocate the child can easily get lost in the shuffle. The child welfare system is no different, except that, by definition, the child's parent is compromised in their ability to look out for his or her needs and interests. The parent is accused of failing to meet the child's needs. Under these circumstances an additional advocate for the child's rights and interests is required.

The legal representative of the child ideally would be expert in the law and the workings of the court system—but would also be knowledgeable in the assessment of parental capacities, risks faced by the child, and the social and emotional needs of a child. The child advocate must understand the importance of identifying the appropriate services and the delicacy of proper pacing in the delivery of those services. The child advocate carries an enormous responsibility, unique in American law. It is no surprise that the evolution of this singular role is taking some time.

1.3 QIC-ChildRep Is Launched

In this context, the Children's Bureau launched the QIC-ChildRep: "to gather, develop and communicate knowledge on child representation, promote consensus on the role of the child's legal representative, and provide empirically-based analysis of how legal representation for the child might best be delivered. Our first task was to determine the current state of knowledge and practice regarding child representation in dependency cases? Where is the state of play today? How did we get here? What is a way forward?

CHAPTER 2

Evolution of Child Representation*

Abstract
This chapter summarizes the academic and policy discussions regarding legal representation of the child in child welfare cases since CAPTA was first enacted in 1974.

2.1   In the Beginning

The creation of the juvenile court and child protection court jurisdiction is an extension of the nineteenth century Progressive Era reform movement, which in turn grew out of the nation's poor laws and policies.[1] Representation of children in child welfare cases developed from the practice of appointing a next friend or guardian ad litem (GAL) for a child who is suing or being sued, in order to protect the child's legal rights. Although the responsibilities of the GAL in child protection are considerably different from what they are for the GAL in civil litigation, this was the term assigned to the child's legal representative.[2]

---

*Part of this chapter is adapted from Duquette and Darwall, *Child Representation in America: Progress Report from the National Quality Improvement Center*, 46 FAM.L.Q. 89 (Spring 2012). Thanks to Julian Darwall for his careful research and synthesis.

1. Marvin Ventrell, *The History of Child Welfare Law, in* CHILD WELFARE LAW AND PRACTICE, (Duquette et al, eds., Bradford Publishing 2016).

2. Brian Fraser, *Independent Representation for the Abused and Neglected Child: The Guardian Ad Litem*, 13 CAL. W. L. REV. 16, 28 (1977).

Children alleged to be abused or neglected have received legal representation for a relatively short time. Before the 1970s courts only occasionally appointed attorneys to represent children. Even today, despite federal and state laws requiring independent representation, there are huge gaps in the appointment of a legal representative of the child. Unlike delinquency law, which mandates independent legal counsel of juveniles accused of a crime under the landmark U.S. Supreme Court case, *In re Gault* (387 U.S. 1 (1967), there is not yet a similar federal or constitutional mandate in child welfare cases.

Federal authority for independent representation of the child comes from the Child Abuse Prevention and Treatment Act (CAPTA). As a condition of receiving Federal child abuse-related funds, CAPTA requires a state to appoint a guardian ad litem (GAL) for a child in every case involving an abused or neglect child that results in a judicial proceeding. CAPTA permits the GAL to be an attorney or a lay advocate or both. It also requires the GAL to obtain, first hand, a clear understanding of the situation and needs of the child and make recommendations to the court concerning the best interests of the child. The GAL is to have appropriate training in the field.[3]

Even prior to the passage of CAPTA in 1974 the GAL, although generally an attorney, was sometimes a non-attorney and sometimes a volunteer.[4] CAPTA also allows for a non-lawyer representative for the child who may be paired with an attorney or serve independently, doing separate investigations and making separate recommendations to the court. Beginning in 1982 the National Court Appointed Special Advocate Association (CASA) produced standards, training and certification for non-lawyer volunteer advocates for the child. Currently the National CASA Association reports that it has 76,000 CASA volunteers around the U.S.:

> ... through a network of 949 community-based programs that recruit, train and support citizen-volunteers to advocate for the best interests of abused and neglected children in courtrooms and communities. Volunteer advocates—empowered directly by the courts—offer judges the critical information they need to ensure that each child's rights and needs are being attended to while in foster care.[5]

But what should be the duties of the child's advocate? What is the advocate's job description? What are they expected to do? CAPTA is a reasonable starting place, but it is far from a comprehensive model. CAPTA is not only silent on a great number of the

---

3. 42 U.S.C. § 5106a(b)(2)(A)(xiii) (2015).
4. Nancy Neraas, *The Non-Lawyer Guardian Ad Litem in Child Abuse and Neglect Proceedings: The King County, Washington, Experience*, 58 Wash. L. Rev. 853 (1983).
5. CASA for Children, http://www.casaforchildren.org/site/c.mtJSJ7MPIsE/b.5301295/k.BE9A/Home.htm (last visited Aug. 18, 2015).

questions about the role and duties of the child's legal representative but also no longer represents the best and latest thinking as to how advocacy services can most effectively be provided to children.

One consequence of the vague direction in CAPTA is that State implementation of CAPTA requirements has been all over the board. We have seen the creation of numerous—and often inconsistent and unclear—models of representation. Some argue that no two models of child representation among the various U.S. jurisdictions are alike.[6] Even within jurisdictions, there is often considerable disagreement as to which model is used and what the role of the representative is within the model. This confusion has undoubtedly contributed to the poor quality of representation children frequently receive in our system.

2.2   Milestones in Development of Child Representation

Since the original CAPTA in 1974, several important milestones mark the national discussion of the proper role of the child's legal representative. The American Bar Association, led by the ABA Center on Children and the Law, has provided consistent guidance and leadership in this field. In 1979 the ABA approved *Juvenile Justice Standards Relating to Counsel for Private Parties,* which include important directions for lawyers representing children in juvenile court matters generally. The ABA recommended that State and local bar associations sponsor training for lawyers representing children and endorsed carefully selected and trained Court Appointed Special Advocates (CASAs). The ABA's most recent contributions, the 1996 ABA Standards and the 2011 Model Act Governing Child Representation are discussed below.

In the 1988 reauthorization of CAPTA Congress mandated a study of "the effectiveness of legal representation through the use of guardians ad litem and court-appointed special advocates."[7] In fulfillment of the mandate, CSR Inc. conducted the first national study of legal representation of children in 1994. The CSR study reviewed three major program models—1) the private attorney model; 2) the staff attorney model; and 3) a CASA model. The effectiveness of the GALs was measured against five major roles as proposed by Don Duquette in a 1990 book, *Advocating for the Child in Protection Proceedings.*[8] Duquette presented a framework for identifying the tasks of the child advocate. Those roles are 1) fact finder and investigator, 2) legal representative, 3) case monitor, 4) mediator and negotiator, and 5) resource broker. CSR defined effectiveness as "the degree to which the GAL performed the five roles identified as essential to GAL work and the related tasks and activities."

---

6. First Star & Children's Advocacy Institute, A Child's Right to Counsel: A National Report Card on Legal Representation for Abused and Neglected Children (3d ed. 2012).
7. P.L. 100-294, 102 Stat 102 (April 25, 1988).
8. Donald N. Duquette, Advocating for the Child in Protection Proceedings: A Handbook for Lawyers and Court Appointed Special Advocates, Lexington Press (1990).

The findings show that no GAL model studied was consistently superior to the others across all five GAL roles. The findings suggest that an optimal approach may involve having a GAL who either has, or has access to, the combined expertise and resources of attorneys, lay volunteers, and caseworkers to perform the broad range of functions and services contained in the definition of the child advocate.[9] A significant short-coming of the CSR study is that they did not use case outcomes as part of their analysis and assessment. CSR did not study whether the actions of the advocates had any impact on the outcomes of the child's case.

In August 1995 the National Council of Juvenile and Family Court Judges produced *Resource Guidelines: Improving Court Practice in Child Abuse & Neglect Cases,* which stress the importance of vigorous representation of children provided by competent and diligent lawyers and urge courts to take action to assure such representation.

In December 1995 attendees at a Fordham University Conference on Ethical Issues in the Legal Representation of Children developed a set of recommendations reported in an influential special law review issue.[10]. The ABA Standards for Lawyers Representing Children were under consideration at that time and were reviewed by the conference.[11] A major issue, then as now, is the extent to which the lawyer for the child should represent the child's *best interests* versus the *stated interests* of the child. That is, should the lawyer for the child be *client-directed* in the same way that a lawyer for an adult is? The Fordham conference attendees recommended that lawyers for children should act in a traditional lawyer role, that is, be *client-directed*.

In 1996, the ABA adopted the influential *Standards of Practice for Lawyers Who Represent Children in Abuse and Neglect Proceedings.*[12] Drawing from the national discussion up to that point, the 1996 ABA Standards recommended that all children subject to court proceedings involving allegations of child abuse and neglect should have legal representation as long as the court jurisdiction continues. Importantly, the Standards and its commentary articulated the practical steps that an assertive lawyer should take in representation of a child at various stages of a case. They reject the notion of a passive, unengaged monitor of the proceedings and set out requirements for a very engaged and active legal representative. The 1996 ABA Standards provide the foundation for the QIC Best Practice Model of Child Representation.

---

9. U.S. Dep't of Health and Human Services, Office of Child Abuse and Neglect, Admin. for Children and Families, Final Report on the Validation and Effectiveness Study of Legal Representation through Guardian Ad Litem (1994).

10. *Proceedings of the Conference on Ethical Issues in the Legal Representation of Children,* 64 Fordam L. Rev. 1301 (1996)

11. Linda Elrod, *An Analysis of the Proposed Standards of Practice for Lawyers Representing Children in Abuse and Neglect Cases,* 64 Fordham L. Rev. 1999 (1996).

12. A.B.A., Standards of Practice for Lawyers Who Represent Children in Abuse and Neglect Cases (1996) [hereinafter 1996 ABA Abuse and Neglect Standards].

The ABA Standards require appointment of either a "child's attorney" (a client-directed lawyer owing the same duties of undivided loyalty, confidentiality, and competent representation to the child as is due an adult client) or appointment of an attorney/guardian *ad litem* "to protect the child's interests without being bound by the child's expressed preferences."[13] The Standards express a preference for the appointment of a child's attorney, choosing a *client-directed* as opposed to a *best interests* approach to lawyer representation.

In December 1996 President Clinton initiated a project called *Adoption 2002: The President's Initiative on Adoption and Foster Care*. Providing some of the strongest Presidential-level leadership on foster care ever, President Clinton addressed the problem of America's foster children spending far too long waiting—deprived of the permanent and stable homes necessary for their healthy development. In an Executive Memorandum of December 14, 1996, President Clinton said: "I am committed to giving the children waiting in our Nation's foster care system what every child in America deserves—loving parents and a healthy, stable home. . . . . Each year State child welfare agencies secure homes for less than one-third of the children whose goal is adoption or an alternate permanent plan. I know we can do better."[14]

Among other things, *Adoption 2002* recommended developing model guidelines for State legislation to achieve these goals. A multidisciplinary workgroup of national leaders in child welfare developed *Guidelines for Public Policy and State Legislation Governing Permanence for Children,* which included recommendations for legal representation of children:

> *Zealous Attorney Representation for Children:* We recommend that States guarantee that all children who are subjects of child protection court proceedings be represented by an independent attorney at all stages and at all hearings in the child protection court process. The attorney owes the same duties of competent representation and zealous advocacy to the child as are due an adult client.[15]

The *Guidelines* address the duties of the advocate separately from the question of who determines the goals and objectives of the child advocate and "tries to avoid a false dichotomy between wishes and best interests and focuses instead on duties of the child's lawyer, regardless of who (or how) the ultimate advocacy goals of the lawyer are determined."[16] No matter whether the advocate represents the child's best interests as determined by the advocate or assumes a client-directed role as recommended by the

---

13. 1996 ABA Standards at 1-A & 1-B.
14. Donald Duquette & Mark Hardin, *Adoption 2002: The President's Initiative on Adoption and Foster Care, Guidelines for Public Policy and State Legislation Governing Permanence for Children,* U.S. Dept. Health & Human Servs, ACYF, Children's Bureau (1999) [hereinafter Adoption 2002 *Guidelines*].Page I-2
15. Adoption 2002 *Guidelines* at VII-11.
16. Adoption 2002 *Guidelines* at VII-19.

ABA Standards, the *Guidelines* expect a vigorous and active participation of the child's lawyer.

In 1997 Professor Jean Koh Peters, director of the Child Advocacy Clinic at Yale Law School, developed a major contribution to the field in her book *Representing Children In Child Protective Proceedings: Ethical And Practical Dimensions* in which she ties theory to a broad view of a child's needs and specific actions by the legal advocate.[17]

In 1998, a survey by the National Council of Juvenile and Family Court Judges (NCJFCJ) determined that 40 States appoint counsel for children in abuse and neglect cases. In 30 of those States an "attorney-guardian ad litem" is typically appointed who serves a dual function of representing both the best interests and wishes of the child. In the 10 other States that appoint counsel for a child, a GAL is appointed in addition to the attorney, so that the attorneys perform the single role of representing the child (i.e., the child's stated wishes). In 10 States, the NCJFCJ reported that an attorney is usually not appointed for the child, but in nine of those States a non-attorney GAL is appointed for the child.[18]

In 2005, a conference informally billed as "Fordham II" convened the major child welfare law players at the University of Nevada Las Vegas, Boyd School of Law. The UNLV conference reaffirmed the Fordham recommendations and promulgated its own recommendations, aimed at empowering child participation. The Working Group on the Best Interests of the Child and the Role of the Attorney "unanimously reaffirmed the Fordham commitment to client-directed representation," stating that a client-directed approach is the preferred approach even in best interests representation and that "the children's attorneys' community has come to the conclusion that ethical legal representation of children is synonymous with allowing the child to direct representation."[19]

The UNLV Conference recommended strengthening the role of the child's voice in CAPTA by mandating that CAPTA comply with the United Nations Convention on the Rights of the Child ("CRC"). The CRC requires a child be given the opportunity to be heard in any judicial proceeding affecting the child.[20] The conference results are reported in a Special Issue of the Nevada Law Journal.[21] A client-directed model

---

17. Jean Koh Peters, Representing Children In Child Protective Proceedings: Ethical And Practical Dimensions (3d ed., LEXUS Law Publishing 2007).
18. Shirley Dobbin et al., *Child Abuse and Neglect Cases: Representation as a Critical Component of Effective Practice,* National Council of Juvenile and Family Court Judges 45 (1998).
19. *Recommendations of the UNLV Conference on Representing Children in Families: Child Advocacy and Justice Ten Years After Fordham,* 6 Nev. L.J. 592 (Spring 2006).
20. U.N. Office of the High Commissioner for Human Rights, *Convention on the Rights of the Child,* art. 7 (Sept. 2, 1990), http://treaties.un.org/Pages/ViewDetails.aspx?src=TREATY&mtdsg_no=IV-11&chapter=4&lang=en.
21. Special Issue on Legal Representation of Children, 6 Nev. L.J. (Spring 2006).

of representation for children of all ages was not the unanimous view of the field, however. Other commentators stood strong on a best interest model for children and youth of all ages.[22] Others advocated for a "bright-line" age limit above which a child received a client directed attorney and below which a child received a best interest advocate charged with including the child's wishes in determining the goals of the case.[23]

After many years of debate, development and consensus building, the ABA Section on Litigation, Children's Rights Litigation Committee collaborating with the ABA Center on Children and the Law, drafted the ABA Model Act Governing the Representation of Children in Abuse, Neglect, and Dependency Proceedings which the ABA House of Delegates adopted in August 2011.[24] The Model Act mandates that a "child's lawyer" who owes essentially the same duties as to an adult client, be appointed for every child in abuse or neglect proceedings. The Model Act provides for a client-directed model of representation but makes careful provision for a client with diminished capacity and provides guidance to attorneys in making the diminished capacity decisions and deciding on protective action to protect the client.

The lawyer for the child is expected to be qualified through training and experience with reasonable caseloads. The child's lawyer is required to complete a thorough and independent investigation, consult the child and otherwise participate fully in all stages of the litigation.[25]

The child's lawyer may request authority from the court to pursue ancillary issues, even those that do not arise in the child protection action, when necessary to ensure the child's needs are met. The Act also provides for the appointment of a "best interest advocate" who may serve in addition to the lawyer.

These milestone events reflect a debate that is at once legal, philosophical, psychological, and political. Does a child have a legal right to counsel? If so, who directs the counsel? Is a child a rights holder in his or her own right? Is a child developmentally capable of directing counsel? Who is going to pay for lawyers for children? And finally, what are the fundamental duties and tasks of a child's lawyer? We begin to unpack these questions with the legal framework.

---

22. Robert F. Harris, *A Response to the Recommendations of the UNLV Conference: Another Look at the Attorney/Guardian Ad Litem Model*, 6 Nev. L.J. 1284 (Spring 2006).

23. Donald N. Duquette, *Two Distinct Roles/Bright Line Test*, 6 Nev. L.J. 1240 (Spring 2006).

24. ABA Model Act Governing the Representation of Children in Abuse, Neglect, and Dependency Proceedings, 2011, https://apps.americanbar.org/litigation/committees/childrights/docs/aba_model_act_2011.pdf.

25. *Id.*, at § 7

2.3 Constitutional Arguments for Child's Right to Counsel

Children arguably have well-defined liberty interests at stake, face a high risk of erroneous deprivation in the absence of attorneys, and states' interests in access to justice may outweigh the financial burden required to provide attorneys.[26] The child has an interest in being protected from harm, but he or she also shares a fundamental right with the parent to remain together without the coercive interference from the state. If the court places the child in the custody of the state, the child has a right to reasonable services and care. Court decisions in a few states addressed and affirmed a child's right to counsel based on the U.S. and state constitutions. [27]

One scholar distinguishes the Supreme Court's decision in *Lassiter,* which held that parents did not have a constitutional right to counsel in termination of parental rights proceedings, from the case of children, who cannot call witnesses, cannot cross-examine witnesses, or do anything that the U.S. Supreme Court considered Ms. Lassiter, an adult, competent to do in the absence of counsel. Children's constitutional right to representation cannot be met with a non-lawyer advocate, such as a Court Appointed Special Advocate (CASA).[28] Others have argued that the similarities between the court's function and role in delinquency and dependency cases suggest the Supreme Court's rationale in *Gault* for requiring counsel for children in delinquency proceedings also applies to dependency proceedings.[29] Others have found a basis for appointment of lawyers for children by analogy to existing victims' rights laws.[30]

2.4 Equal Dignity for Children in the Judicial Process

A number of commentators have argued that appointing attorneys for children is critical to respecting child's right to participate in the judicial decisions affecting their lives.[31] Katherine Hunt Federle argues that children's right to participate arises as a

---

26. Erik Pitchal, *Children's Constitutional Right to Counsel in Dependency Cases*, 15 TEM. POL. & CIV. RTS. L. REV. 663 (2006); Jacob E. Smiles, *A Child's Due Process Right to Legal Counsel in Abuse and Neglect Dependency Proceedings,* 37 FAM. L.Q. 485 (2003)

27. Roe v. Conn, 417 F. Supp. 769, 780 (M.D. Ala. 1976); Kenny A. ex rel. Winn. v. Perdue, 356 F. Supp. 2d 1353 (N.D. Ga. 2005); Matter of Jamie TT, 191 A.D.2d 132, 599 N.Y.S. 2d 892 (1993). *See also* Barbara Atwood, *The Uniform Representation of Children in Abuse, Neglect, and Custody Proceedings Act: Bridging the Divide Between Pragmatism and Idealism*, 42 FAM. L. Q. 63, 85-86 (2008).

28. Gerald F. Glynn, *The Child Abuse Prevention and Treatment Act—Promoting the Unauthorized Practice of Law,* 9 J. L. & FAM.STUD. 53 (2007).

29. LaShanda Taylor, *A Lawyer for Every Child: Client-Directed Representation in Dependency Cases*, 47 FAM. CT. REV. 605, 612 (Oct. 2009). *See also* Pitchal, *supra* note 26, at 681 ("[T]he Gault argument has power . . . because all children in state custody are at the whim of state officials to decide where they will live at any given moment.").

30. Myrna Raeder, *Enhancing the Legal Profession's Response to Victims of Child Abuse,* 24 CRIM. JUST. 12 (2009).

31. Katherine Hunt Federle, *Looking for Rights in All the Wrong Places: Resolving Custody Disputes in Divorce Proceedings,* 15 CARDOZO L. REV. 1523, 1564 (1994) [hereinafter Federle

remedy for powerlessness, situating children on equal footing to challenge subordination. Empowering children to contribute to decisions about their future often contributes to children's psychological well-being. Another scholar notes that society has a broader interest in providing attorneys than the mere protection of children.

Providing attorneys is critical to preserving the dignity of the parties that come before the governmental decision maker and preserving the dignity of the judicial process.[32] Many commentators have described the therapeutic nature of the attorney-client relationship for children involved in the child welfare system.[33] Through the counseling and advice process of the attorney-client relationship, children are told what to expect, given a chance to talk confidentially with someone about their legal needs and desired outcome, given advice about the likelihood of their desired outcome, and often given options for expressing their desires to the decision-makers.[34] Children who feel a sense of participation in the process may be more likely to abide by the court's decision, often take an enhanced interest in the proceedings that affect their futures, and may more readily provide important information to their attorneys.[35]

One scholar suggests that from the child's perspective, a lawyer's failure to advocate his views might be one more betrayal by the adult world or insult to dignity by the foster care system and courts charged with caring for the child.[36] One commentator has also argued that greater bar involvement in the cases of children in foster care would have a salutary effect on the legal culture generally.[37]

2.5 The Critique of Attorneys for Children

A few commentators argue against attorney representation for children in dependency proceedings. Martin Guggenheim has maintained that children's lawyers commonly fail to accurately distinguish between serious safety cases and those in which the child

---

Looking for Rights]; Katherine Hunt Federle, *The Ethics of Empowerment: Rethinking the Role of Lawyers in Interviewing and Counseling the Child Client*, 64 FORDHAM L. REV. 1655, 1658 (1996); Barbara Atwood, *Representing Children: The Ongoing Search for Clear and Workable Standards*, 19 J. AM. ACAD. MATRIM. L. 183, 194-95 (2005); Taylor, *supra* note 29, at 613-14.

32. Pitchal, *supra* note 26, at 689.

33. Emily Buss, *"You're My What?" The Problem of Children's Misperceptions of Their Lawyers' Roles*, 64 FORDHAM L. REV. 1699, 1746 (1996); Manuela Stötzel & Jörg Fegert, *The Representation of the Legal Interests of Children and Adolescents in Germany: A Study of the Children's Guardian from a Child's Perspective*, 20 INT'L J. L. POL'Y & FAM. 201 (2006).

34. Glynn, *supra* note 28.

35. Taylor, *supra* note 29, at 619; Buss, *supra* note 33, at 1760-61. *See also* Victoria Weisz et al., *Children and Procedural Justice*, 44 CT. REV. 36 (2007); Keri K. Gould & Michael L. Perlin, *Johnny's in the Basement/Mixing Up His Medicine: Therapeutic Jurisprudence and Clinical Teaching*, 24 SEATTLE U. L. REV. 339, 359-71 (2000).

36. Atwood, *Representing Children*, *supra* note 31, at 221.

37. Emily Richardson, *Lawyers Were Children Once: An Ethical Approach to Strengthening Child Abuse and Neglect Legislation*, 31 J. LEGAL PROF. 357, 365 (2007).

faces no serious risk of suffering serious harm.³⁸ For Guggenheim, allowing lawyers freedom to determine for themselves what position to advocate to a court threatens a balanced application of the rule of law.³⁹ Commentators have argued that children's attorneys may improperly insert their own worldview into individual client representation, may regard the child in isolation from his or her family and culture, and may primarily serve the state's interest in exercising broad control over impoverished families.⁴⁰

Annette Appell has suggested that the unimproved condition of children and the lack of research about the effectiveness of attorneys leave the value of attorney representation unclear.⁴¹ She argues that the increased number of children's attorneys arose from a series of policy decisions defining child welfare in individual rather than social and economic justice terms. For Appell, these individual legal solutions amount to "tinkering" with individual rights within existing frameworks, at the expense of broader community development remedies.⁴²

Others have questioned the suitability of the adversarial legal system in matters addressing complex interpersonal relationships.⁴³ One survey of empirical studies suggested that the involvement of a CASA volunteer in a case, compared to advocacy by an attorney alone, may improve key factors in child representation, such as face-to-face

---

38. Martin Guggenheim, *How Children's Lawyers Serve State Interests*, 6 Nev. L.J. 805 (2006).
39. *Id.*
40. *Id.* at 806 & 832; Annette Appell, *Representing Children Representing What?: Critical Reflections on Lawyering for Children*, 39 Colum. Hum. Rts. L. Rev. 573, 623 (2008). *See also* Naomi Cahn, *Family Boundaries: Symposium on Third-Party Rights and Obligations with Respect to Children, State Representation of Children's Interests*, 40 Fam. L.Q. 109, 110 (2006).
41. Appell, *supra* note 40, at 605. *See also* Marvin Ventrell, *The Practice of Law for Children*, 28 Hamline J. Pub. L. & Pol'y 75, 94 (2006) ("lawyers [with a 'child-saving' mentality] are frequently seen as an impediment to producing good outcomes").
42. Appell, *supra* note 40, at 620 (citing Robin West, *Re-Imagining Justice*, 14 Yale J.L. & Feminism 333, 340 (2002) (noting how rights discourse may side-step systemic problems and reform); Report of the Working Group on the Role of Race, Ethnicity, and Class, 6 Nev. L. J 634, 670-72 (2006)
43. Mary Kay Kisthardt, *Working in the Best Interest of Children: Facilitating the Collaboration of Lawyers and Social Workers in Abuse and Neglect Cases*, 30 Rutgers L. Rev. 1 (2006). *See also* Hollis Peterson, *In Search of the Best Interests of the Child: The Efficacy of the Court Appointed Special Advocate Model of Guardian ad Litem Representation*, 13 Geo. Mason L. Rev. 1083, 1110 (2006); Janet Weinstein, *And Never the Twain Shall Meet: The Best Interests of Children and the Adversary System*, 52 U. Miami L. Rev. 79, 138-139 (1997); Appell, *supra* note 40, at 620; Susan L. Brooks, *Therapeutic and Preventive Approaches to School Safety: Applications of a Family Systems Model*, 34 New Eng. L. Rev. 615, 618 (2000); Susan L. Brooks, *A Family Systems Paradigm for Legal Decision Making Affecting Child Custody*, 6 Cornell J. L. & Pub. Pol'y 1, 3-4 (1996). *Cf.* Ann Haralambie, *Humility and Chidl Autonomy in Child Welfare and Custody Representation of Children*, 47 No. 1 Judges' J. 23, 26 (2008) (emphasizing that children are necessarily involved in child welfare cases, and that denying them representation will not shield them from a dispute and its ramifications).

contact, and may improve services ordered and number of placement moves.[44] Attorneys for children also constitute a financial burden on states.[45]

2.6 The Role of the Child's Attorney: Competing Models

2.6.1 Best Interests or Client Directed

While providing attorneys for children is recognized as necessary by the child welfare field, opinions differ as to the role attorneys should adopt. The traditional controversy pits "best interests" models—in which attorneys represent the child's best interests—against "expressed wishes/client-directed" models, where the attorney advocates for the child client's wishes in the traditional attorney-client role. Best interests models typically find greater favor with judges and lawmakers, while the preferred model among child advocates and child welfare academics is the expressed wishes model.[46]

Jean Koh Peters has suggested that child competency is a "dimmer switch," in that the client can shed light on some aspects of the representation, even though she cannot participate in all of it.[47] Don Duquette notes that even a best interests model might charge the attorney to express and advocate the child's preferences according to age and maturity since it may be in the best interests of the child to have his voice expressed and advocated for.[48] Emily Buss has maintained that few attorneys adopt an absolutist position under either model.[49] Duquette has also argued that the field might embrace both attorney models, with older youth receiving a client-directed attorney and younger children receiving a best interests attorney. Some authors consider the actual percentage of cases in which a child's best interests and expressed wishes conflict to be relatively small and many warn against a preoccupation with the subtleties of the child's voice in directing the attorney at the expense of exploring other dimensions of quality attorney practice.[50]

---

44. Davin Youngclarke, et al., *A Systematic Review of the Impact of Court Appointed Special Advocates*, 5 J. CENTER FOR FAMILIES, CHILD. & CTS. 109 (2004). For history and structure of CASA program, see *id.*, at 109-112; *see also* Rebecca Ellis, *The Heartbeat of Texas Children: The Role of Court-Appointed Special Advocates in the Wake of the 2005 Family Code Amendments*, 38 TEX. TECH. L. REV. 1065 (2006).

45. *See* Harris, *supra* note 22, at 1294 (citing In re B.K., 833 N.E.2d 945 (Ill. App. Ct. 2005)). *But see* Taylor, *supra* note 29, at 614 (noting that the cost of counsel may be mitigated by the financial benefits of increased permanency).

46. Atwood, *Representing Children*, *supra* note 31, at 91-92

47. Koh Peters, *Representing Children*, *supra* note 17, at §3-2(b)(2).

48. Donald N. Duquette, *Legal Representation for Children in Protection Proceedings: Two Distinct Lawyer Roles are Required*, 34 FAM. L. Q. 441, 442 (2001).

49. *Id. See also* Buss, *supra* note 33, at 1705. ("Those advocating the traditional attorney approach necessarily exclude children too young to speak, and most require that the children be old enough to engage in a rational decision-making process about the particular issue in question. Those advocating the guardian ad litem role for most children, generally still concede that at some age—at least in the late teenage years—children should be able to direct their counsel, on some, if not all, issues.")

50. Glynn, *Unauthorized Practice*, *supra* note 28, at 62.

2.6.2 Child Representative as Advocate for the Child's Best Interests

Those who advocate the best interests lawyer model argue that children lack the maturity or the cognitive capacity for appropriate decision-making in their own interests. The best interests model is characterized as flexibly allowing for individualized client advocacy. Young children may appear more appropriately served by a best interests model than a client-directed model, which offers little guidance in the case of the nonverbal child or the infant.[51] Advocating for the child's legal interests may even defeat the major rationale of the client-directed approach, because it provides no guarantee of attorney objectivity.[52] A lawyer should not employ her skills to advocate a position exposing the young child client to serious harm, nor should attorneys owe "robotic allegiance" to each directive of minimally competent young children.[53]

Practical realities of representation are also argued to favor the best interests model. Lawyers will often have to determine the goals and objectives of the representation with little input from the child. Children may face pressures from families, the court process, or other circumstances that lead them to misidentify their own interests.[54] A lawyer emphasizing best interests considerations may more ably communicate and forge agreement with state social workers, therapists, teacher, or counselors in the child's case.[55]

Requiring children to be responsible for taking difficult positions and decisions may constitute too heavy a psychological burden.[56] Society has a greater obligation to protect children from their own bad judgments.[57] And because overworked caseworkers may be unable to provide relevant information to the judge, unless the child's attorney provides a full factual picture in court, the judge will be not be in a position to make a determination of the child's best interests.[58]

As a practical matter, a statutory right of children to best interests attorneys is often considered more politically realistic because state legislators and judges have favored

---

51. Duquette, *Bright Line Test*, *supra* note 23.
52. Duquette, *Two Roles Required*, *supra* note 48; Harris, *supra* note 22, at 1291.
53. Atwood, *Uniform Representation*, *supra* note 27, at 79; Marvin Ventrell, *Legal Representation of Children in Dependency Court: Toward a Better Model—The ABA (NACC Revised) Standards of Practice*, NACC CHILDREN'S LAW MANUAL SERIES (1999 ed.).
54. Buss, *supra* note 33, at 1702-03.
55. Jean Koh Peters, *The Roles and Content of Best Interests in Client-Directed Lawyering for Children in Child Protective Proceedings*, 64 FORDHAM L. REV. 1505, 1514 (1996).
56. Robert E. Emery, *Children's Voices: Listening—and Deciding—Is an Adult Responsibility*, 45 ARIZ. L. REV. 621, 622 (2003); Atwood, *supra* note 27, at 194; *cf.* Buss, *supra* note 33, at 1702-03.
57. *See* Buss, *supra* note 33, at 1702-03.
58. *Id.*; Sarah H. Ramsey, *Representation of the Child in Protection Proceedings: The Determination of Decision-Making Capacity*, 17 FAM. L. Q. 287, 304-05 (1983).

this model.⁵⁹ Debra Lehrman has suggested that client-directed models may be rooted less in the needs of children than a desire of adults to understand themselves as respecting children.⁶⁰ Barbara Atwood contends that those who criticize best interests lawyering because lawyers lack expertise to make such determinations unfairly envision lawyers as litigating in a vacuum.⁶¹ Further, Atwood argues that other standards emphasizing the client-directed model nevertheless allow considerable discretion under complex substituted judgment assessments.⁶²

2.6.3 Problems with the Best Interests Model of Child Representation

Critics of best interests models contend that the best interests role is outside the requirements of professional ethics.⁶³ The drafters of the 2009 ABA Model Act argue that consistency with previous ABA Model Rules of ethics require that the child's lawyer form an attorney-client relationship which is "fundamentally indistinguishable from the attorney-client relationship in any other situation and which includes duties of client direction, confidentiality, diligence, competence, loyalty, communication, and the duty to advise."⁶⁴ The Model Rules of Professional Conduct require attorneys to maintain confidential communications with the client (Rule 1.6); not use confidential information adverse to the client without informed consent (Rule 1.8); abide by the client's determinations as to the objectives of the litigation (Rule 1.2); maintain client loyalty (Rule 1.2); refrain from intentionally or knowingly engaging in any activity which creates a conflict of interest (Rule 1.7); and refrain from testifying in cases in which

---

59. Duquette, *Bright Line Test*, *supra* note 23, at 1249; Duquette, *Two Roles Required*, *supra* note 48, at 441; Merril Sobie, *The Child Client: Representing Children in Child Protective Proceedings*, 22 Tuoro L. Rev. 745, 791-93 (2006); Haralambie, *supra* note 43, at 23; Sarah L. Marx, *Seen But Not Heard: Advocating For Children in New York State*, 25 Tuoro L. Rev. 491, 514 (2006); Jane Spinak, *When Did Lawyers for Children Stop Reading Goldstein, Freud and Solnit? Lessons from the Twentieth Century on Best Interests and the Role of the Child Advocate*, 41 Fam. L. Q. 393, 409 (2007).

60. Debra H. Lehrmann, *Who Are We Protecting?* 63 Tex. B.J. 123, 126 (2000). *See also* Atwood, *Representing Children*, *supra* note 31, at 193-94.

61. Atwood, *Uniform Representation*, *supra* note 27, at 95.

62. *Id. See also* Haralambie, *supra* note 43, at 23.

63. Jennifer L. Renne, *Special Issues for Guardians ad Litem*, *in* Legal Ethics in Child Welfare Cases, 79 (American Bar Association 2004); Federle, *supra* note 31; Taylor, *supra* note 29, at 618; Atwood, *Uniform Representation*, *supra* note 27, at 92-93; Glynn, *Unauthorized Practice*, *supra* note 28. *See also* Tania M. Culley, *What Does It Mean to Represent Delaware's Abused, Neglected, and Dependent Children?*, 4 Del. L. Rev. 77, 87 (2001). *Cf.* Atwood, *Representing Children*, *supra* note 31, at 207 ("The lawyer for the impaired client is impliedly authorized under Model Rule 1.6(a) to reveal information about the client to the extent necessary to protect the client's interests.").

64. *Report and Working Draft of a Model Act Governing the Representation of Children in Abuse, Neglect, and Dependency Proceedings*, 42 Fam. L.Q. 145, 147-48 (2008) [hereinafter 2009 ABA Model Act Report].

they are also advocates (Rule 3.7).[65] Best interests attorneys often break the Model Rules when disclosing to the court all relevant and necessary information provided by the child. Attorneys in the best interests role may not necessarily advocate for their child client's desired litigation objectives.

Critics also contend that attorneys lack expertise required to adequately determine children's interests, because legal training does not prepare a person to make the nuanced judgments the determination requires.[66] Even specially trained attorneys may not be equipped to make these determinations.[67] With an infant or young child, the pure best interests approach fails to set out principles to guide the advocate's discretion in identifying the child's best interests.

Another objection is that the best interests role is a substituted judgment model that inappropriately substitutes the view of a lawyer for that of the child while at the same time usurping the role of the court to make such determinations.[68] Additionally, critics contend that best interests representation does not respect children as rights-bearing individuals and that the paternalism involved in best interests approaches disempowers children.[69] These critiques will be discussed further as reasons to adopt client-directed models.

---

65. *See* ABA Model Rules of Professional Conduct. *See* Taylor, *supra* note 29, at 621-22; *Introduction, Recommendations of the UNLV Conference on Representing Children in Families*, 6 Nev. L.J. 592 (2006) ("[T]he children's attorneys' community has come to the conclusion that ethical legal representation of children is synonymous with allowing the child to direct representation."); Buss, *supra* note 33, at 1715–1745.

66. Atwood, *Uniform Representation*, *supra* note 27, at 92-93; Appell, *supra* note 40, at 599-600; 2006 UNLV Recommendations, *supra* note 65 ("[T]hese often well-meaning professionals and systems sometimes substitute their own interests or ideas about what children need for the wisdom of the children and their families, and provide solutions that are neither welcome nor responsive to the need."); 2009 ABA Model Act Report, *supra* note 64, at 147-48 ("Children's lawyers are not social workers or psychologists and should not be treated as such. To the extent that courts need information about what is in the child's best interest, the court should use a court appointed advisor or an expert, subject to the rules governing all court experts.").

67. Haralambie, *supra* note 43, at 24

68. Duquette, *Two Roles Required*, *supra* note 48.

69. Ventrell, *supra* note 41, at 96; Federle, *supra* note 31; Taylor, *supra* note 29; Buss, *supra* note 33, at 1703-05. *See also Special Populations: Mobilization for Change*, 25 Touro L. Rev. 467 (2009) (breakout session transcript) ("There is no real right [to counsel for children in New York] at this point because the law guardian can substitute his or her judgment as an attorney for that of the young person.").

2.6.4 Client-Directed Child Representation

Most recent academic and practitioner commentary has favored a client-directed role for attorneys representing children in dependency proceedings.[70] Client-directed representation also finds support abroad.[71]

Those who advocate assuming the traditional attorney role, argue that best interests attorneys usurp the role of the judge in determining the child's best interests.[72] The judge should be able to base her decision on the evidence elicited through an adversarial process, and the child has the right to have his position zealously advocated.[73] Proponents of the traditional attorney model also emphasize that lawyers' lack of psychology and social work expertise and training that should disqualify them from making best interest judgments.[74] As discussed at II.B, supra, allowing children a voice in their own proceedings empowers children.[75] This is also justified as a restorative measure, given children's status disempowered status under the circumstances that bring them into custody.[76]

---

70. KOH PETERS, REPRESENTING CHILDREN, *supra* note 17, at § 2(a)-3(c)(2) ("[F]rom Guggenheim on, the vast majority of literature has resoundingly embraced the traditional lawyering role for children above a certain age); Sobie, *supra* note 59, at 794; Taylor, *supra* note 29, at 615 (arguing that the legal profession supports providing attorneys for children in dependency proceedings.); Glynn, *supra* note 28, at 63-64 ("There is a growing scholarly consensus that children need, at a minimum, a lawyer in these proceedings. . . ."); Martin Guggenheim, *Reconsidering the Need for Counsel for Children in Custody, Visitation and Child Protection Proceedings*, 29 LOY. U. CHI. L. J. 299, 301 (1998) ("[A] growing consensus of scholars and practitioners increasingly insist that personality, personal opinions, values, and beliefs should play as small a role as possible in carrying out the responsibilities of representing a child in a legal proceeding);" Atwood, *Uniform Representation*, *supra* note 27, at 90-91 ("The literature evinces a significant distrust of any model of lawyering that authorizes the lawyer to make decisions for the child based on the lawyer's independent assessment of the child's welfare"); Aditi Kothekar, *Refocusing the Lens of Child Advocacy Reform on the Child*, 86 WASH U. L. REV. 481, 484 (2008) ("National conferences establish a growing consensus"). *See also* Appell, *supra* note 40, at 634-65 ("Despite the broad-based and growing critique of lawyers' and the law's use of children as vehicles to advance dominant norms, many attorneys persist in using a model of representation focusing on the best interests of the child . . ."); Haralambie, *supra* note 43, at 24 ("There is consensus among commentators to move in the direction of child-directed representation . . .")

71. Andy Bilson & Sue White, *Representing Children's Views and Best Interests in Court: An International Comparison*, 14 CHILD ABUSE REV. 220, 223, 236 (2005).

72. Martin Guggenheim, *The Right to Be Represented but Not Heard: Reflections on Legal Representation for Children*, 59 N.Y.U. L. REV. 76, 81 (1984); Jane M. Spinak, *Simon Says Take Three Steps Backwards: The National Conference of Commissioners on Uniform State Laws Recommendations on Child Representation*, 6 NEV. L.J. 1385, 1390; Kothekar, *supra* note 70.

73. Buss, *supra* note 33, at 1703-05.

74. *Id.*; Appell, *supra* note 40, at 634-65. *See also* Guggenheim, AAML's Revised Standards, *supra* note *, at 264

75. Ventrell, *supra* note 41, at 96; Bilson & White, *supra* note 66, at 236.

76. Buss, *supra* note 33, at 1703-05.

Two practical considerations are also important to note in evaluating client-directed advocacy. Attorneys are often influenced and inspired by the wisdom of children, whose judgment about their best interests often proves sound.[77] Children may effectively prevent decisions the children oppose from being effectively implemented, and the child's sense of inclusion in the court process may be critical to the success of placements and services.[78]

2.6.5 Problems with Client-Directed Representation

It is difficult to understand just what client-directed representation means for young children who cannot speak or express a point of view or whose ability to make considered judgments is lacking.[79] Client-directed representation might also under-protect children who lack sufficient fore- sight or understanding of the future or may leave them with a burdensome psychological responsibility in the context of complicated relationships.[80]

2.6.6 An Alternative Model: The Bright Line Test

Duquette has expressed the concern that neither a best interests model nor client-directed lawyer can meet the needs of all children, given their differing levels of development.[81] The older child needs a traditional attorney; the youngest child is incapable of directing counsel and requires a representative to define and advocate for his or her best interests. Under a "Two Distinct Lawyer Roles" model the court must appoint either a best interest lawyer or a traditional attorney under certain conditions defined in the law. Duquette has proposed that a bright line age standard should determine which sort of representative a child is provided. Above a certain age, e.g. seven, the youth would receive a client-directed advocate, and below that age a child would receive a best interests advocate.[82]

2.6.7 ABA Model Rule 1.14

The ABA Model Rule of Professional Conduct 1.14 is provides some of the most authoritative guidance to practitioners in those states which have adopted it.[83] It pro-

---

77. *Id.*
78. *Id.*; Stötzel & Fegert, *supra* note 33.
79. Duquette, *Two Roles Required, supra* note 48.
80. John Anzelc et al., *Comment on the Committee's Model Act Governing Representation of Children in Abuse and Neglect Proceedings*, 12 MICH. CHILD WELFARE L. BAR. J. 4; Emery, *supra* note 56.
81. Duquette, *Two Roles Required, supra* note 48.
82. Duquette, *Bright Line Test, supra* note 23.
83. ABA 2011 Model Act, Section 7(e): "Consistent with Rule 1.14, ABA Model Rules of Professional Conduct (2004), the child's lawyer should determine whether the child has sufficient maturity to understand and form an attorney-client relationship and whether the child is capable of making reasoned judgements and engaging in meaningful communication."

vides: "When a client's capacity to make adequately considered decisions in connection with a representation is diminished, whether because of minority, mental impairment or for some other reason, the lawyer shall, as far as reasonably possible, maintain a normal client-lawyer relationship with the client."[84] The commentary to Rule 1.14 says: "Furthermore, to an increasing extent the law recognizes intermediate degrees of competence. For example, children as young as five or six years of age, and certainly those of 10 or 12, are regarded as having opinions that are entitled to weight in legal proceedings governing their custody." The default position, therefore, is for the child's lawyer to maintain as normal an attorney-client relationship as possible.

Rule 1.14 requires the lawyer to determine whether the child has diminished capacity. The lawyer is permitted to consult others but is ultimately left to his or her own subjective judgment as to capacity. It further complicates the question that a child may be competent for some things and not for others. ("A determination of incapacity may be incremental and issue-specific."[85]) Yet there is little direction as to *how* the diminished capacity determination is to be made.

Lawyers are not trained in child development. The question of competency and maturity is an evolving and elusive judgment that doctoral level psychologists have a difficult time making. In the case of the very young child or the older child, the question of competence to instruct counsel may not be so difficult. If the client is an infant and cannot speak, the client cannot instruct counsel.

If a client is a normally developed 15- or 16-year-old, however, he or she is quite likely to have clear and reasonable views as to the proper decisions affecting his or her life. Those views should be aggressively argued to the court and most would urge traditional client-directed representation for the older youth. But determining capacity for the middle-years child, from 8 to 12 for instance, or the immature or mentally challenged child, and the weight to be given to that child's preferences is perhaps the most difficult question in child advocacy today, and it does not yet have a clear answer.

Despite its limitations in guiding the determination of client competency, however, Model Rule 1.14 provides helpful guidance as to what an attorney is to do if the client is determined to have diminished capacity. Rule 1.14(b) provides: "When the lawyer reasonably believes that the client has diminished capacity, is at risk of substantial physical, financial or other harm unless action is taken and cannot adequately act in the client's own interest, the lawyer may take reasonably necessary protective action, including consulting with individuals or entities that have the ability to take action to protect the client and, in appropriate cases, seeking the appointment of a guardian ad

---

84. The older version of the Model Rules refer to a client who is *impaired*, rather than with *diminished capacity*. The term "diminished capacity" better reflects the current understanding of child development as a process in which a child may be competent for some matters and not others and competent some days and not others.

85. *Id. See also* ABA 1996 Standards.

litem, conservator or guardian." Rule 1.14(b) gives the child's attorney broader guidance on what "other protective action" might be appropriate, including allowing consultation with other persons or entities.

Further, the 2002 Rule 1.14(b) provides more guidance regarding the previous trigger for acting ("only when the lawyer reasonably believes that the client cannot act in the client's own interest") to include situations in which the client "is at risk of substantial physical, financial or other harm unless action is taken and cannot adequately act in the client's own interest." This change reflects the loosening of the confidentiality rules under some circumstances.

The Comment to the new Rule 1.14 provides helpful guidance to the child's attorney wishing to take protective action on behalf of the child client:

> [5] If a lawyer reasonably believes that a client is at risk of substantial physical, financial or other harm unless action is taken, and that a normal client-lawyer relationship cannot be maintained as provided in paragraph (a) because the client lacks sufficient capacity to communicate or to make adequately considered decisions in connection with the representation, then paragraph (b) permits the lawyer to take protective measures deemed necessary. Such measures could include:
>
> - consulting with family members,
> - using a reconsideration period to permit clarification or improvement of circumstances,
> - using voluntary surrogate decision-making tools such as durable powers of attorney or consulting with support groups, professional services, adult-protective agencies or other individuals or entities that have the ability to protect the client.
>
> In taking any protective action, the lawyer should be guided by such factors as the wishes and values of the client to the extent known, the client's best interests and the goals of intruding into the client's decision-making autonomy to the least extent feasible, maximizing client capacities and respecting the client's family and social connections.
>
> [6] In determining the extent of the client's diminished capacity, the lawyer should consider and balance such factors as: the client's ability to articulate reasoning leading to a decision, variability of state of mind and ability to appreciate consequences of a decision; the substantive fairness of a decision; and the consistency of a decision with the known long-term commitments and values of the client. In appropriate circumstances, the lawyer may seek guidance from an appropriate diagnostician.
>
> [7] If a legal representative has not been appointed, the lawyer should consider whether appointment of a guardian ad litem, conservator or guardian is necessary

to protect the client's interests. Thus, if a client with diminished capacity has substantial property that should be sold for the client's benefit, effective completion of the transaction may require appointment of a legal representative. In addition, rules of procedure in litigation sometimes provide that minors or persons with diminished capacity must be represented by a guardian or next friend if they do not have a general guardian. In many circumstances, however, appointment of a legal representative may be more expensive or traumatic for the client than circumstances in fact require. Evaluation of such circumstances is a matter entrusted to the professional judgment of the lawyer. In considering alternatives, however, the lawyer should be aware of any law that requires the lawyer to advocate the least restrictive action on behalf of the client.

The new Comment 4 to Rule 1.14 provides that in "matters involving a minor, whether the lawyer should look to the parents as natural guardians may depend on the type of proceeding or matter in which the lawyer is representing the minor." Even in the child welfare context where parents are accused of neglect or even abuse, the child's attorney may find helpful insights and guidance from the parents on custody alternatives as well as child's needs and preferences, important persons in the child's life, education and health care.

2.6.8 Analysis

The vast majority of legal scholars and authorities who have addressed this issue recommend that a lawyer should take direction from his or her child client if the child is determined to have developed the cognitive capacity to engage in reasoned decision making. The national trend is in the direction of a more traditional lawyer role, giving more deference to the child's wishes and preferences on as many issues as possible, and turning to a more objective process for determining the child's position when that is required. Determining the decision-making capacity of any particular child and the weight to be given to that child's preferences remains a difficult and elusive question, however.[86]

2.7 Promising Practices for Child's Attorneys

The intense debate on who directs the child's lawyer and how, has often detracted from consideration of what that child representative should actually do. That is, what are the duties and practices that create successful representation?[87]

---

86. DONALD DUQUETTE & ANN M. HARALAMBIE, *Representing Children and Youth, in* CHILD WELFARE LAW AND PRACTICE: REPRESENTING CHILDREN, PARENTS, AND STATE AGENCIES IN ABUSE, NEGLECT, AND DEPENDENCY CASES (Duquette et al. eds., 3d ed. 2016).

87. Buss, *supra* note 33 at 1749 ("I am convinced, however, that it matters far less which role is assumed than that the role is communicated to the child"); Katherine Kruse, *Standing in Babylon,*

2.7.1 Basic Duties and Characteristics

The 1996 ABA Standards maintain that attorneys for children should:

- obtain copies of all pleadings and relevant notices;
- participate in depositions, negotiations, discovery, pretrial conferences, and hearings;
- inform other parties and their representatives that they are representing the child and expect reasonable notification prior to case conferences, changes of placement, and other changes of circumstances affecting the child and the child's family;
- attempt to reduce case delays and ensure that the court recognizes the need to speedily promote permanency for the child;
- counsel the child concerning the subject matter of the litigation, the child's rights, the court system, the proceedings, the lawyer's role, and what to expect in the legal process;
- develop a theory and strategy of the case to implement at hearings, including factual and legal issues; and
- identify appropriate family and professional resources for the child.[88]

The 1996 ABA Standards, upon which the QIC Best Practice Model of Child Representation is based, reflects a considerable national consensus on the duties of the child's representative, i.e., what it is that the advocate for the child should actually do.[89] In a similar vein, the UNLV Conference attendees recommended that children's attorneys should be able to recognize issues that require the services of other professionals and know how to access those services. Children's attorneys should have sufficient knowledge of other disciplines to formulate requests for evaluations and services from other professionals and to evaluate and use professional opinions.[90]

2.7.2 Understanding the Child Client

Commentators note that awareness of the client's individual context is necessary to reducing the role of race, culture, or class biases in representation.[91] According to Jean Koh Peters, the child's attorney "whether assigned to represent a child's wishes or her

---

Looking Toward Zion, 6 Nev. L.J. 1315, 1316 (suggesting that the UNLV conference was an ultimately practical endeavor that can inform a lawyer's day-to-day ethical choices); Glynn, *Unauthorized Practice*, *supra* note 28 ("In the debate about best interests versus articulated wishes, the value of legal counseling and advice is often lost"). *See also* Duquette, *Bright Line Test*, *supra* note 23, at 1249 ("how to determine the best interests of a child. . .is among the least developed part of our jurisprudence and should be a central focus of our discussion as a field").

88. 1996 ABA Abuse and Neglect Standards, at B-1.
89. *Id.*
90. *Id.* at (1)(A)(2)(a)(ii). *See also* 2007 ULC Model Act, § 7 cmt.
91. Peter Margulies, *Lawyering for Children: Confidentiality Meets Context*, 81 St. John's L. Rev. 601, 617 & 630 (2007); Taylor, *supra* note 29, at 615; Kisthardt, *supra* note 43; Stötzel & Fegert, *supra* note 33, at 220; 2007 ULC Model Act § 11.

best interests, must ground her representation in a thickly textured understanding of the child's world and the child's point of view."[92] The UNLV Recommendations emphasize that attorneys should continually reflect on and assess the extent to which their personal opinions, values, and biases may affect the representation of their child clients, and attempt to understand their individual client's needs and interests, resisting boilerplate responses.[93] A child's age, legal status, and social attributes can mask the child's individuality, leading to decisions and processes that marginalize the child's identities, needs and interests.[94]

Ann Haralambie and Lauren Adams discuss the importance of planning for relationship building.[95] Building client relationships is crucial not only to understand the individual client, but also because the attorney must establish rapport with the child before the child is likely to provide much useful information. The attorney should learn as much background information as possible before speaking with a child client from caseworkers, social workers, teachers, coaches, family members, friends, school records, case reports, medical records, police reports, or other historical documents.

Meeting with a child client in the child's environment provides the attorney with important information for representation and may allow the client to feel more at ease in developing a relationship. Important elements of relationship include building trust by keeping promises, maintaining honesty, and by managing client expectations about what the attorney is able to provide. Attorneys may strengthen rapport by not rushing children during interviews, actively listening during meetings, being aware of how their own responses may be perceived, and arranging for a trusted adult to emphasize that the attorney may be trusted.

The UNLV recommendations note that attorneys should have competency in child cognitive development, effective child interviewing skills, and should structure all communications to account for the individual child's age, level of education, cultural context, and degree of language acquisition.[96] Emily Buss has examined the importance of understanding children's development in their representation.[97] The 2011 ABA Model Act expects attorneys to be able to gauge the developmental capacity of their child clients.

The UNLV conferees also maintained that children's attorneys should become familiar with the child's family, community and culture, and should take precautions to avoid imposing the lawyer's own standards and cultural values.[98] Children's attorneys

---

92. KOH PETERS, REPRESENTING CHILDREN, *supra* note 17.
93. 2006 UNLV Recommendations, *supra* note 65, at (1)(B)(1).
94. *Id.*
95. Ann Haralambie & Lauren Adams, *Lawyering—Child Client Interviewing and Counseling*, NACC GUIDE (2010); *see also* KOH PETERS, REPRESENTING CHILDREN, *supra* note 17, at § 4-3(a)(3).
96. 2006 UNLV Recommendations, *supra* note 65, at (1)(C)(2)(b), 1996 ABA Abuse and Neglect Standards A-3; 2007 ULC Model Act § 7.
97. Buss, *supra* note 33.
98. 2006 UNLV Recommendations, *supra* note 65, at (1)(A)(2)(a).

should engage the entire family, and help the family understand how they can participate in the proceedings.[99] Children's attorneys should recognize the importance for most clients of maintaining connections to their families and communities.

Attorneys should solicit feedback from clients and families as to their representation.[100] Attorneys should challenge policies and practices that purport to protect the safety of lesbian, gay, bisexual or transgender children solely by isolating them from other children, and children's attorneys should challenge policies and practices that criminalize or pathologize adolescent sexual behavior that is typical or common from a developmental perspective.[101]

2.7.3 The Role of Children in Dependency Proceedings

Commentators argue for a renewed emphasis on the child's status as a full party to the proceedings, with the appropriate level of the child's presence, participation, and involvement.[102] Children, as parties, should be represented throughout the proceedings, receive all papers and communications with the court, attend all hearings, participate in formal discovery, including depositions, participate in settlement agreements, present evidence, including the calling of witnesses, and make arguments to the court.[103]

In 2007, the ABA resolved to provide "all youth with the ability and right to attend and fully participate in all hearings related to their cases."[104] Along these lines, the UNLV Conference recommends strengthening the role of the child's voice in CAPTA by mandating compliance with the United Nations Convention on the Rights of the Child Article 12, allowing that a child be given the opportunity to be heard in any judicial proceeding affecting the child. The UNLV Recommendations also maintain that children's attorneys should promote the development of organizations that support the engagement of youth in child welfare processes.[105]

On a broader level, attorneys should advocate that youth, including youth representing diverse experiences and perspectives, participate in developing policies and practices affecting children and their families.[106]

---

99. *Id.* at (1)(A)(2)(i)
100. *Id.* at (1)(B)(2)(g).
101. 2006 UNLV Recommendations, *supra* note 65, at (3)(C)(2)(d).
102. Sobie, *supra* note 59, at 747. See also Glynn, *Unauthorized Practice*, *supra* note 28 at 70 (enumerating state statutes on child's status as a party to the litigation); 2007 ULC Model Act, at II cmt. (describing state law on party status); Jonathan Whybrow, *Children, Guardians and Rule 9.5*, 34 FAM. L.Q. 504 (2004) (describing English law on party status.) On a child's right to choose counsel, see Sobie, *supra* note 59, at 769-71; *see also* Barry J. Berenberg, *Attorneys for Children in Abuse and Neglect Proceedings*, 36 N.M. L. REV. 533, 561-564 (2006).
103. Glynn, *supra* note 28.
104. ABA Resolution 104a, adopted August 2007. Youth Transitioning from Foster Care (Youth at Risk), available at http://www.abanet.org/child/parentrepresentation/PDFs/060.pdf.
105. 2006 UNLV Recommendations, *supra* note 65, at (3)(A)(2)(b).
106. *Id.*, at (3)(B)(2).

Emily Buss has described her own experience of involving clients directly in proceedings, which increased the quality of attorney-client interaction. She argues that there is value in children seeing precisely what happens in court, because understanding how the court functions is essential to a child's understanding of how the lawyer functions in that system, and how the system makes decisions on the child's behalf.[107]

2.7.4 Systemic Pressures Confounding Child Representatives

A variety of systemic pressures that significantly impede the quality of representation are acknowledged in the literature.[108] Commentators have emphasized the difficulty of providing quality representation in states with overburdened foster care systems.[109] Inadequate representation and adjudication often result from unreasonably high caseloads and crowded dockets.[110] Attorneys with high caseloads are unable to carry out the most basic tasks required for legitimate representation according to any model, including client meetings.[111] Overwhelmed judicial caseloads result in delays.[112] In many jurisdictions, attorney compensation is limited, and is sometimes inadequate to compensate attorneys for basic statutory duties.[113] Inadequate compensation is also cited as an issue internationally.[114]

---

107. Buss, *supra* note 33, at 1760-61.
108. Glynn, *Unauthorized Practice*, *supra* note 28, at 58; Adoption 2002 Guidelines, at 1-5.
109. Kruse, *supra* note 87, at 1316; Buss, *supra* note 33, at 1761; Lois A. Weinberg, et al., *Advocacy's Role in Identifying Dysfunctions in Agencies Serving Abused and Neglected Children*, 2.3 CHILD MALTREATMENT 212, 212 (1997).
110. Taylor, *supra* note 29, at 621-22 (describing state statistics and guidelines); Howard Davidson & Erik S. Pitchal, *Caseloads Must Be Controlled So All Child Clients Can Receive Competent Lawyering*, in THE SPECIALIZED PRACTICE OF JUVENILE LAW: MODEL PRACTICE IN MODEL OFFICES (National Association of Counsel for Children, 2006); Glynn, *Unauthorized Practice*, *supra* note 28, at 58; Randi Mandelbaum, *Revisiting the Question of Whether Young Children in Child Protection Proceedings Should Be Represented by Lawyers*, 32 LOY. U CHI. L.J. 1 (2000); Marx, *supra* note 59, at 531. See also Nolan Clay & Randy Ellis, *National Panel Faults Oklahoma County System*, THE OKLAHOMAN, Apr. 27, 2008 (assistant public defenders in Oklahoma County had caseloads between 1000 and 1250 children).
111. Buss, *supra* note 33, at 1759-61; Margulies, *supra* note 91, at 621; Sobie, *supra* note 59, at 825; Kisthardt, *supra* note 43, at 11; Marcia Robinson Lowry & SaraBartosz, *Looking Ahead to the Next 30 Years of Child Advocacy Symposium Presentations*, 41 U. MICH. J.L. REFORM 199 (2007); Marx, *supra* note 59, at 531.
112. 2006 UNLV Recommendations, *supra* note 65, at (5)(D)(2)(d).
113. See Charlotte A. Carter-Yamauchi, *Issues Relating to Guardians Ad Litem*, HAWAII LEGISLATIVE REFERENCE BUREAU (2003); Marx, *supra* note 59, at 531; Barbara Glesner Fines, *Pressures Toward Mediocrity in the Representation of Children*, 37 CAP. U. L. REV. 411, 440-446 (2008); Kisthardt, *supra* note 43; Melissa Breger et al., *Building Pediatric Law Careers: The University of Michigan Law School Experience*, 34 FAM. L. Q. 531, 532-33 (2000); Richardson, *supra* note 37. See also Jean Koh Peters, *How Children Are Heard in Child Protective Proceedings, in the U.S. and Around the World in 2005: Survey Findings, Initial Observations, and Areas for Further Study*, 6 NEV. L.J. 966, 1074 (2006) (surveying state practice in appointing counsel for children in dependency cases).
114. Stötzel & Fegert, *supra* note 33, at 222.

Attorney training and competence are recognized as a shortcoming in many jurisdictions.[115] Children's lawyers are not social workers or psychologists, and commentators emphasize the benefit of multidisciplinary decision-making.[116] Children's legal representatives often lack funding for important support personnel, for example, social workers and paralegals.[117]

Commentators have described additional pressures arising from the context of child welfare proceedings. Martin Guggenheim argues that too few children's advocates are guided by a presumption in favor of family unification because insisting upon a child's prompt reunification poses a risk to their professional reputations. Judges, as well, are rarely criticized in public for wrongfully ordering the removal of a child. The media focuses its attention on the notorious "false negative" cases, where children are not removed but later suffer serious harm or even death. This skewed media attention creates intense pressure to "err on the side of safety," and the prevailing culture offers emotional rewards for children's lawyers to play a "heroic" role in rescuing children from risk, without a similar reward for minimizing disruption of their lives by providing in-home safety plans and the like.[118] Howard Davidson notes that advocates must constantly be wary of the "rubber stamp" of judicial approval of agency actions. Overextended courts systems do not often have sufficient or qualified staff to understand the needs of children placed with foster agencies.[119]

Commentators have also noted that ambiguity of the representative's role and the lingering notion of the attorney as an agent of the court creates pressure toward general passivity in representation,[120] and that relationships and communication between attorneys and social workers may be strained because of their different languages and training.[121] The informality of proceedings is also noted to be an issue, contributing to

---

115. Fines, *supra* note 113, at 412; *Fostering the Future: Safety, Permanence, and Well-being for Children in Foster Care*, PEW COMMISSION ON CHILDREN IN FOSTER CARE (2004); *Hearing Children's Voices and Interests in Adoption and Guardianship Proceedings*, ABA Child Custody & Adoption Pro Bono Project, 41 FAM. L.Q. 365, 381 (2007); ABA Resolutions on Foster Care and Adoption: Foster Care Reform, Aug. 2005 (urging development and implementation of national protocols and standards for reasonable attorney caseloads); Lowry & Bartosz, *supra* note 111, at 207; Susan A. Snyder, *Promises Kept, Promises Broken: An Analysis of Children's Right to Counsel in Dependency Proceedings in Pennsylvania*, JUVENILE LAW CENTER 38 (2001), http://www.jlc.org/File/publications/pkpd.pdf; Appell, *supra* note 40, at 609-611.

116. 2009 ABA Model Act, *supra* note 64, at 147-48; Kisthardt, *supra* note 43; Haralambie, *supra* note 43, at 24.

117. Fines, *supra* note 113, at 413-14; Davidson & Pitchal, *supra* note 110.

118. Guggenheim, *State Interests*, *supra* note 38, at 830-31; Margulies, *supra* note 91, at 620 (describing the asymmetry of penalty and reward facing attorneys for children).

119. Howard Davidson, *Federal Law and State Intervention When Parents Fail: Has National Guidance of our Child Welfare System Been Successful?*, 42 FAM. L.Q. 481, 482 (2008).

120. Fines, *supra* note 113, at 440–46.

121. Kisthardt, *supra* note 43.

attorney-driven outcomes, an insufficient focus on children, limitations on appellate review, and weakened child confidence in judicial proceedings.[122]

2.7.5 Problem-Solving Courts and Holistic Representation of Children

Alternative or problem-solving court systems such as unified courts, family drug courts, and domestic violence courts are discussed in the academic literature. According to Sarah Ramsey, these courts tend to downplay the role of the court as decision-maker and enforcer, instead emphasizing a service function, team decision-making, and a focus on ultimate outcomes benefiting the litigants and community.[123] These courts are noted to raise due process concerns, such as the blending of criminal and civil proceedings and the potential for judicial bias, but may be structured to incorporate due process protections.[124]

The UNLV Recommendations maintain that jurisdictions should permit lawyers to represent youth in more than one system, engaging in concurrent or dual representation.[125] Ramsey also describes how lawyers may participate in programs such as medical-legal partnerships that seek to improve children's health.[126] Additional models have been thought to strengthen the relationship between representation in court and service delivery.[127] Foster care review panels may also provide oversight of children's cases.[128]

2.8 Caseloads

What is a reasonable caseload for lawyers representing children? Crushing caseloads in urban settings have been a troubling feature of child welfare law practice for many years. The 2005 ABA resolution and Pew Commission recommendations also included standards for reasonable attorney caseloads.[129] In 2005, the finding in Kenny A. that children have a constitutional right to adequate legal representation resulted in a

---

122. Pitchal, *supra* note 26, at 686-687; Buss, *supra* note 33, at 1760-61; Kothekar, *supra* note 70, at 504-05.
123. Sarah Ramsey, *Child Well-Being: A Beneficial Advocacy Framework for Improving the Child Welfare System?*, 41 U. MICH. J.L. REFORM 9, 19-20 (2007).
124. *Id.*
125. 2006 UNLV Recommendations, *supra* note 65, at (5)(D)(2)(a).
126. Ramsey, *supra* note 123, at 21.
127. Shelly L. Jackson, *A USA National Survey of Program Services Provided by Child Advocacy Centers*, 28 CHILD ABUSE & NEGLECT 411, 412 (2004); Gail Chang Bohr, *Ethics and the Standards of Practice for the Representation of Children in Abuse and Neglect Proceedings*, 32 WM. MITCHELL L. REV. 989 (2006); Gail Hornor, *Child Advocacy Centers: Providing Support to Primary Care Providers*, 22 J. PEDIATRIC HEALTH CARE 35 (2008).
128. *See* Youngclarke et al., *supra* note 44, at 112.
129. ABA Resolutions on Foster Care and Adoption: Foster Care Reform, Aug. 2005, http://www.abanet.org/child/foster-adopt.shtml. *See also* Adoption 2002 Guidelines (urging that compensation of children's attorneys should closer to that for attorneys handling matters of similar demand and complexity).

settlement agreement limiting caseloads to 90 children per attorney in DeKalb County.[130] A 2006 survey for the NACC showed that 18 percent of respondents had more than 200 cases and an addition 25% had between 100 and 199.[131]

The NACC recommends a standard of 100 active clients for a full-time attorney.[132] The NACC based this recommendation on a rough calculation that the average attorney has 2000 hours available per year and that the average child client would require about 20 hours of attention in the course of a year.[133] In *Kenny A* the court heard expert testimony from NACC along these lines and this evidence became a key consideration in the court's finding that foster children have a right to an effective lawyer in dependency cases who is not burdened by excessive caseloads.[134]

A 2008 caseload study by the Judicial Council of California based on time and motion measures recommended a caseload of 77 clients per full-time dependency attorney to achieve an optimal best practice standard of performance.[135] The California Judicial Council set 141 as the maximum ceiling of cases a full-time attorney may carry. The Council also recognized the value of multidisciplinary representation when it proscribed a modified *maximum* caseload standard of 188 clients per attorney if there is a 0.5 FTE investigator/social worker complement for each full-time attorney position. New York law sets the maximum caseload at 150.[136]

The Massachusetts Committee for Public Counsel Services, which provides counsel for children and parents in dependency cases, enforces a caseload of 75 open cases.[137] In a systematic study a Pennsylvania workgroup carefully broke down the tasks and expected time required throughout the life of a case and matched that to attorney hours available in a year. They concluded that caseloads for children's lawyers should be set at 65 per full time lawyer.[138]

---

130. Kenny A. ex rel. v. Perdue, 356 F. Supp. 2d 1353 (N.D. Ga. 2005).
131. Davidson & Pitchal, *supra* note 110.
132. National Association of Counsel for Children, *Child Welfare Law Guidebook*, 2006, at 54
133. Erik S. Pitchal et al., *Evaluation of the Guardian ad Litem System in Nebraska*, NACC 42-43 (2009), http://c.ymcdn.com/sites/www.naccchildlaw.org/resource/resmgr/nebraska/final_nebraska_gal_report_12.pdf
134. In re Kenny A, *supra* note 130. Also see Pitchel, note 133 at 43.
135. Dependency Counsel Caseload Standards: A Report to the California Legislature, Judicial Council of California Administrative Office of the Courts, April 2008, http://www.courts.ca.gov/documents/DependencyCounselCaseloadStandards2008.pdf.
136. 22 N.Y. Comp. Codes & Regs. Tit. 22 § 127.5(a).
137. Massachusetts Committee for Public Counsel Services, Policies and Procedures Governing Billing and Compensation, revised November 2011, https://www.publiccounsel.net/private_counsel_manual/CURRENT_MANUAL_2010/MANUALChap5links3.pdf.
138. 2014 Pennsylvania State Roundtable Report: Moving Children to Timely Permanency through high quality Legal Representation (May 9, 2014) http://www.sdgrantmakers.org/Portals/0/AboutUs/2014%20PA%20Roundtable%20Report%20Moving%20Children%20to%20Timely%20Permanency.pdf.

2.9 Implementing Training Programs

Both the 1996 and 2011 ABA Standards recommend training content for lawyers representing children. Trial judges who are regularly involved in child-related matters should participate in training for the child's attorney conducted by the courts, the bar, or any other group.[139] Attorneys must understand applicable state and federal statutes, case law on applicable legal standards; agency and court rules; authoritative representation guidelines and standards; the family court process, service implementation, and key personnel in child-related litigation, including custody evaluations and mediation; child development, family dynamics, and communicating with children.[140] In 2005, the ABA passed a resolution that included an exhortation to Congress, states, and territories to enact policies consistent with the recommendations of the May 2004 Pew Commission on Children in Foster Care. The Pew recommendations included federal and state support for attorney training; and development, implementation of, and funding for, qualification and training standards.[141]

The UNLV Recommendations note that bar associations and other legal organizations should provide continuing legal education ("CLE") so attorneys can stay current in related subject areas and the operations of other systems affecting children and families.[142] The 2009 First Star state survey found that 34 jurisdictions require attorneys for children to have training prior to appointment or CLE after appointment.[143]

The NACC developed a Child Welfare Law Specialist certification currently available in 43 jurisdictions.[144] The 2008 Fostering Connections to Success and Increasing Adoptions Act expanded the availability of federal funds to train attorneys representing children in child protection proceedings.[145]

Certain commentators examined the increasing role of child advocacy education in law schools, including clinical programs.[146] Like the UNLV Recommendations, these

---

139. 1996 ABA Standards I-1; 2011 ABA Standards, Section 4; *see also* Fines, *supra* note 113; Marx, *supra* note 14, at 507; Taylor, *supra* note 29; Harris, *supra* note 22, at 1294.

140. 1996 ABA Standards, at I-2.

141. ABA Resolutions on Foster Care and Adoption: Foster Care Reform, Aug. 2005, http://www.abanet.org/child/foster-adopt.shtml.

142. 2006 UNLV Recommendations, *supra* note 65, at (2)(F)(3)(a).

143. First Star, A Child's Right to Counsel: A National Report Card on Legal Representation for Abused & Neglected Children (2009), http://www.firststar.org/library/report- cards.aspx.

144. NACC Certification is currently available in 42 states. *See* NACC Certification, NACC Website, http://www.naccchildlaw.org/?page=Certification. See also Marvin Ventrell & Amanda George Donnelly, *NACC Certifies Nation's First Child Welfare Law Specialists*, CHILDREN'S VOICE MAG., Apr. 1, 2007.

145. Fostering Connections to Success and Increasing Adoptions Act of 2008, P.L. 110-351, 122 Stat. 3949; Taylor, *supra* note 29, at 620.

146. Donald N. Duquette, *Developing a Child Advocacy Law Clinic: A Law School Clinical Legal Education Opportunity*, 31 U. MICH. J. L. REF. 1 (1997); Ventrell, *The Practice of Law for Children*, *supra* note 41; Christina A. Zawisza, *Two Heads Are Better Than One: The Case-Based Rationale for Dual Disciplinary Teaching in Child Advocacy Clinics*, 7 FLA. COASTAL L.

writers emphasize the importance of multidisciplinary education, practice-oriented modeling, and collaboration with related fields such as a social work.[147] Child law education must also support law students and graduates in pursuing "pediatric," i.e. child welfare law, careers.[148]

2.10 Literature Review Conclusion

The recent literature on child representation has analyzed the law defining child representation; assessed whether a lawyer must be appointed for the child; debated the roles of the child representative; examined the recommendations and standards contributed by authoritative bodies and conferences; illustrated preferred practices for child representatives; and emphasized systemic challenges and progress.

The academic and policy literature supports the view that children require legal representation in child welfare cases, yet point out that the current child representation is inadequate to the need. Commentators recognize the value of individual child advocacy in getting each individual child the specific and unique supports necessary for their safety and well-being in an extremely complex social system, but identify many technical, practical and philosophical issues that must be addressed.

The current academic literature provides an essential theoretical context for framing the QIC Best Practice Model of representation, but the Best Practice Model must be considered in the practical and day to day context of child representation. We turn to that next.

REV. 631, 631 (2006); Fines, *supra* note 113; Kisthardt, *supra* note 43; Breger et al., *supra* note 113, at 532-33.

147. *See also* 2006 UNLV Recommendations, *supra* note 65, at (2)(A)–(F) & (3)(E) ("Bar associations and other legal organizations should promote collaborative approaches to learning and provide cross-disciplinary education . . ."); Zawisza, *supra* note 146, at 631

148. Breger et al., *supra* note 113, at 532-33.

CHAPTER 3
National Needs Assessment

Abstract
This chapter explains how the QIC Needs Assessment examined data and empirical research from:

- State laws
- Stakeholder Discussions
- Surveys of State Report Cards on child representation
- Focus Groups, and
- Reviews of the few existing empirical studies of child representation.

Using that data, the project identified an emerging consensus as to duties and tasks of the child's legal representative and system supports that would allow high practice standards to be realized.

3.1 State Law

In addition to tracing the evolution of the child's attorney role as reflected in federal law, authoritative recommendations and the academic literature, the QIC needs assessment reviewed the current state laws governing lawyers for children. We analyzed all the state laws and posted them on our website in a common template.[1] Some state laws

---

1. See http://www.improvechildrep.org/ChildRep2010/ StateLaws.aspx The organizing template is the same as that for the 1996 ABA Standards and for the QIC Best Practice Model of Child Representation. The website includes state legal authority governing child representation

do an excellent job providing the needed legal structure for children's lawyers while others come up seriously short. Most reflect the general understanding as to core child lawyer functions but there are exceptions. State laws vary in the specification of the duties and tasks of the lawyer while others fail to require legal representation for all children in the child welfare system.[2] Despite the requirements of federal law (CAPTA), in some states children in dependency cases are not appointed counsel (or even a lay advocate) at all.[3] A serious lack of enforcement of CAPTA requiring a representative for each child contributes to this gap between national standards and the practice on the ground.[4]

Our findings are consistent with other commentators who have noted that law defining child representation is quite unsettled. The variation across jurisdictions may decrease the quality of representation and create confusion simply because the attorneys are not clear on what is expected of them. Prevailing opinion calls for increased clarity on the role of children's legal representation. A 2005 survey indicated that there are at least 56 variations in child representation models among the 50 states.[5] A variety of models are also present internationally.[6]

The law on the books may not reflect the "law in practice," however. Subsequent to the QIC Needs Assessment, the Children's Advocacy Institute (CAI) at the University of San Diego School of Law and First Star, a national child advocacy organization, produced a series of influential reports framed as "report cards" with respect to state laws regarding attorneys for abused and neglected children and do not paint a pretty picture of the status of child representation nationally.[7] Despite exemplary legal structures in

---

with links to the authoritative electronic compilation of each state's laws governing child representation.

2. Fla. Stat. § 39.822(1); Burns Ind. Code Ann. § 31-32-4-2; (Rev. Code Wash. § 13.34.100(6)(f)

3. *Shame on U.S.: Failings by All three Branches of Our Federal Government Leave Abused and Neglected Children Vulnerable to Further Harm*, (2015) at 59; available at http://www.caichildlaw.org/Misc/Shame%20on%20U.S._FINAL.pdf

4. Glynn, *The Child's Representation under CAPTA: It Is Time for Enforcement*, 6 Nev L.Rev. 1250 (Spring 2006)

5. Jean Koh Peters, *How Children are Heard in Child Protective Proceedings, in the U.S. and Around the World in 2005: Survey Findings, Initial Observations, and Areas for Further Study*, 6 NEV. L.J. 966 (2006); See also Jean Koh Peters, Representing Children in Child Protective Proceedings, 3d Edition, Lexis Nexis 2007.

Worldwide (2005), available at www.yale.edu/rcw.

6. Koh Peters, Representing Children, supra note 2. See also Bilson & White, supra note 66; Whybrow, supra note 123; Stötzel & Fegert, supra note 22; Patricia O'Kane, The Developing Role of the Guardian Ad Litem under the Children, 12 Child Care in Prac. 157 (2006); Drews & Halprin, supra note 174

7. A Child's Right to Counsel: A National Report Card on Legal Representation for Abused and Neglected Children, Third Edition, May 8, 2012. http://www.caichildlaw.org/Misc/3rd_Ed_Childs_Right_to_Counsel.pdf

some states, there is plenty of room for improvement in the vast majority of states. In the third edition: 15 States earned an A or A+; 11 States earned a B; nine States earned a C; six States earned a D; and 10 States earned an F. Only 61% of states require the appointment of attorneys for abused or neglected children. More than 39% of states do not require that all abused and neglected children have legal representation. Only 24% of states require multidisciplinary training or education for child's counsel. Only 31% of states currently mandate the appointment of client-directed representation for the child.[8]

The CAI and First Star recognize the potential gap between law on the books and the law in practice when the report concludes: "Grades do not imply any correlation between a state's law and the enforcement of, or compliance with, such law. . . . Our assumption is that good law is the cornerstone of any state's commitment to the rights of its children."[9]

3.2. Law in Practice

3.2.1 Method

Recognizing that the "law on the books" tells only part of the story of child representation in any given State, the QIC sought to assess the "law in practice," or at least perceptions of the "law in practice," through several additional means: 1) Stakeholder discussions in 10 sample states; 2) Survey of all state reports to the Federal government; 3) Focus groups with key stakeholders; 4) Notable office visits; and 5) Existing empirical evaluations of child representation.[10]

3.2.2 Stakeholder Discussions

Using ten sample states,[11] QIC developed and implemented structured interviews for key informants from each state, including, the U.S. Health and Human Services Administration for Children and Families (ACF) Regional Office staff person most familiar with the state, the CIP Director or equivalent knowledgeable person, two judges, five attorneys two child welfare caseworker supervisors and two to three CASAs. We were interested in how the duties set out in state laws compared with the law in practice as reflected by the key informants.[12] The discussions yielded a large amount of descriptive

---

8. *Id.* at 11
9. *Id.* at 15
10. QIC Phase II Implementation Plan, September 2010 Report to Children's Bureau, available at www.ImproveChildRep.org
11. The ten sample states are: California, Colorado, Connecticut, Delaware, Georgia, Illinois, Iowa, New York, Texas, and Washington State.
12. The process of analyzing state laws, conducting the structured interviews with key state informants, focus groups etc, is reported on the QIC website, www.ImproveChildRep.org.

data, which was organized into tables, allowing analysis of the responses and comparisons within states, across all states, and among the stakeholder groups. The themes from these key state informants are as follows:

- **Performance is highly variable.** All reported much individual variation, with low marks given to attorneys who do not specialize in dependency cases. Lower variability was reported for attorneys under centralized state oversight or working for dedicated specialty offices, which received the best reports. Stakeholders cited training, oversight and guidelines as reducing variability.
- **Attorneys need more contact with the child.** In a variety of contexts, informants from every group raised the concern that attorneys do not really know their clients. Even some attorneys admitted that they do not have adequate time to spend on home visits with children. Many cited the standard practice of quickly touching base with children in the courthouse just prior to hearings.
- **Attorneys often have little support.** Informants reported very few supports for attorneys representing children. Attorneys often cited peers or even child welfare agency caseworkers as their sole sources of support. In comparison, attorneys in specialized offices received a range of supports, most commonly access to a social worker.
- **More training is needed.** Throughout the interviews, stakeholders mentioned the need for more attorney training. Stakeholders raised this issue frequently throughout the interviews. A caseworker comment reflected the opinions expressed by all stakeholders: "It takes more than a law degree to do this kind of work." Across the board, every stakeholder group wanted to see more training, especially in child and family issues and courtroom practice.
- **Attorneys act as problem solvers.** Stakeholders described attorneys using their negotiating skills to resolve issues outside the courtroom. They noted that when attorneys actively advocate on behalf of their clients, they are also better able to resolve issues outside the courtroom.
- **Attorneys try to accommodate the child's wishes.** Regardless of the formal role, i.e., best interest or expressed wishes, attorneys found ways to accommodate the child's wishes, most often by bringing them to the attention of the court. They saw this more as an issue of determining the child's capacity, since age and maturity play a large factor in whether the attorney will take the child's wishes into account.
- **Caseloads are thought to be too high.** The consensus in most places is that attorneys simply do not have the time necessary to perform all the functions of their jobs. Attorneys described frustrations such as not being compensated for travel time.
- **CASA use varied among the jurisdictions we surveyed.** In some places, informants felt the CASAs form an essential component to the system. Where they are relied upon heavily, their main role is reported as contacting the child and collaterals and providing information to the court and to the attorneys.

3.2.3 State Reports to the Federal Government

QIC surveyed and analyzed reports that the 50 states themselves prepared for the Federal government regarding child welfare practices, including the CIP (Court Improvement Program) Annual Program Assessments and the Child and Family Service Reviews, to determine whether state policy makers identified priorities and challenges in child representation and if they had undertaken initiatives to support or improve practice. Within these reports states are not required to report on child representation, so the reporting is selective and not comprehensive. Despite these limitations, QIC uncovered some important points related to quality of child representation:

- **Training.** Training is routinely offered to child representatives, but the subjects reflect a broad range of topics, with no systematic approach. Only five states reported using a standard curriculum. Only a few states described measuring or evaluating need for training or the results of training. Twenty-eight states require training before appointment. Of the states listing barriers to representation, most cited lack of attorney training and preparation.
- **Oversight and Monitoring.** Only 14 states reported on specific initiatives to oversee attorneys through oversight and monitoring. Five states described statewide systems to ensure quality of representation.
- **Availability of Representation.** Ten states identified a shortage of qualified attorneys as a challenge.
- **CASAs.** Five states listed lack of CASAs as a challenge to providing quality representation. They described the CASAs' key activities as facilitating visitation, visiting clients and "supporting additional advocacy." Twenty-one states assisted volunteer advocate as a way to support better quality representation.
- **Contact with Children.** During CFSR stakeholder interviews, youth in three states said they had had infrequent contact with their attorney or GAL, and foster parents in one state reported not knowing the name of their foster child's attorney.

3.2.4 Focus Groups with Key Stakeholders

QIC conducted focus group sessions with representative of key stakeholders, including the National Council of Juvenile and Family Court Judges, Court Appointed Special Advocates, Midwest Child Welfare Tribes, the American Humane Association, and former foster children.

3.2.4.1 Judges

A focus group of judges said that good training is the key to good advocacy. The judges also said that sometimes a separate attorney must be appointed because attorneys don't have knowledge about collateral issues, such as immigration, or navigating the educational system. Overall, judges said they feel an important role of the attorney is that of problem solver. They believed that in representing children, most attorneys try to reflect the child's wishes to the court. Resources are an issue for paying lawyers and providing proper training. They emphasized the resource limitation they feel and also said, "Don't build us a Cadillac," meaning they would like to see models that are easily replicable and do not require a great deal of additional funding.

3.2.4.2   Court-Appointed Special Advocates (CASA) Focus Group

CASAs reported variability in attorney representation, but agreed that legal representation is necessary. They saw their role as providing information and helping balance the viewpoint presented by the child welfare agency. Participants reported the attorney role as representing the best interests of the child, and some said they work with the attorney and share information. CASAs said that they can spend more time on their cases than any attorney, and that they have more of an opportunity to get to know the child. They noted that they receive quality training and supervisory support, unlike most attorneys for children. Their recommendation for improving child representation includes better training, especially in interacting with children, and more uniform standards and expectations.

3.2.4.3   Tribal Focus Group

The tribal court system has a unique function in that it must meet cultural needs as it also metes out legal decisions affecting its members. In order to understand the specific considerations in representing Native American children, the QIC team conducted focused conversations with judges, attorneys and child welfare professionals at the Midwest Child Welfare Tribal Gathering.

The conversations revealed that tribal members place relatively less emphasis on legal representation in general and focus more on the community coming together to solve family issues. They place a great deal of importance on attorneys helping children maintain community connections and noted that the child's future is so connected with the tribe that the best interests of the child and the best interests of the tribe are interwoven and must be considered as one. Interventions in tribal communities should be crafted to respect and maintain the strong community approach and emphasis on problem solving. Any tribal interventions must take into account the cultural contextual variables.

3.2.4.4   American Humane Association Conference Attendees

Attendees at the American Humane Association Conference on Family Group Decision-making sounded themes consistent with other stakeholder groups. They said they would like to see attorneys get to know their clients better and that attorneys needed specialized training in how to communicate with children. Agency workers said attorneys should attend meetings and family group conferences which would give them a better perspective on their cases and sometimes soften their attitudes toward relative placements. A judge called his court a "problem solving court," and he said he encourages attorneys to find out of court solutions. Attendees also said attorneys need clearer expectations coupled with some form of oversight and accountability.

3.2.4.5 Foster Care Alumni Focus Group

To put the findings into perspective, the QIC gathered the viewpoint of foster youth, those served by the service delivery systems under study. A conference call was held with foster care alumni at the Youth Council Meeting at the University of Minnesota-Duluth. The youth reported they felt the most important aspect of effectively representing children and youth is a need for the advocate to actively come to know the child. This echoed the responses of other stakeholders, who felt attorneys should be thoroughly familiar with the children they represent.

The youth believed that unless the attorney had gotten to know them, and came to understand their background and circumstances, he or she could not accurately convey their wishes. Youth noted their situations are extremely complicated and nuanced. They emphasized the difficulty of opening up to someone they hardly know, and emphasized that trust is necessary to building a relationship with their representative. The youth also said they would like to see more collaboration, with everyone coming to the table to work together for them. They felt planning for their future was an area where attorneys could be most helpful.

3.2.5 Notable Child Law Offices

In order to identify best practices, as well as organizational structures that support the achievement of good legal service delivery, the QIC visited five notable offices known nationally for setting and achieving high standards. They are all devoted solely to the representation of children. After consultation with the QIC Advisory Group and other national contacts, these, five were visited:

- **The Children's Law Center,** Washington, D.C.
- **Kid's Voice,** Pittsburgh, Pa.
- **Lawyers for Children,** New York, N.Y.
- **Legal Aid Society's Juvenile Rights Practice,** New York, N.Y.
- **The Connecticut Center for Child Advocacy,** Hartford, C.T. (which differs from the four above in that it represents a statewide model for oversight and delivery of legal representation for children)

At each site the QIC investigators spoke to supervisors, attorney and staff. They also spoke to human resources personnel and court staff, and attended case conferences and meetings which gave insight into the approach to representation. The QIC used a standardized protocol structured around the ABA Standards of Practice. It was evident that these programs were delivering representation in a format largely consistent with the ABA Standards of Practice. In particular, programs emphasized:

- Timely appointment
- Meeting with the child to promptly assess the child and his needs
- Thorough investigation
- Attorney knowledge of case strategy and goals
- Supports and expertise
- Active in-court representation

All programs provided supports for attorneys, with four-of-the-five providing a teamed approach. All provided close supervision and mentoring, and frequent and comprehensive training. Though the offices differ in size, scope and emphasis, similarities exist which reflect common approaches and themes. Generally, all offices enforced strict initial training requirements, and mandated ongoing training. They all had orderly management structures, with hands-on supervision of attorneys. Attorneys worked with other staff in a teamed approach, with the attorney taking the lead on court matters. The programs made a variety of other supports available to their staff, including administrative support, specialized experts and computer tools, such as electronic case management. All the programs sought to keep caseloads reasonable.

3.3 Review of Existing Empirical Research on Child Legal Representation[13]

One of the major goals of the QIC-ChildRep Project is to conduct empirical research on child representation to determine what approaches to child legal representation result in more desirable outcomes and what behaviors of the representative are likely to be most beneficial. To inform development of a QIC research design, we searched for research articles and evaluations specific to topics of child representation. In addition to traditional searches in law and social science literature, and the secondary literature identified by internet searches and the U.S. Children's Bureau Child Welfare Information Gateway, we asked members of the project's Advisory Committee and Study Team to suggest or provide any articles or evaluations they thought would be helpful. This process identified fourteen evaluations of child representation. Nine of these

---

13. Karl Ensign, Cynthia Samples and Robyn Ristau, of Planning and Learning Technologies in Alexandria VA contributed substantially to this section. The full reports of these research studies are available on our QIC-ChildRep website at: http://www.improve childrep.org/ChildRep2010/EvaluationsofChildRepresentation.aspx

evaluations involved lawyer representation. Another five involved CASA representation. Only one of the evaluations was an experimental design.

Each of these articles and evaluations were reviewed to address the following questions:

- What topics within the field of child representation have been subject to empirical research?
- What types of research designs were utilized?
- What were the general findings from the previous empirical research?

Information was reviewed and synthesized to address each of the three main questions. The following table lists of all of the evaluations that were included in this review. The primary findings from this review are the following:

- The majority of evaluations have focused on comparing *who delivers* child representation and attendant measurement of impact. Specifically the studies examined the impact of using CASAs as well as the role of private attorneys, staff attorneys, law students, and lay volunteers (not CASA).
- Less commonly evaluated subjects include the impact of caseload standards and training. Data collection and analysis of stakeholder perceptions and attitudes has also received relatively less attention.
- The most common type of evaluation design utilized was quasi-experimental, which reflects the difficulty of carrying out random assignment experimental design of systemic court interventions. Both historical and same-time comparisons were made between treatment and non-treatment groups.

Information was reviewed and synthesized to address each of the three main questions. The following table provides a listing of all of the evaluations that were included in this review.

Evaluation/Research Article	Topic/Focus	Research Design
Abramson, S. (1991). *Use of court-appointed advocates to assist in permanency planning for minority children.* Child Welfare, Volume 70, Number 4, July-August 1991.	Court-appointed special advocates (CASA)	Experimental Design
Berliner, L., Fitzgerald, M. and Alving, M. (1998) *Court appointed special advocates for children in Washington State: A review of effectiveness.* Washington State Institute for Public Policy, November 1998.	Court-appointed special advocates (CASA)	Descriptive

Evaluation/Research Article	Topic/Focus	Research Design
Caliber Associates. (2004). *Evaluation of CASA representation: Final Report.*	Court-appointed special advocates (CASA)	Quasi-experimental
Calkins, C. and Millar, M., Ph.D. (1999). *The effectiveness of court appointed special advocates to assist in permanency planning.* In, Child and Adolescent Social Work Journal Volume 16, Number 1, February 1999.	Court-appointed special advocates (CASA)	Quasi-experimental
CSR, Inc (1995). *Final report on the validation and effectiveness study of legal representation through guardian ad litem.* Washington DC: NCCAN, DHHS.	Guardian ad litem	Descriptive
Duquette, D.N. and Ramsey, S.H. (1987). *Representation of children in child abuse and neglect cases: an empirical look at what constitutes effective representation.* University of Michigan.	Type of representation and training	Quasi-experimental
Goodman, G.S., Edelstein, R.S., Mitchell, E.B., and Myers, J.E.B. (2008). *A comparison of types of attorney representation for children in California juvenile court dependency cases.* In, Child Abuse & Neglect 32 (2008) 497–501.	Type of representation	Quasi-experimental
Hess, C., Swanke, S. and Batson, A. (2007). *An evaluation of the North Dakota guardian ad litem project.* HB Consultation and Evaluation Associates, Grand Forks, ND	Guardian ad litem project in North Dakota	Descriptive
Judicial Council of California. (2004). *Dependency counsel caseload study and service delivery model analysis.* San Francisco, CA: Administrative Office of the Courts.	Caseloads	Descriptive
Litzelfelner, P. (2000). *The effectiveness of CASAs in achieving positive outcomes for children.* Child Welfare; Mar/Apr 2000; 79, 2.	Court-appointed special advocates (CASA)	Quasi-experimental
Lukowski, G.A and Davies, H.J. (2002). *A challenge for change: Implementation of the Michigan lawyer-guardian ad litem statute.* The American Bar Association Center on Children and the Law for the Governor's Task Force on Children's Justice.	Guardian ad litem statute in Michigan	Descriptive
Pitchal, E.S., Freundlich, M.D., Kendrick, C. (2009). *Evaluation of the guardian ad litem System.* Nebraska. National Association of Counsel for Children.	Guardian ad litem system in Nebraska	Descriptive

Evaluation/Research Article	Topic/Focus	Research Design
Stotzel, M. and Fegert, J.M. (2006). The *representation of the legal interests of children and adolescents in Germany: a study of the children's guardian from a child's perspective*. International Journal of Law, Policy and the Family 20, (2006), 201-224	Guardian ad litem	Descriptive
Zinn, A. E. & Slowriver, J. (2008) *Expediting Permanency: Legal Representation for Foster Children in Palm Beach County*. Chicago: Chapin Hall Center for Children at the University of Chicago.	Legal Aid's Foster Children's Project	Quasi-experimental

The full reports of these research studies are available on our QIC-ChildRep website at: http://www.improve childrep.org/ChildRep2010/EvaluationsofChildRepresentation.aspx

3.4 Consensus Begins to Emerge

During the first year Needs Assessment, the QIC-ChildRep team reviewed all academic literature, studied state laws, and talked with judges, attorneys, caseworkers, CASAs, state regional office directors, tribes, and former foster youth themselves. Given the varied viewpoints included in the Needs Assessment, as well as the geographic and population diversity, it is striking that the informants and the academic literature raised such similar issues and concerns. But in addition to criticisms of the current state of child representation, a shared positive vision of the child's lawyer also came to light:

- Attorneys must develop a relationship with their client. Attorneys should be actively engaged with their clients in order to understand their needs and advocate effectively. Attorneys must engage with children more by having frequent and more meaningful contact, and should understand the child's living situation, school, and home life.
- Effective representation includes a thorough investigation in order to develop a clear theory of the case and effectively advocate in court. Attorneys must gain a thorough understanding of their cases in order to develop effective strategies and advocate zealously for their clients.
- Attorneys effectively solve problems for their clients by engaging in active out-of-court advocacy. Negotiating solutions and settlements is an important function of the attorney role. By actively seeking solutions on behalf of the child, attorneys can resolve problems quickly and cooperatively.
- Attorneys should take a holistic view of the child's needs. A child in the dependency system often has needs that cannot be met by the dependency system alone.

Often, an attorney must monitor a vast array of services, as well as coordinate other legal issues, such as financial assistance, or educational programs.
- Practice in this area requires comprehensive training which includes child and family issues. Attorneys need to understand child and family issues, as well as agency policies and procedures. They should also have solid courtroom skill and grounding in children's law. Current training of attorneys is ad hoc, lacking a standard curriculum or protocol.
- Attorneys must meet initial and ongoing qualification standards. Children's law is a highly specialized and complex area of law. Attorneys should meet basic qualifications in order to practice in this area, and should have to meet ongoing requirements, which are monitored and overseen.
- Supports help attorneys accomplish the multiple tasks which allow them to be successful advocates. Attorneys need supports in order to accomplish all the duties with which they are tasked. Some supports reported to make a difference include administrative help, investigators, social workers, and strong supervision.
- Caseloads must be reasonable in order for attorneys to accomplish the essential duties of their jobs. Quality practice requires that the system support adequate time and resources for attorneys.[14]

The Needs Assessment did not resolve the controversy on whether the child's legal representative should be client-directed or serving in the best interest of the child. But even best interest jurisdictions tend to agree that the child's wishes should be considered as the child's lawyer determines his or her position. It may also be in the best interests of a child to have their views clearly and aggressively advocated for in court. Informants agree that greater weight should be given to a child's stated goals as the child gains in age and maturity. Achieving harmony between the client directed and best interests view is discussed in the next chapter. The divide is not as wide as many assume.

But no matter how the goals of the case are established and no matter who sets the objectives of the case, whether as directed by the child or by a substituted or best interest judgment of the lawyer, there seems to be an emerging consensus as to the duties and tasks of the legal representative of the child. As the 1996 ABA Standards say: "The chief distinguishing factor between the [client-directed and best interests] roles is the manner and method to be followed in determining the legal position to be advocated."[15]

---

14. QIC Phase II Implementation Plan, September 2010 Report to Children's Bureau, page 18, available at www.ImproveChildRep.org.

15. 1996 ABA Standards, A-2 Commentary.

An ideal view of child representation practice emerged which includes lawyers selected because of a passion for the work who are highly skilled, well qualified, well informed, and held accountable to a high standard that includes engaged-client interaction and a problem-solving ethic. The informants also identified system supports that would allow high practice standards to be realized. This emerging consensus forms the basis of the QIC Best Practice Model of Child Representation.

CHAPTER 4
Emerging Consensus and the QIC Best Practice Model

Abstract
This chapter describes the QIC Best Practice Model and the rationale behind the Six Core Skills. It compares and contrasts the QIC Model with the 1996 ABA Standards and the ABA Model Act of 2011. The models agree the following are needed to better equip attorneys to represent children:

- Approach each child through a developmental lens based on his or her age and demographics;
- Better understand and determine a child's ability to direct counsel; and
- Partner children in dependency cases with dedicated attorneys who take a holistic approach to each case.

The chapter also discusses how differences between client-directed representation and best interests representation have narrowed.

4.1 Emerging Consensus
The national needs assessment provides the foundation for the QIC Best Practice Model. Our review of the literature, national standards, conference recommendations and stakeholder opinion reveals an emerging consensus on *nearly all* aspects of the role and duties of the child's legal representative. The exception stems from the

long-standing best interests versus client directed debate, and there is a narrowing of differences on that point too. From that consensus we framed the QIC Best Practice Model (Appendix A) to reflect this general agreement by practitioners, academics and child welfare policy makers across the country as to what the role and duties of the child's legal representative ought to be.

This chapter provides a description of the model, its origins and its rationale, leading to the Six Core Skills training package. This chapter also compares and contrasts the QIC Model with the 1996 ABA recommendations and the 2011 ABA Model Act.

The policy statement of the ABA 1996 Standards echoes a central premise: *"All children subject to court proceedings involving allegations of child abuse and neglect should have legal representation as long as the court's jurisdiction continues."* Given the challenges and deficiencies of America's child welfare system, and its enormous complexity, stakeholders recognize the need for individualized child advocacy—getting each child the unique supports necessary for that child's safety and well-being. There seems strong, although not yet universal, agreement that the child needs a *legal* advocate in these important proceedings. Major law firms are paid substantial amounts of money to help corporate clients navigate complex government bureaucracies. America's child welfare bureaucracy is no less complex, the needs of the child client no less compelling. A child needs expert advocacy to guide her through it.

Our review also found few persons fully satisfied with the current policy and practice of child representation. People remain dissatisfied with the gap between the need and the reality.

A key component of law and policy around which this consensus has developed is that a child in the child welfare system requires an engaged, active, involved lawyer—just like a lawyer for any other party in any other litigation. There also appears to be a consolidation of views as to the core functions of the child's representative, something that has eluded the field until recently.[1] The QIC Best Practice Model reflects that consensus and sets out in substantial detail the recommended tasks and duties of the child representative. The QIC tasks and duties are based upon and are essentially consistent with the *1996 ABA Standards of Practice for Lawyers Who Represent Children in Abuse and Neglect Cases* (see Appendix B) but updated to reflect another 15 years of national discussion and development.

4.2 Aba Model Act of 2011

After many years of debate, development and consensus building, the ABA House of Delegates adopted the *ABA Model Act Governing Representation of Children in*

---

1. Barbara Ann Atwood, *The Uniform Representation of Children in Abuse, Neglect and Custody Proceedings Act: Bridging the Divide Between Pragmatism and Idealism*, 42 FLQ 63, (Spring 2008) at 64.

Abuse, Neglect and Dependency Proceedings[2] in August 2011. (The 2011 ABA Model Act is included in Appendix C.) The 2011 Model Act focuses specifically on the role and duties of lawyers representing children. Although it anticipates that a court might appoint a best interest advocate—a lawyer or a lay person—the Model Act specifically does not address the best interests role.[3] The Model Act focuses on the child's lawyer who owes the same duties to the child as are due to an adult client. The CAI and First Star Report Card says: "This 'A+' model law embodies the best practices analyzed in this Report Card for the representation of children. Advocates in states with poor grades can develop legislation to implement this model law in their home states."[4]

Between the ABA Model Act and the QIC Best Practice Model there is considerable overlap and essential agreement. Although the 2011 Model Act passed a full year after development of the QIC Model, it is not surprising that our conclusions are so consistent since these two independent processes drew from the same well of expert opinion and state experience. Except for some differences in organization and level of practice detail, the ABA Model Act and QIC Model are in essential harmony as to duties of counsel.

The 2011 Model Act and the QIC Best Practice Model complement one another very well. The ABA Model provides the essential legal structure setting out the duties of the child's lawyer while the QIC Model, reflected in the Six Core Skills training, fills in the clinical knowledge and skills lawyers require to properly fulfill those duties. States should adopt the 2011 ABA Model Act.

4.3 QIC Best Practice Model Compared with the 2011 ABA Model Act and the 1996 ABA Standards

Here are some major comparisons of the ABA recommendations and the QIC-Child-Rep Best Practice Model: This chapter discusses the client-directed/best interest question separately, in section 4.7 below.

Definitions: By defining *child's representative* (CR) to include an individual or a multidisciplinary office the QIC expressly anticipates that the child may be represented by an individual lawyer or by a team of multidisciplinary professionals that includes a lawyer plus social workers, paralegals and/or lay advocates. (See Chapter 12 for the

---

2. *2011 ABA Model Act Governing Representation of Children in Abuse, Neglect and Dependency Proceedings.* The ABA Model Act "focuses on the representation of children in abuse and neglect cases to ensure that states have a model of ethical representation for children that is consistent with the [1996] ABA Abuse and Neglect Standards, ABA Policy, and the ABA Model Rules of Professional Conduct." (2011 Model Act Report, p. 18).

3. "Because this Act deals specifically with lawyers for children, it will not further address the role of the best interest advocate." ABA 2011 *Model Act Governing the Representation of Children in Abuse, Neglect, and Dependency Proceedings*, Section 3, commentary.

4. *Id.* At 6

results of a QIC empirical study supporting the effectiveness of such multidisciplinary representation.)

Appointment: The QIC expressly asks that the child's representative begin service *in advance* of the first hearing. The first hearing is a critical opportunity to protect the child with minimal disruption to the child's life thus easing possible unintended trauma. The first hearing can often set the course of the entire case and a strong child advocate presence there can significantly benefit the child. Like the ABA Standards and Model Act, the QIC requires that the child representative serve until the court's authority over the child ends. Unlike the ABA policy recommendations, which apply only to lawyers, the QIC applies to the entire child representative office, including the non-lawyers.[5]

Assertive: A critically important similarity among the models is that all three anticipate a child representative who is an engaged, assertive, and active participant in the proceedings—both in and out of court. The Model Act enhances the child lawyer role by specifically requiring a meeting with the client prior to each hearing and at least once per quarter.[6]

As to *basic obligations* the three recommendations differ slightly in that the QIC emphasizes the importance of the lawyer being engaged in *all* placement decisions ". . . to disrupt the child's world as little as possible . . . remove the danger not the child . . . and help identify placement alternatives."[7]

As to *Out of Court Actions to be taken*, there is considerable overlap between the recommendations with these additions in QIC. In *meet with the child* the QIC emphasizes, even more than the two ABA policy recommendations, the foundational importance of developing a trusting relationship with the child. QIC expects the child's representative, whether client-directed or best interests, to carefully communicate that the lawyer is directed as much as possible by the child.

In *identifying relatives* QIC expects that the child will have important preferences and likely helpful information as to relatives who might provide emotional support or even placement for the child. As to *outside meetings,* increasingly people recognize that events outside the regular court hearings affect the well-being of the child and the course of their child welfare case. The 1996 ABA encourages such attendance for purposes of *investigation*. But the QIC requires that the child's representative (lawyer or non-lawyer advocate or both) attend these, including treatment meetings and school conferences, not only for investigative purposes, but also as a forum for *advocacy* and *persuasion*.

Services: Like the ABA Standards and Model Act, QIC expects the CR to seek appropriate services for the child and his or her family. QIC frames this somewhat

---

5. The ABA Rules of Professional Conduct also apply to non-lawyer representatives, however.
6. Model Act, s 7(b)(5).
7. QIC Best Practice Model (1)(d).

differently and identifies several services not listed in the ABA Standards—long-term foster care, adoption, education, recreation or social services, housing and, as required by the Federal Law *Fostering Connections,* an appropriate discharge plan and aging out services.

Conflict resolution: QIC augments the ABA call for participating in negotiation by asking the child's representative to "adopt a problem-solving attitude and seek cooperative resolution of the case whenever possible" and, recognizing the "child's sense of time" to seek expeditious resolution of the case.

In-Court: When it comes to hearings and active participation in the hearings, the ABA and QIC match up well. The ABA Model Act focuses and roots the lawyer activity on in-court advocacy and obtaining appropriate court orders. The ABA Standards emphasizes the child as witness more, but QIC certainly does not disagree with those recommendations. The ABA Model Act underlines the importance of the child's presence in court, a position consistent with the QIC but not as strongly emphasized there. Likewise the ABA and QIC recommendations coincide as to post-hearing, appellate advocacy and cessation of representation.

Administration: Apart from discussing fees and expenses, the ABA Model Act does not address the organizational structure for delivering legal services to children, perhaps because that was considered beyond its scope. But both the 1996 ABA Standards and the QIC recognize the essential role that the organizational structure plays for assuring quality representation for the child. There are slight variations in the presentation but both call for the child's lawyer to be independent and for clear court rules governing procedure.

QIC adds that the structure for appointment, support and accountability should be transparent. QIC asks that the administration assure that lawyers are properly qualified, have training programs and mentors available, and that specialty certification be encouraged. Both standards emphasize the need for proper lawyer compensation while QIC asks that lawyers be provided other supports such as for copying, phone, service of process, and transcripts. QIC also specifically speaks to the need for manageable caseload size.

Certainly the 1996 ABA Standards were critical in the emerging consensus that the QIC found. We made remarkably few updates or additions given the passage of 15 years and a fair amount of policy discussion and debate during this period. Likewise, the ABA Model Act further articulates this consensus. One hopes that state legislators and other law makers looking to make their child advocacy reflect the modern best practice will find plenty of guidance and direction in these recommendations.

4.4 Consensus: Adopt a Developmentally Sophisticated Approach to the Child and His or Her Needs.

Across the client-directed/best interests divide it is widely accepted that whether the lawyer serves as a best interests or a client-directed advocate, the lawyer must understand:

- the child's developmental stage and competencies,
- understand the child's family and culture, and
- develop a relationship with the child.

Ann Haralambie and Lauren Adams reflect this consensus when they write: "To effectively represent a child, it is important to understand the child's developmental stage and competencies [including the impact of maltreatment and trauma.]". . . It is difficult to represent a child, either as a client-directed attorney, a best interests attorney or a guardian ad litem without developing a relationship with the child." . . . "Building a relationship and communicating effectively with a child client gives the child a voice in the proceedings and enables the attorney to get the information required to represent the child effectively." [8]

Professor Jean Koh Peters says that the child's attorney "whether assigned to represent a child's wishes or her best interests, must ground her representation in a thickly textured understanding of the child's world." [9]

The 1996 ABA Standards require that a child's attorney structure "all communications to account for the individual child's age, level of education, cultural context, and degree of language acquisition." [10] The ABA 2011 Model Act, addressing client-directed counsel, says: "In a developmentally appropriate manner, the lawyer shall elicit the child's wishes and advise the child as to options." [11] The ABA Model Act also expects attorneys to be able to gauge the developmental capacity of their child clients as they determine whether the child has diminished capacity, that is, whether the child has the ability to direct counsel. [12]

---

8. Ann Haralambie and Lauren Adams, "Interviewing and Counseling Legal Clients Who Are Children," CHILD WELFARE LAW AND PRACTICE, 3d Edition (Duquette, Haralambie and Sankaran, Eds.). They also say: 'Older children may be able to articulate their own needs quite accurately. Younger children may demonstrate their needs more through their behavior or emotions." (Id.)
9. KOH PETERS, REPRESENTING CHILDREN. See also discussion in Chapter 2 above, 2.6 and following.
10. 1996 ABA Standards, A-3.
11. ABA Model Act, Section 7(c).
12. ABA Model Act, Section 7(d).

Similarly, the recommendations of the UNLV Conference in 2006 would require attorneys to have competency in child cognitive development, effective child interviewing skills, and become familiar with the child's family, community and culture.[13]

It is widely agreed that lawyers for children must understand child development and have the skills to be able to talk with a child, understand the child's world and needs, and use this foundation in counseling and advocacy. The QIC Best Practice Model reflects this consensus and captures it in the first of the Six Core Skills—"Enter the Child's World."

4.5 Consensus: Child's Wishes Are Always Relevant

It is widely acknowledged that children should participate meaningfully in dependency proceedings. We find a national consensus in the view that, regardless of whether or not a child is considered competent to direct the attorney and even if the role of the attorney is defined as other than purely client-directed, the wishes and preferences of the child are always relevant and should be communicated to the court unless limited by privilege.[14]

No matter what weight is given to the child's preferences in determining the goals of advocacy, the attorney should elicit the child's preferences in a developmentally appropriate manner, advise the child, and provide guidance. The child's attorney should communicate the child's wishes and preferences to the court. The lawyer also has a duty to explain to the child in a developmentally appropriate way information that will help the child have maximum input in the determination of the particular position at issue. According to the child's ability to understand, the lawyer should inform the child of the relevant facts, the applicable laws, and the ramifications of taking various positions, which may include the impact of such decisions on other family members or on future legal proceedings.[15]

Federal law requires that permanency plans for children 14 and older must be "developed in consultation with youth."[16] State law often requires that the stated wishes and preferences of the child are to be presented to the court.[17]

---

13. 2006 UNLV Recommendations 1(C) (2)(b).

14. These include the ABA STANDARDS OF PRACTICE FOR LAWYERS WHO REPRESENT CHILDREN IN ABUSE AND NEGLECT CASES, AND THE NACC REVISED VERSION (SEE APPENDIX A); ADOPTION 2002, THE PRESIDENT'S INITIATIVE ON ADOPTION AND FOSTER CARE, GUIDELINES FOR PUBLIC POLICY AND STATE LEGISLATION GOVERNING PERMANENCE FOR CHILDREN (1999) [Hereinafter ADOPTION 2002 GUIDELINES]; the FORDHAM CONFERENCE ON ETHICAL ISSUES IN THE LEGAL REPRESENTATION OF CHILDREN, 64 FORDHAM L.REV (MARCH 1996); and. the UNLV CONFERENCE ON REPRESENTING CHILDREN IN FAMILIES: CHILDREN'S ADVOCACY AND JUSTICE TEN YEARS AFTER FORDHAM, 6 NEV. L. J (SPRING 2006).

15. Duquette & Haralambie, *Representing Children and Youth*, in CHILD WELFARE LAW AND PRACTICE, 3d Edition, Bradford Publishers, 2016 at §31.4.2.

16. 42 USC §675(5)(C).

17. For example, FLA. STAT. § 39.807(2)(b)(1), ME. REV. STAT. tit. 22, §4005(1)(E). Michigan, MCL 712A. 17d (1).

4.6 Consensus—A Vigorous and Active Child's Lawyer

The 1996 ABA Standards, the 2011 ABA Model Act and the QIC Best Practice Model all reflect the emerging national consensus on the actual day to day advocacy duties of the child's legal representative. The ABA Standards say: "The chief distinguishing factor between the [client-directed and best interests] roles is the manner and method to be followed in determining the legal position to be advocated." Similarly, QIC says: "Whether the lawyer takes his or her direction from the child or makes a best interest judgment as to what the goals of the litigation should be, once the goals are determined the lawyer is expected to aggressively fulfill the duties and obligations set forth here." The 2011 ABA Model Act sets out very similar fully-engaged, assertive set of duties consistent with the 1996 Standards and the QIC Model.[18]

The U.S. Children's Bureau publication, *Guidelines for Public Policy and State Legislation Governing Permanence for Children,*[19] also grasped this fundamental agreement: No matter whether the advocate represents the child's best interests as determined by the advocate or assumes a client-directed/champion role as recommended by the ABA Standards, these Guidelines expect a vigorous and active participation of the child's lawyer."[20] The *Guidelines* go on to endorse the 1996 ABA Standards as to the specific duties of the child's attorney and say: "State standards should clearly define the duties of the child's attorney. Objective standards make it easier for judges and other review bodies to assess the lawyer's performance on behalf of a client."[21] On this the child advocacy community agrees.

There is a clear national consensus that regardless of how the goals of the cases are identified, whether the lawyer takes his or her direction from the child or makes a best interest judgment, once the goals are determined the lawyer is expected to aggressively fulfill the duties and obligations set forth in these three authoritative recommendations. The child welfare community can build on that foundation. But now let's move to the area of lesser agreement—how to address the fact of child client incapacity to direct counsel at certain ages and stages.

4.7 Client Directed Versus Best Interests?

4.7.1 Common Ground? Narrow the Differences?

This emerging consensus identified in our national needs assessment covers *nearly all* aspects of the child representative's role—save one. The question around which consensus eludes the field is: Should the child's legal representative be *client directed*, that is, represent the stated wishes of the child arrived at after a period of lawyer-client counseling just as would happen with an adult client? Or should the lawyer represent what

---

18. Section 7 (a) & (b) of the 2011 ABA Model Act.
19. ADOPTION 2002 GUIDELINES.
20. *Id.* at VII-12.
21. *Id.* at VII-12.

the lawyer believes to be in the *best interests* of the child? Despite the strong support for *client-directed* representation in the academic community and the national child advocacy community, state legislatures retain an affinity for a *best interest* approach to child representation. Are we doomed to an irresolvable conflict of opinion? Will this best interest/client directed debate continue to paralyze the field for another two decades? Maybe not.

Theoretically the controversy is framed as opposites—the client-directed lawyer advocates for the *child's* stated wishes and the best interest lawyer advocates for the outcome that the *lawyer* thinks is best for the child. But in practice few attorneys adopt an absolutist position under either approach. Some authors consider the actual percentage of cases in which a child's best interests and expressed wishes conflict to be relatively small.[22]

When the two approaches are analyzed carefully there is a great deal of common ground in the lawyer's child development savvy approach to the child, the importance of the child's voice and wishes in determining the goals of the advocacy, and the vigor and assertiveness of the child's lawyer once the direction of the advocacy is established. Without denying the essential differences between the approaches, there may be significant points of harmony that allow the field to move forward.

The major theoretical difference between the two approaches seems to come down to two: 1) determining the child's capacity to instruct counsel; and, 2) in light of the determination of capacity, deciding how much weight is to be given to a child's wishes and preferences in deciding the objectives of the case?

4.7.2 Determining a Child's Capacity to Direct Counsel

In a best interests regime the lawyer essentially *presumes* that the child client lacks capacity to instruct counsel. On the other hand, a client-directed regime *requires the lawyer to determine* whether the child has diminished capacity.[23]

Both the best interests lawyer and the client-directed lawyer require a more nuanced understanding of the child's capacity to direct counsel for reasons discussed below. This shared need for a better understanding of the child leads both types of lawyers to engage in certain actions to inform the determination of capacity. These *common actions* further link the best interests role and the client directed role and further narrows the differences between the approaches.

Both client-directed and best interests lawyers need to assess the child's capacity and the steps an attorney takes to do so are similar no matter the role. That is, both types of lawyers would meet with the child, develop as much trust and rapport as possible, and would consider the various dimensions that we summarize as the first QIC

---

22. Emily Buss, *You're My What? The Problem of Children's Misperceptions of Their Lawyers' Roles,* 64 FORDHAM L. REV. 1699, 1746.

23. 2002 ABA Model Rules of Professional Conduct, §1.14; 2011 ABA Model Act (7)(d).

Core Skill, "Enter the Child's World," such as the child's developmental stage, level of trauma, general intelligence, and existing relationships.

Similarly, Comment 6 to ABA Model Rule 1.14 provides guidance—to both client directed and best interest lawyers—saying lawyers should consider and balance factors like:

- Client's ability to articulate reasons leading to a decision;
- Variability of state of mind;
- Ability to appreciate consequences and fairness of a decision; and
- consistency of a decision with the known long-term commitments and values of client.

If appropriate, lawyer may seek guidance from an appropriate diagnostician.

The best interests lawyer needs to take these steps to inform their best interests advocacy position in the proceedings and to maximize the input of the child into that decision as is the prevailing practice.[24]

The client-directed lawyer will encounter children unable to direct counsel and must be able to assess their capacity objectively. 2011 ABA Model Act typifies the client-directed approach when it requires the *lawyer* to determine whether the child has diminished capacity but provides little guidance as to how to do this[25]. Apart from the limited guidance of the ABA Model Rule 1.14, the lawyer is left to his or her own unfettered and subjective judgment. The lawyer is permitted to consult others and the commentary recognizes that a child may be competent for some things and not for others. "A determination of incapacity may be incremental and issue-specific."[26] Yet there is little direction in the Model Act in *how* the diminished capacity determination is to be made. (The ABA Model Act is very helpful in its discussion of how to proceed *after* a determination of diminished capacity is made, however. We turn to that below.)

Lawyers are not trained in child development. The question of competency and maturity is an evolving and elusive judgment that doctoral level psychologists have a difficult time making. In the case of the very young child or the older child, the question of competence to instruct counsel may not be so difficult. If the client is an infant and cannot speak, the client cannot instruct counsel.

If a client is a normally developed 15- or 16-year-old, however, he or she is quite likely to have clear views as to the proper decisions to be made affecting his or her life. Those views should be aggressively argued to the court and most would urge traditional client-directed representation for the older youth. But determining capacity for the middle-years child, from 8 to 12 for instance, or the immature or mentally challenged child, and the weight to be given to that child's preferences is perhaps the most difficult question in child advocacy today, and it does not yet have a clear answer.

---

24. Duquette and Haralambie supra note 14 at §31.5.1.
25. ABA Model Act (7)(d).
26. Id.

The imprecision of this important determination exacerbates the existing risk that similarly situated children will get quite different representation depending on the subjective view of their lawyer as to their maturity and ability to understand the situation. Lawyers need more guidance in making this important determination and the Model Act, for all its virtues, fails on this point.

There are risks in the best interests approach too. The best interests lawyer is even more untethered than the client-directed lawyer. There are even fewer guideposts in determining basic competency. Given that amorphous situation it is easy for the lawyer to override the wishes of a child because the lawyer disagrees with the child. Disagreement with the lawyer's own judgment can easily be seen as clear evidence of a child's incompetence.

The ABA Model Act helps in the question of determining capacity when it allows the state to establish a *bright-line age* at which a child is presumed capable of directing counsel at a particular age and presumed incapable below that age. Several states have adopted this bright line approach.[27] Under this approach the presumption of diminished capacity may be rebutted if the lawyer determines that the child is capable of directing representation.[28] This alternative reflects the view that neither a best interests model nor the client-directed model can meet the needs of all children, given their widely differing level of development. The older child needs a traditional attorney and the younger child requires a representative who can define and advocate for his or her best interests.[29]

States that have opted for this approach reflect most legislators' preference for the paternalism and perceived protectiveness of the best interests approach (with which I disagree). A bright-line approach may represent a political compromise in that the youngest children would get a best interests advocate but the voice of older youth would be strengthened by preserving a client-directed attorney. More youth may get a stronger advocacy for their views.

Caution is warranted in that some of the statutory bright-line ages are set higher than psychological and medical research would dictate.[30] The bright line could be drawn at quite a young age, say at 10. The rule would only create a presumption of competence, of course, and the lawyer would have the guidance of the ABA Model Act, if adopted by their state, and of ethics rules MRPC 1.14 when that capacity is questionable. The difficulty of making the determination of a child's competence has been explored in the literature.[31]

---

27. New Mexico at 14, Wisconsin at 12 Washington State at 12.
28. 2011 ABA Model Act (7)(d).
29. Duquette, Two Distinct Roles/Bright Line Test, 6 NEVADA L.J. 1240 (Spring 2006).
30. Hei Lei, Helen No, and Sarah Plotnick, *A Guide to Accommodating a Child's Wishes: The Progression of Agency*, on the QIC website www.ImproveChildRep.org.
31. Rachel Martin, Jena Gutierrez, Jerome Galang, *Evaluating the Decision-making Capacity of Children: A Guide for Legal Practitioners*, on the QIC website www.ImproveChildRep.org.

The U.S. Supreme Court addressed the analogous question of when a youth should be held fully culpable for homicide and adopted a categorical rule barring imposition of the death penalty for offenders under the age of 18. In *Roper v. Simmons*,[32] the Court rejected a case-by-case approach and adopted a categorical age-based prohibition of the death penalty. "It is difficult even for expert psychologists to differentiate between the juvenile offender whose crime reflects unfortunate, yet transient immaturity, and the rare juvenile offender whose crime reflects irreparable corruption."[33]

Largely because of the difficulty in determining maturity and culpability, the court drew a bright line at 18, 'the point where society draws the line for many purposes between childhood and adulthood."[34] We will not go into further depth here except to urge that we continue to explore this pressure point. The main purpose is to highlight the *determination of capacity* as one of the most significant elements where consensus in child representation still eludes us.

4.7.3 How Much Weight to Wishes of Child with Diminished Capacity?

The *weight* given to a child's stated wishes and preferences in determining the case theory and goals of the advocacy generally depends on the lawyer's determination of a child's mental competence and maturity. As described above, that is a difficult determination for a lawyer to make—and re-make since the wishes and preferences of the child must be elicited throughout the case, not just at a single point, and capacity may well change in the course of a single case.

For the client-directed lawyer the statements of the *competent* child provide the clear answer, subject only to the same counseling that a lawyer would provide an adult or corporate client. But both the client-directed lawyer and the best interests lawyer face the same question if the child is determined to have diminished capacity: How much *weight* is to be given to the child's stated preferences in determining the goals of the advocacy?

The trend identified by the QIC national needs assessment is to encourage a more traditional lawyer role for both best interests and client directed lawyers in which the lawyers give more deference to the child's wishes and preferences. This is a position consistent with the vast majority of legal scholars and with the MRPC Rule 1.14 admonition for the lawyer to maintain a normal client-lawyer relationship with the diminished capacity client. Even in a best interest jurisdiction it is often seen to be in the child's best interests for the child's views to be fully argued to the court.

The ABA Model Act addresses how the lawyer is to deal with children's varying capacity in several ways, tracking the provisions of MRPC 1.14. When a child is

---

Hei Lei, Helen No, and Sarah Plotnick, *A Guide to Accommodating a Child's Wishes: The Progression of Agency*, on the QIC website www.ImproveChildRep.org.

32. *Roper v. Simmons*, 543 U.S. 551 (2005).
33. *Id.* at 572.
34. *Id.* at 573.

determined NOT to have capacity to instruct counsel, the ABA Model Act allows the lawyer to take reasonably necessary protective action where the client has diminished capacity and is at risk of serious harm. The 2011 ABA analysis rests squarely on existing rules of professional responsibility that apply to clients generally, without finding the need to carve out different or separate rules for children. The protective action may include "consulting with individuals or entities that have the ability to take action to protect the client and, in appropriate cases, seeking the appointment of a best interests advocate or investigator to make an independent recommendation to the court with respect to the best interests of the child."[35]

The best interests and client directed approaches merge on this point so as to be practically indistinguishable. Capacity is not an either-or proposition, particularly for the middle-years child. Children mature at different rates and may be capable for some judgments and not for others. Professor Jean Koh Peters creates the image of a sliding scale or "dimmer switch" in which the child's capability is not an "on or off" phenomenon where a child is either capable of directing the lawyer or not.[36] A child's capacity, then, is a broader spectrum where children may be able to contribute various amounts to guide the representation if the lawyer properly incorporates the child's unique individuality.

State law and practice may incorporate the "dimmer switch" concept in authoritative directions to the lawyer. If the lawyer is appointed to represent the "best interests of the child," for instance, some state statutes recognize the child's growing capacity. In Michigan, for example, the duties of the lawyer/guardian-ad-litem include:

> (h) To make a determination regarding the child's best interests and advocate for those best interests according to the lawyer-guardian ad litem's understanding of those best interests, regardless of whether the lawyer- guardian ad litem's determination reflects the child's wishes. *The child's wishes are relevant to the lawyer-guardian ad litem's determination of the child's best interests, and the lawyer-guardian ad litem shall weigh the child's wishes according to the child's competence and maturity.* Consistent with the law governing attorney-client privilege, the lawyer-guardian ad litem shall inform the court as to the child's wishes and preferences.[37] (Emphasis added)

---

35. 2011 ABA Model Act (7)(e) The commentary says that recommendation of a best interests advocate is to be reserved for extreme cases.

36. JEAN KOH PETERS, REPRESENTING CHILDREN IN CHILD PROTECTIVE PROCEEDINGS 53-54 (1997). "Competency, in this context, is a dimmer switch: the client can shed light on some aspects of the representation, even though she cannot participate in all of it."

37. MCL 712A.17d(1)(h). Where there is a disagreement between the lawyer-guardian ad litem and the child as to the child's best interests, the lawyer is to bring the question before the court and the court may appoint an attorney for the child who as the same duty of zealous representation as for an adult and serves in addition to the lawyer-guardian ad litem (MCL 712A.17d(2).

Under Michigan law, when formulating the litigation goal the lawyer gives increasing weight to the preferences of the child according to the child's age and maturity. The idea is that at some point the weight given to the child's wishes becomes stronger and stronger, and the benefit to the child of merely having his or her position strongly advocated similarly grows stronger, so that approach taken by a best interests lawyer becomes hardly distinguishable from the client-directed approach.

The best interests and wishes of the child merge and the lawyer-GAL ends up representing the stated wishes of the child. If, however, a conflict remains between the child and the lawyer-GAL regarding the child's best interests, the lawyer-GAL should bring the matter to the court, which may appoint an *attorney* for the child who serves in addition to the lawyer/GAL.[38] (It seems more consistent for a best interest advocate to request a client-directed attorney than for a client-directed lawyer to jeopardize loyalty to a client by seeking a best interest advocate who by definition would generally advocate for something other than what the child wants. A client-directed lawyer asking for a best interest attorney telegraphs disagreement between lawyer and child-client.)

4.8 QIC Approach

The "wishes or best interest" debate has dominated the child representation field for four decades. Some would say it has distracted us from settling other fundamental questions about the child attorney role. That continued disagreement within the child advocate community presents a major obstacle to strengthening the law and practice governing child representation and deters robust development of the child representative work force. Despite the fundamental philosophical difference between client-directed and best interests, there is also considerable overlap in the practical approach that may allow the field to move forward.

The QIC tried to finesse the disagreement by asking the lawyer to "**accommodate the child's wishes**" as much as possible, whether operating under a client-directed or best interests state law. The two states in which we experimented with the QIC Best Practice Model were different. One was client-directed (Washington State) and the other best interests (Georgia—at the time of the research, but no longer). Under the QIC Model, lawyers are asked to recognize the importance to a child personally and to the entire child welfare process of having the child's voice and views strongly presented to the court. The voice of the child should not be merely *stated*, but *advocated for* and pursued in a strategic manner, trying from one hearing to another to eliminate the obstacles to realizing a child's position.

---

38. MICH. COMP. LAWS § 712A.17d(1)(h). Where there is a disagreement between the lawyer-guardian ad litem and the child as to the child's best interests, the lawyer is to bring the question before the court, and the court may appoint an *attorney* for the child who has the same duty of zealous representation as for an adult and serves in addition to the lawyer-guardian ad litem. MICH. COMP. LAWS § 712A.17d(2).

Even in best interest jurisdictions the QIC Model urges lawyers to follow the ABA Model Rule 1.14, "The lawyer shall, as far as reasonably possible, maintain a normal client-lawyer relationship with the client." We urge the best interests lawyers to enter the child's world as much as possible and really listen to the child; understand what is important from the child's perspective and how decisions will impact on the child's experience of his or her life. We urge lawyers to act with humility when considering taking a position contrary to the child's express wishes.

We urge lawyers in best interests states to recognize the best interests benefits of the child having his or her voice fully expressed. Advocating for the child's stated goals is often in the child's best interests and thus consistent with that model because of the perception of fairness and procedural justice. The child benefits from being fully heard, respected and treated with fairness and dignity. A fully presented voice of the child may also help the court understand the situation better and arrive at overall better decisions, which would, of course, certainly reflect the best interests of the child.

Once the wishes and preferences of the child are given their appropriate weight and the objectives of the case are established, the lawyer activities are essentially the same. Whether client directed or best interests, the lawyer remains vigorous and active, in-court and out of court. Under either role, the lawyer counsels the child and communicates the child's wishes to the court.

4.9 Conclusion

The Children's Bureau's quest for consensus as to the role of the child's legal representative is slowly being realized by the national standard setting bodies as updated by the QIC Best Practice Model. A consensus has emerged around the *core tasks and duties* expected of the child's legal representative—whether client directed, best interests or some combination. It is not surprising these independent processes should come to such similar conclusions about the fundamental tasks and duties of the child's representative. Both the QIC and the ABA recommendations are influenced by the same pool of academic writings and research and the experiences of individual states as they try to develop and implement law and policy governing individual child representation.

We have not found any other duties for the child representative substantially different from what is described here or that is considered equal or superior. Having arrived at this position, we turn to the question of how to train lawyers to implement this assertive model of child representation. Then we evaluate the effect of training lawyers to implement this QIC model. Our research theory is that fully implementing this model will improve child representation and contribute to better outcomes for children.

CHAPTER 5
QIC Six Core Skills and the QIC Best Practice Training

Abstract

The chapter describes:

- The Six Core Skills and how to teach the QIC approach in two days using an easy-to-retain, adult learning format.
- How to reinforce the Six Core Skills, through regular coaching and pod meetings.
- QIC Six Core Skills training materials.

5.1   Six Core Skills Derived from QIC Best Practice Model

Three processes were underway in 2011 within the QIC Project that led to the final articulation and formulation of the Six Core Skills:

- First, the QIC Team was identifying at a basic, phenomenological level, specific lawyer behavior required to realize each element and task of the QIC Best Practice Model.
- Second, we were identifying the potential observable and measurable outcomes for our research component.
- Third, we were experimenting with various ways to organize and present an effective, adult-learning style training in the QIC Model.

From these exercises the Six Core Skills emerged as an organizing structure that we hoped would communicate the QIC Model in a clear and cogent way.[1]

We broke down each element of the QIC Model to specific lawyer behaviors required to fulfill it and from that identified curriculum goals and objectives. The application of the Six Core Skills is not linear. The desired attitudes, behaviors and skills are required from the beginning to the end of the court process; they are manifest in the lawyer's many interactions with the child and others participants in the child welfare process. Connecting each element of the QIC Model to specific lawyer knowledge and behavior also informed the design of our research instruments and the articulation of the Six Core Skills.

The framing of the Six Core Skills and the QIC Training reflects two constraints—the realities of adult learning style and the practicality of how much time attorneys would have available for the training. As to adult learning styles, we tried to make the training memorable and easy to absorb. We wanted to maximize the chances that the training would be deeply internalized by the trainees so that it resulted in knowledge acquisition *and* a change in lawyer behaviors. A prolonged period of lecture on the QIC Model might result in confidence that every single element of the Best Practice Model was actually presented and discussed—but passive lecture is of limited effectiveness and has modest impact on changing professional practice.[2] Thus it was critical that we used training techniques with the greatest likelihood of sustained effect.

A second external constraint on how we presented the Best Practice Model was a judgment that two days of training was about the limit of how much time could reasonably be expected of the attorneys we wished to train. Taking more than two days away from a practice, even though they received incentive payments and CLE credits, was thought to be impractical.

Once the two-day limit was decided we faced the challenge of communicating a fair amount of material and skills within a few hours. We could not make every part of the child attorney skill set a priority. Our view was that the main focus of the two-day training should be on elements that distinguish the QIC approach. We tried to identify elements that were unique or of essential importance to realizing the QIC Model. That judgment led us to make two critical assumptions. We decided to assume that the lawyers knew the basics of their state law and procedure and that they had fundamental trial practice skills.

The theory of change logic model for Attorney Behaviors is as follows:

---

1. The architects of the final training package were Melissa Carter of Barton Child Law Center at Emory University, Timothy Jaasko-Fisher of University of Washington CITA program, and Don Duquette. Frank Vandervort of University of Michigan Law School provided the initial structure and content for the conflict resolution and Advocacy Corollaries" sections and later participated in the first trainings in Georgia.

2. Knowles, Malcomb. (1984). Andragogy in Action. San Francisco: Jossey-Bass.

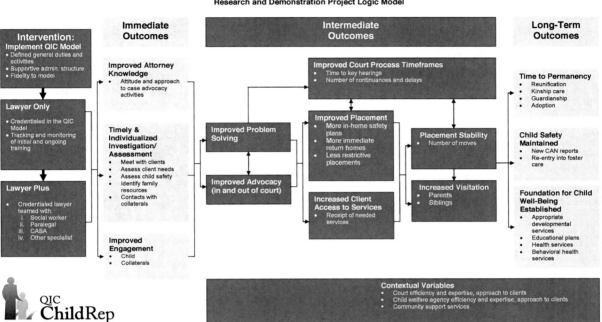

Figure 5.1
Quality Improvement Center on the Representation of Children in the Child Welfare System
Research and Demonstration Project Logic Model

5.2 QIC Six Core Skills

The Six Core Skills add the QIC Best Practice knowledge and clinical skills to the basic lawyer expertise required to be a successful legal representative for an alleged maltreated child. Figure 5.2 summarizes the Six Core Skills along with the graphic used throughout the training and elsewhere as a mnemonic to remind lawyers of its components. The graphic emphasizes three dimensions of advocacy—*listen, counsel* and *advocate* and places the Six Core Skills in that context.

1. *Enter the Child's World:* Engage with the child, learn their needs, guide them, counsel them and advocate for their needs while accommodating their stated interests consistent with state law.
2. *Assess child safety* and protect the child but without *over-reacting*. "Remove the danger, not the child," whenever that can be done consistent with child safety. Distinguish between case plan and safety plan.
3. *Actively Evaluate Needs:* Facilitate an appropriate assessment of the needs of the child and his/her family. Diagnose the problem.
4. *Advance Case Planning:* Facilitate development of an appropriate case plan.

5. *Develop Case Theory*: Develop an active and forward looking theory of the case. What is going on here? Adopt, and maybe rule-out, alternative and tentative theories of the case. Provides force and direction to the advocacy. (Drive the bus.).
6. *Advocate Effectively*: Use advocacy corollaries in meeting a child's needs that stress problem-solving and non-adversarial approaches - but which include traditional adversarial modes when appropriate.

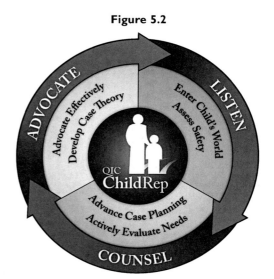

Figure 5.2

The Six Core Skills Training focused on certain principles, lawyer attitude, and clinical skills required to drive the Six Core Skills and thus the Best Practice Model. Establishing certain principles and realizing adjustments in attitude and clinical skills is more likely to generate lasting change than a how-to cookbook approach listing remedies and responses for various situations. Besides we figured the attorneys would also enjoy a problem-solving approach that respected their existing knowledge and experience.

Once the lawyers are focused on one of the QIC principles, the various legal authorities, strategy, and practical approaches for achieving those goals are readily identified by the lawyer. A lawyer focusing on safety for instance, or theory of the case or any of the other Six Core Skills, would conduct legal research or fact investigation or advocacy strategies using conventional methods just as a lawyer responds in any other legal case. A linear cookbook approach would be cumbersome and hard to internalize. The fundamental principles of the Six Core Skills are intended to frame and guide their advocacy and open up new perspectives.

While these Six Core Skills represent our last and best articulation of the skill set necessary to represent children, they are hardly the last word. Others will tailor them to the uniqueness of their own jurisdictions and their own needs. The two-day training approach articulated here was the major research intervention that we evaluated. We found that lawyers receiving this particular training and supported by the coaching and pod meetings, changed their advocacy behavior to reflect the Six Core Skills, which resulted in some improvements in case outcomes for the children.

5.3 Six Core Skills Two-Day Training—Day One
5.3.1 Agenda and Materials

The training was designed with up to 30 participants in mind. A total of 130 lawyers received the training. As implemented in Georgia and Washington State, the number of participants per session ranged from 10 to 28. In March and April of 2012, 67 lawyers from Georgia received the training and in May 2012 63 lawyers from Washington State. In preparation for the training each attorney was asked to view a short, five-minute video that described the QIC Project, the Six Core Skills, and what was expected of them as "QIC Attorneys." Participants were also asked to read the QIC Best Practice Model in advance. At the day of the training participants received a binder of training materials and a copy of the NACC "Red Book," (Duquette and Haralambie, Eds; *Child Welfare Law and Practice: Representing Children, Parents and State Agencies in Abuse, Neglect and Dependency Cases*, Second Edition (2010)). The Agenda follows as Figure 5.3.

Figure 5.3   QIC Training Agenda

NATIONAL QUALITY IMPROVEMENT CENTER ON THE REPRESENTATION OF CHILDREN IN THE CHILD WELFARE SYSTEM

QIC TRAINING AGENDA
DAY ONE:

8:00	Welcome, Introductions and Logistics
8:30	Appreciating Differences: Race, Class and Culture Circle Exercise
9:10	Entering The Child's World
	Introduction
	Understanding the Child's Developmental Level
9:45	BREAK
10:00	Rephrasing Exercise
	Adolescent Development
	Effects of Trauma and Loss on Child Development
	Treatment Needs
11:30	LUNCH
12:15	Interviewing the Child Client
1:45	Counseling the Child: Accommodating the Child's Wishes in Setting Case Goals
2:30	BREAK
2:45	Counseling the Child (cont.)
3:30	Child Safety Decision-Making
4:20	Group Reflection on the Day
4:30	END

QIC TRAINING AGENDA - DAY TWO

8:00	Marco's Case - Marco and Lily at Preliminary Hearing
9:15	BREAK
9:30	
1.	Actively Evaluate Needs
2.	Develop a Forward-looking Theory of the Case
3.	Non-adversarial Case Resolution
11:30	**LUNCH**
12:15	Increasing the Case Plan's Likelihood of Success
1:15	Marco's Case—Disposition
2:15	BREAK
2:30	Monitoring Well-being; Aging Out
3:00	Marco's Case—Permanency Planning
4:00	Wrap up and Evaluation
4:30	**END**

Training Materials Available:
The power point slides, handouts and videos used in the training are available on the websites of the QIC-ChildRep and the ABA Center on Children and the Law.

The available materials are found here: www.ImproveChildRep.org and http://www.americanbar.org/groups/child_law.html .

5.3.2 Introduction

The training begins with an introduction of the presenters and an orientation to the overall plan and objectives of the training. The Six Core Skills are again summarized. Lawyers are told that knowing the law and procedure of the jurisdiction is essential to good child representation as are courtroom practice skills. They are not, however, sufficient for doing a good job for a child. A child's attorney also has to develop an array of *clinical* knowledge and skills to cope with the challenges. Many of these clinical skills are unique to child representation, which is why they are emphasized in the course.

The course does not address Six Core Skills one-at-a-time. The skills are employed at various parts of the process and aspects of the lawyer relationship to the child and the case. The discussions, particularly in the second day, were intended to demonstrate the integration and unity of the Six Core Skills concept.

The course begins with "Enter the Child's World," a concept that embraces engaging with the child, learning about the child's life and needs, and counseling him or her when faced with significant life decisions. Lawyers are asked to recognize the importance to a child personally and to the entire child welfare process of having the child's voice and views strongly presented to the court. Even in a best interests jurisdiction, the

QIC SIX CORE SKILLS AND THE QIC BEST PRACTICE TRAINING

voice of the child should be accommodated as much as possible by the advocate. The voice of the child should not be simply stated, but rather advocated for and pursued in a strategic manner as the lawyer tries to eliminate obstacles to realizing a child's position from one hearing to another.

5.3.3 Identity Circle Exercise: Race, Class and Culture

After a general introduction and as a first step toward "entering the child's world," participants explored their own identity and discussed how awareness of these personal and immutable characteristics impact both lawyer and the client.[3] Youth in child welfare cases are sometimes asked to give up a part of their identity. The child's lawyer must be aware of this and be willing to explore the issue with the client to decide how best to respond.

The Identity Circle Exercise asks the participants to create a pie chart of their identity.

The exercise identifies immutable characteristics of individuals including age, race, disability, religious culture, ethnicity, social class culture, sexual orientation, indigenous heritage, national origin, and gender. The Identity Circle pie charts are discussed as a group. (This graphic is an example of a lawyer's Identity Circle.)

One of the high points of the exercise is an interchange with persons who had more than 50% of their identity as "family" or some role in family such as mother, father, etc. The person would be asked if they would be willing to give up that part of their identity—even for a brief period of time. Would they be willing to give that up even if there were studies or experts who said that giving up that part of their identity was "good" for the participant?

Most participants are not willing to change their identity in any way, yet many times we ask youth in foster care implicitly or explicitly to reject parts of their identity (i.e. your parents are dangerous drug addicts, experts agree that going to a different school and leaving your current friends would be "best" for you, etc.). How might the participant's identity differ from that of their client? The participants were asked to think of their last youth client. What do they think that youth's identity circle would look like? How is it the same or different from the participant, and how might that impact representation of that client?

---

3. The Identify Circle exercise was adapted from the University of Michigan School of Social Work's Cultural Humility workshop by Kathleen Faller and Robert Ortega.

5.3.4 Understanding the Child's Developmental Level and Effects of Trauma

Our premise is that the child's lawyer cannot understand the shaping of the child's world until he or she has entered it and understood it. The client needs extra help understanding what will be shaping his world and who all the new adults in his life are. We start this section with a quote from Professor Jean Koh Peters:

> Just as every lawyer must start "where the client is" in the representation, *the lawyer must strive for as specific an understanding as possible of how the child sees her situation* in the representation. Otherwise, the lawyer's attempts to counsel the client, negotiate with the client, negotiate for the client, translate the client's wishes into legal terms for the court, or otherwise carefully involve the child in the legal proceedings around her, are *doomed*."[4]

A child psychologist presents the child development section of the course using a participatory lecture approach.[5] The four facets of development were addressed—cognitive, emotional, social and physical. Not every child fits neatly into a pattern of development. And it is important to keep in mind that children often regress when exposed to trauma or under stressful situations.

So the lawyer should get to know the client and the client's circumstances before making any assumptions about capabilities. The presenters provided the basic parameters of child development at various ages and stages of development to help the lawyers understand how a child is able to process information and communicate and manage the events of his life.

To reinforce the language acquisition points, the facilitator led a "Rephrasing Exercise" in which typical sentences an attorney might use are reworded to fit the child's age and development. Trainees were encouraged to use language that was: simple, short, clear, and concrete and to check for the child's understanding of what the attorney is saying. Attorneys were asked to try to see the exchange from the child's perspective.

Effects of trauma and loss on child development and a child's ability to cope were addressed. Attorneys were urged to be alert to cues that the child is experiencing the effects of trauma in order to get the right intervention for the child and to adjust their own communication with a child who has been traumatized. The "still face" video[6]

---

4. JEAN KOH PETERS, REPRESENTING CHILDREN IN CHILD PROTECTIVE PROCEEDINGS: ETHICAL AND PRACTICAL DIMENSIONS (3d ed. 2007)

5. Dr. Katherine Rosenblum of University of Michigan developed and presented the material on child development and was the principal presenter for the Georgia trainings. The Washington trainings were handled by Dr. Frances Lexcen.

6. The "still face experiment" by Edward Tronick, available on YouTube and in the QIC Training materials, is a powerful demonstration of the bonding connection between mother and baby. In the video, an infant and a mother interact warmly, normally and then the mother turns

had a powerful impact in demonstrating that significant and important developmental processes were occurring in babies. Discussing the physical consequence of trauma and stress and of the neurotoxic effects of the human stress hormone cortisol was impactful.

The presenters connected these psychological points to their applicability to lawyers, and particularly to lawyers for children. For example, it is important to get to know the traumatized child first-hand and establish trust. It is easy to misinterpret a child's behavior as acting out or depressed when it could be masking the consequences of trauma. Supporting a trusting, safe and predictable environment is especially important as is supporting caregivers trying to provide a safe, secure and reliable environment while faced with the challenge of understanding the child's miscues. The lawyer role in getting appropriate evaluations and assessments was addressed as was framing treatment appropriately.

5.3.5 Interviewing and Counseling Child Clients
5.3.5.1 Interviewing

Interviewing and counseling skills are the primary and most familiar tools lawyers have for identifying advocacy goals on behalf of a client. This is our main portal into any client's world, including the child's world. What information we elicit and how skillfully we do it generally determines our advocacy position. We assume that communication with children and youth is a skill that can always be improved, no matter how much experience one might have as a child's representative. Even if the fundamentals are not new to the participant, there are always some new ideas, tricks, or techniques that can enhance practice. An important training point is that building trust and "entering the child's world" is something that occurs gradually over time and number of contacts. Trainees were consistently invited to share ideas and experiences and

> **INTERVIEW OUTCOMES**
>
> What were the major goals of this meeting? Were they accomplished? What subjective and objective facts were gathered? Which information is necessary for your advocacy at the next hearing? Which is important for out-of-court advocacy before/after the next hearing?
>
> - Concern for / attachment to Lily
> - Safety concerns (being whooped), Marco does not perceive risk to his own safety, feels Lily is also safe
> - Wants to go home
> - Existence of Auntie Ruby and superficial exploration of relationship

---

non-responsive and expressionless. The baby tries to get the interaction into its usual reciprocal pattern and when these attempts fail, the infant withdraws and flairs in despair. The video demonstrates that these relationship bonds are immensely powerful and important.

> **INTERVIEW TECHNIQUES**
>
> What techniques were used?
>
> - Gentle tone
> - Slow rate of speech and shorten sentences
> - Attentive body language, eye contact
> - Facilitative expressions ("uh-huh" suggesting agreement, encouragement to continue)
> - Restating to indicate clarity of understanding
> - Adopted child's language ("Auntie Ruby," "whooped")
> - Seek clarification, further understanding ("what do you mean by ____?")
> - Allow the child time to process questions and respond, avoid interruptions
> - Ask simple, open-ended, concrete questions free of abstract ideas, suggestions and double-negatives
> - Ask the client to repeat back what you have stated to ensure clarity of understanding
> - Summaries, reiterates positions

these exchanges, building on one other's expertise, were an essential part of the training.

Each part of the interviewing section generally started with a question to the group. For instance, "How are children different from adults?" Responses were written on a board or flip chart. Another example, "What are the formal goals of interviewing a child client? A participant would offer that it was essentially what they are for any client—1) Get the Facts, 2) Set case goals; and 3) Counsel. And the presenter would reinforce the point with the slide and commentary and maybe further questioning. Through question and response dialogue with the trainees, the main points identified in the curriculum were elicited. The lawyer trainees were generally responsive and seemed to appreciate sharing their views with peers. (See the website for details of the Interviewing presentation: www.ImproveChildRep.org and http://www.americanbar.org/groups/child_law.html . Once the foundation points were made we provided an opportunity to reinforce and think critically about their application.

Trainees read the first part of "Marco's Case" and then discussed what the challenges are for this contact with a youth at the first court hearing and what they wanted to know ahead of the interview. The group then viewed the video of a simulated attorney client interview occurring at a preliminary (detention, shelter care) hearing.

Discussion followed the interview. The videotaped interview was purposely not perfect so there were plenty of issues to discuss. Using the dialogue technique, the trainer elicited and emphasized the major take-away points as to desirable interview technique and outcomes. Positive critiques of the video generally included the interviewer's good rapport with the client and lead to a discussion of rapport-building strategies. The negatives included the scarcity of legally relevant factual detail elicited—details critical to the immediate hearing.

5.3.5.2 Counseling

Marco's case also provided the vehicle for the counseling discussion. Participants viewed an interview clip called "Marco's Choice" set at the Permanency Planning stage of a proceeding in which the youth's wishes and opinions about termination of parental rights, reunification with parents, on-going relationship with parents, longer-term caregiver are central.

When does a child have the capacity to direct counsel in these important decisions? The guidance from Rule of Professional Conduct 1.14, adopted in both states, was discussed. Washington State attorneys were accustomed to having clients over 12 and the practice there is clearly client directed, but they still had the occasional youth with diminished capacity and some were occasionally appointed as guardian ad litem. Georgia attorneys on the other hand were, *at that time*, charged with best interest representation and represented children from infancy to late teens. Nonetheless, Georgia lawyers seemed generally receptive to the idea that it is in the interests of the child to have his or her point of view elicited, presented and advocated for within the court proceedings. The wishes of the child were always relevant, even in the best interests context. The training made the point that it may be in the child's best interests to give more weight to the child's views as the child is older and more mature and competent.

The counseling discussion continued with the question of what foundation is required prior to a successful counseling session. As elicited by the trainer, lawyers shared their experiences and examples from their own practice in gaining the trust of the child and developing a solid relationship. The child should understand that the attorney will give advice and reasons but that it is the child who finally sets the goals—but the court who ultimately decides.

Many lawyers shared experiences that it helped their young clients understand the relationship when they said something along the lines of "You are my boss." Children found that relationship with an adult unusual—but often liked it too. The training emphasized that counseling was NOT simply talking the child into accepting what the lawyer thinks is best. It was also important to listen as much as, or more than, you talked.

5.3.6 *Assess Child Safety*

The core skill, **"Assessing child safety"** encourages the lawyers to "remove the danger, not the child," whenever that can be done consistent with child safety. The trainees are introduced to an ABA risk assessment model in which the lawyer (and the court and child welfare agency) assesses the *threat* of danger, the *vulnerability* of the child and *protective capacities* of the caregivers and the child. The ABA Lund & Renne[7] (2009) model is pretty straightforward and easy to apply and consistent with existing state law

---

7. ABA Lund & Renne (2009).

and many state agency practices. For more information see Child Safety: A Guide for Judges and Attorneys, available through www.shopABA.org.

The model encourages careful thought behind the decision to remove a child (and keep a child in placement) and seeks to protect the child without over-reacting. At the end of a case the model distinguishes between *case plan* meant to address all the problems that caused a child to come under court jurisdiction and a *safety plan* where a child could be safely protected at home and returned even where the parent has not fulfilled every element of the court-ordered safety plan.[8]

The overview emphasized that the attorneys need to understand how safety is assessed by the agency responsible for child welfare in their state.

The model requires identification of *threats* to the child, a determination of whether the child is *vulnerable*, and an assessment of *protective capacities* to mitigate threats. The model is designed as a way of structuring thinking around safety to make sure all important factors are considered. If there are insufficient protective capacities to protect a child from threats to which the child is vulnerable, then the child is not safe.

This model may be used to assess a biological parent's home, a potential relative placement, or even a foster home. The model is useful for the initial removal and placement question but also for the question of when a child may safely be returned home. There is considerable concern that once a child enters care, he or she is often kept longer than pure safety concerns might warrant.

Using the dialogue technique, the concepts of *threat, vulnerability* and *protective factors* are explored with the group. The *threat* must be specific, observable, out of control, immediate or imminent, and severe. Is *this child* vulnerable to this threat? *Protective factors* could include behavioral, cognitive, and emotional characteristics.

A *safety plan* is identified as a situation where the child is "safe" because there are no threats to which the child is vulnerable or where there are sufficient protective capacities present to protect the child from threats to which they are vulnerable. For

---

8. Timothy Jaasko-Fisher developed this element of the QIC training approach, including the helpful triangle, which communicated this concept so simply and so clearly.

example, is a backyard swimming pool safe? It certainly can present a threat, but is the child vulnerable? A toddler certainly is; but the 14-year-old swim team member not so much. If there is a threat and if the child is vulnerable, will a fence around the pool may provide sufficient protective factors? This paradigm was explored in various examples.

A threat/no threat 10 minute exercise rounded out this section. Participants were asked to stand to one side of the room. They were presented with a brief scenario and asked whether there was a threat or no threat to this child. If a threat they were asked to move to one side of the room, if no threat, to another side of the room. (This was a great exercise at the end of a full day when some physical activity was especially welcome.) For example: 1) Sixteen-year-old Margo is left at home alone in the evening while her mother works the night shift. Or 2) Seven-year-old child is in a home that regularly has only peanut butter, bread and ramen noodles to eat.

Some lawyers were quick to identify potential risks in scenarios—but speculative risks that failed the requirement of being "specific, observable, out of control, imminent, and severe." The trainer emphasized the need for facts, not fears. We do not want to expose a child to danger; but neither do we want to cause harm to a child through an unnecessary removal from his or her home. These exercises reinforced the abstract structure of the concept and required careful thought about applying the construct to a particular fact situation.

5.3.7 Group Reflection on the Day
Based on what they learned today, each participant was asked to write down one thing that they could do differently in their practice next week. Then the cards were exchanged among the participants for review. The reviewers ranked each card's entry on a one to five scale, with one being low and five high. ("Wish I would have thought of that.") The cards were exchanged until each card had 5 comments. The fifth person added the scores up. Then the leader asked for how many 25s, what was it? How many 24s; what was it? And so forth until the top five or six take-away learning points were identified.

5.4. Six Core Skills Two-Day Training—Day Two
5.4.1 *Marco's Case #1—Exercise in Emergency Removal and Placement*
Day Two begins with a brief overview of the Six Core Skills and what was covered the previous day. The trainees are asked to review the Marco's Case Exercise Part One (See www.ImproveChildRep.org and http://www.americanbar.org/groups/child_law.html), which puts them in the position of a child's lawyer at the initial hearing. They have all been in the situation where they know little or nothing about a case before they walk into the courthouse. They are asked to work through the scenario step by step in their small groups and determine what they need to do next. "Please identify what

considerations you would make and what you would do from here?" The Small Group Instructions summarizes the Six Core Skills with questions relating to the first court hearing.

1. **Listen**. How do you learn from the child? What are the child's wishes and needs? To what extent do you accommodate the child's wishes at this point?
2. **Listen**: Safety Assessment. Will your client be safe? Please identify the elements you would consider in making the Safety/Removal decision. What will be your recommendation to the court?
3. **Counsel**: Assess the Case/Evaluate the Evaluations: What are the needs of the child and family? How can you facilitate an appropriate assessment of the child and the family in order to diagnose and define the problem and thus give proper direction to the case?
4. **Counsel**: How can you advance adoption of an appropriate case plan that addresses the properly defined needs of the child and family and addresses the child's needs, including the needs for safety and permanency?
5. **Advocate: Case Theory**: What is going on here? What is the "big picture"? Where is this case going? Drive the bus!
6. **Advocate: Next Steps**: What steps should you take to address the child's needs? Problem-solve, negotiate, argue? What position do you take before the court?

After 20-25 minutes the group is reconvened to compare notes and the reasoning of each group.

The leader circulates around the room to unobtrusively monitor the discussions of the groups and keep them on track if needed. The monitoring can also reveal notable conversations and take-away points to surface in the later discussions.

Upon reconvening, the leader relies on the Discussion Guide (see Marco Case #1), which has not been shared with the trainees, to surface as many of the critical considerations as time allows. The plenary discussion is not intended to surface every element related to the Six Core Skills that a lawyer should or could consider in this case. Rather it is intended to open the trainees' minds to these dimensions of representation and case preparation that they might not have considered. The small group discussion accomplishes much of this.

In the plenary discussion the leader might start with questions such as: "What position do you advocate for Marco and why?" "How does the safety assessment go as to Marco? What's the threat? Is he vulnerable? Are there protective capacities to be called upon?" These and similar questions usually generated a good discussion from the group. This challenge for the teacher is to channel and guide the conversation to surface the educational goals. The main take-away points are reinforced verbally or by writing down on a whiteboard or poster.

The Marco #1 exercise provides a good opportunity to introduce the Core Skill of "Develop Case Theory." *Case Theory* proved to be a less intuitive concept and more difficult to communicate to the trainees than others. The term is generally used in trial practice and that could have caused confusion. The following questions, or questions similar to these, help communicate the concept and its relevance going forward.

- Of course this is early in the life of a case, but what are your early thoughts?
- What is going on here?
- What are the possible dynamics that explain what might be going on in this family?

Once they understand you really want some speculation (based on the facts as currently known), trainees will offer competing explanations. There could be different and inconsistent hypotheses. For example:

Theory #1: This is a case about a mother who is using drugs or engaging in other criminal activity during the night, rather than caring for her children and her children are suffering as a consequence.

Theory #2: This is a case about a single mother in poverty who is doing the very best she can with two challenging children.

Theory #3: This is a case about an out-of control teenager who is sneaking out at night carousing with bad company, maybe abusing alcohol and other drugs.

The concept is introduced at this point but the full presentation follows later in the afternoon. The point is for the lawyer to think through these alternative explanations early, but hold them lightly.

5.4.2 Actively Evaluate the Needs of the Child and Family

After a teaser "Twilight Zone" sound track and the promise of traveling to "A New Earth," this section begins with a short lecture. The players in a dependency court case cannot solve a problem unless the problem is properly defined. Apart from pure emergencies, beware of responding to the family issues without an appropriate assessment of the needs of the child and family. The lawyer must not only gather information relating to what is contained in the dependency petition, but must also understand what is necessary to advocate for the health, safety, and wellbeing of the client. From a legal perspective, begin by thinking about what the court must legally consider at a given hearing. Beyond the legal requirements, one should consider the developmental needs of the child.

One simple framework for evaluating wellbeing is Maslow's hierarchy. Using such a model reminds us to consider the child's physiological needs, need for safety, love and a sense of belonging, esteem, and ultimately self-actualization. These domains are not offered in a strict sense, but rather as a framework for helping to remember that to

> **MASLOW'S NEEDS**
>
> *Physiological:* food, water, sleep
> *Safety:* security of body, family, health, property, employment, morality
> *Love / Belonging:* friendships, family, intimacy
> *Esteem:* self-esteem, confidence, achievement, respect by and for others
> *Self-actualization:* morality, creativity, spontaneity, problem solving

adequately advocate for a client's needs, one must consider those needs in a holistic manner. Remember also that to understand some of these needs, you may need to ask for assistance by requesting evaluations of your client.

On the one hand, evaluations to help the lawyer understand issues such as a client's unique mental health, educational, or physical needs can be very useful. It is likely most clients have been exposed to significant trauma, and are at higher risk of both physical and mental health problems than their peers.

On the other hand, it is also important not to try to evaluate your way to a resolution of the case. Sometimes difficult judgments and choices are required and no amount of additional assessment—drug screens, psychological evaluations etc.—will remove that burden. The attorney should understand that a full battery of psychological tests may not be required in every case. It can save time, not to mention money, for the system, if scarce resources are carefully targeted.

Most professional evaluations answer very specific types of questions related to your client. The more specific you can be about the question, the more likely the evaluator will provide a helpful evaluation. So before asking for the evaluation, be clear on what you expect and consider what you hope to learn might fit into your overall case theory. Ultimately, deciding what information you pursue is more of an art than a science. Don't be afraid to be curious and test your "gut" theories about where the case may need some attention. Also, don't forget to ask your client what they think you need to know—particularly in a client-directed model of representation this may be a powerful way to direct your inquiry.

The presentation continues to identify some information sources and statutes governing access such as HIPPA and FERPA. Strategies for obtaining information are highlighted. Mental health or social agency evaluations are central to dependency cases. Lawyers need to understand what evaluations are required and under what circumstances. Lawyers need to know how to evaluate the quality of an evaluation. The discussion surfaced some elements lawyers could use in evaluating an evaluation, including:

- Did evaluator have right qualifications?
- Experience in administering the tests given?
- Were referral questions answered?
- Subjects evaluated over time?

- Limitations and generalizability of the evaluation addressed?
- Were multiple sources of information used?
- Child's developmental level taken into account?
- Are clinical judgments clearly laid out?

The "Journey to New Earth" exercise[9] was intended to sensitize the lawyers to how the person *about whom* the data was collected evaluates what's important, compared to what the professionals gathering the information think is important. The exercise presumes a need for a two to three year journey to an ultimate place of safety, an obvious reference to the foster care journey their clients are embarking on. Because people on the journey may have difficulty with memory and judgment the government has appointed "Gatherers"—people who compile records and recommend evaluations for those being evacuated to help look after their health and wellbeing as they make the journey.

Participants were evenly divided into Evacuees and Gatherers. In five minutes Gatherers compile a list of things on individual post-it notes that they believe is important to the Evacuee they are talking to. Then they switch roles.

Trainees post their notes, of different colors for Gatherers versus Evacuees, on a Maslow scale affixed to the wall Trainees were asked to notice differences between what was important to them as Gatherers versus what was important to them as Evacuees. The variance was clear and illuminating.

5.4.3 Develop a Forward-Looking Case Theory

Develop an active and forward looking theory of case is a Core Skill. Our concept is similar to, but different from, the *theory of the case* notion that we use in trial practice. The similarities are that a theory should explain what is really happening in the family and be consistent with the available evidence and evaluations. It should be logical and consistent with people's perceptions as to how things really work. But our concept is different from the trial practice theory in that it is forward-looking and anticipates competing and even inconsistent theories as to "what's going on here?"

After an introduction of the topic the leader asked: When you walk into a courthouse and pick up a case for the first time, review the petition, the caseworker's notes and get your first look at the players, ideas began occurring to you, right? Your thoughts naturally generate notions of what could be going on here. What are the real issues here? What is happening here? Where is this case going? Where is this likely to end up?

You do not act on these preliminary notions, do you? You need to carefully gather information and check your intuitions against firmer data. But these intuitions, these

---

9. Developed by Tim Jaasko-Fisher.

tentative thoughts have value in the problem-solving process. Physicians proceed along similar paths as they use the technique of *differential diagnosis* in which they consider what could lie behind a certain set of symptoms. They gather information and do tests to *rule out* this possibility or rule out that. We lawyers can proceed similarly.

We encourage the lawyers to adopt *preliminary* or tentative theories of the case—but do not rush to judgment. Just because a certain explanation, say drug abuse, is what *could possibly* explain what is going on here, does not mean it is so. We encouraged the trainees to "Develop a theory or theories early; but hold them lightly." The theory of the case will evolve as the facts are developed and different legal theories are considered. This is true both pre-adjudication and throughout the dispositional phase of a proceeding.

For instance, the child's lawyer may take the position early in the case that the parent's conduct, while neglectful, is not so serious as to merit an early movement toward an alternative permanency plan. But as time goes by and the parent fails to take advantage of treatment services or attends them but is unable to derive any benefit, the theory of the case may change from a neglectful parent who needs services to safely care for her child to a parent who is unable or unwilling to take the steps necessary to provide a safe home for the child.

What is the advantage of coming to a tentative theory of the case early, or of entertaining alternative explanations of what is going on here? This mental exercise, exploring in one's mind what could possibly explain the situation, is also a way to give *force* and *direction* to the advocacy.

The trainer asked the trainees whether this concept ring true to them and asked for some examples. Examples emerged either from the trainees, trainers or both. For instance, in a case in which a parent has a drug abuse problem which impairs his capacity to care for this child, the theory may be "This is a case about a father whose drug addiction has interfered with his ability to provide a fit home for his child so the court must take jurisdiction of the child and direct the father to become drug free so that the child may be returned to him within the next 12 to 15 months."

The point is for the lawyer to think through these alternative explanations early. Just as a physician might in differential diagnosis, the attorney should collect information (or see that information is collected for the court), to rule out this or that possibility or rule in this or that possibility. Further facts and assessment may confirm or disconfirm one of a lawyer's theories. But having different theories of "what's going on here," even if discounted later on, can guide the lawyer advocacy to be sure that all avenues are explored, the case is assessed thoroughly and all options are considered.

Thinking broadly about a case at this stage may open up possibilities for investigation, assessment, placement, or support and services that wouldn't otherwise emerge. Alternative theories can give force and direction to the lawyer's advocacy and help the court in getting all relevant information before it. The next question is what does the lawyer or the court need to do to exclude or confirm any or all of your hypotheses?

The introductory comments and discussion are followed by an exercise using "Danny's Case." (See website.) In small groups the trainees developed possible theories of the case. In plenary these were compared and discussed and the *theory of the case* concept clarified. What explains what is going on? Where should this case be going? What ideas for investigation or assessment, problem-solving or advocacy are triggered by the theory? A theory, even alternative theories, can give force and direction to your advocacy. A forward-looking approach can harness your ability to work a case and moves you to an aggressive, assertive, and positive role. Not just a "gotcha" role or "putting the state to its burden.

Danny's Case also served as segue to another of the Six Core Skills—*Advocate Effectively*.

5.4.4 Advocate Effectively/Non-Adversarial Case Resolution[10]
5.4.4.1 Needs and the Advocacy Corollaries

Before one advocates, one must identify the goals for the client and his case. Developing the theory of the case helps the lawyer identify *goals* for the case, both long- and short-term. The primary long-term goal, of course, is the permanency goal. The *theory of the case* is the "big picture"—what the case is about and where you want it to go eventually.

The *needs* of the child and family are the smaller bits that move the case toward the ultimate goal. The needs of the family may be those of the child or a parent. Generally, both need to be addressed if the child is to return or maintain a relationship. The *needs* of the child or family are the "intermediate goals" such as obtaining a necessary evaluation or finding an appropriate relative with whom the child may be placed. The intermediate goals may also address issues of safety and well-being.

Intermediate goals include such things as addressing the child's emotional dysregulation that might result from the chaotic home environment provided by the parent, putting in place an appropriate educational plan, seeing that the child has a needed medical assessment, or ensuring that the parent's treatment plan adequately addresses all the issues in the case and is tailored so as to equip them to meet the child's needs. The question is: What needs to happen to move the family toward the ultimate permanency goal?

Danny's Case was used to communicate this concept. The trainees were asked to identify the child's needs, parent's needs and the intermediate goals that will move the case in the direction of achieving the ultimate goal. After analyzing and identifying the child's needs, the lawyers match a form of advocacy with each need. Each identified

---

10. Frank Vandervort developed much of this section.

need has an advocacy corollary. Identifying the corollary turns on this question: What is the quickest, least adversarial way of meeting that need?

For instance, if the child needs a medical examination, the lawyer should ask, "What is the quickest, least adversarial way of getting that examination?" Perhaps it is to request that the parent take the child to a pediatrician, or ask the worker to ensure that the examination is scheduled. If these methods do not work, then the advocate should be prepared to file a motion asking the court to order that such an examination take place.

After laying out this matching of a "need" or "intermediate goal" to one or more acts of advocacy, trainees are asked to identify one or more needs of the various parties to the case—the child and the parent. These are listed on a white board. When a list of "needs" or "intermediate goals," is generated, each is matched with an act of advocacy (e.g., calling the worker, talking to a supervisor or perhaps the agency's attorney, filing an appropriate motion)

Advocacy Corollary

Need/Goal	Advocacy Corollary
• Identify a child's or parent's need.	Matches need to at least one method of advocacy.
• Identify goal	Try least adversarial first. Be prepared to use more adversarial methods if necessary to address need or realize goal.

5.4.4.2 Non-Adversarial Case Resolution (NACR)

The QIC Model emphasizes non-adversarial and problem-solving approaches to child welfare cases. Many jurisdictions use formal mediation or some form of family group conferencing as a routine part of dependency cases. The QIC attorneys were generally familiar with these processes and many had participated in them. The Non-Adversarial Case Resolution (NACR) section of the QIC training exposed the trainees to mediation-type techniques they can use in day to day practices, whether or not a case is part of a formal alternative dispute resolution process.

Through an interactive lecture some of the benefits of a non-adversarial, collaborative approach were identified. Collaboration assumes a shared objective. The child's lawyer can generally find common ground with other players as to goals and objectives. In child welfare cases, a safe and successful return of the child home is a common shared goal, at least at the outset.

Most everyone wants what is best for the child, even though views of what is

Different professional ethics and behavioral expectations

• Caseworkers	• Lawyers
– May find "zealous advocacy" disagreeable and aggressive	– More comfortable with spirited debate and disagreement
– Often expect complete openness and honesty	– May negotiate strategically (e.g., withhold information)
– Tend to be more relational	– Tend to be more analytic

"best" may vary. The importance of searching for common ground was emphasized as was the need for solid working relationships with the caseworkers, other lawyers and service providers. Friendly, or at least respectful, encounters outside of court can build a trusting relationship that can serve as a foundation for resolving difficult disagreements. Professional rapport takes time, but pays dividends when a conflict or need arises.

Group discussion identified some of the characteristics of a strong working relationship:

- Understanding each other's backgrounds, job responsibilities, point of view
- Good communication
- Responsiveness
- Trust
- Mutual respect
- Teamwork
- Preferred modes of communication

Ideally disagreements should be about differences in judgment or professional opinion and not based on power struggle or concerns about malevolent intent or bad character.

Child welfare cases are uniquely collaborative. More than lawyers are required and cross-disciplinary exchange is essential. The players often become frustrated with one another when someone does not understand or consider the differences in disciplinary approaches or the requirements of the law.

There are different professional ethics and norms in play that can cause confusion and engender distrust. Lawyers may be comfortable with spirited debate and disagreement while caseworkers find confrontive zealous advocacy disagreeable and overly aggressive. Lawyers may negotiate strategically and withhold certain information while caseworkers expect complete openness and honesty. Lawyers tend to be more analytical and caseworkers more relational.

Recognizing these different approaches and accommodating them can help facilitate good exchanges of information and perspective and encourage problem-solving.

The trainees were guided on a discussion of fairly routine exchanges of information and negotiation with caseworkers. The conversation emphasized civility and patience urging the lawyers to use their best diplomatic side whenever possible. "What techniques do you use?" the leader asked. Trainees all had experience with collaborative approaches. Certain approaches were highlighted such as:

- State concerns clearly and concisely but not in a judgmental fashion.
- Restate and reframe points in neutral, not blaming, language.

- Avoid critical accusatory language.
- Where there are points of disagreement, narrow them and define them carefully.
- The agency attorney may be able to help craft a solution.
- It is very useful to understand the caseworkers world, their limits and the scope of their authority.

There are "urban legends" among caseworkers. That is, there may be understandings of policy and practice that are clearly wrong. Increasingly policy is posted on line and can be clarified. Give the agency the courtesy of a chance to resolve a question. Even if there is a policy, the caseworker or supervisor can often waive. Of course the lawyers will use the court process to resolve questions as needed.

These collaborative tools can promote problem-solving and professional civility and maybe even lower blood pressure, but they will not resolve every dispute. Sometimes one has to escalate to a higher authority in the agency or use the litigation options in court. Do so professionally, of course. One lawyer said "You can only circle that drain so long." Although the QIC Model emphasizes non-adversarial and collaborative methods and problem-solving, the attorneys are encouraged to use traditional adversarial modes when appropriate. Reasonable people can differ. Sometimes the best way to resolve a conflict is to present the matter vigorously to a judge.

5.4.5 Advance Case Planning

Facilitating development of an appropriate case plan is one of the lawyer's Core Skills. Case planning should not be left entirely in the hands of the agency and service providers. Both child clients and the parents have a great deal riding on whether the case plan identifies the true needs of the family and whether the services are appropriately focused and targeted to address those needs.

The child's lawyer should be closely involved in that process. The case plan sets the direction of the case going forward and the parents are evaluated according to how well they succeed or not. In most cases the child's future rests on how accurately the case plan targets rehabilitative services for the entire family so as to address the conditions that caused the child to come under the jurisdiction of the court.

The trainer asks "How do we increase the case plan's likelihood of success? What are your experiences with developing case plans?" That generated some experiences, positive and negative, which allowed for follow-up from the trainer: "Are the parents and child consulted?" Is the plan based on an adequate assessment? Is the case plan driven by the identified needs of the family or by the readily available resources of the agency and community?

- Specific
- Measureable
- Achievable
- Relevant
- Time Specific

How well does the case plan directly and specifically relate to the reasons the child cannot live at home safely? Or are they standard, "cookie cutter" plans? Do the plans target threats of danger and conditions that affect the parents' protective capacities? Does the case plan differ from the safety plan? Is it realistic?

The attorney role is to get to know the child client and understand not only what her needs are, but also what she wants. And it is most often the case that the child wants more than anything to return home. An effective way to achieve the child's goal is to ensure the case plan is designed in a way that logically addresses the parents' particular issues in a way that makes success possible and even likely.

This discussion allows the trainer to identify characteristics of good case plans, based as much as possible on comments made by the trainees. The case plan should be SMART, that is: Specific, Measureable, Achievable, Relevant, and Time Specific.[11] It should be simple and clear for the benefit of all providers and for the family. Simple and clear plans make it easier to hold both the agency and the parents accountable. Clear plans facilitate later court review of whether the agency made reasonable efforts to reunify the child and parents.

Several case plan examples are presented and critiqued based on the SMART criteria. Generally lawyers raise questions about options they might have to improve upon the original framing of a case plan or enforce provisions not being implemented properly or timely.

Next the trainer introduces a discussion of what services are available locally? Are they appropriate for your case? Unfortunately, in most communities services and service providers come and go. The state contracted providers go and in out of business. It is a tough job to stay current on what is available and on the quality. But it is part of the attorney's job to do so. How does a busy lawyer stay up on local services? The trainees are assured that we will discuss this question now, but will follow up on this topic in the subsequent QIC training meetings, the Pod Meetings.

The trainees are asked: "Is understanding what services are available and how to evaluate their quality and suitability for a particular client or family really a lawyer responsibility?" What do you think? What experiences have you had?

Discussion should surface:

- Rules of professional responsibility require counseling a client even on non-law matters.
- Poor services or the wrong services can set your client's cause back dramatically — no matter how good your legal advocacy is otherwise.

---

11. Adapted from *Solution-based Casework for Judges, Lawyers and Other Court Professionals,* a training created in collaboration with the University of Washington School of Law's Court Improvement Training Academy, Partners for Our Children, and the Washington State DSHS Children's Administration.

- Even though it is part of our job, but we are not trained to make these judgments. We often lack the tools to evaluate service quality effectively. (It is not beyond our duties; it is beyond our control.)
- All we can do is adopt an intelligent consumer model. Ask, is this service worthwhile? How can we evaluate what our client gets?

The conclusion is that keeping up to speed on availability and quality of services is indeed part of the obligations of the child's lawyer.

WHAT kind of service related information does a lawyer need to keep up on? What is the range of services potentially relevant to a child welfare case? What are your ideas? Discussion should identify:

- Evaluators, mental health providers and qualifications
- Mental health clinics
- Health clinics
- Doctors and dentists who take Medicaid
- Inpatient mental health and substance abuse programs and how they are paid for
- Levels of foster care and services available at each level
- Whether families can take advantage of resources in neighboring communities and if reimbursement is available for travel and expenses
- Neighborhood facilities
- Community centers
- Services available through the schools
- Recreational opportunities for the child, e.g., camp, lessons, sports

How do you learn what is potentially available in your jurisdiction? How do you evaluate the quality of any particular service? How do you evaluate its appropriateness in any given case? What ideas do you have for doing this?

Discussion should identify:

- Look to practices that have evidence of effectiveness.
- Evidence-based practice is gradually becoming the norm. Demand proof of the effectiveness of the services offered your clients.
- Talk to caseworkers, to other lawyers, to other trusted professionals. During time waiting for your case to be called, schmooze with the caseworkers, ask questions, get opinions.

5.4.6 *Marco's Case #2—Exercise in Case Planning and Disposition*

Part 2 of Marco's Case brings the case beyond adjudication to case planning and dispositional order. The scenario is designed to reinforce some of the skills covered up to this point. The facilitator briefly summarizes the Six Core Skills again, introduces exercise and instructs each table of 4 to 6 to work through this scenario step by step in the next 30 minutes. Each group is asked to identify what considerations they would make using the six QIC core skills and ultimately what position they would take at the dispositional hearing.

The educational objectives are to reinforce how to identify the immediate, mid and long term needs of the child including the value of learning and accommodating the child's wishes. Trainees should learn the importance of doing a careful investigation, consulting with others, and doing a safety assessment. Trainees should learn the importance of the child's attorney developing a cogent theory of the case—even though the theory may change as the facts develop further. Trainees should recognize the importance of framing an advocacy agenda from the beginning.

In the plenary discussion, the facilitator asks one or two groups to report what they decided to advocate for at the Dispositional Hearing and why. The goals of the discussion are to identify and clarify various positions and recommendations for Dispositional Hearing according to the Core QIC skills. Lawyers commonly recognize a potential conflict between the interests of Lilly and Marco and that they may not be able to represent them both.

The facilitator elicited the needs of Marco and what additional assessment information is required. The Safety Assessment process is reviewed and the question asked: Is Marco safe? Consider safety for Lily, even though she is not the client, Marco cares about what happens to her. It is a closer question to which there is no clear answer. Marco's greatest need might be to gain some stability.

The trainees generally have good ideas about school interventions by themselves or the caseworker, visits for the family, mentorship for Marco, maybe by the coach. Marco's presence at the hearing is encouraged, pros and cons addressed, court resistance acknowledged. Trainees are asked to frame a theory of the case and elements of the case plan that they would advocate for at the hearing itself. Finally, trainees are asked to develop an advocacy plan between now and next hearing. What are the key events, services, and so forth that need to be done to keep the case progressing to some satisfactory resolution?

5.4.7 Monitoring Well-Being; Aging Out

This section on advocacy for child well-being was presented via interactive lecture with brief group exercises. The learning objectives are: To understand substantive law addressing a child's well-being and the attorney's role in monitoring and advocating for a child's well-being needs. During this period in foster care many things affecting the child's overall well-being are at risk. The attorney has a significant role in protecting the child's relationship with parents, defending sibling connections, getting proper medical care and educational placement and services. Some youth age out of foster care and face especially complex legal and bureaucratic and personal challenges as they move to independent living.

Ensuring the child's well-being means taking a proactive approach, which requires out of court advocacy beyond being prepared for court hearings. In addition to regular contact with the child, the attorney must get regular reports on the child's general condition and needs.

The section begins with a group exercise in which the trainees imagine their child being moved to the home of a stranger and you have a few minutes to talk with the caseworker in charge of his case. What do you ask for? What do you tell the caseworker about the child? Facilitator lists responses on the whiteboard and then draws the trainee attention to the fact that most of the items listed are not specific statutory items, not explicitly identified in law. These "things that mean the most" depend on the individual child's world. We must get to know our child clients so that we can identify their needs, monitor any changes, and advocate as necessary.

Monitoring Well-Being
REGULAR REPORTS

- Health status
- Educational Status
- Visitation
- Behavioral Issues
- Progress in therapeutic interventions
- Parents' progress on the case plan goals
- Placement

Lawyers have access to regular reports about a child. The trainees are asked what they want to know about each of these items. Each of these can be critically important to the child client if not addressed properly.

The 2008 Fostering Connections Act provides child advocates resources and tools to protect a child's well-being. This is one of the few areas of substantive law included in the QIC training. Key elements covering notice to relatives, sibling placement and visitation, supports for older youth, health care planning and educational stability are discussed.

The Fostering Connections points are reinforced with a group exercise in which the participants are asked: What can the attorney do to preserve the child's connections? The group generates a list and the facilitator then recaps and summarizes.

Possible responses:

- Search for relatives at beginning and ongoing, even if goal is reunification
- Request more frequent and longer visits, in more natural settings
- Consider whether supervision is necessary; if so, think creatively about visit supervisors
- Consider which family members should attend the visits; seek and enforce sibling visitation
- Advocate for placement as close to home of origin as possible

- Advocate for child to remain in same school
- Facilitate speedy ICPC for out-of-home placements
- Monitor concurrent planning efforts for meaningfulness
- Ensure child is engaged in community activities that are important to him

Throughout your entire representation of the child, establishing permanency in a timely manner is at the forefront of the lawyer advocacy. Permanency planning begins as early as removal. The child's attorney is in a powerful position of influence over the outcome of the case. The lawyers are encouraged to know their client and his family situation, be assertive and not overly rely on the caseworker or an expert to provide the direction.

Permanency

- Permanency Options
  - Reunification
  - Adoption
  - Permanent Guardianship
  - Permanent Custody to a Relative
  - Another Planned Permanent Living Arrangement (AAPLA)
    - Must be justified by a compelling reason why no other preferred permanency option is in the child's best interest

The facilitator elicits commonly recognized permanency options and lists them on the whiteboard. Facilitator then asks participants of examples of when one of these options may be better than then others. The discussion may identify:

- When a child is in a relative placement and is secure (happy, attached), but the relative will not adopt it may be better to have a permanent guardianship with that relative than find an adoptive home.
- Reverse is true too. If the relative become engaged after child has been doing well in a pre-adoptive home and has been there a long time, the established non-relative home may be in the child's best interests.

Finally, trainees were asked what kind of permanency they have seen in their cases. The point is to show that there is a considerable variation in practice—beyond return home or adoption.

5.4.8 Marco's Case #3: Exercise in Permanency Planning Options

The trainees are asked to work through Part III of Marco's case in their small groups to reinforce the application of the Six Core Skills to client counseling and permanency planning. Trainees are asked to read through the developments since the last hearing and decide what they would do next and why? What are the permanency options for Marco? What will they recommend?

In the plenary discussion groups are asked what their position will be in court and why? Process points to highlight include the importance of understanding Marco and what he has gone through the past years. This lawyer really has "entered the child's world." What are the young man's needs? Is there any information lacking at this point? One would think that there would not be after this long under the court and agency care with a pretty attentive lawyer. But children, especially traumatized children, may have undisclosed experiences even after lengthy times in care.

What is the "big picture" here, your culminating theory of the case? The lawyers are quick to move to assessing the legal options and these are listed on the whiteboard. The facilitator tries to get the group to think broadly and keep an open mind until all options are presented and discussed. Legal permanence includes emotional and psychological stability but also attention to financial aspects of the plan. How will Marco be financially supported? A state may have some peculiarities of eligibility for adoption or guardianship funding. Knowledge of these technical details is essential for the advocate.

The process of coming to a decision is the most important goal of the exercise. But as to outcome, the general view was that Marco should stay with Aunt Ruby permanently with the legal status of permanent guardianship, so long as it could be subsidized. Lawyers wanted to preserve the possibility of maintaining a relationship with Hector Troy, Marco's father. Even if the decision is made that only Marco is the client, what happens to Lily is relevant because he wants to maintain a connection to her and preferably live in a home with her. Her options are less clear, especially since Aunt Ruby is no blood relative of hers. Some of the lawyers had quite unique and creative solutions to this dilemma that depended in part on what subsidies were available and whether one found willing and flexible decision-makers in the agency and in the court.

5.5 Wrap-Up and Evaluation of Training

At the conclusion of the second day the trainees were asked to write down three things that they learned in the training that they would implement in their practice next week. Then the group discussed these "take-away" points as a means of reviewing and reinforcing the content of the day. The trainees evaluated the QIC program quite highly.

5.6 Pod Meetings and Coaching

The purpose of coaching and supplemental pod meetings was to maximize the attorneys' retention of the Six Core Skills and to ensure fidelity to the intervention model through frequent and continuous contacts.[12] The intention was that each experimental (QIC) attorney would confer at least once per quarter with a resource attorney (a "coach") and would also meet once per quarter in small group "pod" meeting with each state's lead attorney trainer and the coach. These contacts were intended to reinforce the two-day training in the QIC model and Six Core Skills and to provide one-on-one guidance to the lawyers as they implemented the model implementation.[13] Pod

---

12. Chapin Hall Final Evaluation Report, p. 54-56.
13. *Id.* at p. 90: Appendix C: QIC Coaching and Supplemental Trainings Protocol; available at www.ImproveChildRep.org/QIC-ChildRepProducts.aspx.

meetings and coaching sessions began in July 2012 in Georgia and in September 2012 in Washington State.

The design of the coaching relied on adult learning theory that was intended "to avoid dogmatic and authoritarian approaches which tend to elicit resistance from adults and thus not work as well as a less directive learner-centered approach."[14] The coach was to initiate an in person or telephone conversation with each treatment attorney at least once per quarter until the end of the project. In that conversation, the coach would "gradually and naturally" elicit how the attorney was engaging with the model in their own practice. This "more organic, less structured, generative approach" was considered more likely to obtain a sense of what the attorneys were actually experiencing and to be less threatening to them.

The coach was expected to reinforce the model skills, not by acting as an authority, but by guiding the attorney to utilize the appropriate core skills for the circumstances of the case. The goal was that the attorney would eventually be able to generalize implementation of the skills from a specific case to their practice more broadly. A coaching contact reporting template was developed to systematically capture the coaches' interactions with the attorneys and to learn how the attorney was applying the model to his or her practice.[15]

The "pod meeting," was designed to maintain a common understanding of the model and provide an opportunity for group reflection on the implementation of its components. It also was intended that the meetings would help build "enduring communities of [child representation] practice" that would support the attorneys as they continued in their practice after the end of the study.

Each pod meeting would last 60 to 90 minutes, with both the lead trainer and coach participating. The trainer would confer with the coach to ascertain which topics were most salient for the treatment attorneys and then design a pod program of training and conversation around one or more of the Six Core Skills. Although the pod meetings were intended to be more directive and structured than the coaching discussions, it was expected that they would allow for some amount of "organic" interactions. It was emphasized in the design that the pod meetings had to be "explicitly tied" to the treatment attorneys' actual experiences utilizing the Six Core Skills. This would occur through discussions at the meetings using prompts such as "How is it going? What is going well? What are the challenges or impediments? What successes have you had?"

---

14. STEPHEN D. BROOKFIELD, UNDERSTANDING AND FACILITATING ADULT LEARNING. 1986.

15. *See* **Chapin Hall Evaluation of the QIC-ChildRep Best Practices Model Training for Attorneys Representing Children in the Child Welfare System Final Evaluation Report**, Britany Orlebeke, Xiaomeng Zhou, Ada Skyles, Andrew Zinn (2016) www.ChapinHall.org; Appendix C (QIC Coaching and Supplemental Trainings Protocol) & Appendix D (Sample Coaching Session Notes)

It was expected that the trainer would have an agenda and goals for each meeting, but would take into consideration: "Start where your [attorney] is."[16]

Generally, the pod meeting format included a check in with the attorneys on their experiences with the model during the quarter, one or more QIC core skills being discussed in-depth, an exercise(s) for the individual or small group discussion with learning shared with the full pod, case scenarios to facilitate knowledge and skill development with the model, and/or information on child-related subjects. Each meeting allowed for attorney comments pertaining to their cases.)

5.7 Conclusion

The two-day Six Core Skill Training plus the coaching and the pod meetings follow up, constitute the QIC intervention. Attorneys liked the training and evaluated it highly, but would they use the Six Core Skills in their practice? Once they get back to their offices does the model make sense? What are the challenges to implementing the QIC approach? How would the courts and agencies react to the trained lawyers? What can we learn anecdotally about the Six Core Skills effect on individual children, on an attorneys practice? Next we examine these questions through the QIC lawyers' comments to the coaches.

---

16. *Id. See* Chapin Hall Evaluation at p. 96 (Appendix E) for an example of a Pod Meeting agenda.

CHAPTER 6

What the Lawyers Say About Implementing the Six Core Skills

Abstract
These comments from coaching reports and interviews reflect attorneys' experiences with the QIC model and highlight challenges and successes of the approach. Attorneys found the Six Core Skills familiar and intuitive while advancing the level of practice.

6.1. Introduction
Pod meetings and coaching sessions were an essential element of the QIC research intervention. Both pods and coaching reinforced the major elements of the two-day training and helped QIC attorneys apply the Six Core Skills elements to specific cases. The first objective of the QIC field experiment was to improve legal representation of children. Empirical data reported in subsequent chapters demonstrate that this objective was achieved.

But how did the lawyers do this? What were their challenges and successes? What were the lawyer attitudes as they struggled with an approach that was new to many of them?

Although the on-going coaching of the lawyers was primarily meant to help improve their child representation, it also provides a window into their day-to-day involvement as they implemented the QIC approach. Any global, generalizable change in practice builds on the case by case efforts of these individual lawyers.

What was their experience? The coaching notes not only document that the coaching sessions occurred, but also provide anecdotal stories of lawyers trying to implement the QIC approach. Their personal successes and challenges and the effect of their advocacy on specific cases make for instructive reading and insight into implementing the Six Core Skills Model.

6.2 Method

In the quarterly coaching phone calls the QIC coaches were instructed to ask open ended questions of the lawyers, get them talking about their experiences, and document their responses. "How is it going?" "What are your challenges or successes?" As part of the intervention, coaches were expected to write and keep a report for each coaching session for each attorney. Notes were to have three sections: *Report*, where the coach summarized the issues the attorney brought up for discussion; *Advice*, where the coach documented what the coach said; and *Follow up/Concerns*, where the coach noted any issues that need to be addressed between coaching sessions.

The coaches sent their reports to Chapin Hall each quarter and each quarter 10 coaching reports from each state were randomly selected for analysis. The number of coaching sessions and the frequency with which the various Six Core Skills were discussed was a way of measuring the implementation of the QIC Model.[1]

All coaching notes were analyzed and organized into the subtopics below. Coaches sometimes quoted the lawyer directly and sometime summarized statements in third person. The initial variation in voice and tense and the summary nature of some of the notes requires some paraphrasing of the attorney comments. Nevertheless, every effort has been made to be faithful to the views and experiences expressed by the reporting attorneys.

6.3 Overall Value of QIC Skills

Overall the lawyers in both states appreciated the six core skill approach. Some found the approach new, even revolutionary, with significant consequences to their approach to cases. Others thought that the QIC approach was pretty "oh hum"—believing the Six Core Skills are essentially what they have been doing right along or are just plain common sense.

A few lawyers noted, even complained, that the model required more time and effort than they were being paid for. While some found their local court and agency receptive and engaged with the QIC ideas, even changing court practices to be more focused on

---

1. The numerical analysis is at **Chapin Hall Evaluation of the QIC-ChildRep Best Practices Model Training for Attorneys Representing Children in the Child Welfare System Final Evaluation Report**, Britany Orlebeke, Xiaomeng Zhou, Ada Skyles, Andrew Zinn (2016) www.ChapinHall.org; pp 54-66. In addition to coaches' notes this compilation includes comments made in follow-up interviews with a small sample of the lawyers in both states conducted by the University of Michigan researchers.

IMPLEMENTING THE SIX CORE SKILLS

the child and the perspective of the child, others were met with great resistance in their local court to an approach different from "how we do things around here."

QIC lawyers said:

- The QIC Model has really helped me to summarize exactly what it is I do when I represent kids, or what I should do, and I think all of those skills are very important.
- My partner and I worked carefully on implementation. When we open cases initially we consciously work on entering the child's world and developing case theory. We meet with the youth differently than before and put an outline of the model on each file and use it as a checklist
- Model is quite easy to implement. The six skills seem to bleed into one another; they are all related, not distinct. Together they have helped me see the case from the youth perspective. Seeing the case from the youth perspective brings an urgency to the work.
- I love the model. I put the outline in every one of my files. I appreciate the rigor; things are too informal in my jurisdiction, this gives a structure.
- I am using the model and having it in mind at almost all meetings with youth, and often when doing other things in my practice.
- I am more intentional in early meetings with youth and trying to develop a relationship with the child. I like getting to know the youth; I feel like I am being a lawyer not just a mouthpiece.

Not everyone was a fan:

- This is nothing new. And I can't be chasing kids around to visit them when there are no pressing issues.
- I have not used any of the model. It is not useful. I just don't have the time, either. Doesn't fit into the way things are done in my jurisdiction.
- Model is not that much different. I was not asked to participate and I am frustrated about the demands. I am not paid to do more.

Some found applicability beyond lawyer representation of children in dependency cases:

- I really like the model, and use it in GAL cases and juvenile justice cases too.
- The overall approach is quite relevant to representing parents too.

Lawyers remarked on the benefit of sharing experiences with other ChildRep lawyers:

- The initial two-day training fades and these pod meetings are the next best thing to keep the learning alive.
- I really appreciate contact with other ChildRep lawyers. It really helps.
- I prefer in-person meetings for a more effective method of engagement.
- It was good to have the pod meetings and then be able to go out and apply the ideas to my cases.
- The pod meetings actually helped to refine some of the skills and practice that come out of the model and the QIC training. Pods talked specifically about how to enter the world of the child and I've gotten ideas how to really do that. I find it very helpful.
- Except for "entering the child's world" I didn't find the model helpful at first. But the pod meetings and discussions with the local lawyers helped me see that the approach is really foundational and applies to our daily work."

6.4 Entering the Child's World

The QIC Six Core Skills training presented information about child development, the effect of trauma on a child, and methods of engaging the child and building trust. The training encouraged lawyers to engage with the child, learn their needs, guide them, counsel them and advocate for their needs while learning and accommodating their stated wishes as much as possible, consistent with state law.

Entering the Child's World (ECW) was generally considered the most helpful and most foundational of the Six Core Skills.

- Entering the Child's World is the most often used skill. That is what is most often in my mind when working with kids. I've been thinking more about the other skills as well and see they flow from ECW. Assessing the client's needs and advocating for those needs in court and in negotiations with other parties has worked well. I am thinking more about those skills and more consciously using them
- I am focusing most particularly on meeting with client in some kind of natural environment and as frequently as possible. Meeting in better settings and more frequently has led to deeper relationship with my clients and I am able to have better conversations.
- I am working on meeting with clients other than just before court, but time constraints make that difficult.
- ECW reminds me to step back and see the case from the child's perspective—home stability, family connections, school, familiar routine—and then fashion solutions around that.
- I am meeting with a client again after the first meeting to develop better relationship. In a recent case I learned about some needs for clothes and such. I got those for the client, which really was a big benefit to the relationship.

- I am trying to stay in the ECW place when working with youth. The temptation is to go back to what is comfortable—being more directive, as with adults. I want youth clients to open up and trust more. The message to the child is "we're on the same team." That is harder to accomplish with youth clients than with adults. Also other relationships have a greater affect on the youth's relationship with his or her attorney than what happens with adult clients
- I am using cell phone, texting and email more to stay in touch with my youth clients.
- I use the model in tribal court too.
- It's hard to get a good relationship with youth but I realize that an earlier relationship can help learn the needs of a youth, assess the situation better, and prevent running.
- (A number of attorneys discussed youth on the run.) It's hard to develop a relationship with a youth on the run. An earlier relationship might help prevent running or at least get youth to look at the child welfare system to address their needs and concerns, rather than running to friends etc.
- Getting past the relationship with the client and then getting into case planning with difficult children is a particular challenge for me. Kids on the run are hard to develop enough relationship with to do concrete planning. Then when I do get some idea of what the client wants, the client does not follow through with plans I've advocated for in court. How do I do real case planning with a client who constantly runs and burns the few bridges available?
- (Several attorneys discussed the use of a "safe run" with the coach in which the youth might flee but maintain contact with someone—including the lawyer or foster parent or other trusted person.)
- I've been trying to schedule visits (or at least contact) with clients regularly, even when there are no hot issues to discuss. I put it on the calendar and protect the time. I find it useful to get to know the person and what their priorities, goals and wishes are. I think this approach is a time saver overall.
- I do not have time to go scheduling meetings with youth when there are no critical issues pending.
- I am trying to see kids more and find it beneficial but I don't know how long this will be sustainable because of my court's compensation structure.
- I used to seek information only for issues raised by the youth. But now I see the need for a broader approach, to understand the youth, inform the youth about what the issues exist and may be important. With a broader approach I am better able to advocate for needs.
- I try not to speak with children directly but to listen to other sources, particularly the CASA. I feel it confuses the child and that children do not understand the difference between attorney role and CASA. I get my best information from others who know the child well.

- After the training I see the kids differently. I used to typically see kids in court on the day of the hearing or in my office. Encouraged by the QIC Model to find more informal settings, I visited an 8 year old client at day camp. The girl very relaxed and we had a great time together. The child opened up to me and talked about her wishes and needs in a way I would not expect in the more formal settings I was used to. It allowed me to understand this child, better, assess her needs, and advocate more effectively and forcefully. The model is a huge enhancement to my work.
- I am more aware of evaluating the case from the kid's perspective.
- Only ECW connected with me at first, but now I am feeling other parts of the model better. They seem to flow from ECW, such as identifying child's needs and coming to a "big picture," a theory of the case.
- I am aware of needing to be a listening ear for clients. Doing better with teens; better connected; this new approach opens doors in ways I did not anticipate. Understanding the kid opens up a new perspective on safety, assessing needs, theory of the case, and advocacy. And my advocacy is stronger and more effective when acting from deep conviction, not just as mouthpiece.
- I am reluctant to visit youth in the community instead of in office or at court because I am concerned about my own safety.
- I am concerned about meeting children in community. There are privacy and attorney-client privilege issues but I also feel personally at risk. But I am experimenting with texting and giving cell phone number. Youth are abusing this less than adults would.

Even though the Entering the Child's World was widely and deeply accepted, it was not universally popular. Several attorneys said they were frustrated. They are paid poorly and not reimbursed for these extra efforts. (Remember, they received encouragement from QIC, but no additional compensation for casework.)

6.5 Safety Assessment

The QIC Safety Assessment encouraged attorneys to evaluate the safety of a child using the risk/vulnerability/protective factors framework of the ABA Renne and Lund model and to use that assessment in decision-making for initial removal and for return home. Some attorneys said they thought the safety assessment framework the most useful part of the training.

- I find the safety assessment framework the most useful part of the QIC training. It has changed my approach.
- I not only use safety framework in court, but also in talks with kids and with social workers. It is a simple, easy to understand framework.
- Safety and risk framework helps with counseling clients.

- "Why is this child not at home?" I love this question. It keeps the focus on permanency.
- I love safety assessment above all. I took the Red Book to a state safety training and told the group about it and read portions of the Red Book to them. Fostering Connections legislation is a key permanency element for my older clients. The safety framework helps planning for these youth.
- I shared the safety assessment framework with CASA to get them on same page. I also shared it with department workers.
- Used safety assessment framework in an argument. Didn't win but it strengthened my argument to the court and in front of the child.
- I constantly push for permanency and used safety assessment framework quite effectively. Got a dismissal of a case at the shelter care hearing using the framework.
- Safety assessment helps; it's more analytical. I used it in a case and the judge left the child with the parent with in-home services, which is a first for this judge.
- Safety assessment is a helpful frame both when I think child should go home and should not go home. Judge is beginning to adopt this approach.
- It is easy to react to a bad set of facts without analyzing the safety threat to the child.
- I tried to use the safety assessment in court, and it didn't work well. No one recognized it.
- Using the safety framework is not coming easily. Hard to understand the conclusion that the tool is designed to reach. (The Coach then talked about the framework being a *structure* for the conversation not a conclusion in itself. Coach discussed how it tracks the statute fairly well, so can provide framework for the conversation with the client as well as for the argument to the Court.)
- There is no safety assessment conversation going on in my county.
- I do not want to be the first in the county to argue the safety assessment structure, but I have used it counseling clients.
- Safety assessment is hard to implement; not consistent with statutory language and not the way people talk about risk in this county.
- (Same state as above.) I love the safety framework above all. It fits the statutory framework really well. The caseworkers are being trained in it. The words used are somewhat different but the concepts are the same. Safety framework is very useful in advocating for permanency.
- As to safety plan, the actual words are not used but the concept is. It is well suited to the state statutory framework.
- I am using the safety assessment to advocate for reunification, and a couple of times recently I argued at shelter care hearing that kid should stay in home and that resulted in dismissals.

- I find Safety Assessment useful and use it to analyze and advocate *for* removal and *against* removal—for return and against return. It helps in counseling clients too.
- Safety assessment helps push return home. Our court won't return the child until the parents have "knocked the ball out of the park."
- I really like the safety plan idea. People in this jurisdiction get caught up in completing the complete case plan, rather than evaluating safety (and allowing child to go home while case plan is being completed.)
- The court does not get the safety framework. It is just not helpful for me.

6.6 Actively Evaluate Needs

The QIC training encouraged lawyers to facilitate an appropriate assessment of the needs of the child and the family. A careful diagnosis of the presenting problem is essential to framing the appropriate legal response. Attorneys commonly thought that entering the child's world skills set up a stronger assessment of the child's needs.

- Seeing the needs assessment, "what's the real problem here?" as a responsibility of the child's lawyer was one of the most significant take-aways from the QIC training.
- I believe that Entering the Child's World helps fashion better understanding of the child and consequently leads to better needs assessment and better dispositions.
- The totality of the model, the energy, and attention paid to child helps me understand the case better.
- The relationship with the child helps the case assessment.
- It's a challenge to assess the child's needs. It doesn't fall into neat boxes.
- I feel more aware of evaluating the case and needs from the child's perspective
- I realize more than before the QIC training, how important it is to get information from the agency promptly. But there are many barriers. Caseworkers are often inexperienced and overworked.
- I am finding this really difficult because it is really hard to get information I need out of the department.
- I have a developmentally disabled client and was frustrated by the agency inertia. I did a lot of work, did my own investigation and assessment of the case, but had to resolve a professional boundary issue. I finally determined that although it was clearly my responsibility to make sure the department made the proper referrals, it was the department job to get it done. They have the resources and the responsibility to adequately assess the case.

6.7 Advance Case Planning

The QIC training encouraged the lawyers to facilitate the development of an appropriate case plan. They were encouraged to engage with that process and not to defer completely to the agency. Attorneys said that the QIC model in its entirety strengthened their influence over developing and monitoring the case plan, in part because they payed close attention to it and in part because of a better understanding of their clients' situations.

- I became more aware of the importance of being critical of the case plan.
- Knowing the child, "entering the child's world" really helps me figure out what the dispositional order should include. QIC training gave me confidence to question the agency on the case plan.
- I've been successful advancing case planning for my child clients. This comes naturally because I do a lot of civil work and clients are always concerned about how slowly their cases are proceeding. I am used to pressing those cases forward.
- Knowing what resources are available is a challenge.
- Case managers may not know what services are available.
- Careful approach to case planning helps with older youth who are aging out. Learning the Fostering Connections law and services available strengthens the advocacy for those youth.
- I'm looking more critically at the case plan, not deferring to the department. I am thinking like a lawyer.
- I realize that I could do more, be more active, in case planning. But I am not there yet.

6.8 Theory of Case

The QIC training asked the lawyers to develop an active and forward looking "theory of the case." They were encouraged to figure out what is really going on in a case and maybe even develop alternative theories that might explain what is going on that would in turn guide their advocacy as the case unfolds. Attorneys were also encouraged to "drive the bus," a slogan that stuck with many and seemed to resonate with them.

The theory of the case was the most difficult of the Six Core Skills to communicate and understand. Nevertheless, several lawyers said theory of the case, seeing the "big picture" and where you want the case to go eventually, is the most valuable of the skills.

- I didn't get the theory of case idea at first. It was only after some discussions in pod meetings and coaching that I saw its value. Now I use it regularly.
- Theory of case, the "end game" planning, really helps on my cases.
- It helps to have the theory written down in file and to refer to it as case progresses.
- Theory of the case has been a success for me. I'm taking time to think about it and write it down. I keep referring back to it with the actions later.
- It helps to repeat the case theory (this is what this case is about) and the goals of the client. It helps to repeat this to the court, but also to the caseworker and others in the case.

- Theory of the case is the most effective. Having a sense of "where are we going with this" helps me—and the court—focus.
- Because of my own theory of the case (what is going on here and where is this case going?) I did own investigation and turned up a grandmother who had been cut off by the parent. Grandmother was willing and suitable to be placement for the child.
- I am using this approach more in my juvenile justice defense cases too.
- ECW was the most intuitive and easiest to accept. Theory of the case isn't so clear and is the hardest to implement.
- I am very resistant to the whole QIC project. But theory of case might have some value. Right now the case is completely driven by the agency. Everyone else reacts. The theory idea asks others to be proactive.
- Case facts are so unclear and change constantly so that it is hard to develop a solid theory of the case. (Coach reminded attorney of training advice to come to a theory but hold it lightly or even develop alternative theories. Facts do change, but better to have a tentative direction than to simply drift in the wind.)

6.9 Advocate Effectively

The QIC model encourages lawyers to use various approaches to advocacy—with a preference for mediation and problem-solving but using traditional motions and litigation as appropriate. A common reaction among the QIC lawyers is that the other skills provide the supportive facts, perspective and foundation for more effective advocacy.

- The other parts of the model really help me be more effective in inserting the child's perspective into the decision-making of the agency and court
- The QIC Model helps set priorities and goals and therefore sets me up to "drive the bus," that is, advocate for the outcomes my client wants or needs.
- Model has resulted in me organizing myself more. And I actually get advocacy advice from my clients.
- The totality of the model (ECW and needs assessment etc.) helps me "drive the bus." I am more involved in the case planning and advocacy for client needs and have more influence because of that QIC foundation.
- The QIC model expects more organization and structure to my advocacy. It is a bit like the organization and structure that comes from having a trial notebook at trial. The QIC model expects more and delivers more.
- I had an experience where I used the QIC safety assessment approach as a counseling tool with a youth. It is simply and easy to explain and understand. The dialogue we had really helped clarify and refine the youth's position and helped me better understand the youth's views. In turn, I became more comfortable with the client's position. This really paid off in the courtroom advocacy where the better

congruence between me and the client moved me beyond being a mouthpiece to being a zealous advocate.
- I am more engaged and advocate more for case assessment and disposition. Case planning and reviews of those plans now have more of my attorney influence.
- Clients a long distance away are a challenge. Taking a broader and longer view of case helped me advocate for permanence for some older youth out of state.
- Because of my relationship with youth and his foster parents, I have been successful in helping him engage in a "safe run" and then advocating giving the youth more chances.
- Meetings that are poor or happen right before court result in less effective advocacy because I am just "mouthing what the client wants" But the QIC approach results in advocating for a more deeply understood position. But, it can be hard to advocate well if I am not getting good interaction with client in meetings and other conversations.
- My court just rubber-stamps the agency position and it is hard to break into that.
- The department runs our cases. It is hard to implement the theory of case idea or to push the agency as "drive the bus" would imply.
- I am motivated and working to advocate hard, to drive the bus. The challenge is that the department seems unwilling to see the case from the youth's perspective. In one of my cases the department is dead-set on TPR even though it is not what the kid wants.

6.10 Local Systemic Challenges

Sometimes the policies and practices of the local court present a challenge to implementing the Six Core Skills.

- There is a challenge getting the court to value the attorney. CASA is free. But the caseworkers are often inexperienced and overworked.
- Delay in initial appointment presents a serious barrier to my effectiveness.
- The court often makes appointments later in the case when the youth seems to be distressed or presenting challenges. Sometimes these are the kids who run, or are at risk of running. An earlier appointment would allow me to develop some trust with the kid and help address some of the issues and maybe prevent a runner. Court misses a preventive opportunity by appointing so late in the case.
- Being appointed after the shelter care hearing means that I am coming in half-blind. So much has happened and the case is already taking a direction.
- It is frustrating to be appointed in the middle of a case.
- Getting information from the department is very hard and makes it difficult to do my job.

- I am not sure what I am supposed to do individually to implement the model. Our court likes some of these ideas and has itself implemented some changes. For instance the court now wants all kids over 12 to come to the hearings.
- I am using what I learned in the Six Core Skills training to convince the court to change some practices.
- The court only expects the lawyers to see the kids right at the courthouse and just before the hearing. Seeing the kid only just before the hearing leaves us playing catch-up. It means that the lawyer will certainly not be "driving the bus."
- Attorneys who do this for most of their practice are better than those who only take a few cases
- I have a huge caseload, over 100, and I find it nearly impossible to do what the QIC model envisions—which I think would be the right way to represent the child.
- I appreciate the model and use it as much as I can. However, caseloads and busy court schedules are the biggest impediments to doing everything I would like.
- The overloaded docket requires much business to be done out of court. The court hearings themselves are very perfunctory.
- I am frustrated with the jurisdiction because court dockets are too heavy. A huge barrier is presented because the department does not share information. It is way too hard to get information from them.
- I am trying to see the kids more and reading the case reports much more carefully, looking for gaps. But it is frustrating. I love the work but may quit because of low pay and limits on pay.
- I drive long distances to see the kids but then only get partial pay.
- The QIC model is the preferred way but the court effectively discourages using the model because of the logistics. I am often appointed after the 72 hour hearing so it is hard to catch up. So much has happened by then. It is really hard to do the job. And the court does not keep the lawyer throughout the case. You might represent a child early on, get released, and then get re-appointed at a later stage of the case.
- The pay structure really discourages doing a good job. I billed for $3000 in a very hard case in which I did really good work for a child. The court reduced my bill to $2000. Also, if attorneys are too vigorous they get taken off the appointment list.
- There were some really good ideas coming from the QIC but our [judicial officer] is set in her ways and does not want to hear different language or a different way to approach a case.
- The QIC encourages advocacy but our judge does not want to hear from the child's lawyer. The judge's mind is made up. If too aggressive lawyers lose appointments.
- I am shocked at how little training other lawyers in the state have had. I am thankful to be in this county. Our judge has high expectations and lets the attorneys do their job.

- Attorney excited about the training but asks "now what"? The hammer is in; there is a new way of thinking, but we need more. It used to be that keeping the chair warm was enough. Clearly it isn't, but we need more.

Most expressed gratitude that their state is doing this. - Sample comment: "I have enjoyed participating in the study and think it's good we're doing this kind of study. Hopefully we can move forward with child representation and finding people who are really interested in working in this area of the law so that these children and families won't be as screwed up as they are with having no resources and no people advocating for their success."

6.11 Conclusion

These anecdotal comments selected from random coaching reports and other interviews with the QIC lawyers reflect the attorneys' experiences with the model. The comments help us understand the challenges and successes in adopting an approach that is common sense and reflects a national consensus and, yet, may be new and novel in some jurisdictions and to some lawyers. It is not surprising that attorneys found the Six Core Skills familiar. The skills are, of course, based on a review of state laws, practice models, and recommendations from leading authorities, most particularly the 1996 ABA standards. The QIC effort synthesized the national conversation into an approach that hopefully would find a sweet spot between being comfortable and maybe even intuitive, yet still advancing the level of practice.

We did not want to propose an approach that deviated too far from the currently accepted views of good practice or that demanded significantly more attorney time for fear that anything too radical would be resisted.

We were also looking for an approach that focused on clinical skills of the lawyer. Good child representation is a three-legged stool of 1) sound state law; 2) attorneys who know the law and how to operate in a court room; and 3) attorneys with the clinical skills to engage with children, assess their problems and advocate effectively. The good news is that so many lawyers embraced the approach and seemed to benefit from it.

The cognoscenti of child welfare law may well react to the Six Core Skills with a collective "oh hum." After all the QIC Best Practice Model is quite consistent with what the leaders in the field have been advocating for some years. But nonetheless it is fascinating—and perhaps even surprising—that so many QIC lawyers saw the approach as new and innovative, a better practice *model*. Some said that it has a freshness and a rigor that they appreciated.

Another pleasant surprise is that so few attorneys complained that we were asking them to do social work. Over the years some lawyers have complained that many of the functions being asked of a child's lawyer were really social work and not "real law." These critics complained that expecting them to be able to speak to children, taking time to develop a trusting relationship, knowing about child development and trauma, understanding the dynamics of dysfunctional families etc., was not what real lawyers do.

It appears, at least for our sample, that that overly narrow and wrongheaded view of lawyering has not taken root. The QIC lawyers seem to understand that lawyers in all specialties need to understand the context in which they practice law. Labor lawyers need to understand labor history and the politics past and present, not just the statutes and court opinions. Construction lawyers need to understand the business and economics of building, not just the law of contracts and remedies. Lawyers representing banks need to understand banking as an industry. Lawyers handling medical malpractice cases learn vast amounts of anatomy and physiology and other medicine in the defense or prosecution of such cases.

Likewise the most effective lawyers in child welfare understand the need for reliable information and skills regarding children and families. Their comments suggest that most QIC lawyers understood that.

The coaching notes reveal the importance of a collaborative community of lawyers committed to the field. Many lawyers talked about how much they learned from one another in pod meetings or other exchanges. The coaching helped lawyers process the Six Core Skills content and apply the model to their specific cases in the practical context of their courts and agency attitude and resources. We thought this on-going follow-up would be an important element of our research intervention and it proved to be so.

We turn now to Chapin Hall's three empirical studies of the Georgia and Washington State lawyers. The effect of the QIC Six Core Skills training on lawyer representation of children (Chapter 10) is at the highest level of research integrity—random assignment—that allows us to draw causal conclusions between the training, lawyer behavior and case outcomes.

CHAPTER 7

Sample Selection and Research Methods[1]

Britany Orlebeke, Xiaomeng Zhou, Ada Skyles, and Andrew Zinn

Abstract

This chapter reports on the methodology and process of implementing the QIC-ChildRep study using data covering 240 lawyers representing over 4000 children. The project was designed to test whether attorneys practicing the QIC-ChildRep Best Practice Model would change their practice, and consequently improve safety, permanency and well-being outcomes for children relative to control attorneys.

7.1 Introduction

The QIC-ChildRep conducted four research studies: (1) A profile of lawyers representing the children (presented in Chapter 8); (2) A description of what the child's lawyer actually does and when and how activities vary by case type and characteristics of the attorney (presented in Chapter 9); (3) Evaluation of the effect of the Six Core Skills Training on case process and outcome in Georgia and Washington State (presented in Chapter 10); and (4) A description and evaluation of a multidisciplinary team representing children in Flint, Michigan (presented in Chapter 12).

Three of these studies, conducted by Chapin Hall at the University of Chicago, are based upon a similar sample of lawyers and cases. This chapter describes the relevant

---

1. Excerpted from the Chapin Hall Evaluation Report: Orlebeke, B., Zhou, X., Skyles, A., & Zinn, A. (2016) *Evaluation of the QIC-ChildRep Training and Coaching Intervention for Child Representatives*. Chicago, IL: Chapin Hall at the University of Chicago. For the unabridged Chapin Hall QIC Evaluation report, go to the Chapin Hall website at: www.chapinhall.org.

samples and methodology related to those three investigations.[2] The methodology and impact of lawyer and social worker multidisciplinary teams representing children in Flint, Michigan is presented separately in Chapter 12.

7.2 The Basis for the Research Findings: Samples

The samples used for the research presented in Chapters 8, 9, and 10 have three dimensions: local judicial jurisdictions, the group of attorneys themselves, and the group of children those attorneys represented during the study period. Data from each of these groups forms a distribution of case type, attorney actions and case outcomes that can be described. Distributions are then compared using methodologies appropriate to the shape of distribution and the question at hand. Comparisons also need to take into account that the distributions are nested within each other and each is a potential source of variation. Jurisdictions have different policies, personnel, and capacities, both in the court and in the local child welfare agency. Attorneys have diverse experience and views about their work and behave in a variety of ways as they do their work. Children have parents with a distribution of capacities, child and family needs, and child welfare history. All three of these groups contribute to the distribution of attorney behaviors and child outcomes observed through data collection.

The interpretation of both descriptive and impact information about these distributions depends first on an understanding of each of these groups. The purpose of this chapter is to describe those groups, the data collected from and about them, and an overview of methodology used to generate knowledge about who these attorneys are, what they do, and the results of the effort to improve their practice using the QIC-ChildRep Best Practice Model.

7.3 Sample: Local Judicial Jurisdictions

7.3.1 Geography

The QIC research and demonstration took place throughout Washington State and in selected counties in Georgia. In both states a large number of attorneys practiced either independently as solo practitioners or in small firms, or in small numbers (under 10 attorneys representing children) in nonprofit legal aid organizations.

In Georgia, participating judicial districts represented 26 percent of Georgia's general child population. The two largest Georgia counties (DeKalb and Fulton) were excluded from the project because attorneys in those two counties practiced primarily as staff attorneys in large legal offices, and random assignment of attorneys to treatment and control groups within the same organization would not have been feasible or reliable.

---

2. Data collected in Georgia and Washington will also be placed in the National Data Archive on Child Abuse and Neglect to support additional research projects.

SAMPLE SELECTION AND RESEARCH METHODS

Figure 7.1 Counties in Georgia Judicial Jurisdictions Participating in the Intervention and Evaluation

Georgia Jurisdictions

Appalachian
Bartow
Chatham
Cherokee
Clarke
Cobb (2 of 4 judges)
Enotah
Forsyth
Haralson/Polk
Houston
Newton
Paulding
Troup

Figure 7.2 Counties in Washington Judicial Jurisdictions Participating in the Intervention and Evaluation

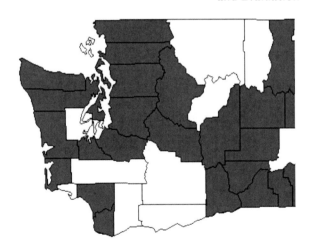

Washington Jurisdictions

Adams	Kitsap
Benton	Kittitas
Chelan	Lincoln
Clallam	Pacific
Clark	Pierce
Cowlitz	Skagit
Grant	Snohomish
Grays Harbor	Spokane
Hells Canyon	Stevens
Island	Thurston
Jefferson	Walla Walla
King	Whatcom

In Washington State, the attorneys were working in 24 judicial jurisdictions, including King (Seattle), Pierce (Tacoma), Clark (Vancouver), Spokane, and a number of medium- and small-sized counties (see Figure 7.2). Together, these 24 districts represented 89 percent of Washington's child population.

7.3.2 State Laws Governing Attorney Appointment

When the research began, attorneys for the child were not mandated in either state. Georgia's statutes in 2012 made attorney representation of the child *discretionary* with the court except for termination of parental rights proceedings (First Star & Children's Advocacy Institute, 2014).[3] If a child's representative was appointed, state law allowed jurisdictions the discretion to assign an attorney as counsel for the child or assign either a Court Appointed Special Advocate (CASA) or an attorney to fulfill the Guardian ad litem (GAL) best interests role. Participating jurisdictions in Georgia varied on whether attorneys were used to fulfill the GAL role. Half of the jurisdictions reported that attorneys were assigned for children in all cases and the remainder assigned an attorney upon request or only as required by state law (*i.e.* in termination proceedings).

In Washington State in 2012, the appointment of an attorney was not mandated at any point in the case for any child. State law provided that "if the child requests legal counsel and is age twelve or older, or if the guardian ad litem or the court determines that the child needs to be independently represented by counsel, the court *may* appoint an attorney to represent the child's position."[4] Local court practice varied, but the majority of courts at least provided for the appointment of a client-directed attorney upon request for children entering or already in out-of-home care at the age of 12 or older.

During the evaluation, state laws changed in both states, expanding the number of children for whom jurisdictions were required to appoint attorneys for children in child welfare cases. On January 1, 2014, almost two years into the intervention, a new law went into effect in Georgia requiring every child in any dependency case to have an attorney.[5]

Jurisdictions' response to the new law varied, but overall, the number of appointments went up in Georgia starting in 2014. In Washington State, as of July 1, 2014, state law required that all children who were legally free (i.e., those whose parent's parental rights had been terminated), or who became legally free after July 1, 2014, must be appointed a client-directed attorney.[6] This change resulted in a modest increase in appointments to studied attorneys, especially among children who had been in care for three or more years.

---

3. Even though Georgia statutes in effect in 2012 (Ga. Code Ann. § 15-11-6(b)) entitled a child to legal representation at all stages of the proceedings, separate counsel was only specifically required for proceedings terminating parental rights (Ga. Code Ann. § 15-11-98(a)). Georgia case law had established that in all other proceedings, when children are placed in the custody of the Department of Human Resources and the Department is represented by counsel, such representation "also constitute[s] representation by counsel on behalf of the children" (Williams v. Department of Human Resources, (1979) 150 Ga. App. 610, 611.).

4. *See* Rev. Code Wash. § 13.34.100(6)(f).

5. *See* Ga. Code Ann. § 15-11-104(c).

6. Rev. Code Wash. § 13.34.100(6).

7.3.3 Best Interests or Client-Directed Representation

Determining whether the attorney was charged with a GAL or "substitute-judgment" role or with a role to represent the child's "expressed wishes" differed in the two states at the time of study.[7] In Washington State, when an attorney was assigned, the attorney's role was almost always to represent the child's expressed wishes.

In Georgia, by contrast, even though the legal authority and practice was quite ambiguous and unsettled throughout the study period, attorneys were commonly, although not always, appointed to serve both roles at once, or in a "dual role." That is, the attorneys served in a substitute-judgment, GAL role unless there was a conflict between the attorney's view of the child's best interests and the child's wishes. If and when that occurred, the attorney was obligated to inform the court and an expressed wishes counsel for the child would be appointed.[8]

Reliable administrative data on the type of representation for which attorneys were appointed was not available in either state. Attorney surveys, however, had a question about the type of representation the child was receiving. According to the attorney survey data, 44 percent of represented children in Georgia received client-directed representation, 23 percent received Guardian ad litem representation and the remainder were being represented by attorneys serving a dual role (32%). In Washington State, children received client-directed representation exclusively.

7.4 Sample: Attorneys

Georgia and Washington partners ensured that most practicing attorneys representing children throughout Washington State and in study counties in Georgia were included in the demonstration. Among those attorneys, response rates to the various surveys were generally high. Consequently, information presented in Chapters 8, 9 and 10 is based on groups of attorneys who likely represent the typical range of ability, experience and motivation of attorneys practicing as child representatives in each state.

As a result, findings have external validity; that is, they are relevant to other jurisdictions to the extent to which the legal and practice contexts of these other jurisdictions are similar to those in Georgia and Washington State

---

7. A Child's Right to Counsel: A National Report Card on Legal Representation for Abused and Neglected Children, Third Edition, May 8, 2012. http://www.caichildlaw.org/Misc/3rd_Ed_Childs_Right_to_Counsel.pdf.

8. In 2012, the Georgia Supreme Court approved a formal advisory opinion of the State Bar, ruling that a dual role attorney, confronted with a conflict between the child's expressed wishes and the attorney's considered opinion of the child's best interest, must withdraw as GAL, and seek appointment of a separate GAL without disclosing the reasons for her withdrawal. The attorney was permitted to continue as the child's (client-directed) attorney, or to withdraw entirely if the conflict was severe. State Bar of Georgia (Formal Advisory Opinion 10-2, upheld Ga. S.Ct. Docket No. S11U0730).

The attorney recruitment process was different between the states based on each partner organization's recommendation of the method that would maximize participation.

In Georgia, the partner organization for the study, the Georgia Supreme Court Committee on Justice for Children Court Improvement Program (J4C), sought and received agreement from presiding juvenile court judges in 13 judicial districts representing 20 counties. These judges agreed to require all attorneys practicing in those jurisdictions to participate in the study. As a result, all attorneys representing children at the start of the study or who began to represent children during the study were automatically enrolled. Over the course of the study, 146 Georgia lawyers who regularly represented children in dependency cases were included in some part of the study.

In Washington State, participation was based on a statewide recruitment and consent process conducted by the Center for Children & Youth Justice and the Washington Office of Civil and Legal Aid, two of the QIC-ChildRep partner organizations in Washington State. Based on the assessment of CCYJ staff members, several of whom had extensive contacts within the child welfare legal community in Washington State, nearly all of the attorneys known to have been actively serving as child representatives in the participating counties at the time of the sample were contacted by CCYJ or OCLA staff. Over the course of the study, 117 Washington State lawyers who regularly represented children in dependency cases were included in some part of the study.

Treatment attorney participation in the three elements of the QIC-ChildRep intervention was voluntary. Compensation was provided primarily as a strategy to incentivize participation in data collection for both treatment and control attorneys and was not linked to attorney participation in pods or coaching, except in the last three quarters the intervention was offered in Georgia jurisdictions. Most treatment and control attorneys were given $1,500 per year as a professional honorarium for participation in general, and for the time associated with data collection in particular.

Three organizations in Washington State precluded their attorneys from receiving stipends directly at any point in the project as a matter of professional ethics. In January 2014, two additional organizations became part of county government and, as a result, additional Washington attorneys stopped receiving direct compensation but remained in the study.

7.5 Sample: Children
7.5.1 Included If Represented by a Treatment or Control Attorney
Children were included in the sample by virtue of having a treatment or control attorney appointed as their legal representative. All children whose attorneys were participating in the project during the study period were considered part of the study. Depending on their placement status at the time or subsequent placement, children were included in the analysis of out-of-home care outcomes or were a part of the attorney

Table.7.1 Total Number of Children Represented by Project Attorneys with Associated Out-of-Home Care Placement

	Children represented by treatment attorneys			Children represented by control attorneys			Total
	2012*	2013	2014**	2012*	2013	2014**	All Years
GA	261	268	389	265	177	417	1,777
WA	220	400	424	162	249	332	1,787
Total	481	668	813	427	426	749	3,564

*"Enrollment" into study started in February 2012 in Georgia and in May 2012 in Washington State.
**The last children were added to the study during the month of November 2014.

behavior analysis (or both). In Georgia, since nearly 30 percent of children who were represented were never placed, the two analysis samples were somewhat different. The attorney behavior sample included children who were never a part of the out-of-home care outcome analysis. In Washington State, a much smaller proportion of children were never placed (14%), so almost all the children about whom attorneys were surveyed were also part of the placement analysis. Between the two analyses, a total of 4,274 children in two states (2,318 children in Georgia and 1,956 children in Washington State) were included.

The observation period for each child with an associated out-of-home care placement depended on when that attorney began to represent the child and, if the child was not already in out-of-home care at the time of appointment, when that child entered out-of-home care. For pairs who became part of the out-of-home care analysis in 2012 (900), the observation window for out-of-home care outcomes ranged from about two to three years. For pairs who became part of the out-of-home care analysis in 2013 (1094), the observation window for out-of-home care outcomes ranged from about 1.25 to 2.25 years. For pairs who became part of the out-of-home care analysis in 2014 (1562), the observation window for out-of-home care outcomes ranged from about 5 months to about 1.5 years. For children who were assigned an attorney within 6 months, almost all children's outcomes could be observed within 6 months of placement.

7.5.2 Timing of Lawyer Appointment

Washington attorneys almost always represented children already placed, whereas in Georgia, almost one-third of appointments were made while a child was not in placement.[9] Looking only at children who were placed at some point after assignment,

---

9. Of children who were appointed attorneys when not in placement, 85 percent were never placed as of the end of the observation period (March 31, 2015).

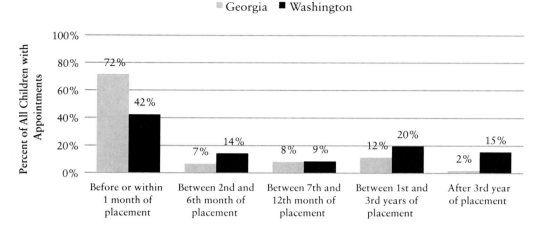

Figure 7.3 Timing of Attorney Appointment for Children Placed

the timing of assignment relative to the beginning of placement is shown in Figure 7.3. Almost three-quarters of appointments in Georgia were made before or within a month of placement (74%). Of children in the Washington sample, 42 percent were appointed before or within a month of placement. On the other end of the distribution, 14 percent of the Georgia and 35 percent of the Washington sample had an attorney appointed after at least a year in placement.

7.5.3 Child's Age at Appointment

Characteristics of represented children reflected differences in state laws. For children who were placed in out-of-home care, the median age of receiving an attorney was 6 years old in Georgia and 11 years old in Washington State. Figure 4 shows the distribution by age at placement. Just under half of the sample of children in Georgia had an attorney appointed for them at age 5 or under. The sample of children for Washington State included very few infants (3%) and few children under age of 5 (12%). Almost half of the sample (48%) were children appointed attorneys at age 13 or older.

Figure 7.4 shows how age at appointment and timing of appointment were related in the two samples. In Georgia, where the age of the child entering care did not have a relationship to attorney appointment, children for whom an attorney was appointed in the first six months had a similar age-at-placement distribution to those who were appointed an attorney later. In Washington State, however, there was a distinct subsample of children who were both older at placement and had an attorney appointed early: Among children for whom an attorney was appointed within the first six months, 68 percent of these children were 12 years old or over (Figure 7.5). Notably, in Washington State, the distribution by age among those appointed an attorney later in placement was similar to the distribution in Georgia.

SAMPLE SELECTION AND RESEARCH METHODS 117

Figure 7.4 Distribution of Age of Child at the Time of Attorney Appointment for Children Placed

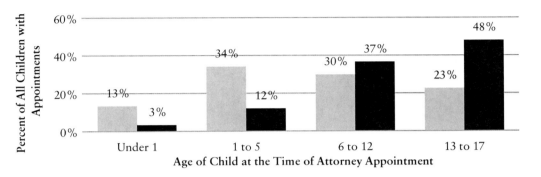

Figure 7.5 Proportion of Children Placed Under and Over 12 Years Old by Assignment Timing

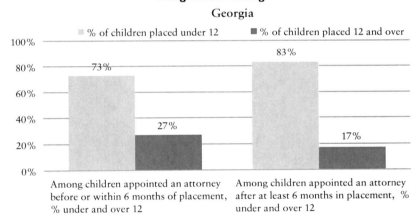

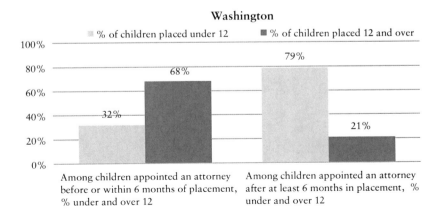

Table 7.2 Child Context Comparison

Sample characteristic	Georgia	Washington
% of children with attorney appointed within 6 months of the start of placement	79%	56%
Median age at assignment (years)	6	11
Median age at assignment, assigned in first 6 months (years)	6	13
Median age at assignment, assigned after first 6 months (years)	4	8
% of assignments while child not in out-of-home placement	31%	14%
% of children in first placement experience	90%	77%
% children associated with sibling group	55%	21%
% of sibling groups represented by one attorney	95%	64%
% of children in family-based care (foster or kinship)	82%	76%
% of children in congregate care	13%	12%

Table 7.2 summarizes the child context in the samples in the two states and provides some additional contextual information. In Washington State, fewer children who were part of sibling groups were represented, and fewer sibling groups were represented by one attorney. Most children in both states were in some type of family-based care (foster home or relative home) at the time an attorney was appointed. Thirteen percent of children in Georgia and 12% of children in Washington State were in congregate care placement at the time of appointment.

7.6 The Basis for the Research Findings: Data Sources

Data was collected for the implementation study from intervention partners, from administrative data sources, and from attorney surveys. Each is described below. There was a strong interest in collecting data directly from children. However, it would not have been possible within the resources of the evaluation to collect enough data to fully describe and analyze the distribution of experiences, even within one local jurisdiction. Previous studies have documented the challenges associated with collecting data directly from children in these contexts.[10]

---

10. Zinn, A. E. & Slowriver, J. (2008) Expediting Permanency: Legal Representation for Foster Children in Palm Beach County. Chicago: Chapin Hall Center for Children at the University of Chicago.

7.6.1 Intervention Data

Evaluators collected the following data during the project for the implementation study:

- Written materials distributed and used for initial two-day training
- Attorney attendance at initial two-day trainings
- Initial two-day training evaluations completed by attorneys at the end of the training
- Quarterly pod meeting attendance by attorneys and which of the Six Core Skills were covered in each meeting
- Quarterly coaching session participation by attorneys and which of the Six Core Skills were covered in each session
- Random sample of coaches' notes from 10 coaching sessions per quarter per site (These are the basis for Chapter 6.)
- Notes from UM QIC attorney and stakeholder interviews in 2013 (UM QIC conducted interviews with randomly selected treatment attorneys in both states to ask, among other subjects, about their views of the coaching and pod meetings. These are the basis for Chapter 6.)
- Interviews with project partners in Fall 2014 (the Chapin Hall evaluation team conducted interviews in the fall of 2014 with team members in each state to obtain their observations and reflections about the coaching and pod meetings)

A member of the evaluation team also observed each initial two-day training and members of the evaluation team attended selected intervention team meetings (for UM QIC and state teams). A member of the evaluation team also attended the last in-person Georgia pod meeting.

7.6.2 Administrative Data

In Washington State, records of attorneys' appointments as legal counsel for children in dependency cases were obtained from the Washington Administrative Office of the Courts' SCOMIS database. SCOMIS data were also used to help determine the date of attorney appointments and the dates of children's legal milestones, including temporary legal custody, disposition, and termination of parental rights. In Georgia, there was no statewide administrative data source for appointments of attorneys or legal milestones. Instead, a system was set up whereby staff from each participating jurisdiction provided information about each appointment on a monthly basis to Chapin Hall and over the course of the evaluation these records were compiled into a database of assignments.

Data about children's substitute care histories, permanency outcomes, and demographic characteristics were obtained from Chapin Hall's Multistate Foster Care Data

Archive. In Washington State, these child-level data were derived from extracts provided by the Washington State Department of Social and Health Services, Children's Administration based on records maintained in their FAMLINK data system. In Georgia, these data were obtained from extracts provided by the Georgia Department of Human Services based on records maintained in their SHINES data system.

7.6.3 Attorney Survey Data
7.6.3.1 Baseline Survey

A baseline survey was administered to attorneys prior to the inception of the evaluation. The questions on the baseline survey covered a number of different domains, including attorney demographic characteristics, practice tenure, contract arrangements with counties, income, caseload size, and continuing legal education and experience in different areas of the law. The baseline survey also contained several questions about attorneys' opinions concerning the level of responsibility that child representatives should assume over various dependency case tasks and the importance of various tactics and objectives vis-à-vis dependency court outcomes. Finally, the survey contained questions concerning attorneys' job satisfaction and perceived impact as child representatives. The response rates for the first baseline survey were 86 percent in Georgia and 93 percent in Washington State. Baseline survey results are used in the analyses presented in Chapter 8.

7.6.3.2 Child-Specific Attorney Surveys

A second set of surveys, referred to as "the milestone surveys," was provided to attorneys through a website where attorneys clicked on links to answer questions for a particular child. Surveys were triggered based on the attorneys' appointment as legal counsel and continued approximately every six months thereafter. For example, a child that stayed in substitute care for at least a year after being appointed an attorney would have a survey generated at two, seven, and 13 months after the date of their attorney's appointment. Also, in Washington State, attorneys were asked to complete additional milestone surveys when children experienced certain legal or service milestones, such as dispositional order, termination of parental rights order, and exit from substitute care.

The milestone surveys contain a number of questions about individual child dependency cases, including the frequency of children's visitation with family members, frequency of contact between attorneys and various parties to a case (e.g., child clients, children's family members), amount of time devoted by attorneys to various case-related activities (e.g., legal case preparation, service advocacy), quality of attorneys' relationships with child clients, and the attributes of children's dispositional hearings and order.

To reduce the burden on attorneys, not every appointment generated a survey. Attorneys were asked to complete milestone surveys for a randomly selected subsample of child cases. The administration of these surveys began in July 2012 in Washington State and in October 2013 in Georgia. The overall response rate for the milestone surveys was 89 percent in Washington State and 82 percent in Georgia.

Milestone survey results are the basis for the analysis of attorney activity in Chapter 9 and the impact analysis of the QIC-Childrep Best Practices Model Training in Chapter 10.

7.7 The Basis for Research Findings: Methodology

The primary objective of the methodology was to assess the impact of the QIC-ChildRep intervention on attorneys' behaviors and consequent case-level outcomes, compared to attorneys who did not receive the intervention. Attorneys were randomly assigned within each jurisdiction to control and treatment groups based on the firms or legal offices in which attorneys practiced (if an attorney was a solo practitioner, she or he was treated as a one-person firm when conducting the random assignment).

For example, if a jurisdiction contained eight attorneys working within four distinct offices, each of these offices would be assigned as a whole to the treatment or control group.[11] This type of randomization design, known as cluster randomized control design, ensured that the two groups of attorneys were, in expectation, statistically equivalent, while also helping to mitigate the extent to which control group attorneys were exposed to the QIC-ChildRep intervention materials.[12] *With random assignment, any statistically significant differences in attorney behaviors or case outcomes could be attributed to the intervention with treatment attorneys, that is to the QIC Training and Pod and Coaching follow-up.*

At the child level, the evaluation design also contained procedures so that the children assigned to each group of attorneys would be statistically equivalent. Evaluators interviewed case assigners in each jurisdiction about the processes they used to determine case assignments. In most cases, assignments were made using rotational lists or some other arbitrary process. For the three years of the evaluation, case assigners agreed to follow a rotational list provided by evaluators and, where the case assignment deviated from that list, to indicate the reason. While deviations from the list did occur, assigners reported it was primarily due to attorneys not being available. Over the course of the study, evaluators were in conversation with case assigners on many

---

11. See for example Kay Wijekumar, John Hitchcock, HerbTurner, PuiWa Lei, & Kyle Peck, *A Multisite Cluster Randomized Trial of the Effects of CompassLearning Odyssey® Math on the Math Achievement of Selected Grade 4 Students in the Mid-Atlantic Region.* National Center for Education Evaluation and Regional Assistance, Institute of Education Sciences, U.S. Department of Education: Washington, DC (2005).

12. Howard Bloom, *Learning more from social experiments: evolving analytic approaches.* New York: Russel Sage (2005) pg. 246.

occasions, and there was no indication of any systematic differences between the cases assigned to treatment attorneys or to control attorneys.

Power estimates[13] indicated that the evaluation had enough power to detect moderate effects on attorney and child outcomes. For the outcomes where no statistically significant results were found, there may have been small average impacts that the evaluation did not have enough power to detect. Detecting small average impacts would have required a greater number of attorneys and cases.

Research methods to analyze the samples took into account the nested structure of the resultant data by using multilevel models with random effects. These models have the effect of comparing the behaviors and case outcomes of treatment and control group attorneys within each jurisdiction and estimating the results over the treatment and control group samples. All analyses were done separately for each state.

Attorneys, regardless of assignment to treatment or control, participated equally in data collection. This full sample was useful to answer questions outside of the impact of the QIC-ChildRep intervention. The analyses in Chapters 8 and 9 are based on the full sample of attorneys practicing in these jurisdictions during 2012-2015.

---

13. Chapin Hall conducted an initial power analysis in 2011 to be included in the RFP for the project. The purpose of the power analysis was to estimate the sample size of attorneys and cases necessary to detect a difference between the treatment and control groups. Before the project began, Chapin Hall concluded that both Georgia and Washington had enough attorneys and cases to detect a moderate impact on attorney and child outcomes. See Jacob Cohen, Statistical Power Analysis for the Behavioral Sciences (2nd Edition). In Jacob Cohen, *Statistical Power Analysis for the Behavioral Sciences (2nd Edition)*. New Jersey: Lawrence Erlbaum. (1988).

CHAPTER 8

Profile of Lawyers Representing Children[1]

Britany Orlebeke and Andrew Zinn

Abstract
We profile child advocates and discuss implications for developing and sustaining a state's child representation. In this study, most children are represented by an experienced lawyer handling only a few cases as part of a diverse legal practice. This has significant implications for training and delivery of legal services for children

8.1 Introduction
Research results presented in this chapter begin to fill the gap in knowledge about the attorneys who serve as the child's representative. The chapter presents the characteristics, experiences, circumstances and attitudes of attorneys representing children in dependency cases throughout the state of Washington and nineteen counties in Georgia in 2013, at the beginning of the experimental evaluation of the QIC-ChildRep Best Practices Model for child representation. These findings give legislators, court staff and policy-makers an understanding of the characteristics, experiences, circumstances and attitudes of lawyers currently representing children in their jurisdiction. These findings also allow attorneys to situate themselves among their peers doing similar work. We

---

1. Excerpted from: Britany Orlebeke, Andrew Zinn, Donald N. Duquette, & Xiaomeng Zhou, *Characteristics of Attorneys Representing Children in Child Welfare Cases*, 49 FAM.L.Q. 477 (Fall 2015) and Andrew Zinn, Britany Orlebeke, Donald N. Duquette, & Xiaomeng Zhou, (in press). The organizational contexts of child representation services in child welfare cases. *Family Court Review.*

also learn that the various employment settings—staff attorney office, private law firm, or sole practitioner—are associated with some interesting similarities and differences.

How representative is this group of attorneys of the broader population of attorneys representing children in child welfare cases across the country? That is, can these findings be generalized so that a policy maker in another state can reliably use these results to understand his or her population of attorneys representing children? That question cannot be answered directly, but this research sample has several advantages. First, almost all attorneys who were practicing in the covered geographic areas were included, so results reflect a general attorney population. Second, the response rate on the survey was quite high: 86% for Georgia attorneys and 93% for Washington State attorneys.

> The QIC-ChildRep baseline survey provided information about:
>
> - Employment Setting
> - Demographics
> - Experience
> - Continuing Legal Education
> - Other Types of Law Practiced
> - Financial Compensation
> - Organizational Supports
> - Responsibilities as Child Representatives
> - Importance of different representation tasks
> - Job Satisfaction and Sense of Impact

Finally, when comparing the characteristics and circumstances of attorneys between these two very different states, the profile revealed many similarities. Thus, we can make stronger claims about the representativeness of this combined sample to the population of child representatives in other jurisdictions.

8.2   Distinctions by Employment Setting

Among Washington State's attorneys, there were enough attorneys working in different employment settings to allow for a comparison of across those settings. In staff attorney offices, the median number of child representatives per organization was nine. In both Georgia and Washington State, most attorneys working in private firms, and, by definition, all solo practitioners, were alone within their respective organizations in their practice of child representation. Throughout this chapter, distinctions in the findings based on employment setting are highlighted.

8.3   Attorney Demographics

Eighty-seven percent of attorneys were white. Ten percent of attorneys in the Georgia jurisdictions were African American and four percent of attorneys in Washington were African American. Very few attorneys indicated Hispanic origin. Only 3% of attorneys were Asian or "Other" race/ethnicity. Most attorneys (84%) did not have other graduate

PROFILE OF LAWYERS REPRESENTING CHILDREN

Table 8.1 Number of and Percent of Responding Attorneys by State and Employment Setting

Employment Setting	Georgia Juris (N = 123)		Washington (N = 117)	
	Freq.	Pct.	Freq.	Pct.
Solo practitioner	95	77%	59	50%
Private law firm	27	22%	19	16%
Employed by private, non-profit organization (i.e., staff attorney)	0	0%	35	30%
Employed by county office	1	1%	4	3%
Total	123	100%	117	100%

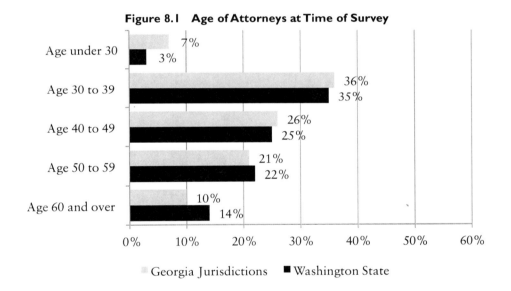

Figure 8.1 Age of Attorneys at Time of Survey

degrees besides a law degree. One-third of attorneys indicated that they had worked with children in capacities other than as an attorney and 56% were a biological, foster or adoptive parent. Attorneys who represented children ranged in age (Figure 8.1). Five percent of attorneys were under 30. Thirty-five percent were in their thirties, 26% were in their forties and 21% were in their fifties. Twelve percent were over 60 years old.

Washington Employment Settings: Attorneys from staff offices in Washington State were younger than attorneys from solo practice or firm contexts. Fifty percent of staff office attorneys were between the ages of 30 and 39.

8.4 Experience as Child Representatives

All the attorneys in the sample had represented, or were representing, children during 2013, but there was a range in how much child representation each attorney was doing. For fifty-two percent of attorneys across both sites, child representation constituted 20% or less of their practice (Table 8.2). For twenty-four percent of attorneys, it constituted 21-40% of their practice. Child representation constituted at least 61% of attorney practice for only 15% of attorneys.

Attorneys were also asked to report the number of cases represented in the last six months. Thirty-seven percent across both samples represented fewer than five cases in the last six months. Twenty-four percent had represented 6-10 cases, 19% had represented 11-21 cases and 20% had represented 22 or more cases. Thus, these "child

Table 8.2 Child Representation Practice

% of Practice that is Child Representation	All	Georgia Jurisdictions	Washington State
0% to 20%	52%	48%	56%
21% to 40%	24%	23%	25%
41% to 60%	8%	9%	8%
61% to 80%	5%	9%	2%
81% to 100%	10%	11%	9%
Number of Cases Represented in Past Six Months	**All**	**Georgia Jurisdictions**	**Washington State**
0 - 5 cases	37%	38%	36%
6 - 10 cases	24%	20%	29%
11- 21 cases	19%	19%	19%
22 or more cases	20%	23%	16%
Years Practicing as Child Representative	**All**	**Georgia Jurisdictions**	**Washington State**
Less than 1 year	13%	10%	17%
1 or 2 years	16%	13%	19%
3 or 4 years	15%	20%	10%
5 or 6 years	16%	17%	14%
7 or 8 years	8%	6%	9%
9 or 10 years	6%	5%	8%
More than 10 years	26%	30%	22%

representatives" were attorneys with a range of experience and specialization in this area of practice, with child representation constituting a minority of their practice for most child representatives.

The majority of attorneys representing children (56%) had been practicing child representation for at least five years. Twenty-six percent had been practicing for more than ten years and 29% had been practicing for two years or less.

Washington Employment Settings: Child representation constituted 20% or less of the practice for about 50% of attorneys from all types of settings, including staff offices. Attorneys from private firms had the highest proportion of attorneys who had represented 5 or fewer cases in the last six months (53%) but had a comparable proportion

Table 8.3 Child Representation Practice by Organizational Setting (Washington State only)

% of Practice that is Child Representation	Solo (n=59)	Private (n=19)	Staff Office (n=35)
0% to 20%	60%	58%	50%
21% to 40%	27%	26%	24%
41% to 60%	10%	11%	3%
61% to 80%	0%	5%	3%
81% to 100%	3%	0%	21%
Number of Cases Represented in Past Six Months	Solo (n=59)	Private (n=19)	Staff Office (n=35)
0 - 5 cases	34%	53%	29%
6 - 10 cases	25%	26%	40%
11- 21 cases	25%	5%	17%
22 or more cases	15%	16%	14%
Years Practicing as Child Representative	Solo (n=59)	Private (n=19)	Staff Office (n=35)
Less than 1 year	7%	21%	32%
1 or 2 years	12%	32%	27%
3 or 4 years	9%	11%	12%
5 or 6 years	15%	16%	12%
7 or 8 years	14%	5%	3%
9 or 10 years	7%	11%	9%
More than 10 years	37%	5%	6%

of attorneys who had represented 22 or more cases in the last six months (16%). Attorneys from staff offices in Washington State had less experience as child representatives: Thirty-two percent had been practicing child representation for less than a year. Solo practitioners reported much more experience, with 37% practicing child representation for more than 10 years.

8.5 Continuing Legal Education

Most attorneys had taken a CLE course in the last two years that had covered at least one topic in child welfare law and policy and child representation practice. Within those two broad topics, differences were revealed across the two sites, with Washington attorneys more likely to have covered state child welfare law, permanency planning, aging out of foster care, federal and state requirements for foster care cases and the Indian Child Welfare Act. Washington attorneys were also more likely to have covered expert witness and interviewing and counseling the child.

However, more than half of the attorneys from either site had not received training on trial practice in maltreatment cases, expert witnesses or interviewing and counseling the child in the last two years. Topics about child and family well-being were the least likely to have been covered in CLEs taken in the last two years, though these topics were clearly available to at least some attorneys in both sites. Differences between the Georgia jurisdictions and Washington were the most pronounced in these topic areas, with Washington attorneys selecting these as covered topics at least twice as much as attorneys practicing in the Georgia jurisdictions.

Nevertheless, more than 50% of Washington attorneys had not received CLEs on child development, child maltreatment, mental health treatment and family dynamics in the last two years. With respect to CLEs on domestic violence and substance abuse, Washington attorneys were more likely to have covered these topics in a CLE in the last two years than attorneys in the Georgia jurisdictions.

Washington Employment Settings: The percentages of attorneys reporting having received continuing legal education credits during the prior 2 years is very similar across organizational settings. Some differences are found, however, with respect to continuing legal education credits pertaining to child welfare law and policy. For example, attorneys in private practice were significantly less likely to report training in state child welfare law (37%) than solo practitioners (66%) and attorneys in staff attorney offices (62%).

8.6 What Other Types of Law Were These Attorneys Practicing?

The professional practice of lawyers representing children included a broad range of legal subjects. In addition to representing children, attorneys were practicing a variety of other types of law (Figure 8.2). At least three-quarters of the Georgia jurisdiction attorneys

Table 8.4 Continuing Legal Education in Prior 2 Years

	All	Georgia Jurisdictions	Washington State
Child welfare law and policy			
Racial disproportionality	60%	99%	18%
State child welfare (i.e., deprivation) law	53%	46%	60%
State case law updates affecting child welfare	51%	47%	55%
Permanency planning	33%	18%	49%
Aging out of foster care	23%	14%	32%
Federal & state requirements for foster care cases	19%	10%	27%
Indian Child Welfare Act	18%	9%	27%
Any of the above (excluding racial dispro.)	70%	64%	76%
Child representation practice			
Alternative dispute resolution (ADR)	63%	99%	25%
Child representation practice	59%	63%	54%
Trial practice in child abuse and neglect cases	34%	30%	38%
Expert witnesses	28%	15%	42%
Interviewing and counseling the child	22%	17%	28%
Any of the above (excluding ADR)	75%	71%	80%
Child and family well-being			
Child development	33%	18%	49%
Child maltreatment	33%	22%	44%
Mental health treatment for children and families	27%	18%	37%
Family dynamics in child maltreatment	22%	14%	31%
Any of the above	49%	32%	67%
Other issues			
Domestic violence	43%	33%	53%
Substance abuse	37%	24%	50%
Educational rights of children	16%	15%	17%

were practicing some other type of child and family law (divorce or paternity, private adoption, truancy, and juvenile justice). The proportion of attorneys who practiced child and family-related law was significantly lower in Washington. Across both sites, 62% were representing adults in criminal cases, 26% were practicing landlord/tenant related law, 18% were involved in real-estate law and 9% were practicing bankruptcy.

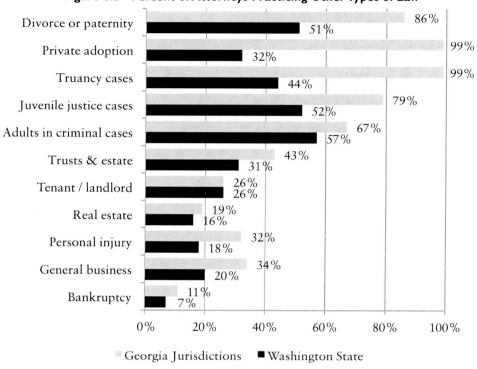

Figure 8.2 Percent of Attorneys Practicing Other Types of Law

■ Georgia Jurisdictions   ■ Washington State

Washington Employment Settings: Attorneys employed by staff attorney offices report significantly less heterogeneity in their recent legal practice than do other attorneys, though even those attorneys did not spend the majority of their time on child welfare cases. In contrast, the level of heterogeneity of practice experience among solo practitioners and attorneys in private firms in Washington was very similar, and was also similar to the prevalence of these practice types in Georgia.

8.7 Financial Compensation and Compensation Arrangements

Attorneys were asked about annual income from the practice of law and had the option to leave this question blank. Twenty-eight percent of Georgia jurisdiction attorneys and fourteen percent of Washington attorneys left the question blank. About half of the attorneys from Georgia and Washington who completed the question indicated incomes from the practice of law between $40,000 and $80,000.

There was an issue with this question, however, because some attorneys may not have been working full-time. Suffice to say that in both states, there were few attorneys doing this work who were earning more than $100,000 from the practice of law: 17% in Georgia and 12% in Washington.

Table 8.5 Adequacy of Compensation

How adequate do you think the level of compensation you receive for child welfare cases is?	All	Georgia Jurisdictions	Washington State
Very inadequate	29%	30%	28%
Somewhat inadequate	38%	41%	36%
Somewhat adequate	29%	28%	30%
More than adequate	4%	2%	6%

Table 8.6 Compensation Arrangement

Compensation Arrangement	All	Georgia Jurisdictions	Washington State
Hourly rate based on voucher	65%	86%	42%
Hourly rate based on voucher with limits	11%	12%	10%
Contract for a monthly or annual payment	8%	2%	14%
Salaried in non-profit or government organization	16%	0%	33%

When asked, "how adequate do you think the level of the compensation you receive for dependency cases is?" the majority of attorneys thought it was short of adequate, indicating either "very inadequate" (29%) or "somewhat inadequate" (38%). Twenty-nine percent of attorneys responded with "somewhat adequate" and a small percent thought compensation was "more than adequate."

Washington Employment Settings Note: Attorneys from different employment settings responded similarly to this question, though no attorneys from private law firms indicated that compensation was more than adequate.

There were several common types of compensation arrangements. Attorneys were paid an hourly rate, paid an hourly rate with limits per case, paid with a monthly or annual payment to handle some or all open cases or were working for a salary in a non-profit or government organization (Table 8.6). In a few jurisdictions, more than one contract arrangement was possible within the same jurisdiction. For example, one jurisdiction used the Office of the Public Defender (salaried attorney) but, if all public defender attorneys had conflicts, the jurisdiction used an outside "conflict attorney" paid by the hour based on a submitted voucher.

The most common compensation arrangement was a submission of a voucher with hours, in which the attorneys were paid an hourly rate without official limits on the number of hours. A few attorneys (10-12%) were paid an hourly rate with a jurisdiction-imposed maximum payment amount. It was more common for Washington attorneys to be paid a monthly amount negotiated as part of an annual contract for handling a certain number of open cases per month. And in Georgia jurisdictions, as discussed previously, there were no attorneys representing children who were staff attorneys either in a government or non-profit agency.

Washington Employment Settings: Attorneys working in private practice and as solo practitioners were more likely to be appointed to individual cases (by a judge or from a rotational list) than are attorneys who work in staff attorney offices. Conversely, attorneys working in staff attorney offices are more likely than other attorneys to report working under contract to courts in which they are remunerated on a per-hearing basis.

8.8 Organizational Supports

Legal research databases and individuals with whom to discuss cases were the most commonly available services. Less commonly available were paralegals and administrative support. Only about a third of attorneys indicated that psychologists or psychiatrists with whom to consult were available often or almost always available. Social workers and other helping professionals and investigative staff were the least likely to be available, though they were more available in Washington than in the Georgia jurisdictions. Social workers and other helping professionals were not at all available to 52% of attorneys in the Georgia jurisdictions and 33% of attorneys practicing in Washington (p<.01). Investigative staff was not at all available to 54% of attorneys in the Georgia jurisdictions and 35% of attorneys practicing in Washington (p<.01).

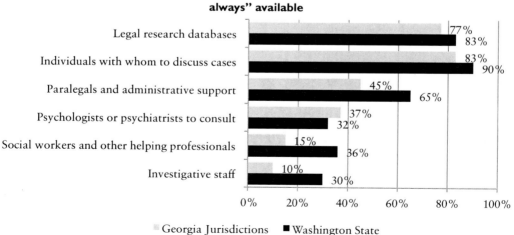

Figure 8.3 Percent of attorneys indicating support was "often" or "almost always" available

Washington Employment Settings: Attorneys in staff attorney offices are found to be more likely to have access to investigative staff and to have greater access to social workers, psychologists, psychiatrists, or other helping professionals, than attorneys in solo practice and private firms. Solo practitioners are found to be less likely than attorneys in private practice to have access to paralegals.

There are no significant differences across organizational settings concerning access to legal databases or individuals with whom attorneys can discuss cases. In both Georgia sites and Washington, when only attorneys practicing in small firms or as solo practitioners are compared, Washington attorneys still had more access to investigative staff, paralegals, and psychologists or psychiatrists than Georgia jurisdiction attorneys but they rate the access to social workers and legal research databases equally.

8.9 Identified Responsibilities of Child Representatives

Attorneys were asked to evaluate seven child representation tasks and indicate on a five-level scale the extent to which each task was "your responsibility as a child's attorney in dependency cases." Each statement and the response distribution are shown on Table 8.7. These questions were not intended to be comprehensive but rather to gauge attorney's opinions of certain tasks associated with an active model of child representation in advance of the evaluation of the QIC-ChildRep Best Practices Model for child representation.

> The QIC-ChildRep baseline survey asked if the attorney had the following level of responsibility: little or no responsibility, other parties are mostly or solely responsible
>
> - limited responsibility, generally the responsibility of other parties
> - shared responsibility with other parties
> - primary responsibility, other parties have limited or delegated responsibility
> - exclusive responsibility, other parties have little or no responsibility

These questions were designed to assess how attorneys understood their responsibility to child clients relative to the duties of other parties with a stake in the case, including public child welfare agency workers, assistant attorneys general representing the state's interests, CASAs, judges and parents. The responses can be used to understand attorney's views on responsibility and to reveal differences in attorneys practicing in these two different state contexts.[2] With respect to attorneys views of responsibility in general, the majority of attorneys considered attending case planning meetings (61%) and establishing the goals that parents need to meet in order

---

2. See Chapter 7 for a description of the state legal and policy context in Georgia and Washington.

Table 8.7 Opinions about responsibilities of child representatives.
The bolded state indicates that group of attorneys from that state rated the task was higher on the responsibility scale.

	All	Georgia Juris.	Wash.
Attending case planning meetings			
Little or none	6%	11%	1%
Limited	16%	24%	7%
Shared	61%	59%	62%
Primary	11%	4%	19%
Exclusive	6%	2%	11%
Advocating for services for children			
Little or none	0%	0%	0%
Limited	2%	3%	0%
Shared	33%	37%	28%
Primary	47%	50%	43%
Exclusive	19%	9%	29%
Identifying caregivers who can serve as foster parents			
Little or none	17%	24%	10%
Limited	30%	31%	28%
Shared	45%	41%	50%
Primary	7%	5%	9%
Exclusive	1%	0%	2%
Identifying potential adoptive homes			
Little or none	32%	37%	26%
Limited	35%	32%	38%
Shared	29%	28%	30%
Primary	4%	3%	4%
Exclusive	0%	0%	1%
Advocating with respect to other legal matters (e.g., education, custody, SSI) for the children you represent in dependency cases			
Little or none	7%	7%	8%
Limited	13%	15%	11%
Shared	33%	36%	31%

Table 8.7 (continued)

	All	Georgia Juris.	Wash.
Primary	32%	32%	32%
Exclusive	15%	11%	19%
Establish the goals that parents need to meet in order to have their children returned to them			
Little or none	8%	7%	9%
Limited	25%	20%	32%
Shared	57%	62%	52%
Primary	7%	10%	3%
Exclusive	3%	2%	4%
Advocating for services for parents			
Little or none	15%	11%	19%
Limited	29%	25%	32%
Shared	45%	49%	41%
Primary	9%	13%	4%
Exclusive	3%	2%	3%

to have their children returned to them (57%) a shared responsibility with other parties to the case.

Forty-five percent of attorneys indicated that identifying caregivers to serve as foster parents was a shared responsibility with other parties to the case and 35% indicated that identifying potential adoptive homes was a shared responsibility. Almost half of the attorneys thought that advocating for services for parents and children was a shared responsibility. Thirty-two percent thought that advocating with respect to other legal matters was a shared responsibility.

For those attorneys who did not indicate a shared responsibility, did they select an option lower or higher on the scale provided? A response lower on the scale indicated less responsibility and a response higher on the scale indicated more responsibility. Across both sites, among attorneys who did not indicate a shared responsibility, more attorneys felt limited or little or no responsibility for the tasks listed, with the exception of attending case planning meetings and identifying adoptive homes.

For those two tasks, responses were not significantly different on either side of "shared responsibility." Comparing sites, attorneys from Washington were more likely to select options higher on the scale than attorneys from the Georgia sites for every task except establishing goals and advocating services for parents. For those tasks, attorneys from Georgia were more likely to select options higher on the scale of responsibility.

Washington Employment Settings: Attorneys' opinions about the responsibilities of child representatives were similar across organizational setting. The one exception to this general finding was that solo practitioners were more likely than other attorneys to ascribe a higher level of responsibility to child representatives for identifying caregivers who can serve as foster parents.

8.10 Opinions about the Importance of Child Representation Tasks

Attorneys were asked to evaluate 10 child representation tasks and indicate on a four-level scale the extent to which each approach was important "for achieving positive and timely court outcomes for the children I represent." Each statement, and its corresponding response distribution, are shown on Table 8.8. Very few attorneys in either site selected "not at all important" for any of the statements, so this response is left off the table.

The distribution of response for the four highest ranked tasks was the same across both sites. The first statement related to how attorneys viewed the importance of communicating the child's wishes. The second two had to do with communication capacities and interactions with child clients. And the fourth related to being culturally sensitive in interactions with the child client. Few attorneys indicated that any of these tasks were less than important, with a comparable proportion (ranging from about 55% to 71%) indicating these tasks were very important.

The remaining six statements related to possible approaches towards representing and interacting with child clients. Washington attorneys had stronger opinions than attorneys from the Georgia jurisdictions about the importance of all six approaches that would be considered part of client-directed legal representation. But it should be noted that the majority of attorneys selected "important" or "very important" for all of the statements with most of the variation concentrated within the top two levels of the scale.

Washington Employment Settings: Child representatives in different organizational settings report generally similar views with respect to the importance of various competencies and practices for achieving timely court outcomes. There were no significant differences in the perceived importance of understanding the cognitive and communication capacities of individual children, or understanding the impact of maltreatment and trauma on children's mental and behavioral well-being. Similarly, there were no significant differences in the perceived importance of keeping children informed of the progress and status of their dependency cases, or making sure that children understand the legal options available to them. However, attorneys in staff attorney offices are more

Table 8.8 Opinions about the Importance of Certain Child Representation Tasks
The bolded state indicates that group of attorneys from that state rated the task was higher on the responsibility scale.

Importance For Achieving Positive And Timely Court Outcomes for Children	All	Georgia Juris	Wash.
Communicating children's wishes and needs to others involved in the case.			
Somewhat important	3%	5%	1%
Important	25%	28%	23%
Very Important	71%	67%	75%
Understanding the impact of maltreatment and trauma on children's mental and behavioral well-being.			
Somewhat important	4%	3%	5%
Important	30%	29%	32%
Very Important	65%	67%	62%
Understanding the cognitive and communication capacities of individual children.			
Somewhat important	9%	11%	7%
Important	37%	36%	38%
Very Important	54%	53%	55%
Being culturally sensitive in your interactions with child clients.			
Somewhat important	8%	11%	5%
Important	35%	38%	31%
Very Important	56%	50%	62%
Establishing and maintaining a relationship with the children you represent.			
Somewhat important	7%	8%	5%
Important	31%	38%	**24%**
Very Important	61%	53%	**70%**
Giving children the opportunity to express their wishes regarding legal objectives			
Somewhat important	8%	13%	3%
Important	33%	46%	**20%**
Very Important	58%	41%	**76%**
Informing children of positions you have taken or will take as their legal representative.			
Somewhat important	15%	25%	5%

(continued)

Table 8.8 (continued)

Importance For Achieving Positive And Timely Court Outcomes for Children	All	Georgia Juris	Wash.
Important	30%	38%	21%
Very Important	54%	36%	74%
Explaining to children the meaning of attorney-client privilege.			
Somewhat important	9%	12%	5%
Important	31%	38%	24%
Very Important	59%	49%	70%
Keeping children informed of the progress and status of their dependency case.			
Somewhat important	12%	19%	4%
Important	36%	42%	30%
Very Important	51%	38%	65%
Making sure that children understand the legal options available to them.			
Somewhat important	6%	10%	2%
Important	31%	45%	17%
Very Important	61%	43%	80%

likely than other attorneys to endorse the importance of giving children the opportunity to express their wishes regarding legal objectives.

8.11 Job Satisfaction and Impact

When asked to rate their impact and job satisfaction, 64% of attorneys "strongly agreed" with the statement, "I find my work as a legal representative for children in dependency cases to be rewarding." Twenty-eight percent "somewhat agreed" and small percentage (8%) selected an option lower on the scale (Table 8.9). When asked to reflect on their impact, 34% of attorneys "strongly agreed" with the statement, "I have a significant impact on the outcomes of the children I represent in dependency cases." Fifty-one percent "somewhat agreed" and the remaining 16% selected an option lower on the scale.

Washington Employment Settings: No significant differences were found across organizational setting in opinions about how rewarding attorneys find their work as child representatives. In contrast, attorneys working in staff attorney offices report a lower level of perceived impact than attorneys in solo practice or private firms.

Table 8.9 Opinions about Personal Rewards and Impact

I find my work as a legal representative for children in dependency cases to be rewarding			
Strongly disagree	0%	1%	0%
Somewhat disagree	2%	1%	3%
Neither agree nor disagree	6%	7%	6%
Somewhat agree	28%	23%	32%
Strongly agree	64%	69%	59%
I have a significant impact on the outcomes of the children I represent in dependency cases			
Strongly disagree	0%	0%	1%
Somewhat disagree	3%	1%	4%
Neither agree nor disagree	13%	11%	14%
Somewhat agree	51%	50%	52%
Strongly agree	34%	38%	29%

8.12 Discussion

8.12.1 Experience of Child Representatives

Most children's lawyers are not specialists, but many are experienced lawyers. Survey results showed that the professional practice of lawyers representing children includes a broad range of legal subjects. Indeed, for a majority of the lawyers, child representation constituted less than 20% of their law practice and income. Even among attorneys in staff offices in Washington State, about half of the attorneys were spending 20% or less time on child representation. The practice portfolio of the attorneys was broad and heterogeneous.

Most attorneys were handling only a handful of dependency cases—one-third report handling five or fewer cases within six months. In discussing delivery of legal services to children, the national cognoscenti of child advocates tend to focus on the specialty child welfare law office where children are represented by a dedicated group of lawyers who develop considerable experience and expertise.[3] This sample shows that most children are not represented by such specialists, but rather by general practitioners handling a limited number of dependency cases.

The survey data show that these child attorneys are not fresh out of law school. Most had practiced law for many years (mean of 13.5 years) and 56% had had

---

3. National Association of Counsel for Children, CHILD WELFARE LAW OFFICE GUIDEBOOK: BEST PRACTICE GUIDELINES FOR ORGANIZATIONAL LEGAL REPRESENTATION OF CHILDREN IN ABUSE, NEGLECT AND DEPENDENCY CASES. (2006)

represented children for 5 or more years. The implications for training and recruitment may be that good child attorneys could be recruited at various stages of a legal career and that training opportunities should be available to prepare not only the beginning lawyer but also the more experienced lawyer looking to add the personally rewarding child representation to an existing practice. A downside could be that attorneys who are already accustomed to representing children in a certain way may be less flexible and reluctant to change and accept practice innovations.

8.12.2 Organizational Supports for Child Representation Practice

Information about the availability of supports to attorneys is important because these supports are often thought to contribute to the quality of representation.[4] Several supports, including legal research databases and individuals with whom attorneys can discuss cases, appeared to be widely available. In contrast, however, several other types of supports, including investigative staff and social workers, appeared to be available to only a minority of attorneys. These supports were the most available to the group of attorneys practicing in staff attorney offices in Washington State.

8.12.3 Compensation and Satisfaction

One of the concerns voiced by legal advocates is that the financial compensation received by child representatives is low, leading to a high level of attrition and diminution in practice quality.[5] However, the findings here paint a somewhat more complicated picture. Although it is true that a majority of attorneys in both states report that the level of financial compensation is either somewhat or very inadequate, it is also true that most report that their work as child representatives is both rewarding and impactful. Moreover, based on their average tenure as child representatives, it appears that the level of attrition among these groups of child representatives may be low.

Taken together, the attorneys' views that the work is personally rewarding but the financial compensation inadequate suggests that there may be other, non-financial factors at play. For example, child representatives may be motivated by altruistic reasons that transcend financial concerns. The personal rewards these attorneys derive from including child representation as part of their practice may serve to countervail the influence of inadequate compensation.

8.12.4 Views of Responsibilities of Child Representative

A majority of attorneys in both states reported that child representatives have shared, primary, or exclusive responsibility over many dependency case tasks. As might be

---

4. *Id.*
5. Theresa D'Andrea, "Money Talks": An Assessment of the Effects of Attorney Compensation on the Representation of Children in the Child Welfare System and How States Speak through Delivery Systems. *Children's Legal Rights Journal*, 32(3), 67-88. (2012)

expected, attorneys acknowledged greater responsibility for tasks that pertain specifically to the child (e.g., advocating for services for children) than they did for tasks pertaining to other parties or matters that were not central to children's dependency cases (e.g., advocating with respect to other collateral legal matters). On the other hand, notable proportions of attorneys saw themselves having limited or no responsibilities for surveyed tasks.

This is consistent with Ross' qualitative study of lawyer's views of the tasks of child representation. She found that "lawyers reported that they represented children in very different ways, reflecting ambiguity about how to interpret these roles and involve children as clients or the subject of best interests representation."[6]

Differences in opinions about responsibility for certain tasks between Washington State and Georgia attorneys may reflect the influence of the best interests versus client directed models of representation used in these respective states at the time of the study. That is, the GAL model used in Georgia may be associated with a narrower, less assertive, purview than that associated with the client-directed model used in Washington State. Alternatively, the more assertive and broader purview associated with Washington State attorneys may be a reflection of the fact that Washington State attorneys served a group of children with an average age of 11, compared to a group of children with an average of 6 in Georgia.

8.12.5 Views of Task Importance for Achieving Positive and Timely Outcomes

Attorney's responses to questions about the importance of different tasks suggest that attorneys in both states put a premium on actively engaging child clients. Reported differences across states appear to be limited to two general types of tasks: eliciting children's input on case decisions and attorneys' efforts to communicate with child clients. For both types of tasks, higher percentages of attorneys in Washington State report that the tasks are very important. As is the case for the questions concerning attorney responsibilities, these differences might reflect differences between the models of representation used in each.

Washington attorneys, who operate under a client-directed model, are required to afford children greater authority over case decisions than are attorneys in Georgia, who operated primarily under a GAL model. The client-directed model may also necessitate a more concerted effort to help children understand the exigencies of their court cases in order to ensure that children's expressed interests are well informed. Alternatively, the differences across states in attorneys' assessments of the importance of these tasks may simply be a reflection of an older, more capable pool of child clients.

---

6. Nicola M. Ross, *Different Views? Children's Lawyers and Children's Participation In Protective Proceedings in New South Wales, Australia.* 27(3) International Journal of Law, Policy and the Family (2013).

8.12.6 Differences Across Organizational Settings

Many of the findings concerning the characteristics and circumstances of attorneys across organizational settings support the general assertion that the manner in which child representation services are organized may have important implications for child representation practice. Some of these findings support the arguments that child welfare legal offices offer a number of advantages.[7]. For example, attorneys working in staff attorney offices are found to have greater access to some types of professional resources (e.g., access to helping professionals) and less heterogeneous case compositions, than other attorneys, a finding that suggests a more specialized, better resourced practice environment. Also, a much higher proportion of attorneys in staff attorney offices report working under contract with courts to handle a specified number or proportion of cases.

In light of the fact that attorneys in nonprofit agencies are salaried employees, while solo practitioners and private-firm attorneys must bill on a case-by-case basis,[8] this finding suggests that attorneys in nonprofit agencies enjoy a greater degree of autonomy from those making legal appointments than other attorneys[9]. It should be noted, however, that not all findings support the superiority of staff attorney offices. For example, attorneys working for staff attorney offices are found to be less experienced and to report lower law incomes than attorneys working in other settings. Also, the assessment of the impact of their work on children's outcomes is lower among attorneys working for staff attorney offices than among other attorneys.

There were also many important similarities across organizational settings. Across all settings, attorneys report having had practice experiences in several areas of law. Attorneys, regardless of setting, appear to share a similar mix of attitudes about the proper approach child representation practice and its impact. The findings of no significant differences in caseload size, the degree to which attorneys find their work as child representatives to be rewarding suggest important similarities in the work environments of these various organizational settings.

Finally, it is important to point out that, although solo practitioners and private-firm attorneys share many differences from attorneys in staff attorney offices, the former two settings do not appear equivalent. Solo practitioners have worked longer as child representatives, report higher incomes from the practice of law, and received more continuing legal education credits in state child welfare law, than attorneys in private firms.

---

7. Leslie Starr Heimov, Amanda George Donnelly and Marvin Ventrell, *Rise of the Organizational Practice of Child Welfare Law: The Child Welfare Law Office*, 78 University of Colorado Law Review 1097-1117 (2007); Donald N. Duquette, with Julian Darwall, *Child Representation in America: Progress Report from the National Quality Improvement Center,* 46 FAM.L.Q. 1 (2012).

8. Based on information obtained from participating attorneys and jurisdictions during sample recruitment.

9. Heimov, supra note 7.

One possible hypothesis for the differences between solo practitioners and attorneys in private law firms is that the former are comprised of attorneys who have worked within other organizational settings, including nonprofits and private law firms. As these attorneys gained greater experience and expertise, they left these settings to set up their own solo law practices.

CHAPTER 9

Lawyer Activities and Their Impact[1]

Andrew Zinn and Britany Orlebeke

Abstract

Drawing from the QIC data, this chapter identifies major activities of a child representative across diverse groups and identifies qualitative distinctions across attorneys. This chapter examines the interrelationships among the different behaviors and draws conclusions about types of practice behaviors. This is important for two reasons: it informs our understanding of child representation practice *and* helps us put into perspective different practice behaviors across QIC groups.

9.1 Introduction

Research results presented in this chapter begin to fill the gap in knowledge about what the child's representative does and when, and how those activities vary depending on the characteristics of the case and the attorney. It is based on the periodic, child-specific surveys completed by attorneys from 2012-2015 as described in Chapter 7. The findings in this chapter are based on a random sample of cases from the QIC-ChildRep sample and only includes children from that group who were placed into substitute care between Feb 1, 2012 and October 1, 2014 and whose dependency cases had been assigned to participating attorneys prior to, or during, children's first two years in substitute care. The final analytic sample includes 166 attorneys (Washington: 94, Georgia:

---

1. Abridged from Andrew Zinn and Britany Orlebeke, **The Nature and Determinants of ChildRepresentation Practice in Child Welfare Cases** [in press, Family Court Review].

72) representing 745 children (Washington: 509, Georgia: 236) within 36 jurisdictions (Washington: 22, Georgia: 14).

These findings give legislators, court staff and policy-makers seeking to provide and improve upon the delivery of legal services an understanding of what these attorneys do in practice and how that varies across cases and attorneys. These findings also allow attorneys to compare how they serve their child clients compared with their peers doing similar work.

While much has been said about what child representatives *should* do, there has been little research about what child representatives *actually* do in practice.[2] Although there have been several attempts to indirectly measure the activities of child representatives, there has yet to be any published study examining these activities on a case-by-case basis.

> The QIC-ChildRep attorney activity surveys provided periodic, child-specific information about:
>
> - Contact with child clients
> - Contact with children's family members
> - Contact with proximate collaterals like caseworkers and parent attorneys
> - Contact with distal collaterals like teachers and medical doctors
> - Time spent on investigation activities and document review
> - Time spent on legal case preparation activities like review of court files and developing a theory of the case

Before discussing the significance or implications of these findings, there are several important limitations of these analyses. First, because attorneys report on their own activities, these data may be subject to recall or social desirability bias. Second, as with the characteristics of attorneys presented in Chapter 8, the sample for the study comes from a limited set of jurisdictions. If the circumstances of child representation (e.g., case characteristics, attorney characteristics, and context-level constraints) in these states differ from those of other jurisdictions, the applicability of these findings to other jurisdictions is limited. Third, the study design is observational not experimental.

This means that the associations between attorney-level and child characteristics and attorney activity rates may not reflect the influence of those characteristics but may be associated with an unmeasured characteristic. Finally, these data contain no case-level characteristics beyond child demographic characteristics and placement history. Thus if certain types of attorneys (e.g., inexperienced or particularly experienced in a certain type of case) are more likely to be assigned certain types of cases, the findings

---

2. Daniel P. Gallagher. *Child Abuse and Neglect Cases in the Colorado Courts 1996-2000: A Reassessment.* Denver: Colorado Court Improvement Committee, Colorado Judicial Branch (2002); Judicial Council of California. *Dependency Counsel Caseload Standards: A Report to The California Legislature.* San Francisco: Judicial Council of California, California Administrative Office of the Courts (2008).

concerning the relationships between attorney characteristics and activity levels could be skewed.

Finally, the significance of the findings depends on whether or not the differences observed are meaningful with respect to either process or child welfare outcomes. Some of the differences are statistically significant, but small. Judging whether or not an increase in contact or time spent on activities of the magnitudes identified has meaning is beyond the scope of these analyses.

9.2 More about Samples and Data

Chapter 7 describes the sources for survey and child-specific data. This study uses information about attorneys themselves from the baseline survey, information about attorney activities from the milestone surveys, and demographic characteristics and substitute care histories of children represented, including the type of substitute care placement in which children were placed at the point in time that milestone surveys were administered.

The milestone surveys were administered at regular intervals after a dependency case was assigned to an attorney. Specifically, an initial survey (i.e., assignment survey) was administered within approximately 45 days of case assignment. Then, if a child's dependency case remained open, two subsequent surveys (i.e., review surveys) were administered at approximately 180-day intervals.[3] The response rates for the baseline and milestone surveys were, respectively 89.2 and 86.3 percent.[4]

The milestone surveys contained two series of questions about activities engaged in on behalf of individual dependency cases. In the first series of questions, attorneys were asked about the frequency of contact between the attorney and various parties, including child clients, children's family members, and various collateral contacts like caseworkers, parent attorneys, and teachers. The response options for these questions were specified as 4-level interval scales, ranging from none or not applicable to more than 5 times. In the second series of questions, attorneys are asked about the amount of time spent engaged in various case-related activities, including assessment, investigation, and legal case preparation. The response options for these questions are specified as 5-level interval scales, ranging from none to many.

For both series of questions, the specific rosters of items differed somewhat across the two sample states. For example, in the surveys administered to attorneys in

---

3. In Washington State, surveys were also administered when specific legal events occurred, including the issuance of a dispositional order, termination of parental rights order, and exit from substitute care.

4. Britany Orlebeke, Xiaomeng Zhou, Ada Skyles, and Andrew Zinn. *Evaluation of the QIC-ChildRep Training and Coaching Intervention for Child Representatives*. Chicago: Chapin Hall (2016); Britany Orlebeke, Andrew Zinn, Donald N. Duquette, and Xiaomeng Zhou. *Characteristics of attorneys representing children in child welfare cases*. Family Law Quarterly, 49(3), 477-507 (2015).

Response options for "frequency of contact questions" were:	Response options for "time spent" questions were:
• none / not applicable • 1 time • 2 - 3 times • 4 - 5 times • more than 5 times	• none • about a half hour or less • about an hour • several hours • many hours

Washington State, there was a question about the frequency of contact with a child's "biological parents," whereas the surveys administered to attorneys in Georgia contained separate questions about contact with a child's "biological father" and "biological mother."

9.3 Analysis Approach

The analysis uses attorney responses on the activity-related survey questions to calculate monthly rates for each activity type. These rates (either singly or in combination with other related activities) are used as the dependent variables in a series of mixed-effect regression models. Also, these models enable us to explore the influence of various case- and attorney-level factors on attorneys practice activities, and to examine the degree to which the overall variability in practice activities is attributable to attorneys per se.

The monthly rates are derived from each survey response as follows. First, based on the response options for each set of questions about attorney activities, we assign numeric values to each response. Because the response options for these two sets of questions are different, however, the values assigned to each set also differ: frequency of contact with various parties (none / not applicable = 0; 1 time = 1; 2 - 3 times = 2.5; 4 - 5 times = 4.5; and more than 5 times = 6), time spent engaged in various case-related activities (none = 0; about a half hour or less=.5; about an hour=1; several hours=3; many hours=5). Second, in order to account for the fact that the time between survey administrations varies from case to case, we divided these assigned numeric values by the time since the last survey and then multiplied that result by thirty, which yields a monthly rate.

The first set of models are used to calculate the average monthly rate for each activity type, controlling for state, length of time in substitute care at the time of the survey, and survey type. The resulting adjusted averages correct for any biases that may occur as a result of differences in the number of completed surveys across states, survey types, and time in care. The second set of models are used to estimate the prevalence of each activity type; specifically, the average likelihood that a particular contact or activity ever occurred during the past six months (or since the prior survey). Like the first set of models, these include covariates for state, length of time in care, and survey type. These models also provide an analysis of how the rate of each attorney activity varied as a function of care spell time.

In the final set of models, monthly rates of individual activity types are averaged to create composite monthly rates for several substantive categories of attorney activities. (See Text Box on page xx). The extent to which child-level characteristics are associated with different activity levels is analyzed and then the extent to which attorney-level characteristics are associated with different activity levels is analyzed. These final models allow inferences about the relative influence of attorney-level characteristics, net of the influence of case-level factors, on the average rates of contact and time spent per case. For example, after controlling for child-level characteristics like age and time in care, we found that attorneys working for private, non-profit law firms report higher levels of in-person contact with children than attorneys working in other settings.

9.4 Attorney Activities: How Often and How Much

Figure 9.1 shows the adjusted average monthly rates of contact with parties to the child's case. This monthly rate is interpreted as the average number of contacts per month per case. Figure 2 shows, for the same contact types, the percent of attorneys who had at least one contact within the past six months. Meeting with proximate collaterals (Figure 9.1) is the most common type of contact reported by sampled attorneys. For example, an average of 94% attorneys report that they had met with case workers in the last six months or since the prior survey, for an average of 1.19 meetings

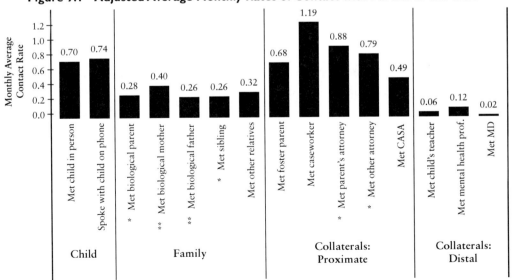

Figure 9.1 Adjusted Average Monthly Rates of Contact with Parties to the Case†

* - Washington only, ** - Georgia only.
†- Monthly adjusted-average based on the intercepts of the initial mixed-effect models. Estimated are adjusted for state, time in care, and survey type.

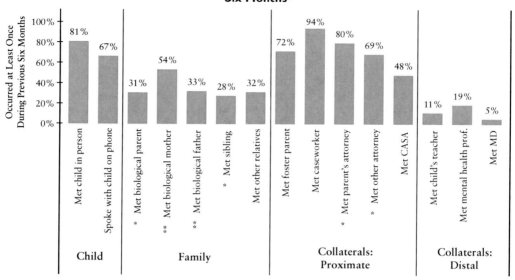

Figure 9.2 Attorneys with at Least One Contact with Parties to the Case in Last Six Months†

* - Washington only, ** - Georgia only.
†- Monthly adjusted-average based on the intercepts of the initial mixed-effect models. Estimated are adjusted for state, time in care, and survey type.

per month. Also, large majorities of attorneys report having met with foster parents (72%) parents' attorneys (80%), and other attorneys (69%) at least once in the last six months. In total, attorneys report an average of 4.03 contacts per month with proximate collaterals.

Attorneys also report relatively high rates of contact with their child clients. For example, at each survey, about four-fifths (81%) of attorneys report having met in person with their child client, for an average of 0.70 meetings per month. At the other end of the spectrum, very few attorneys report meeting with distal collaterals like teachers (11% during prior 6 months, an average of 0.06 times per month) and medical doctors (5% during prior 6 months, an average of 0.02 times per month). In total, the average rate of contact with children's family members (1.52 times per month) is also relatively low, at least in comparison to the rates of contact with other parties. For example, less than a third of attorneys report having met with siblings (28% during prior 6 months, average of 0.26 times per month) or other relatives (32% during prior 6 months, average of 0.32 times per month).

Figure 9.3 shows the adjusted average monthly hours per month of activity on behalf of the child's case. These monthly rates are interpreted as the average number of hours per month per case. Figure 934 shows, for the same activity types, the percent of attorneys who spent at least some time on that activity within the past six months.

LAWYER ACTIVITIES AND THEIR IMPACT

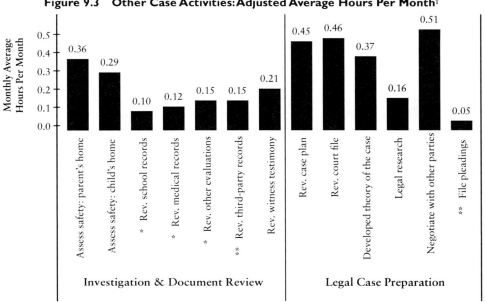

Figure 9.3 Other Case Activities: Adjusted Average Hours Per Month[†]

* - Washington only, ** - Georgia only.
[†]- Monthly adjusted-average based on the intercepts of the initial mixed-effect models. Estimated are adjusted for state, time in care, and survey type.

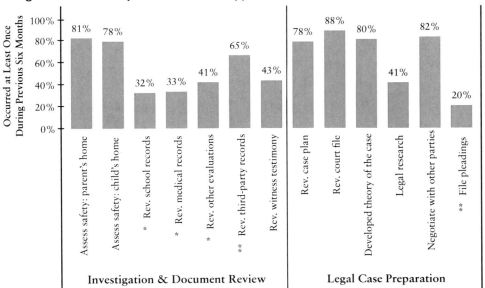

Figure 9.4 Attorney Activities that Happened at Least Once in Last Six Months[†]

* - Washington only, ** - Georgia only.
[†]- Monthly adjusted-average based on the intercepts of the initial mixed-effect models. Estimated are adjusted for state, time in care, and survey type.

Attorneys report spending more time on legal case preparation activities (avg. of 2.01 hours per month) than investigation and document review (avg. of 1.38 hours per month). The case activities on which attorneys report spending the most time include negotiating with other parties (average of 0.51 hours per month), reviewing case plans (average of 0.45 hours per month), and reviewing court files (average of 0.46 hours per month).

There are also considerable differences in the rates of activities within substantive activity categories. While certain types of legal case preparation activities, like reviewing court files and negotiating with other parties appear to consume a greater amount of attorneys' time, others, like legal research (41% spent at least some time during prior 6 months, average of 0.16 hours per month), consume much less time.

Similarly, while certain types of investigation and document review activities, like assessing the safety of the homes of parents (0.36 hours per month) and children (81% spent at least some time during past 6 months, average of 0.29 hours per month), appear to occupy a greater proportion of attorneys' time, others like review of school (32% during prior 6 months, average of 0.10 hours per month) or medical (33% during prior 6 months, average of 0.12 hours per month) records consume much less time.

9.5 Timing of Attorney Activities

Figures 9.5 and 9.6 present the average monthly rates for each activity type by time since entry into substitute care. Figure 9.5 presents the average rates for the survey questions about contact between attorneys and different parties, and Figure 9.6 presents the average rates for the questions about other types of case activities. The y-axis of each chart indicates the average monthly activity rate, and the x-axis indicates the time since children have entered care. The shape of each curve describes how the rate of each activity varies as a function of time since a child enters care. For example, in the chart under the heading "Child" in Figure 9.5 are plotted the rates of in-person and phone contacts between attorneys and their child clients. These curves indicate that the level of contact between attorneys and children is highest at the point in time that children enter substitute care. For both types of contact, the monthly rate then decreases steadily through the first year in care, and subsequently rebounds somewhat during the second year in care.

This general pattern—relatively steep decline in activity during the first year followed by a partial recovery during the second year—is also observed for many other types of attorney activities. However, there are several notable departures from this pattern that warrant discussion. First, the average rates of contact with all types of distal collaterals (fifth panel of Figure 5), start and remain low throughout the two-year observation period. Second, there are several types of activities for which the rates start low and subsequently increase. For example, unlike contact with other relatives (third panel of Figure 9.5), the average rate of contact with biological fathers doubles during

LAWYER ACTIVITIES AND THEIR IMPACT

Figure 9.5 Contact with Parties: Adjusted Average Monthly Rate by Time in Care†

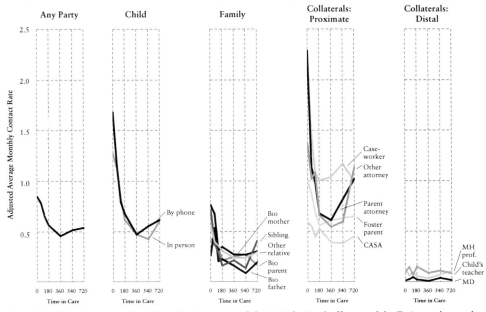

† - Monthly adjusted-average based on the intercepts of the initial mixed-effect models. Estimated are adjusted for state, and survey type.

Figure 9.6 Other Case Activities: Adjusted Average Hours Per Month by Time in Care†

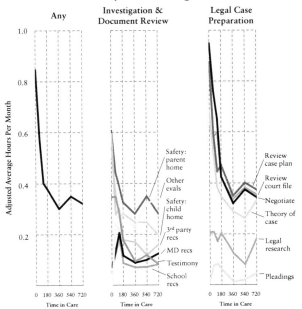

† - Monthly adjusted-average based on the intercepts of the initial mixed-effect models. Estimated are adjusted for state, and survey type.

the first 90 days after entry. Third, during the second year after care, several distinct patterns of change are observed.

For example, as described above, there are a number of activities for which average rates continue to increase throughout the end of the second year after entry to care; examples include contact with parent attorneys and other attorneys (fourth panel of Figure 9.5). Conversely, there are a number of activities that appear to peak at 540 days after entry; examples include contact with caseworkers and several types of investigation and document review activities. Finally, the relative degree of the initial decline, or subsequent increase, in activity rates varies considerably across activity types. For example, the initial rate of contact with caseworkers and parent attorneys (fourth panel of Figure 9.5) are both relatively high, and both exhibit steep declines during the first 6 months after entry to care. However, while the level of contact with caseworkers starts to increase again at six months after entry to care, the average rate of contact with parent attorneys continues to fall through the end of the first year. Nevertheless, during the second year, the average rate for parent attorneys increases steadily, resulting in approximately equal average rates of contact with caseworkers and parent attorneys by the end of the second year.

9.6 How Child-Level Characteristics Are Associated with Attorney Activity Levels

Table 9.1 summarizes the relationships among several child-level characteristics and the composite measures of attorney activities. The bottom row of the table shows the average monthly rate before taking into account child-level characteristics. These average rates are analogous to the monthly rates presented in Figures 9.1 and 9.2. The top section of Table 1 shows the differences in the average monthly composite rates that are associated with each child characteristic. Using the average rate and the estimated difference, we are able to calculate the percentage change in each composite activity measure associated with each child characteristic.

Child age is positively associated with the frequency of contact between attorneys and their child clients. Specifically, with each additional year of child age, the monthly rate of contact is found to increase 0.032 contacts. Based on the average rate (0.734), which is listed in the bottom row of Table1, this estimate corresponds to an increase of about 4.4 percent (0.032 ÷ 0.734 = 4.36%) per month. To put this into perspective, the estimated rate of contact with a 13-year-old adolescent would be almost 45 percent higher than the estimated rate of contact with a 3-year-old toddler. Child age is also found to be positively associated with the rate of attorney contact with family members (B=0.008, 1.7% increase per year), and distal collaterals (B=0.004, 4.4% increase per year). In contrast, child age is found to be associated with a slight decrease in the frequency of contact between attorneys and proximate collaterals (B=-.009, 1.1% decrease per year).

Table 9.1 Mixed-Effect Regression Models of Composite Activity Measures: Child-Level Characteristics

Child Characteristics	Frequency of Contact with Parties				Time in Case-Related Activities	
	Contact: Child	Contact: Family	Collaterals: Proximate	Collaterals: Distal	Investigation & Document Review	Legal Case Preparation
Age	0.032***	0.008**	−0.009†	0.004*	−0.002	−0.001
Female (vs. male)	0.149***	0.064***	0.043	0.025*	0.002	0.023
Race / Ethnicity (vs. white)						
Black	0.014	0.006	0.051	−0.004	−0.016	0.020
Hispanic	−0.015	−0.033	−0.032	−0.020	−0.047*	−0.020
Other	0.027	−0.018	−0.086	−0.005	−0.003	0.037
Placement Type (vs. non-relative foster home)						
Relative (kinship) foster home	−0.022	−0.007	−0.010	−0.018	0.003	−0.018
Residential / congregate care	−0.208***	−0.084*	−0.075	−0.001	−0.014	−0.045
Other or unknown	−0.064	0.016	−0.071	−0.011	−0.007	−0.014
Adjusted-average monthly rate	0.734	0.485	0.846	0.091	0.248	0.405

*** - p <.001, ** - p <.01, * p <.05, † - p <.10. Note: regression models include control variables for state, time in care, and survey type (not shown).

Across several composite activity measures, attorneys report higher levels of activity with female clients compared to male clients. For example, the estimated monthly rates of contact with child clients (B=0.149), and meetings with children's family members (B=0.064), are, respectively, 20 and 13 percent higher among female clients than among males. Also, the estimated monthly rate of contact with distal collaterals is 27 percent higher for female clients than male clients.

Children's race/ethnicity is not found to be significantly (i.e., statistically) related to the rates of contact with children, children's family members, or collaterals. However, the rate of investigation and document review is found to be 19 percent lower for Hispanic children (B=-0.047) than among white children.

The rate of contact between attorneys and children is substantially lower for cases in which children are placed in residential or congregate care facilities (B=-0.208) than it is for children placed in non-relative (28% lower) and relative (26% lower) foster homes. Similarly, the monthly rates of legal case preparation activities (B=-0.069, 13% lower), and contact between attorneys and children's families (B=-0.084, 17% lower), are lower among children in residential or congregate care than for children in non-relative foster homes.

9.7 How Attorney-Level Characteristics Are Associated with Attorney Activity Levels

To explore the association among attorney-level characteristics and composite activity measures, we estimated a final set of models that included controls for time in care, survey type, state, and child characteristics, as well as a several attorney-level characteristics. The results of these models are presented in Table 9.2.

In general, the attorneys' demographic characteristics are found to be weakly associated with activity rates. The length of an attorney's tenure representing children in dependency cases is found to exhibit significant, but nonlinear, relationships with several composite activity measures. In brief, attorneys who have less than 1 year experience representing children in dependency cases report significantly higher rates of contact with their child clients (B=0.206, 29% higher), contact with proximate collaterals (B=0.195, 23% higher), and legal case preparation activities (B=0.103, 19% higher) than attorneys with more than one year experience in dependency cases

The size of attorneys' dependency caseloads is found to be significantly negatively associated with the rates of investigation and document review activities and legal case preparation activities. Specifically, a 1-standard-deviation increase (20 cases) in the size of dependency caseloads is associated with a 22 percent decrease (B=-0.054) in the monthly rate of investigation and document review, and a 9 percent decrease (B=-0.049) in the monthly rate of legal case preparation activities.

Attorneys working for private, nonprofit law firms report significantly higher rates of contact with children (B=0.113) than solo practitioners (13% lower) and attorneys

Table 9.2 Mixed-Effect Regression Models of Composite Activity Measures: Attorney-Level Characteristics

Attorney Characteristic	Frequency of Contact with Parties				Time in Case-Related Activities	
	Contact: Child	Contact: Family	Collaterals: Proximate	Collaterals: Distal	Investigation & Document Review	Legal Case Preparation
Race (vs. white)						
African American	−0.101	−0.020	−0.137	0.043	−0.059	−0.071
Other	0.018	−0.079	−0.049	−0.021	−0.026	0.062
Age	−0.021	−0.022	−0.010	−0.011†	−0.005	0.001
Tenure < 1 year	0.206**	0.063	0.195*	0.040	0.043	0.103†
Dependency case caseload‡	−0.008	0.007	0.001	−0.013	−0.054***	−0.049*
Employment Setting (vs. sole practitioner)						
Private law firm	−0.069	0.023	0.092	0.004	0.035	−0.007
Private, non-profit organization	0.113*	−0.050	−0.041	0.079**	−0.045	−0.036
State / county office	−0.003	0.193	−0.025	0.141†	0.160	0.119
Percent of law practice that involves representing children in dependency cases‡	0.082***	0.043*	0.053†	0.011	0.054**	0.054†
Child representation compensation is 'very inadequate'	0.141†	0.091†	0.067	0.073	0.098**	0.062
Assumed-responsibility scaleΔ	0.154*	0.119**	0.069	0.006	0.048	0.006
Representing children in dependency cases is rewarding‡	0.044	0.036	0.086*	0.010	0.053**	0.063†
Adjusted-average hours per month	0.740	0.470	0.841	0.085	0.243	0.539

‡ - Independent variable has been standardized. Δ - Item measured on a 5-point Likert scale. *** - p <.001, ** - p <.01, * p <.05, † - p <.10. Note: regression models include control variables for state, time in care, survey type, and child characteristics (not shown).

working for private law firms ((-0.069) - (0.113) = 21% lower). Attorneys working for private, non-profit law firms (B=0.079), and state or county offices (B=0.141), report significantly higher rates of contact with distal collaterals than solo practitioners and attorneys working for private law firms.

The proportion of an attorney's practice that involves dependency cases is significantly associated with the rates of several types of activities. For example, a 1-standard-deviation increase (28 percent) in the proportion (i.e., percentage) of dependency cases is associated with a 11 percent increase in the rate of contact between attorneys and child clients (B=0.082). Similar increases are found with respect to the rates of contact with children's families (9% increase), contact with proximate collaterals (6% increase), investigation and document review (22% increase), and legal case preparation activities (10% increase).

The association between attorneys' perceptions of the adequacy of financial compensation they receive in dependency cases and composite activity measures is found to be negative. Specifically, attorneys who report that the level of compensation is 'very inadequate' are found to have higher rates of contact with children (B=0.141, 19% higher), contact with children's families (B=0.091, 19% higher), and investigation and document review (B=0.098, 40% higher) than other attorneys.

The assumed-responsibility scale, which indicates an attorney's professed level of responsibility for dependency-case-related tasks, is found to be positively associated with the rates of contact with child clients and children's family members. Specifically, a 1-unit increase (e.g., primary vs. shared responsibility) in the assumed-responsibility scale is associated with 21 and 25 percent increase, respectively, in the rates of contact with child clients (B=0.154) and children's family members (B=0.119).

Finally, attorneys' opinions about the degree to which their work in dependency cases is rewarding are found to be positively associated with the rates of several types of activities. A 1-unit increase in the degree to which dependency work is rewarding is associated with increased rates of contact between attorneys and proximate collaterals (B=0.086. 10% increase), investigation and document review (B=0.053, 22% increase), and legal case preparation activities (B=0.063, 12% increase).

9.8 Discussion

9.8.1 *Phenomena at Various Levels*

Collectively, the variability in the rates of different types of activities appears to be a function of phenomena operating at various levels, including organizations, attorneys, cases, and case time (i.e., time since entry to care). Interestingly, this variability does not appear to be a function of court- or jurisdiction-level influences. Indeed, based on the intra-class correlation coefficients from the mixed-effect models of composite attorney activity measures, approximately 3 percent of the variability in these measures is attributable to the jurisdiction level. In contrast, the degree of variability in composite attorney activity measures that is attributable to attorneys and children is substantial for all activity categories.

The findings also suggest that the level of attorney effort expended by attorneys varies significantly across activity type. For example, the average number of times attorneys meet with caseworkers per month (1.19) is 70 percent higher than the number of times they meet with children (0.70) and over 10 times higher than the number of times they meet with children's teachers (0.11). Similarly, the findings suggest that the level of attorney effort varies considerably across individual cases, with the top quartile of cases experiencing rates that are in excess of five times that for the bottom quartile.

The variability in activity rates—both across cases and activity types—appears to be partially explained by a combination of case, child, and attorney characteristics. As discussed in the next section, these differences suggest several competing hypotheses about the mechanisms underlying the differences in the level of attorney activity.

9.8.2 Differences Across Case Time

The findings suggest that the passage of time after a child enters care (i.e., case time) is an important source of variability in attorney activity rates. The general pattern observed for many types of activities is that of a lopsided bathtub: a relatively high initial rate followed by a steep decline through the end of the first year and partial recovery during the second year. This pattern likely reflects changes in court objectives and requirements as dependency cases progress through various legal and service milestones. Specifically, during the first 6 months or so of a dependency case, when attorneys are working towards adjudication and disposition, they are occupied with a number of different activities required to develop and advocate their case. Then, after a period of relative calm, attorney activity begins to increase during children's second year in care, which may reflect the combined demands of permanency plan reviews, termination proceedings, and service advocacy (e.g., placement with kin and siblings).

Although this bathtub-like pattern appears to hold for many types of activities, there is considerable variability across activity types in the magnitude and timing of changes over case time. Some of these differences may reflect changes in attorneys' tactics that accompany changes in court objectives and demands as cases progress. For example, although the rate of contact with caseworkers is initially lower than the rate of contact with attorneys, this pattern is reversed after children's first 6 months in care, which may reflect a pivot from court-based work related to adjudication and disposition to service issues related to meeting the requirements of children's case plans.

Alternatively, some of the differences in activity rates over case time may reflect processes governing the availability of different parties or resources. For example, the spike in contact with biological fathers at 60 days post-entry may reflect the fact that many fathers are often not involved or aware of dependency proceedings until they are served notice, which may take a number of weeks to accomplish. Similarly, the observed spike in medical and school record review occurring at 120 days post-entry may reflect the time required to request and receive these records from community organizations

9.8.3 Differences Across Child Characteristics

The parameter estimates from the mixed-effect models of the composite measures of attorney activities suggest that there are significant differences in activity levels across child characteristics. These differences may be a reflection of two distinct types of phenomena. First, observed differences in activity rates across child characteristics may reflect differences in the needs and capacities of different groups of children. For example, the finding that attorneys have higher levels of contact with older children and the families of older children may reflect that older children are more communicative than younger children and, thus, meeting with them is perceived as being more productive or useful.

Older children may, on average, experience more complex legal problems and, thus, may necessitate more frequent communication with their attorneys than younger children. Similarly, lower levels of attorney contact with children and their families among children placed in residential care (vs. children placed in foster homes) may reflect challenges associated with these children's behavior problems or the restricted or remote nature of some residential care facilities. Finally, the higher level of attorney contact with distal collaterals among older children may reflect the fact that these individuals (e.g., teachers, mental health providers) are more likely to work with older (school-age) children than with younger children.

An alternative explanation for the observed differences in activity levels across child characteristics is that they are a function of attorney-level preferences or biases. For example, more frequent contact with older children may be more a reflection of the ease of communicating with these children than an indication of greater need. Similarly, although the higher rates of contact with girls may reflect unmeasured differences in behavior across gender, they may also indicate attorneys' preferences based on gender.

Finally, it is important to note that the parameter estimates from the mixed-effect models of the composite measures of attorney activities suggest that there are no differences across child race/ethnicity or between children placed with relative vs. non-relative foster families. This is interesting because a number of studies have found significant differences in child welfare service and dependency court outcomes across child race/ethnicity, child age, and substitute care placement type.[5] Thus, if the service

---

5. Indeed, a number of studies have found significant differences in child welfare service and dependency court outcomes across child race/ethnicity, child age, and substitute care placement type. See Akin (2011) for a review of child welfare service outcomes. Examples of dependency court outcome studies include Barth et al. (1994), Festinger and Pratt (2002), Zinn and Cusick (2014), and Zinn and Peters (2015).

and court outcomes of the children represented by sampled attorneys differ across these groups, it would not seem to be the result of systematic differences in attorney activity.

9.8.4 Differences Across Attorney Characteristics

The parameter estimates from the mixed-effect models of attorney activities also suggest that there are significant differences in activity levels across attorney characteristics. These differences may reflect a combination of factors, including attorney-level capacities and attitudes and context-level resources and demands. For example, the respective findings that higher ratings on the assumed-responsibility scale, and more positive assessments of perceived impact, are positively associated with some activity levels suggests that attorney effort is a product of attorney-level attitudes about the importance of their role as child representatives. Similarly, the finding that less-experienced attorneys report higher levels of activity may be a reflection of attorney-level work efficiency; less experienced attorneys are still learning when, and for whom, different types of activities are needed and, thus, they expend more effort than more seasoned attorneys.

Alternatively, the findings of differences in activity rates vis-à-vis caseload size, employment setting, and the proportion of law practice devoted to child representation could be due to context-level phenomena. For example, the negative relationship between child representation caseload size and activity rates may reflect the added burden placed on attorneys' time as the number of clients increases. Also, the higher rates of contact with children and families among attorneys working for private, non-profit organizations could reflect the differences in organizational-level resources and culture that are thought to be associated with different employment settings[6]. Similarly, the positive relationship between the proportion of an attorney's practice devoted to child representation and attorney activity levels could reflect the benefits of specialization that come with a more concentrated caseload.

It is also important to acknowledge that attorneys who are effective, enthusiastic child representatives may be more likely choose to work under certain working conditions, which then leads to the erroneous conclusion that these conditions are responsible for a higher level of practice. For example, these attorneys may be more likely to

---

6. Leslie Starr Heimov, Amanda George Donnelly, and Marvin Ventrell. *Rise of the organizational practice of child welfare law: The child welfare law office.* University of Colorado Law Review, 78, 1097-1117 (2007); Quality Improvement Center on the Representation of Children in the Child Welfare System. *Needs assessment: Discussions with stakeholders* (2010). Retrieved from http://www.improvechildrep.org/Portals/0/QIC%20Child%20Rep%20Discussions%20with%20Stakeholders.pdf; Andrew Zinn, Britany Orlebeke, Donald N. Duquette, and Xiaomeng Zhou, X. *The Organizational Contexts of Child Representation Services In Child Welfare Cases.* Family Court Review (in press).

Donald N. Duquette and Julian Darwall, *Child Representation in America: Progress Report from the National Quality Improvement Center,* 46 FAM.L.Q. 87 (Spring 2012).

decide to work for private, non-profit organizations, more likely to specialize in child representation law, and more able to exert (greater) control over their caseloads. Thus, the higher activity rates associated with private, non-profit organizations could, in fact, be a function of average-level differences on attorney-level characteristics.

Finally, the mixed-effect model parameter estimates of the relationship between attorneys' activity rates and their opinions about the adequacy of their financial compensation appear, at first glance, to be counter-intuitive. Attorneys who report their compensation as being 'very inadequate' report higher rates of contact with children and families, and higher rates of document review and investigation, than other attorneys. Although it is possible that lower levels of financial compensation somehow induce attorneys to work harder, this explanation seems to strain credulity. A more plausible explanation may be that, because the compensation received by child representatives is relatively fixed (at least in the short- to mid-term), attorneys who devote more time to child representation cases, receive a lower effective per-hour rate than other attorneys—thus, yielding a negative association between compensation adequacy and attorney effort.

CHAPTER 10

Findings of the Evaluation of the QIC-Childrep Best Practices Model Training for Attorneys[1]

Britany Orlebeke, Xiomeng Zhou, Ada Skyles and Andrew Zinn

Abstract

Our research shows that the QIC attorneys in both Washington State and Georgia applied the Six Core Skills:

- They *changed the way they represented children* and were significantly more likely to engage in behaviors considered best practice.
- These best practice *behaviors resulted in measurable improvement* in case outcomes for children.
- The model resulted in *greater contact with the child* and increased communications with the other players.
- The QIC lawyers in both states were also *more actively involved in conflict resolution and negotiation* activities and showed a commitment to moving the case forward.
- Children represented by the trained QIC attorneys tended to *exit care sooner* than the controls.

---

1. Excerpted from the Chapin Hall Evaluation Report: Orlebeke, B., Zhou, X., Skyles, A., & Zinn, A. (2016) *Evaluation of the QIC-ChildRep Training and Coaching Intervention for Child Representatives*. Chicago, IL: Chapin Hall at the University of Chicago. For the unabridged Chapin Hall QIC Evaluation report, go to the Chapin Hall website at: www.chapinhall.org.

- Children represented by QIC attorneys in Washington State were *40% more likely to experience permanency* within six months of placement than children represented by control attorneys.

10.1 Introduction

Chapters 5 and 6 describe the Best Practice Model and the specific manifestation of the model that took place in Georgia and Washington State. This chapter presents the experimental evidence addressing the impact of those efforts to improve attorney practice. It addresses two primary questions: Did treatment attorneys change the way they handled their dependency cases, compared to attorneys who continued to practice as usual? Did children served by treatment attorneys experience different outcomes than children served by control attorneys?

The questions about attorney behavior were examined using responses to child-specific attorney surveys. Questions about outcomes were examined with links to state administrative data systems. The evaluation had sufficient statistical power to detect moderate effects. Chapter 7 provides the methodological basis for the research findings, and Section 7.4 briefly explains the randomized-controlled design, power analysis and analytic methods. The unabridged Chapin Hall evaluation report presents the full methods explanation.

With respect to child outcomes, the evaluation does not address the question of whether representation by an attorney (versus a lay *guardian ad litem* only) is associated with a different distribution of outcomes. All children in the evaluation were represented by an attorney.

The scope of the evaluation of the QIC intervention—37 local judicial districts, 263 attorneys and 4,274 children—was both its strength and its weakness. This large sample, with randomization of attorneys within jurisdiction to account for jurisdiction-level influences, provided a more rigorous test of impact. For impact to show through, the intervention had to generate a detectable difference in many places. But the scope limited the data that could be collected and analyzed. In order to answer the question posed (would the pilots in Georgia and Washington State yield a general, detectable difference), data had to be collected from a large number of attorneys about a large number of cases.

These data were limited to those which could be asked on a survey and those in administrative data. So for example, the evaluation does not speak to comparisons of children's perception of representation or to differences in specific services received by children or their caregivers.

With respect to child outcomes, only experiences that applied to most children (the timing of exit from care, placement type, and placement stability) could be rigorously analyzed. Experiences of subsets of children would yield samples too small to fairly judge impact. This was the case for sibling placements (only some children had siblings coming into care) and the likelihood of placement in the first place (only some children had attorneys assigned prior to placement).

This would also have been the case for evaluating preparedness for independent living (only a few children would have left care to live independently). However, the outcomes that were evaluated—the likelihood of early reunification, rates of kinship placement, and rates of movement within one year of assignment—are among the foundational outcomes of any child welfare system.

Finally, even for the outcomes that could be measured, the evaluation was designed to detect moderate average effects on attorney and child outcomes. Detecting small average impacts would have required a greater number of attorneys and cases. For the outcomes where no statistically significant results were found, there may have been small average impacts that the evaluation did not have enough power to detect.

10.2 Implementation of Intervention

Almost all Georgia and Washington State attorneys attended the initial two-day training. Only 7 out of the 131 attorneys assigned to the treatment group missed the initial training.

Attorney participation in pod meetings and coaching sessions following the two-day training differed in the two states. In Georgia, fewer sessions were offered and participation rates ranged from 10 percent to 60 percent of treatment attorneys; on average around 45 percent of treatment attorneys attended each offered session. In Washington State, participation was consistent and usually ranged from between 70 and 80 percent of treatment attorneys for the majority of offered sessions. The median number of pod meetings attended by Georgia attorneys was three (out of seven offered) and the median number of coaching sessions among Georgia attorneys was also three (out of eight offered). In Washington State, treatment attorneys attended a median of seven pod meetings (out of ten offered) and participated in a median of nine coaching sessions (out of ten offered).

Pod meetings and coaching sessions were implemented with greater fidelity to the intervention plan in Washington State than in Georgia. Five out of seven Georgia pod meetings were conducted as online meetings, whereas all Washington State pod meetings were done in person. Coaching sessions in Washington State followed a consistent format, whereas Georgia coaching sessions did not.

Evaluators also collected data from attorneys about which core skill or skills were discussed in each pod meeting or coaching session. From these data, participation is characterized by how many attorneys covered each core skill at least three times over the course of the post-training period. Georgia's treatment attorneys were exposed to the core skills less due to fewer post-training offerings and lower participation.

Still, about two-thirds of attorneys had covered the core skill "enter the child's world" at least three times. About half had covered the core skills "evaluate needs,"

Table 10.1 Six Core Skills—Frequency of Discussion Post Initial Two-Day Training

	Percent of All Treatment Attorneys Discussing Skill at Least 3 Times	
Core Skill	Georgia	Washington
Enter Child's World	68%	92%
Evaluate Needs	52%	89%
Advocate Effectively	56%	89%
Assess Safety	47%	78%
Advance Case Planning	27%	89%
Develop Case Theory	14%	79%

"advocate effectively," and "assess safety" at least three times and half had not reached this threshold. Most attorneys had not had at least three discussions with state team staff about "advance case planning" and "develop case theory." Washington's treatment attorneys were exposed to all Six Core Skills more widely and consistently. The percentage of all treatment attorneys discussing a particular core skill at least 3 times ranged from 78 percent to 92 percent.

10.3 Measuring Attorney Behavior

Whether and how attorney behavior changed because of the intervention was measured with the child-specific surveys of attorneys described in Chapter 7 and used for the analyses in Chapter 9. The surveys contained questions addressing the hypothesized links in attorney behavior to child outcomes that could be reasonably measured through surveys. Surveys were triggered based on the attorneys' appointment as legal counsel and continued at approximately six-month intervals thereafter. In Washington State, attorneys were asked to complete additional milestone surveys when children experienced certain legal or service milestones, such as dispositional order, termination of parental rights order, and exit from substitute care.

The evaluation of attorney behavior change was based on attorney self-reports. Because attorneys report on their own activities, these data may have been subject to recall or social desirability bias. While problems relating to recall are probably equally distributed among treatment and control attorneys, it is possible that treatment attorneys may have overstated their activities on measures they knew were expectations of the Best Practice Model.

A total of 3,787 survey records of the randomly selected cases associated with 198 attorneys were used in the analysis. Survey data collection operated for more than a

FINDINGS OF THE EVALUATION

Table 10.2 Attorneys by Number of Surveys Completed

		# of Attorneys			% of Attorneys		
		Treat.	Control	Total	Treat.	Control	Total
GA	1-3 surveys	8	14	22	18%	30%	24%
	4-10 surveys	16	18	34	36%	38%	37%
	11-25 surveys	17	11	28	39%	23%	31%
	26+ surveys	3	4	7	7%	9%	8%
GA Total		44	47	91	100%	100%	100%
		Treat.	Control	Total	Treat.	Control	Total
WA	1-3 surveys	2	6	8	4%	13%	8%
	4-10 surveys	15	4	19	26%	9%	18%
	11-25 surveys	11	10	21	19%	22%	20%
	26+ surveys	29	26	55	51%	57%	53%
WA Total		57	46	103	100%	100%	100%

year longer in Washington State than in Georgia, so more surveys were completed by Washington attorneys (2,840) than by Georgia attorneys (947).

Because of variation in the number of cases that these child representatives served during this period, the number of surveys completed by each attorney also varied (Table 10.2). Fewer Washington State attorneys completed only a small number of surveys because survey data collection started a year earlier.

> Each distribution of survey responses was analyzed for three types of survey groups:
>
> - All surveys regardless of type
> - Assignment survey only
> - Review surveys only

Forty-nine attorney opinions and behaviors were analyzed with child-specific surveys. Each question was analyzed over all survey types and separately for assignment surveys and review surveys. In addition, similar composites of common response types used in the analyses for Chapter 9 were created and analyzed. To reduce the burdens on some attorneys, not every assignment generated a survey. For these attorneys, the models contained adjustments to reflect the total number of these attorneys' cases.[2]

---

2. Selected cases were weighted based on the inverse of the probability of being selected for a survey within each attorney.

Table 10.3 Odds Ratio (OR): Treatment effect on times attorney met in person, spoke on the phone, e-mailed, or texted with...

	Georgia			Washington		
	All Surveys	Assignment	Review	All Surveys	Assignment	Review
Type of Individual	OR	OR	OR	OR	OR	OR
Biological parent or original caregiver				1.48†	1.16	1.84†
Mother	1.45	1.18	2.16†			
Father	1.62*	1.89**	1.06			
Siblings				0.90	0.97	0.67
Other individuals related to this child (e.g., grandparent)	1.36	1.40	1.20	1.27	1.13	1.61
Foster parent or substitute caregiver	1.69*	1.92*	1.64	1.59*	1.62**	1.92*
Caseworker(s)	1.80*	1.64	1.97	1.34	1.18	1.51
Attorneys	1.25	0.98	2.32*			
Attorney for this child's parent's				1.16	0.89	1.70
Other attorneys or legal professionals				1.64†	1.19	3.22*
CASA	1.46	1.82	1.95†	1.40†	1.09	1.43
Teacher or other education professional	1.47*	Δ	2.36	1.23	1.41	1.05

** p-value < 0.01, * p-value < 0.05, † p-value < 0.1, Δ Not estimable.

Attorney behavior results are grouped in four domains: questions relating to the frequency of contact with individuals related to the case (see Tables 10.3 and 10.4), time spent on selected activities (see Tables 10.5 and 10.6), frequency of occurrence of certain events (see Table 10.7), and relationship and advocacy activities (see Table 10.8). The analysis of the surveys showed some differences between treatment and control attorneys across all of these domains. Not every question was asked in each state, and some questions were asked differently. In these cases, the associated boxes are blank.

Table 10.4 Average Scales: Treatment effect (Beta or B) on times attorney met in person, spoken on the phone, e-mailed, or texted with...

	Georgia			Washington		
	All Surveys	Assignment	Review	All Surveys	Assignment	Review
Average Scales	B	B	B	B	B	B
Family Members	0.12*	0.09	0.12	0.04	0.00	0.05
Proximate Collaterals [a]	0.22*	0.19†	0.28*	0.17†	0.05	0.31
Distal Collaterals [b]	0.06	0.10	0.08	0.06	0.02	0.08

** p-value < 0.01, * p-value < 0.05, † p-value < 0.1, Δ Not estimable.
[a] Includes caseworkers, other attorneys, and foster parents.
[b] Includes teachers, CASA, and health professionals, and other service providers.

10.4 Treatment Attorneys Changed Their Behavior

The following tables and summaries demonstrate that lawyers receiving the Six Core Skills Intervention changed their approach to child representation in the hypothesized direction.

Georgia treatment attorneys were more likely to communicate with fathers near the time of assignment and were more likely to communicate with mothers at the time of review. More communication occurred with proximate collaterals at all survey points. Differences were also observed for contact with CASA at review. Across all surveys, the differences observed between the treatment and control attorneys were communication with fathers, foster parents, and caseworkers, and teacher or other education professional.

Washington treatment attorneys were more likely to communicate with a biological parent or original caregiver, foster parent or substitute caregiver, other legal professionals and CASA across all surveys. More communication occurred with proximate collaterals at all survey points. In addition, differences were also observed for contact with other legal professionals at review. The largest differences observed between the treatment and control attorneys were for communication with foster parent or substitute caregiver at the time of assignment.

Georgia treatment attorneys responded in the hypothesized direction in most of the activity measures. The QIC intervention seems to have had the strongest impact on consulting or negotiating with other parties to the case and conducting interviews or reviewing interview notes across all surveys. Differences were also observed for developing the theory of the case and assessing child's safety with respect to current placement. In addition, treatment attorneys were more likely to review the child's case plan and third-party records; perform more drafting and filing pleadings, motions, and

Table 10.5 Odds Ratio (OR): Treatment effect on time spent involved in the following activities.

	Georgia			Washington		
	All Surveys	Assignment	Review	All Surveys	Assignment	Review
Activity	OR	OR	OR	OR	OR	OR
Developing the theory of the case	2.34*	2.64†	2.28	1.90**	2.1**	2.81*
Legal research	2.38	2.35	2.89	0.98	1.08	1.28
Consulting or negotiating with other parties to the case	2.72**	2.85*	2.14†	1.19	0.85	1.76
Obtaining / reviewing this child's court file	1.13	0.93	1.21	0.79	0.80	0.85
Obtaining / reviewing third-party records	1.72†	1.40	2.09			
Reviewing this child's school records				0.88	1.00	0.97
Reviewing this child's medical records or assessments				1.07	1.17	1.18
Reviewing other evaluations and assessments				0.96	0.86	1.22
Conducting interviews or reviewing interview notes	2.55**	2.54**	2.64†	0.91	0.83	1.20
Drafting and filing pleadings, motions, and court orders	2.18	1.99	3.24*			
Assessing this child's safety with respect to removal or return to their home of origin	1.43	1.49*	1.56	1.35	1.20	1.70
Reassessing child's safety with respect to home of the original care taker				1.19	0.96	1.92
Assessing this child's safety with respect to current placement	1.69*	1.46†	3.14**	1.01	0.92	1.41
Reassessing this child's safety with respect to current placement				1.33	0.90	1.87†
Reviewing, assessing or seeking to influence this child's case plan	1.87†	2.11*	1.58	1.14	0.94	1.69

** p-value < 0.01, * p-value < 0.05, † p-value < 0.1, Δ Not estimable

FINDINGS OF THE EVALUATION

Table 10.6 Average Scales: Treatment effect on time spent involved in the following activities in furtherance of this child's case

	Georgia			Washington		
	All Surveys	Assignment	Review	All Surveys	Assignment	Review
Average Scales	B	B	B	B	B	B
Legal Case Preparation [a]	0.25*	0.24†	0.21	0.03	0.00	0.14
Investigation & Document Review [b]	0.25*	0.21*	0.29†	−0.04	−0.06	0.05

** p-value < 0.01, * p-value < 0.05, † p-value < 0.1, Δ Not estimable.
[a] Includes developing strategy of the case, consultation and negotiation, drafting pleadings and other court documents, reviewing court file, and seeking to influence child's case plan.
[b] Includes third-party record review, witness interviews, and assessing safety.

Table 10.7 Odds Ratio (OR): Treatment effect on whether attorney participated in the following events since the last survey

	Georgia			Washington		
	All Surveys	Assignment	Review	All Surveys	Assignment	Review
Event	OR	OR	OR	OR	OR	OR
Mediation	0.70	1.10	3.19	1.81	1.48	Δ
Family team or treatment team meeting	2.83*	Δ	1.32	1.27	0.81	2.08**
Other judicial, administrative, or educational proceedings	1.35	2.00	0.90	0.81	0.81	0.87
Hearing on placement change				0.91	0.89	1.14
Pre-trial hearing/ settlement conference	1.85	2.88*	1.29			
Motion hearing (non-reunification, placement change, etc.)	0.98	Δ	1.11	1.17	0.90	1.78*

** p-value < 0.01, * p-value < 0.05, † p-value < 0.1, Δ Not estimable.

court orders for treatment attorneys at the time of review; and assessing the child's safety with respect to removal or return to their home of origin right after the time of assignment.

In Washington State, although there were not many statistically significant findings in time spent on various activities, the robust difference in time spent developing a

Table 10.8 Odds Ratio (OR): Treatment effect on relationship and advocacy activities

	Georgia			Washington		
	All Surveys	Assignment	Review	All Surveys	Assignment	Review
Activity	OR	OR	OR	OR	OR	OR
Number of times spoken, emailed or text with child	2.47†	2.19†	3.13*	1.03	0.94	1.26
Number of times met in person with child	2.18*	2.69*	1.68	1.04	1.04	1.31
Met child in their home or placement	1.87	1.26	2.56†	1.17	1.18	1.50
Have you made any efforts to initiate a non-adversarial case resolution process	1.84	2.24	2.06	2.09*	1.62	2.94*
Did you argue for, or make other concerted efforts to change, the array of services provided to this child	2.35*	2.32*	2.62†	1.22	1.26	1.31
Did you argue for, or make other concerted efforts to change, the array of services to this child's family	2.15*	2.34*	2.57*	1.36	1.29	1.64
Quality of relationship with child	1.46	1.28	1.87	1.04	1.09	1.04
Your level of understanding of child's goals and objectives	1.61	1.61	2.65	0.79	0.75	0.81
Your advocacy agreed with child's wishes				0.60†	0.70	0.73

** p-value < 0.01, * p-value < 0.05, † p-value < 0.1, Δ Not estimable.

theory of the case was notable. It showed that Washington treatment attorneys were more likely to spend time developing the case theory at different points of the surveys. At the time of review, treatment attorneys were also more likely to spend time reassessing their client's safety with respect to the placement.

Georgia treatment attorneys participated more in family team or treatment team meetings across all surveys, and attended more pretrial hearing/settlement conferences near the time of assignment.

Washington State treatment attorneys participated more in family team meetings at the time of review. Also at the time of review, a difference was observed in motion hearings in the hypothesized direction.

Georgia treatment attorneys were more likely to speak, e-mail or text the child client, and meet in person with the child at all survey points than control attorneys. Differences were also observed for arguing for or making other concerted efforts to change, the array of services provided to the child and the child's family in the hypothesized direction. It was also shown at the time of review that Georgia treatment attorneys were more likely to meet the child outside of the court.

In comparison to control attorneys, Washington treatment attorneys initiated non-adversarial case resolution process more frequently both across all surveys and at review. However, their advocacy was less likely to agree with the child's wishes.

There were no statistically significant differences in either state between treatment and control attorneys' assessment of the degree to which dispositional orders agreed with the goals of the child.

10.5 Child-Level Outcomes

10.5.1 Each Child Had an Attorney

To be included in the child outcome sample, a child must have had a treatment or control attorney assigned to represent them at some point prior to leaving out-of-home care. Every child in the out-of-home care sample was represented by an attorney at some point. (Chapter 7 shows the distribution of the timing of an assignment to an attorney.) Using this sample, the evaluation addressed the question of whether children assigned to attorneys who received the intervention experienced differences in permanency outcomes, rates of kinship placement, and rates of movement within one year of assignment compared to children assigned to control attorneys.

> Each child in the outcome analyses was represented by either a treatment or control attorney. All children had an attorney, so the results do NOT speak to the question of impact of having or not having an attorney.

As with the attorney surveys, the number of children represented by each attorney varied. The overall distributions of attorneys by the number of represented children from the two states were similar—more concentrated in the middle and lower at the two ends (Table 10.9). Approximately 61% of the Georgia attorneys represented fewer than 11 children during the study while a smaller percentage 54% of the Washington State attorneys were in the same category. When looking at the numbers by treatment and control status, the distributions in Washington State were more or less equivalent between the two groups, which was not the case in Georgia. In Georgia, a much lower percentage of treatment attorneys represented 11 or fewer children than control

Table 10.9 Attorneys by Count of Number of Children Represented with Associated Out-of-Home Care Placement

		# of Attorneys			% of Attorneys		
		Treat.	Control	Total	Treat.	Control	Total
GA	1–3 children	10	20	30	16%	27%	22%
	4–10 children	20	34	54	32%	45%	39%
	11–25 children	22	11	33	35%	15%	24%
	26+ children	10	10	20	16%	13%	15%
GA Total		62	75	137	100%	100%	100%
		Treat.	Control	Total	Treat.	Control	Total
WA	1–3 children	11	12	23	19%	22%	20%
	4–10 children	21	18	39	36%	33%	34%
	11–25 children	16	15	31	27%	27%	27%
	26+ Children	11	10	21	19%	18%	18%
WA Total		59	55	114	100%	100%	100%

attorneys over the course of the study, while a significantly higher percentage of attorneys represented 11 or more children.

10.5.2 Placement Moves and Placement with Kin

Among Georgia children studied, 17 percent of children were placed with kin at placement or as the next placement after assignment to a treatment or control attorney. Among Washington children studied, 17 percent of children were placed with kin at or as the next placement after assignment to a treatment or control attorney. Among Georgia children studied, 61 percent of children did not experience a placement move within a year after assignment to a treatment or control attorney (or prior to exiting care, whichever came first). Among Washington children studied, 69 percent of children did not experience a placement move within a year after assignment to a treatment or control attorney (or prior to exiting care, whichever came first).

Children represented by treatment and control attorneys did not appear to have different experiences of placement moves or placement with kin. Effects were in the expected, positive direction with the exception of the likelihood of placement with kin associated with treatment attorneys in Washington State. There, the model showed that treatment attorneys were associated with a lower likelihood of placement with kin, though the result was not statistically significant.

Table 10.10 Estimated Hazard Ratios of Placement with Kin and Movement

State	Outcome	H.R.	Sig.
Washington	Placement with kin	0.75	0.18
	No placement move within 1 year of assignment	1.21	0.19
Georgia	Placement with kin	1.05	0.84
	No placement move within 1 year of assignment	1.32	0.14

H.R. = Hazard ratio. For kinship analysis, hazard ratio of greater than 1 indicates greater likelihood of placement with kin. For movement analysis, hazard ratio of greater than 1 indicates greater likelihood of a stable placement (no movement).
Sig = Statistical significance level.

10.5.3 Measuring Permanency Outcomes

A child's experience of permanency after out-of-home care placement has two dimensions: whether the child leaves care to a permanent family and how long the child spends in out-of-home care placement before that happens. Two of the primary goals of the child welfare system are to *maximize* the frequency with which children leave out-of-home placement to a permanent family (as opposed to aging out or running away, for example) and *minimize* how long that takes. Once all children in the group being summarized have left care, the distribution of both of these dimensions can be summarized and compared for groups of children served. All else being equal, groups of children for whom permanent exits are more prevalent and whose time in substitute care is less are assumed to reflect "better" outcomes.

A common feature of this type of analysis is that the experiences of some subjects are still in progress at the time observation ends. That is, neither exit type (to a permanent family or not) nor the total time in care are known for all children. For example, at the end of the observation period covered by this evaluation (March 31, 2015), about half of the children represented were still in care as of March 31, 2015 (49% in Georgia and 52% in Washington State; See Table 10.8). Chapter 7, Section *Observation Period for Out-of-Home Placement Impacts*, explains that observation period for out-of-home care ranged from 5 months to 3 years. In order to properly address this issue, a class of statistical models know as hazard models were employed.[3]

Variations in the timing of attorney assignment also presented an additional analytic wrinkle. Groups of children who are early in their placement experience are more likely to exit to reunification and to do so relatively quickly. Groups of children who have been in care longer are more likely to exit to adoption than groups of children who

---

3. For the permanency outcomes, discrete time hazard models were used, with a binary dependent variable indicating whether the child had achieved permanency. The discrete time hazard model accommodated differences in the timing of assignment to an attorney.

Table 10.11 Exit Status from Out-of-Home Care by Permanent and Other Exit Types for All Assignments to Project Attorneys (Observed through March 31, 2015).

	Georgia		Washington	
Exit Type	#	%	#	%
Exit to family/relative	652	37%	451	25%
Guardianship guar	90	5%	51	3%
Adoption	64	4%	225	13%
All Permanency Exits	806	45%	727	41%
Other Exits	104	6%	134	8%
Still in care on 3/31/2015	867	49%	926	52%
Total	1,777	100%	1,787	100%

have recently entered care. This is apparent in the Washington State sample, where adoption exits represented 13 percent of observed exits. This reflects the fact that more children who had been in care longer were assigned attorneys in Washington State than in Georgia. As described in Chapter 7, almost three-quarters of appointments in Georgia were made before or within a month of placement (74%). Of children in the Washington sample, 42 percent were appointed before or within a month of placement. On the other end of the distribution, 14 percent of the Georgia and 35 percent of the Washington sample had an attorney appointed after at least a year in placement.

To fully address the challenges of incomplete observation and variation in attorney assignment, the permanency analysis was done using three different models. The first analysis evaluated the average treatment effect on permanency to date for the complete sample, including all assignment timings. This model represents a strong test of impact, as the differences between treatment and control attorneys on the timing of permanency would have to show up in a variety of situations, both early in the child's out-of-home placement and later on, where achieving permanency may be more complex for a variety of reasons, such as child characteristics, ongoing family issues, or the availability of adoptive homes. The results of this model are shown in Table 10.11 as Model 1 and in the first bar of Figure 10.1. In both states, no significant differences in permanency between treatment or control group attorneys were observed, even though the effects were positive and in the expected direction.

The second model introduced the distinctions of both assignment timing as well as early vs. later permanency. The second model evaluated the interaction between the treatment effect and the likelihood of permanency within six months and the interaction between the treatment effect and the likelihood of permanency after six months.

FINDINGS OF THE EVALUATION

Figure 10.1 Percent Difference in Hazard of Exit to Permanence between QIC and Control Groups by State and Observation Period

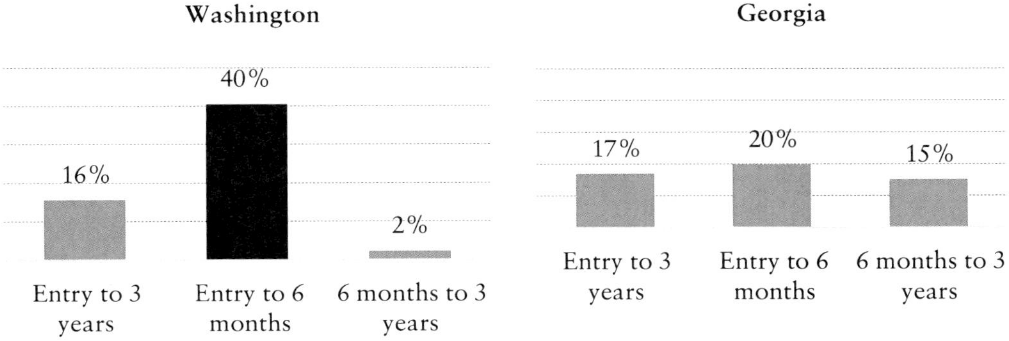

Washington

- Entry to 3 years: 16%
- Entry to 6 months: 40%
- 6 months to 3 years: 2%

Georgia

- Entry to 3 years: 17%
- Entry to 6 months: 20%
- 6 months to 3 years: 15%

Note: Black column represents statistically significant difference.

This approach serves two purposes. For children who were assigned an attorney within 6 months, almost all children's outcomes could be observed within 6 months of placement. Thus, the permanency findings can speak to the impact of treatment or control attorney assignment observable within six months for almost all children. The second purpose is to allow a separate evaluation of the impact of the treatment on early vs. later permanency.

The distinction in the second model also had the effect of creating a sample in the Washington State site that reflected both early appointment (within six months) and older children coming into care. In the Washington sample, 78% of children who were appointed counsel within six months were *over* age 12. As shown in Figure 5 in Chapter 7, the opposite was true for the later appointment group in Washington and both the early and late appointment groups in Georgia: Between 73 and 83 percent of these children were *under* age 12. By virtue of Washington State's law favoring the appointment of client-directed attorneys to children age 12 and over, the evaluation had a sample with which to evaluate the impact of the QIC intervention that was of special interest to the field: mostly older children, appointed an attorney early in their out-of-home placement experience, who received client-directed representation.

10.6 Improved Permanency Outcomes

The results of the two parts of the second model are shown in Table 10.11 as Model 2 and in the second and third bars of Figure 10.1. Note the statistically significant finding: *The group of children assigned a treatment attorney in Washington State were 40 percent more likely to experience permanency within six months of placement than the group of children represented by control group attorneys.* Although it did not rise to the level of statistical significance, the exit to permanency rate for *all* Washington children represented by a treatment attorney was 16% better than that of the control group.

Table 10.12 Estimated Hazard Ratios of Exit to Permanence for Children Represented by QIC vs. Control Group Attorneys

State	Observation Period	H.R.	Sig.
Washington	Model 1: First 3 years after entry to care	1.16	0.2994
	Model 2: First 6 months after entry to care	1.40	0.0318*
	Model 2: 6 months to 3 years after entry to care	1.02	0.8861
Georgia	Model 1: First 3 years after entry to care	1.17	0.2027
	Model 2: First 6 months after entry to care	1.20	0.1980
	Model 2: 6 months to 3 years after entry to care	1.15	0.2808

H.R. = Hazard ratio. Hazard ratio of greater than 1 indicates faster permanency during observation period.
Sig = Statistical significance level.

In Georgia, the likelihood of permanency was greater for the treatment group, +17% from entry to 3 years (+20% for the within 6 months of placement period.) Although the permanency effect was positive in Georgia, it did not reach statistical significance.

In both states, there were no significant differences in permanency between treatment or control group attorneys for when the attorney was assigned after six months, though the effects were positive and in the expected direction. For this group, the observation period is incomplete for many children, though for some children, the observation period was as long as three years.

CHAPTER 11
Reflections on QIC Empirical Findings

Abstract
What do these findings mean in the context of this study? What are the lessons learned going forward? What insights do the data provide for the practitioner? What further questions do the data raise for future research and policy development?

11.1 QIC Field Experiment Limitations

There are a couple of other things to keep in mind in discussing the QIC data. First, the QIC intervention changed no other part of the child welfare system, except for encouraging the lawyers to adopt the Six Core Skills. The child welfare agency practices, the local services available and the functioning of the court all remained unchanged. Participation of the lawyers themselves was voluntary. Even though the QIC lawyers were paid a modest stipend for data reporting, the amount and manner of compensation for representing a child was not changed. The only element of the local child welfare system that was changed in this field experiment is the training and encouragement received by the QIC attorneys.

Second, attorney behavior measures are based on attorney self-reports and limited to aspects of behavior that could be quantified based on survey questions. Not everything that counts can be counted. That is, there could be QIC effects that are not detected. We cannot measure the specific ways in which attorneys interacted with children. Nor can we measure if a child feels more engaged or respected because of his or her attorney's attentiveness or if a child feels less anxious because of the lawyer's counseling and attention. A child comfortable and safe in the relationship with the lawyer may disclose personal history, feelings and wishes more clearly and candidly, thus enhancing the attorney's legal advocacy.

In addition, our data does not measure quality of the behaviors that are counted. There may be the same number of contacts with other case participants, but the QIC lawyers are more focused and qualitatively better. QIC attorneys may have contacted the child just as many times as they would prior to our intervention but are doing it better as a result of the intervention.

Similarly, the statistical models analyze average impact of the QIC intervention so that the fact that an average difference is not found does not mean that some *individual* QIC attorneys within a jurisdiction did not change their practice in ways that benefitted their clients as a result of the QIC intervention. Maybe there were other qualitative benefits realized by children because of the robust level of attorney engagement that could not be measured.

With respect to child welfare outcomes, these data only report what is available through existing administrative data, which were limited to permanency and other substitute care outcomes. There are other outcomes affected by the QIC attorneys that we cannot measure. For instance, the data revealed that for both experimental and control groups the advocacy of children's lawyers was usually in agreement with the recommendations of the public child welfare agency.

Is that because all the lawyers are simply compliant and generally go along with the agency recommendations without question? Or is it because a high level of agreement was a product of more effective negotiation and problem solving initiated by the child's lawyer upstream of the dispositional hearing. Our data would not detect those qualitative dynamics.

11.2 Procedural Justice as an Outcome

Children's legal interests are seriously implicated in child protection proceedings. A child may be at risk of harm from their parent or other caregiver and depending upon effective government intervention to protect them. On the other hand, children face an invasion of their personal liberty under the supervision of the state or when physically in state custody. Children's legal interests, including fundamental constitutional rights, remain at risk and require and deserve procedural justice as part of due process fairness.

Due process requires that their interests and wishes be presented and advocated before the court. When adults face a significant challenge to liberty from the government, they get a lawyer to represent them and protect their interests. Adults facing loss of liberty generally get counsel whether or not the lawyer affects the ultimate outcome. Lawyers representing persons accused of crime are not evaluated on the basis of whether their legal advocacy actually achieves the outcomes their client wants. And the lawyers are certainly not evaluated on whether their representation achieves the interests of the state or saves the state money. Due process and procedural justice is considered a value in and of itself.

There is something troubling about evaluating lawyers based on outcomes desired by the state. Protecting a child's liberty interest should be a value in and of itself. Perhaps outcomes like permanency, placement stability and placement with kin are not the appropriate criteria for evaluating effective representation of children?

Nonetheless the QIC hypotheses are that improved representation of children would benefit not only the children's experience with the legal process but also the ability of the system to deliver desirable outcomes for each child. We hypothesize that lawyers practicing according to the QIC Best Practice Model will indeed result in more carefully calibrated interventions into the family and more efficient handling of cases thus saving the government money enough to justify enhancing legal representation.

The benefits of good representation of the child exist regardless of whether it saves money or otherwise benefits the state. The child at risk of being separated from his or her family by the government certainly deserves and requires a competent lawyer to protect his or her interests. Legal representation is required as a matter of principle and as a matter of law—any benefits to the system are bonus points.

11.3 Lawyers Implemented the QIC Six Core Skills

Does the QIC Best Practice Model, as distilled into the Six Core Skills improve the *process* of legal representation and the *outcomes* for children? The answer is a qualified "yes." The approach worked to change practice and to some modest extent the approach affected outcomes. Importantly, it appears that, among other things, the model resulted in greater contact with the child and increased communications with the other players, which has important implications for procedural justice, i.e., being heard and being treated fairly. Improved communication with others also suggests more careful and deliberate collective decision-making. The QIC lawyers in both states were also more actively involved in conflict resolution and negotiation activities and showed a commitment to moving the case forward.

11.3.1 Enter the Child's World

A principal hypothesis of the QIC study is that attorneys trained in the Six Core Skills would be more attentive to the child client, listen more carefully and frame their advocacy more in keeping with the child's needs and wishes. The consequences of "entering the child world" are relevant not only to possible outcome improvements, but also to the important procedural justice aspects. Any litigant faced with a liberty deprivation at the hands of the state has a due process interest in having their voice and interests fully advocated. We anticipated that "entering the child's world" would lead both the client-directed lawyer and best interests lawyer to better accommodate the child wishes and enhance procedural justice for the child. The data support this expectation.

By significant margins, Georgia QIC lawyers spoke to, emailed and texted their child client more than the control and met more often in person with the child throughout the court process. The Georgia QIC lawyers were also more likely to meet the child outside of the court. (Chapter 10, Table 8) When the Georgia lawyers assessed the effect and importance of their relationship with the child on their advocacy, all measures were in the hypothesized direction. That is, the Georgia QIC lawyers were more likely to have engaged with the child.

On the other hand, the Georgia data does not reflect that the Georgia QIC lawyers advocated for the *child's wishes* any more than the Georgia control attorneys did. Our hypothesis that QIC lawyers would defer more to the child's wishes, even in a mostly best interests state as Georgia was at the time of the study, was not borne out. The lack of difference could be attributed to the fact that the child clients in Georgia were very young, average age is 6. Or perhaps the best interest culture was so ingrained it was not changed? This is interesting because Georgia QIC lawyers changed their behaviors in other domains.

Washington QIC lawyers engagement with the child was only slightly stronger than the control group, and not significantly so. We expected trained lawyers would be more likely to understand, appreciate, and advocate for the child's wishes. There may have been qualitative improvements, but we found no measurable differences in that direction.

Many factors could explain the relative lack of difference in child engagement in Washington despite the emphasis of child engagement in the QIC training. Primary is that Washington is a client-directed state and all attorneys are likely accustomed to taking direction from the child client—as they would from an adult. Since the over-all Washington practice culture was client-directed, the community culture likely reflects and supports that position already. Also the Washington children were older (average age 11, versus 6 in Georgia) so that both treatment and control lawyers might also have an easier time engaging with each child.

In fact, not only did the Washington State QIC lawyers not advocate more for the child's wishes, our findings show that the trained Washington lawyers were actually *less* likely to advocate for the child's wishes than the control group. Two related Washington findings are somewhat surprising on this point.

When asked what the attorney's level of understanding of the child's goals and objectives of the case were, the QIC experimental attorneys rated their understanding lower than the control attorneys, though the result was not statistically significant. (Chapter 10, Table 8) Similarly in response to the question: "To what extent has your advocacy in court on behalf of this child agreed with this child's expressed interests?" Washington QIC attorneys reported their advocacy was *less likely to agree with the child's wishes* than the control group. By a significant margin (meaning that the training in Six Core

Skills was a causal factor) attorneys in this client-directed state were less likely to be client-directed. This is unexpected. What would make the QIC attorneys less likely to advocate for the child's expressed interests in this client directed state?

Perhaps as a result of the QIC training, lawyers "entering the child's world" were more likely to understand the varied cognitive and emotional capacity of children at different ages and stages of maturity and the effects of trauma on intellectual functioning and judgment. An attorney more knowledgeable in child psychology may be less likely to overlook signs of trauma and impact on judgment. A properly trained lawyer might be better able to appraise the competence of the child client accurately and less likely to overrate the child's understanding of the situation. Thus the trained lawyers may be less willing to adopt without questioning a child's stated wishes.

Another possible explanation is that because the QIC attorneys better understood the complexity of these situations, perhaps the QIC lawyers counseled the child to a different position than the one the child started out with. Our data would not pick up the extent to which a lawyer faced a child's stated desire, but counseled them to a somewhat different formal position for purposes of the litigation.

Another explanation might be that the data would not discern the extent to which control lawyers might have modified the advocacy goals on their own? Maybe the control lawyers interpreted the client-directed responsibility rather flexibly so that "robotic allegiance" to the child's stated wishes is not actually required. The QIC lawyers, being better trained in child development, may be more familiar with the developmental limitations of children, more mindful that they are accommodating to those limitations, and more willing to report it on their surveys.

11.3.2 Service Advocacy

QIC attorneys were urged to pay attention to services for the child *and* the child's family. We expected a boost in advocating for services for the child as well as the family, something that is generally in the child's interests but not always recognized by child's lawyers. Georgia QIC lawyers meet that expectation. (Chapter 10, Table 8) They were significantly more likely to advocate for services for the child *and* services for the family. But Washington lawyers scored no significant differences on either of these measures, although the findings trend in the expected direction. (Chapter 10, Table 8) Perhaps *all* Washington lawyers, in a relatively unambiguous client-directed role with older youth able to communicate their needs and wishes, are already paying close attention to services for their child client? Thus there might not be "room to grow" on this measure. Also, perhaps because Washington lawyers were more likely to enter a case mid-stream, that is, after the initial intervention because of a child reaching age 12, the assessment and case plan were already set and there was less opportunity to affect it at that stage?

11.3.3 Improved Communication with All Players

The QIC trained lawyers *communicated significantly more* with various players, most notably with foster parents and other caregivers and other attorneys in the review stage. Each of the Six Core Skills requires more communication and more contacts with more players. The Six Core Skills training encouraged QIC lawyers to understand the child's developmental needs and consider the effects of child trauma.

We asked them to advocate for a thorough safety assessment to prevent unnecessary or unnecessarily long placement, assess the family carefully, then advocate for services needed by the child and family, and that they develop a cogent theory of the case. The data show that QIC attorneys in both states did as we asked. The data support a conclusion that the QIC model and training worked to increase the amount of interaction among the principal players. This finding supports the goal of procedural justice in that the active lawyer is more likely to communicate (and realize) the needs and interests of the child.

Is an increase in communication a positive thing by itself? Most people would say so and would expect that increased communication would improve the handling of the child welfare case, even irrespective of whether the increased communication is linked to the state's preferred case outcomes. Communication with other players may reflect a more careful investigation and assessment of the case, more focus on problem-solving and conflict resolution, more engagement between lawyer and child, and more exchange of views among the principles - the attorneys, caseworkers, parents and other caregivers. An increase in communication may reflect a more careful decision-making in the child welfare process—an overall goal of the whole system. It also reflects attention to the due process interests of the child.

11.3.4 Time Spent

The QIC lawyers spent their time differently from the control group at significant levels doing tasks that reflect the Six Core Skills training. The Georgia lawyers really responded strongly. They spent more time influencing the case plan, developing a theory of the case, negotiating with other parties, and conducting interviews or reviewing notes. (Table 5) Similarly, at quite robust statistical levels, Washington State QIC lawyers were more likely to spend time developing a theory of the case and time reassessing child's safety in the current placement. These are very important to the progress of a child's case and to the due process goal of treating a child fairly when personal liberty rights are at stake.

The differences in time spent are also notable because the trained QIC lawyers did not receive additional compensation or additional hours. They simply chose to spend what time they had in these ways.

11.3.5 Promoting Case Resolution

Both Washington and Georgia experimental (QIC) attorneys participated more in family team meetings. There are also significant differences in pre-trial hearing/settlement conferences for Georgia and motion hearings in Washington. In Washington QIC attorneys are more likely to initiate non-adversarial case resolution (NACR) processes. The QIC lawyers seem to be pressing for movement on cases and seem more likely to seek non-adversarial problem-solving approaches.

11.4 Child Outcomes

Our study revealed differences in rates of achieving permanency between the experimental and control groups. That is, children represented by the trained QIC attorneys tended to exit care sooner that the controls. In both states the experimental effects were in the hypothesized direction—that is tending toward quicker exits from care by children represented by the QIC lawyers. (Table 11) Note the *statistically significant* outcome finding:

Children represented by treatment attorneys in Washington State were 40% more likely to experience permanency within six months of placement than children represented by control attorneys. Even though QIC attorneys achieved quicker permanency at the beginning of a case, there was no QIC advantage discernable once the placement extended beyond six months. Similarly, where a lawyer was appointed for a child who had been in care for some period of time prior to the lawyer appointment there is no detectable advantage to the QIC attorneys. Thus the big impact of the QIC trained lawyers appears to be at the beginning of the case, rather than at the beginning of the lawyer appointment.

In Georgia, the likelihood of permanency was also greater for the treatment group, +17% from entry to 3 years (+20% for the within 6 months of placement period.) Although the permanency effect was positive in Georgia, it did not reach statistical significance.

What explains the QIC lawyer impact early in a case and not later? It could be that an attorney performing well in the role (versus one performing less well) can reduce the time in placement for children whose family issues can be resolved *relatively quickly*, but for more complicated situations associated with longer placements, the influence of the well-trained attorney on outcomes is not detectable.

There are so many independent variables and independent players in these cases that the attorney's ability to influence the actual case outcome on longer term cases may be limited. Once a case is assessed and once the "easy wins" are identified and addressed, the longer-term cases require sustained attention from many other professionals and the court itself. Some cases may fall into a pattern where is hard to accelerate the rehabilitative or long term planning process—for example, substance abuse treatment, mental health diagnosis and treatment, or sexual abuse cases.

The inter-agency and bureaucratic complexity of the longer case may make it harder for a single player to affect the outcome. Once the child is safe and a proper assessment and case plan is in place, the attorney's ability to influence the result may be limited—even when he or she practices according to a Best Practice Model. It may be that when we compare QIC-trained attorneys to business-as-usual attorneys there is not a huge incremental difference in longer-term case outcome because so many other professionals and the court itself are engaged and working toward a similar outcome.

11.5 Community of Practice

Formal and informal "learning communities" offer one approach to building and enhancing a sophisticated child representation workforce. Children's lawyers are often independent and somewhat isolated from one another. The QIC attorneys expressed an appetite for learning from experts and from each other about child representation. There are some lessons learned from the QIC experience that may be helpful to states interested in encouraging a community of practice among their child welfare lawyers or for researchers who wish to replicate a study such as this one. The QIC data also found an impressive willingness of attorneys to assist others in their child representation. Despite the fact that most attorneys were solo practitioners, more than 80% said that individuals were often or almost always available to discuss cases with them.

Participation rates by the QIC lawyers demonstrate that when offered the opportunity to receive more specialized training and participate in a community of child lawyers, they did so. There seems to be an appetite among the lawyers for gaining more skills and improving their practice. They were receptive to learning new methods and adopted new approaches even where there was no increase in compensation or time available and even when their approaches might be inconsistent with the general way cases might be handled in their jurisdiction. They seem to be saying: "Tell me what good child representation is and I will do it." The hunger and receptiveness of the attorneys has lessons for those training and recruiting child's attorneys. The latent motivation among attorneys may be a force to build on and harness for future efforts.

In the QIC experience there are some interesting state-to-state variations in participation. Nearly all the treatment attorneys from both states attended the two-day QIC Best Practice Model training and rated it highly. But even though attorneys from both Georgia and Washington State participated reasonably well in the follow-up pod and coaching sessions, there was still considerable differences between the two states. Pods and coaching were implemented with greater fidelity to the Six Core Skills model in Washington State than in Georgia. All Washington pod meetings were done in person and coaching sessions in Washington followed a consistent format focused on the Six Core Skills. More than three-quarters of the Washington State lawyers participated in full, which is a high level of commitment for such a complicated and long lasting project. The Washington State pods meetings were all live; they decided not to use the option of a virtual meeting. As reported above, not only was the attendance quite robust but the participant reviews were very positive.

On the other hand, while Georgia lawyers engagement with the pod meetings and coaching was considerably less. After a disappointing attendance in the first pod meeting it was decided to use a virtual alternative for the remaining sessions. It turns out that the best-attended session was the very first, in-person session. One explanation for the difference in attorney engagement may be the fact that the Georgia sessions were virtual, not live, and so lacked some of the camaraderie and community building that might result from regular in person meetings.

Another explanation for the difference in engagement may lie in how the lawyers were recruited into the project. Maybe lawyers just like to be asked? Each Washington attorney was personally enrolled and signed an individual agreement whereas Georgia judges pledged that the attorneys from their jurisdiction would participate and the lawyers were never asked individually. Georgia lawyers never complained about the way they were "delivered" into the project and, as we discuss below, they embraced the Six Core Skills approach quite impressively. The data show that the GA attorney participation was in fact voluntary. There was no forced participation or any consequences for failing to participate. There is no evidence that judges ever compelled an attorney to participate. So the dynamic at work may not be that the Georgia approach was particularly *negative* but rather that obtaining a personal and individual commitment from each Washington lawyer was a *positive,* resulting in greater commitment to the project. In Washington State there were 118 separate conversations (one with each participating lawyer) about the possible state and national benefits of the study and how each lawyer's involvement was critical. The approach showed respect and elicited their personal commitment. In retrospect, that might have been a better approach in Georgia, even though it would have taken more time and energy.

Maybe lawyers found the coaching and pods unrewarding because the sessions were overly directive and did not allow them enough time to talk and discuss? Attorneys like to talk; they also like to hear from their peers and discuss matters. In adult learning there is an ethic—"less teacher, more student." Although the lawyers doing the coaching in both states were very experienced and respected, the facilitative approach recommended in our coaching and pod protocol is not an approach with which all lawyers and potential coaches are comfortable. Matching the skill set to the need is an important element of a project such as this.

The Washington coach, like his Georgia counterparts, was an experienced lawyer with much trial experience, a former supervisor and well known and liked throughout the state. But in addition, he possessed an MSW degree and was personally comfortable with the facilitative, non-dogmatic, non-authoritarian and less directive approach anticipated in the QIC Protocol. In the pod meetings there was an emphasis on being supportive to one another and on professional growth from meeting to meeting.

Targets and goals were set for each participant, helping them to build a "reflective practice." This framework seemed very popular with the attorneys.

But even though popular among the Washington attorneys, was consistent participation in the coaching and pod meetings actually necessary to achieve the QIC goals? There were an impressive number of significant differences in how the Georgia lawyers handled their cases—even more so than in Washington. Our research design assumed the need for constant refreshment and encouragement to get the lawyers to actually use the QIC approach, but perhaps change can be accomplished without as much of the "community of practice" follow-up?

On the other hand, even though Georgia attorney participation in pods and coaching was less, the Six Core Skills of the QIC experiment were constantly brought to their attention in other ways. Lawyers were asked to provide data monthly and received an impressive amount of communications from our Georgia partners by email, phone and personal contacts in the courthouse. Those repeated contacts probably insured that the original Six Core Skills training was never too far from their mind. Repetition, refreshment and reminders seem necessary to seed a significant change in behavior, however it is done.

11.6 Implications for Practice and Policy

There is a wealth of information in the QIC policy and empirical research. Chapter 13 draws on some of that with recommendations for practice and policy, but we do not think we have exhausted the lessons available in these data. We hope that others will review and study this material and draw further lessons from this experience.

CHAPTER 12

The Flint MDT Study: A Description and Evaluation of a Multidisciplinary Team Representing Children in Child Welfare

Robbin Pott

Abstract

Children in Genesee County (Flint), Michigan, represented by a team of a lawyer and social worker were compared with children only represented by an attorney. Despite the cultural challenges of lawyers and social workers collaborating together, multidisciplinary teams (MDT) improved case outcomes and the experience of children facing foster care. The MDT approach led to quicker case resolutions and preserved family connections more often.

12.1 Introduction

Multidisciplinary team approaches are considered one of the best ways to improve the quality of representation *for court-involved children in the child welfare system.*[1] Pro-

---

*Robbin Pott, JD, MPP is a lawyer and researcher at the University of Michigan Law School's Child Advocacy Law Clinic, where she serves as the assistant director of the QIC-ChildRep. She also serves as the executive director of the Detroit Center for Family Advocacy, a multidisciplinary civil legal aid provider to families involved in the child protection system in Wayne County and has represented parents and children in child welfare proceedings.

1. **Author's note:** I want to express my sincerest gratitude to Don Duquette for providing me with the opportunity and support to pursue this research, to the Genesee County Court who provided generous access to their data, and especially to the courageous professionals who agreed to take on this project and allowed me to observe. *See National Quality Improvement Center on the Representation of Children in Child Welfare's National Needs Assessment at* http://www.improvechildrep.org/NeedsAssessment.aspx. (The QIC-ChildRep conducted a national needs assessment in its first year by talking with judges, attorneys, caseworkers, CASAs, state regional

fessionals who practice in multidisciplinary teams (MDTs) believe these teams benefit case investigation, assessment and management, and lead to more efficient and accurate services for children and families. To date, however, there is little empirical evidence of the effectiveness of MDTs in legal representation of children.

The Flint MDT study was designed to provide insight into how MDTs are formed and operate and to provide some of the first empirical evidence on outcomes for children represented by an MDT. The study aims to address the following questions: 1) What does the process of designing and implementing a multidisciplinary team approach to representing children look like? 2) Do children have better outcomes when represented by an MDT compared to children represented by an attorney alone? and 3) What are the key elements to a successful model?

The study uses qualitative data to describe the events, attitudes, successes, and challenges experienced by a group of five lawyers and two social workers collaborating to advocate for the needs of children in child welfare proceedings. The study is also a randomized control trial, designed to detect evidence of differences in outcomes between the intervention (MDT) and control group. Participating lawyers represented both treatment and control group children and the study randomly assigned cases to be either represented by just the lawyer or by the lawyer and a social worker (MDT). The outcome evaluation sample includes 409 children from 216 families.

Both the social workers and attorneys reported that the MDT approach had a positive impact on cases, and the empirical data confirmed their perceptions. The MDT impacts include quicker resolutions for some cases and better preservation of family ties. Cases represented by the MDT were more likely to be dismissed rather than have an adjudication of jurisdiction. For children ever removed from their homes, they were more likely to be placed with relatives and less likely to be placed in non-relative foster care. And parents of children represented by the MDT had fewer petitions to terminate their parental rights filed.

The study identified three key components to the MDT's effectiveness. The attorneys' respect for the social work skillset allowed the social workers to provide creative advocacy for their clients. The social workers also effectively collaborated with the child welfare agency to build alliances and tear down barriers. Lastly, the social workers provided intensive advocacy early in the case, which often changed the case trajectory.

While the quantitative findings demonstrate that MDTs improve the quality of representation for children, the study also illuminates the barriers to effectively implementing and employing such approaches. The MDT resulted in quicker resolution of some cases and the preservation of more family connections, despite the observed

---

office directors, tribes, and children across the country.) See also NACC, Child Welfare Law Office Guidebook, 2006 at 50.

professional cultural differences that significantly impaired the teams' ability to collaborate. The MDT also never established adequate protocols for protecting client confidentiality. The study concludes that in order for multidisciplinary teams of attorneys and social workers to thrive in child welfare, the social workers need autonomy to be creative in how they handle cases and respect as professionals, and that clear protections for client confidentiality are needed.

12.2 Current Understanding of MDTs

Multidisciplinary approaches in the field of child welfare are not new, but they are understudied and untested.[2] There are a few MDT evaluations, mostly on doctors who work with law enforcement, but none on attorneys who work with social workers.

Overwhelmingly, these studies focus on the benefits of a team approach without examining the potential problems and challenges.[3] And, there are no published randomized controlled trials on outcomes from MDT approaches to child welfare proceedings.[4]

The research that has been done on multidisciplinary approaches demonstrate that professionals (medical, law enforcement, social service agencies, and legal) who work in MDTs believe that the team is better able to get to know the child's particular problems and therefore provide better services.[5] The assumption is that by producing more thorough investigations that incorporate diverse perspectives, an MDT can make better assessments and provide more appropriate interventions.

Child Advocacy Centers (CAC) use multidisciplinary approaches to interviewing children in child abuse cases. Their philosophy is that responses to child abuse need to focus on the needs of the child and the family, and that they are most effective when the different skillsets addressing the problem are coordinated.[6] A quasi-experimental study of four CACs found that, "Communities with CACs had greater law enforcement involvement in child sexual abuse investigations, more evidence of coordinated

---

2. Marina Lalayants & Irwin Epstein, *Evaluating Multidisciplinary Child Abuse and Neglect Teams: a Research Agenda* (2005). (Summarizes the history of MDTs in child welfare cases and provides a comprehensive review of existing evaluations of MDTs.)

3. *Id.*

4. *Id.*

5. *See e.g.* Marcia M. Boumil, Debbie F. Freitas, & Cristina F. Freitas, *Multidisciplinary Representation of Patients: The Potential for Ethical Issues and Professional Duty Conflicts in the Medical-Legal Partnership Model*, 13 J. Health Care L. & Pol'y 107 (2010); Jeffrey R. Baker, *Necessary Third Parties: Multidisciplinary Collaborations and Inadequate Professional Privileges in Domestic Violence Practice*, 21 Colum. J. Gender & L., 283 (2012), Maryann Zavez, *The Ethical and Moral Considerations Presented by Lawyers/Social Workers Interdisciplinary Collaborations*, 5 Whittier J. Child & Fam. Advoc. 191 (2005).

6. Theodore P. Cross, Lisa M. Jones, Wendy A. Walsh, et al, *Evaluating Children's Advocacy Centers' Response to Child Sexual Abuse*, OJJDP Juvenile Justice Bulletin, August 2008.

investigations, better child access to medical exams, more referrals for child mental health treatment, and greater caregiver satisfaction with the investigation process."[7]

However, little is written about how MDTs work in practice and even less is known about lawyers who work with social workers.[8] The process of building a functional multidisciplinary team of attorneys and social workers to provide representation for children involved in the child welfare system has not been well documented in the literature.[9]

Differences in professional values and ethics are known sources of tension inherent when attorneys and social workers work together.[10] One example is the differences in ethical duties to maintain confidentiality. Most states do not include attorneys but do include social workers in their mandated reporting statutes.[11]

While the ABA Model Rules of Professional Conduct allows an attorney to share a client's confidences if she becomes aware of likely harm to the client or others,[12] states' adoption of that rule varies, which can lead to conflicting ethics guiding professionals on the same team.[13] There are core differences in their trainings, too.

Social workers are trained to identify and help resolve the underlying issues that are causing problems and lawyers are trained to protect the rights that are at risk due to the problems.[14] Lawyers are singularly focused on their client while social workers are focused on systems (e.g. families). While the literature consistently insists that collaboration between these two professions is critical, there is also the recognition that this collaboration "does not come easily."[15]

In truth, professional relationships between lawyers and social workers can sometimes be described as "sharply polarized, hostile, and resentful."[16] Power struggles,

---

7. *Id.* Pg 2.

8. Lalyants & Epstein, *supra* note 2. But see, Lisa A. Stranger, *Conflicts between Attorneys and Social Workers Representing Children in Delinquency Proceedings*, 65 Fordham L. Rev. 1123 (1996), which provides a description of ways social workers can help attorneys.

9. Paula Galowitz, *Collaboration Between Lawyers and Social Workers: Re-examining the Nature and Potential of the Relationship*, 67 Fordham L. Rev. 2123 (1999); Frank P. Cervone & Linda M. Mauro, *Ethics, Cultures, and Professions in the Representation of Children*, 64 Fordham L. Rev. 1975 (1996).

10. Frank E. Vandervort, Robbin P. Gonzalez & Kathleen C. Faller, *Legal ethics and high child welfare worker turnover: An unexplored connection*, 30 Children and Youth Services Review 546 (2007).

11. Maryann Zavez, *The Ethical and Moral Considerations Presented by Laywers/Social Workers Interdiscplinary Collaborations*, 5 Whittier J. Child & Fam. Advoc. 191 (2005) pg 192.

12. Rule 1.6(b)(1).

13. See MRE 1.6—Michigan did not adopt that particular rule.

14. Lisa A. Stranger, *Conflicts between Attorneys and Social Workers Representing Children in Delinquency Proceedings*, 65 Fordham L. Rev. 1123 (1996) pg 1150.

15. Mary K. Kisthardt, *Working in the Best Interest of Children: Facilitating the Collaboration of Lawyers and Social Workers in Abuse and Neglect Cases*, Rutgers Law Review, Vol. 30, No.1, (2006) pg 1.

16. Tamara Walsh, *Lawyers and Social Workers Working Together: Ethic of Care and Feminist Legal Practice in Community Law*, Griffith Law Review (2012) vol. 21 no. 3, pg 755. See

such as "turf disputes" and confusion about ownership of cases,[17] contribute to this reality. In one study the social workers in MDTs that reported high levels of tension tended to feel that they were not valued or trusted, and that they were not given the professional autonomy to undertake interventions they deemed necessary.[18] The Walsh study suggests that to overcome this dynamic, professionals need to respect each other's specialized knowledge, and be open to a division of labor based on each other's strengths.[19] However, despite the tensions reported in these types of collaborations, participants tend to agree that they were providing high quality and effective services to their clients.[20]

Since 2011, Colorado has been piloting multidisciplinary legal offices (MDLOs), where lawyer-guardians ad litem and social workers collaborate to represent children in child welfare.[21] Collaborators presented their findings in January 2014 and stated, "While the multidisciplinary model could benefit youth by integrating legal and social work expertise, preliminary evidence suggests this multidisciplinary collaboration involves inherent challenges, and outcomes have not been well assessed."[22]

Challenges include lack of a supervision structure among the team, a need for a more formal and consistent collaboration process, communication problems, power differential between the attorneys and social workers that led to tensions, and role confusion resulting from overlapping responsibilities. The evaluators concluded that these challenges, the reasons for them, and ways to alleviate them are "worthy of further study" because they also found a strong belief between both professional groups that these MDLOs are having a positive impact on the children they serve.[23]

12.3 Methods

12.3.1 Two Parts: Process Observation and Randomized Control Trial

The Flint MDT study uses a mixed-method approach with two distinct components. The first is an observation of the process of designing and implementing a multidisciplinary approach to representing children in child welfare proceedings from the perspective of the child's representation. The study uses qualitative data collected from individual interviews, group meetings, and other observations to construct an in-depth

---

also, Colorado's Multidisciplinary Law Office (MDLO) presentation summary on their pilot evaluation at the Society for Social Work Research conference at https://sswr.confex.com/sswr/2014/webprogram/Paper21252.html.

17. Lalayants & Epstein, *supra* note 2, pg 454.
18. Walsh, *supra* note 16, p 768.
19. Id.
20. Id. p 769.
21. More information about the Colorado MDLOs can be found at http://www.coloradochildrep.org/about-ocr/multidisciplinary-law-office-project/
22. https://sswr.confex.com/sswr/2014/webprogram/Paper21252.html.
23. Jenna Brill, Jocelyn Durkay, and Timothy Ridley, *What do MDLOs Look Like and How Do They Function?*, University of Denver, 2013, unpublished.

description of the process, and to discern the essential components of an effective approach. The second component is a randomized controlled trial designed to assess outcome difference between children who are represented by the MDT (intervention) and those represented by a single attorney (control). The study analyzes quantitative administrative court and agency data to evaluate the differences in outcomes, and qualitative data to explain those outcome differences.

12.3.2 Study Site

The study chose Genesee County (Flint), Michigan as its site. Its juvenile court has a contract with one nonprofit law firm to handle its child representation. This law office consists of five attorneys who exclusively represent children in child welfare and juvenile justice cases. The law office had served the county for ten years, and the same five attorneys have been law partners in this law office the entire time. The law office had no hierarchy; attorneys essentially had sole discretion on how they perform his/her own job. The study agreed to provide two social workers for at least two years to the attorneys for their cases assigned to the intervention group.

The Genesee County court has five juvenile court judges, and each judge's courtroom has a closed group of attorneys that handle all of the child welfare cases for that judge. Specifically, each judge has one attorney who represents all the mothers, one attorney who represents all the fathers, and one attorney who represents all the children as the lawyer-guardian-ad-litem. One prosecutor provides legal counsel to the agency in all cases for each courtroom as well.

Michigan's child protection statute requires a lawyer-guardian-ad-litem (L-GAL) be appointed to children at the first court hearing.[24] The L-GALs are to "serve as the independent representative for the child's best interest."[25] The statute requires that in determining the best interests of the child, the L-GAL give weight to "the child's wishes according to the child's competence and maturity."[26] Attorneys in Michigan must maintain a "normal client-lawyer relationship" to the extent possible when clients may have diminished capacity.[27] The statute states the L-GAL's duty is to the child and not the court, and protects attorney-client privilege.[28]

Michigan's rules of professional conduct allow an attorney to reveal confidences if the attorney becomes aware of "the intention of a client to commit a crime and the information necessary to prevent the crime."[29] Social workers in Michigan abide by the

---

24. MICH. COMP. LAWS § 712A.17c(7).
25. MICH. COMP. LAWS § 712A.17d(1)(b).
26. MICH. COMP. LAWS § 712A.17d(1)(i).
27. MRPC 1.14.
28. MICH. COMP. LAWS § 712A.17d(1)(i).
29. MRPC 1.6(c)(4).

National Association of Social Workers Code of Ethics[30] and are considered mandatory reporters.[31]

12.3.3 Process Observation Design

The study was designed to provide the resources to create a multidisciplinary team of attorneys collaborating with social workers to represent children in child protection proceedings in order to observe the process. The study did not impose a predetermined structure on the team and was not meant to test a specific model. The study did facilitate the team's exploration of how different MDTs operate, and provided guidance as they made decisions about how theirs would. The study did not directly interfere with how the team was functioning but did sometimes act to facilitate communication between the attorneys and the social workers.

12.3.4 Randomized Control Evaluation Design

The study examines the impact of a multidisciplinary approach (intervention) on outcomes for individual children using a within-subject, randomized controlled design.[32] It is within-subject because the same attorneys served as both intervention and control case participants. A within-subject design removes the threat of errors in data analysis due to natural variance in characteristics between different intervention and control group participants. It also conserves resources since it requires half of the number of participants that a between-subjects design requires. The one concern with the design is the possibility of carry-over effects—the possibility that the attorneys would use what they learn from the intervention cases on their control cases. Carry-over effects could potentially improve outcomes for all cases and make it harder to detect the intervention's effect.

Cases were randomly assigned on two levels - to an attorney and to a study group. The Genesee County Court was already randomly assigning cases to judges prior to the implementation of the study because of state court rules and joint local administrative orders.[33] As described above, each participating attorney exclusively practiced in front of the same judge in a particular courtroom. Therefore, for the study, the random assignment of filed petitions to judges at the court level provided for, in effect, the random assignment of cases to the attorneys. Then, if the court authorized a petition at the

---

30. *See* http://www.nasw-michigan.org/?page=Ethics.
31. MCL 722.621 et seq.
32. *See generally,* Howard Seltman, Experimental Design and Analysis, Ch. 14 Within-Subjects Designs. (2009).
33. Case assignment is governed by MCR 8.111(B), except for allowable deviations provided in Joint Local Administrative Order, 2006-8J (circuit), 2006-5J (probate) Family Court Plan; Local Administrative Order, 2009-3, Re-Assignment of Cases—Baby Court; and Local Administrative Order 2013-4, Case Assignments.

preliminary hearing (i.e. found probable cause that one or more of the allegations in the petition are true and that the case should more forward to adjudication), the study randomly assigned the case to the intervention or control group within a week.

Thus, the potential impact of the MDT begins after the preliminary hearing. For cases randomly assigned to the intervention group, the attorneys were to collaborate with the social workers to provide legal representation for their child/youth clients. For cases randomly assigned to the control group, the attorneys represented their child/youth clients without the assistance of a social worker, as they normally would.[34]

The group of study participants was necessarily small. When looking for a site, the study prioritized finding a valid control group. Child welfare legal practice varies widely from county to county due to a myriad of factors such as level of experience and training of practitioners and judges, the socio-economic conditions of their populations, and county-controlled funding for family and children services, to name a few. It would be impossible to control for all of the variables that would confound a county-to-county comparison. By using a within-subject design in this particular jurisdiction (given that each courtroom makeup of attorneys does not change between its child welfare cases) there were no other differences between the intervention and control group cases other than whether the child's attorney had access to a social worker for the case.

Random assignment of cases ensured that all of the various factors that could potentially influence a case outcome, such as which judge heard the case, the age of the child, the severity of the allegations, or other services/programs the child and family were receiving, were equally distributed to both groups. This created two statistically equivalent groups where the only difference between them was the method used to deliver legal representation. Differences observed between the two groups of cases can be directly attributable to the intervention.

12.3.5 Data Collection

The qualitative data collected included notes transcribed during periodic individual interviews with the participating attorneys and social workers, notes from regular team meetings and meetings with each group of professionals, and other observations made during routine interactions with the team through email and in-person settings. The meeting agendas always included a discussion of what was working well, what could be done better, and of shared examples of success stories and challenges. Individual

---

34. The number of cases the attorneys handled did not change. The study only altered their ongoing practice by making a social worker available to them on their new child welfare case that were randomly assigned to the intervention group. Also, there was an absolute ban on the attorneys employing the social workers in any way on their control cases, which was captured in the agreement between the University of Michigan and the attorney participants. All participants were routinely asked about the ban and there was never an indication of it being violated.

interviews were semi-structured so that each individual conversation touched upon the same topics.[35]

The study collected administrative and other data from the court's web-based database and paper files. Those data include child and family demographics, court hearing dates and hearing results, placement information, allegations, disposition court ordered and additional services for parents and children, sibling contacts, and permanency outcomes.

12.4 Creating an MDT Approach to Representing Children
12.4.1 Getting Started

The attorneys got to choose the two social workers for the project. One of the social workers hired was an individual who had worked in the courts as a juvenile probation officer for many years, was well known by the attorneys, and was considered an effective advocate for children, even though she did not have direct experience in child welfare. This candidate did not have a master's in social work, but was the type of social worker the attorneys anticipated potentially wanting to hire—someone with a good reputation in their courts for being an effective advocate for children. The other candidate was not known to the attorneys, but held an MSW and had several years' experience in the child welfare field.

The social workers' job initially lacked direction. Neither the attorneys nor the social workers had experience working as an MDT, there was no existing supervision structure, nor were there written office policies or procedures manuals. The attorneys acknowledged that they really did not know how these social workers would be best put to use on their cases. So, the MDT spent the first few weeks getting oriented and developing a structure.

The attorneys had a two-week training schedule for the social workers that included shadowing each of the attorneys at different types of court hearings, training on office procedures and the web-based case management tool, and reviewing existing case files. There was a full team meeting the first week to begin to discuss the challenging issues that the team could expect to face. The team also traveled to New York City to visit two law offices that practice child welfare law in multidisciplinary teams.[36] These early

---

35. The study attempted to interview youth aged 14 and older about their experience with their representation, but had to abandon that data collection effort due to the difficulty locating the youth after the case closed. A month of active recruiting, including an afternoon tracking youth in the community, yielded one interview. The study determined that it did not have the resources for such an intensive effort.

36. The Legal Aid Society's Juvenile Rights Practice and Lawyers for Children agreed to host the entire team at their offices for a day each. Both of these offices were profiled for the QIC-ChildRep's Need Assessment as model MDT practices. See http://improvechildrep.org/NeedsAssessment/NotableOffices.aspx

implementation activities were designed to build confidence in each other and to assist them in formulating their own MDT practice.

In reality, the first few weeks the social workers were in the office were harder than expected, and core challenges revealed themselves immediately. For example, the first team meeting exposed a deep divide between the two professional groups. The group participated in conversations about the common challenges to an MDT practice, including understanding and managing the differences in their professional ethics, the possibility of having the social workers testify in court, and confidentiality expectations. The team constructively explored the first two topics, but the conversation about confidentiality turned contentious. The attorneys wanted the social workers to abide by the attorney/client privilege and viewed the social workers' role as an extension of theirs for the clients. When the MSW social worker expressed concerns about the risks to her licensure, which made her a mandated reporter, the tone of conversation escalated into a confrontation. Specifically, one of the attorneys stated, "We will sue you, and then take your license if you report against any of our clients."

The study team reminded the group that they would have the opportunity to explore how other offices approach this issue when they travel to New York. However, this incident did permanent damage to the social worker's attitude. This was one of several examples of the difficult culture to which the social workers were being asked to acclimate.

The climate challenges between the two professions, aggravated by the ambiguity of the initial lack of project structure, quickly proved unworkable for the MSW social worker. Within the first two weeks, she and the attorneys clashed in regards to case management, court appearances, and general professional conduct. The social worker was offended by the attorneys' unfiltered, direct, and often impolite styles of communication. The attorneys thought that the social worker dressed inappropriately for court, lacked promptness, and was unable to collaborate. At the beginning of the third week, it was clear that this social worker was a bad fit and she left the project.

Meanwhile, the other social worker was performing well. She had previously worked with the attorneys as a juvenile probation officer for youths the attorneys represented in juvenile justice cases and was well aware of their personalities. Despite the tensions with the other social worker, she remained enthusiastic about the project and was willing to be flexible and think creatively during its implementation. Fortunately, another top candidate with an MSW and experience working in foster care was hired and joined the project a few weeks later. Study case assignments began five weeks after the project started.

12.4.2 First Six Months

Early on, all participants agreed that the teams were adding value to the work with cases. Individual participants, however, held different perspectives on how well things were working and how things could be better. The social workers reported a wide range of attorney attitudes about how they prefer to collaborate, ranging from two of the attorneys wanting to do the first visit with the child before or with the social worker and who expressed, "Don't do anything without me," to two giving free rein and expressing, "Do what you need to do and get back to me," and one attorney in the middle of those two perspectives. The attorneys mirrored what the social workers said. Some attorneys described how they directed the social workers, and stated "They are doing what I want them to do," while other attorneys discussed how they let the social workers dive into the cases and said they told the social workers that, "They don't have to ask permission. Just do it. I don't want them to tell me how to handle the legal issues so I don't want to tell them how to do the social work."

During the first few months of the study, the attorneys seemed willing to try the MDT approach but, to various degrees, were struggling with handing over some control over their cases. In fact, during the trip to New York, the majority of the attorneys shared that they expected to have a hard time "letting go" because for a long time, they have felt accountable for all aspects of their young clients' lives.

Most of the attorneys slowly began to afford social workers the liberty to be creative with the MDT cases and expressed appreciation for the social workers' ability to do so. The social workers, by contrast, expressed reservations about some of the attorneys' commitment to the MDT approach, citing a lack of access to them and the unwillingness from some of them to fully use the social workers' skillset on their cases.

Despite these differences, everyone had examples of how the social workers were having a positive impact. The social workers felt they were helping by building rapport early on with the children and families and keeping the case kid-focused. The attorneys especially appreciated the additional visits and the assessments that the social workers were providing. They were identifying needed services and then working to ensure that the services were provided.

The team also believed that the social workers were helping to keep cases moving. For example, one social worker attended a hearing for which the attorney needed an alternate attorney to stand in. The day of the hearing, the alternate attorney did not know a sufficient amount about the case and wanted to ask for an adjournment. But, the social worker was able to brief the attorney before the hearing and spoke directly to the judge during the hearing. As a result, the case was closed instead of being adjourned.

In a separate example, a client needed a placement change but the attorney was in trial that entire day. The social worker was able to participate in the decision with the agency and keep the attorney informed of the progress throughout the day. Having a social worker on the case avoided delay and ensured that the child's voice was represented in an important decision.

Sometimes the social worker's contribution changed the trajectory of the case. For example, the social worker's assessment of one case convinced the court to refer the parent to Baby Court[37] instead of ordering the agency to pursue termination. Many of these impacts occurred early in the cases, in particular for three the attorneys who took a more hands-off approach to what the social workers were doing.

While the participants agreed the MDT approach was working, perceptions differed sharply regarding the office climate. The attorneys thought that the social workers were fitting in, but the social workers reported feeling like outsiders. The attorneys' long work history together created a family-like environment in the office, both in terms of camaraderie and conflict.

The attorneys came and went without much conversation or interaction. The social workers were treated the same way the attorneys treated each other. There was no concerted effort made to help them feel comfortable or welcome on an ongoing basis. The attorneys thought that the social workers had blended well, but to the social workers, the environment felt cold and disrespectful.

Communication was the one challenge everyone recognized. The social workers said that it was sometimes hard to get the attorneys' attention on their cases, that they were not meeting regularly, and they expressed wanting more frequent and regular access to the attorneys. The attorneys admitted that communication was not great, but felt it was getting better. But all of the attorneys admitted that they could be spending more time with the social workers.

The team continued to make steady progress in developing how they approached multidisciplinary representation of children. The social workers expanded the types of support they were providing the attorneys, which included emotionally preparing and supporting child witnesses, finding and developing resources for children and families, defusing tensions between the agency and parents/caregivers, and speaking on the record both informally and through sworn testimony. The attorneys were learning to trust the social workers and how to let go of having total control over their cases. When the attorneys were asked why they were able to do this, one attorney said, "I could see the benefit. I get to be the lawyer and not have to be the social worker also."

Communications improved somewhat over time. The teams found a rhythm of email, text and phone contacts that helped keep them up to date, and case materials got to the social workers more reliably. The social workers were diligent about typing their notes into the law office's web-based case management system, and the attorneys said they relied on those notes. But routine meetings between the attorney/social worker pairs continued to not happen, and the social workers felt that the communication tended to flow one way.

---

37. The county has an intensive infant-toddler court team program called Baby Court. See Zero to Three's Safe Babies Court Teams for information on the model used in Flint. http://www.zerotothree.org/maltreatment/safe-babies-court-team/.

At hearings, different courtrooms treated the social workers differently. In two, the social workers were at the table with the attorney and were always introduced. In two other courtrooms, the social workers were present but were called upon only when needed. And in one courtroom, the judge was not willing to hear directly from the social workers and they were never recognized on the case.

Despite the operational challenges, the social workers were satisfied with the work they were doing with the children and felt they were making a difference in their lives. And, the attorneys had glowing praise for their contributions. In the words of attorneys, "It's been awesome," "They get the whole picture," and after describing a successful case, "They couldn't have done more."

There was a sense that the child's voice was clearer in court hearings and that the MDT cases were keeping the focus on the children. For example, one social worker developed a rapport with one client such that the youth stated he no longer wanted to visit with his previous caregivers from a disrupted adoption. The social worker worked with the youth and the youth's therapist to prepare a letter supporting those wishes for the next hearing. The social workers took part in family team meetings, advocated for the children outside of court such as ensuring kids were able to stay in their home schools after a removal and ensuring caregivers received proper reimbursements. They were regularly visiting institutionalized youth, doing independent investigations of the cases, and identifying needed services for the children. In fact, the attorneys saw that the up-front work that the social workers did on the MDT cases resulted in the court dismissing cases at the adjudication phase.

But closing cases quickly was not the social workers' mandate; the social workers were focused on keeping the children safe and on serving their wellbeing. In a few cases, the social worker's assessments led to the court taking additional actions against the parents. For example, the children in one case were about to be placed with their father, who was not listed on the petition. The social worker did an independent investigation of the home for the attorney and discovered an unsafe environment and criminal activity. The social worker's investigation prevented the placement and a potential future removal for the children.

The social workers felt varying degrees of being valued among the attorneys. One attorney engaged with them regularly, would ask, "What do you suggest?" and would act on their recommendations. Three attorneys gave the social workers freedom to work their cases, but did not really collaborate with them as a team. One attorney was half-engaged with one social worker and seemed to be actively avoiding the other. Overall, the social workers generally felt that they were "carrying the cases" without consistently getting the "right amount of credit" for their work.

When asked individually, four of the attorneys felt that they were fully utilizing the social workers' services, but seemed unaware of the perceived lack of credit being given for their contributions. One attorney admitted that if anything, they were overly relying on the social workers and that they probably should spend more time on the MDT cases.

The social workers had an easier time getting information from the agency workers than the attorneys did. The social workers seemed to have a gentler approach and could relate more with the agency workers compared to the attorneys. The attorneys acknowledged that they were not able to track the agency's actions between hearings like the social workers could. The social workers were able to better ensure the agency was doing what it was supposed to between hearings. And, when the agency failed to perform, the social workers' tracking was used in the hearing against the agency. The social workers sometimes even provided an assessment of the case that differed from the agency. For example, an agency worker reported in court that an infant had attachment issues with its mother. The MDT social worker started attending visitations to make an independent assessment and observed that the infant was comfortable in mom's presence and looked to her for help, and that the mother was affectionate and attentive.

By six months, the social workers were enjoying their freedom to work on their cases, but now wanted to strengthen working as a team. They continued to feel like outsiders and were struggling to get the attorneys' attention on the cases they shared. As a result, the social workers sometimes acted unilaterally. For the most part, the social workers were operating on their own and updating the attorneys through the notes they kept in the law office's web-based case management tool or in person right before a hearing. The attorneys were also acting without consulting with the social workers first, but would often bring the decision to the social worker's attention, after the fact, to get their opinion.

12.4.3 Team Climate Issues Come to the Forefront

At eight months into the project, the social workers disclosed that the office climate was deteriorating and was increasingly hostile, in particular, between them and two of the attorneys. Ultimately, these two attorneys decided to withdraw from the study.

The withdrawals did not surprise the rest of the team, but at the first meeting with the remaining team members there was a sense of uncertainty about how to move forward. C

Conversations leading up to this moment highlighted core obstacles to making the MDT approach work for both professionals. The three remaining attorneys acknowledged that the climate in the office was difficult at times, and explained that these tensions existed before the introduction of the social workers. When asked what they needed from the attorneys to make this work, the social workers replied, "Respect, to be treated professionally, and to have greater access to the attorneys."

Specifically, they wanted more one-on-one time with the attorneys, a uniform way of presenting their work at hearings, and a protocol for handling problems. The attorneys understood that they needed to provide the social workers with a comfortable and appropriate working environment, and they communicated a commitment to meet that need. One attorney specifically said she wanted the social workers to be happy working there because they were doing such great work. Soon afterwards, the social workers reported that things were better.

12.4.4 The Second Year

At twelve months, the remaining three attorneys were treating the two social workers with more courtesy but they still did not make themselves available to the social workers more. The de facto MDT structure was the attorney and social worker working the cases separately and then coming together only at critical moments, such as during a crisis or for a hearing. And this is how the team operated for the duration of the project.

While there was consensus that this approach was having a positive impact on cases and clients, the social workers continually expressed wanting more communication with the attorneys. Over the course of the subsequent year, the social workers gradually gave up trying to engage the attorneys. They stopped going to every hearing and asked the attorneys to request their presence if they wanted them there. The attorneys rarely did.

With six months left in the two-year project, the team met to explore the possibility of continuing the social worker services after the study ended. The attorneys still very much appreciated what the social workers were doing. However, when the attorneys were presented with potential funding options that they could pursue to continue the MDT, they had concerns about meeting the bureaucratic demands for such funding.

And at this point both of the social workers had decided that they did not want to work for the law firm after the study. Case assignments stopped as scheduled and the team took three months to wind down the study cases. At the end of the project, the attorneys no longer had social worker support on any of their cases.

12.5 Primary Findings from the Evaluation[38]

12.5.1 MDT Resulted in Quicker Resolution of Some Cases and the Preservation of More Family Connections

The data confirm what the MDT reported—that the multidisciplinary approach impacted cases in positive ways. The study found that children represented by the MDT

---

38. The author collaborated with the University of Michigan's Center for Statistical Consultation and Research (CSCAR) on the outcome evaluation. Thank you to Kerby Shedden, Ph.D, Professor of Statistics and CSCAR Director, who assisted with designing the study, performed the preliminary power analysis, and conducted all analyses.

were more likely to have their cases dismissed at adjudication rather than have the court take jurisdiction. When children were removed, they were more likely to be placed with relatives and less likely to be placed in foster care. Parents of children served by the MDT had fewer petitions to terminate their parental rights filed. Observationally, the MDT group had 38% fewer removals after the intervention was assigned.

12.5.2 Sample

The quantitative data include 409 individual children involved in 216 child abuse and neglect petitions authorized (accepted for consideration by the court) in Genesee County, MI. The study included every new case assigned to a participating attorney's court between March 17, 2014 and October 30, 2015.[39] The court randomly assigned a filed petition to a judge/attorney pair and the attorneys participated in the preliminary hearings. If the court authorized the petition, the study assigned the case to the intervention or control group within a week, so the potential impact of the MDT begins after the preliminary hearing. Forty-five percent of children were still in their homes at the time their petitions were authorized. The remaining 55% were either placed shortly before the initial hearing on an emergency basis or at the initial hearing.

A greater proportion of control cases were already in placement when the intervention began (61% vs 50% for the MDT group). Because social workers began assisting with the cases randomly assigned to receive the MDT representation after the preliminary hearing, this difference is not a result of the MDT.

Observations ended January 31, 2016. Overall, 60% of the cases were assigned to the MDT group and 40% were assigned to the control.[40] See Table 12.1 for distribution of demographics. There were no significant differences in distribution of these categories between treatment and control group.

12.5.3 Analytical Approach

The study used regression analyses[41] for dependent data to assess the relationships of each outcome with the intervention. The correlation between individual child outcomes

---

39. For the attorneys who withdrew from the study, the sample includes all of their intervention and control cases that were closed at the time of their decision to withdraw. All of their cases that were open were removed from the study. The study included 15 cases and removed 7 for one attorney, and included 25 and removed 14 for the other.

40. The social workers' caseloads started small and accumulated over time. For the first six months of case assignments, individual cases had a 2/3 chance of being assigned to the intervention group so that the social workers' caseloads accumulated faster to capacity. After six month, the chance was reduced to 50%. After six months, each social worker carried an average of 51 active child/youth clients, with the range being 37–67 at any given time.

41. For binary and count outcomes, the study used logistic and Poisson regression, respectively, fit using generalized estimating equations (GEE). The study fit models using only the

Table 12.1 Sample Demographics

	Frequency	Percent
Sex		
Female	208	51%
Male	201	49%
Age		
0-5 years old	239	58%
6-11 years old	100	24%
12 & older	70	18%
Race		
White	203	50%
Black	158	39%
Bi-racial	39	9%
Other	9	2%
Severity level[1]		
Abuse	176	43%
Neglect	233	57%

1. Cases were coded as "abuse" if there were allegations of physical or sexual abuse, and coded "neglect" for cases that did not have allegations of physical or sexual abuse.

and family outcomes was nearly 1 (.98) making the study's effective sample size for analyses 216 (number of families). The models accounted for this. The analyses also controlled for age range, gender, race, judge, and severity level. Since the intervention groups were randomized, these other factors are unlikely to be confounding. But to the extent that they are independent predictors of outcomes, power for assessing the intervention effect is increased by controlling for such factors.[42]

12.5.4 Study Limitations

There were still about half of the cases still open at the end of the study. There may have been differences in how those cases were resolved, had the intervention continued, that the study will not detect. While the study's internal validity is high (almost every confounding factor was controlled to isolate and measure the intervention's impact),

---

intervention status as a predictor, and separately fit models with intervention status and other relevant potential predictors.

42. Reported statistics include the controls.

the external validity may be lower in that the study had a small group of participants in an idiosyncratic environment. However, the current MDT literature predicted the study's challenges and successes, which suggest the lessons learned here are likely to be broadly applicable.

12.5.5 Impact Analyses

The first impact the study tested was adjudication, that is, whether the case was dismissed (and therefore closed) during the adjudication phase, or whether the court found it had jurisdiction to continue involvement with the case. This decision point was reached for nearly all cases in the study and included cases where children had been placed prior to this point. Cases served by the MDT were more likely to be dismissed and closed (31% compared to 11%) without the court finding it had jurisdiction (Table 12.2).

The second impact analyzed for all cases was the frequency of termination of parental rights (TPR) petition filings and orders. Parents of children served by the MDT had fewer petitions to terminate their rights filed (16% v. 30% for mothers, 20% v. 30% for fathers) but equivalent percentages of TPR orders.

The third set of impacts analyzed for all cases was the proportion of children who were placed at some point and whose cases were closed because of reunification, guardianship or adoption. Because all children in both the MDT group and the control group could have experienced a placement and a discharge, this analysis also includes all children. There were no significant differences in these impacts: children were equally likely to have been placed and discharged to permanency.

The fourth impact analyzed was for children who were still in their homes at the time their petitions were authorized and their case was randomly assigned to the MDT or control condition. There were too few cases of subsequent removals in this subgroup to test significance of this finding, but observationally, among these children, 15% of the children served by the MDT and 23% of the control group were removed[43] after the intervention was assigned.

The fifth set of impacts analyzed was for children who were ever removed. Among this group, the children represented by the MDT group were more likely to be ever placed with relatives (61% compared to 46%). In a closely related finding, fewer children in MDT cases who were ever removed were ever placed in non-relative foster care (46% compared to 64%).[44]

There were too few petitions (6) subsequently authorized after the close of the family's original case to evaluate whether the intervention affected reentry rates.

---

43. For the purpose of this study, a child was considered "removed" if the child was removed from her original home to anywhere but a biological parent's home.
44. The study calculated if the child ever had each type of placement. The categories are not mutually exclusive and do not necessarily total 100%.

Table 12.2 Analyses of Case Outcomes

	MDT		Control	
	Freq	% of Sample/ % with outcome	Freq	% of Sample/ % with outcome
All Children Randomly Assigned	243	100%	166	100%
Adjudication—almost all	242	100%	163	98%
Dismissed at or prior to adjud.***	75	31%	18	11%
Termination of Parental Rights - all	243	100%	166	100%
Petition for Mother**	38	16%	49	30%
Petition for Father*	49	20%	50	30%
Order for Mother	18	7%	16	10%
Order for Father	20	8%	17	10%
Permanency - all	243	100%	166	100%
Case closed after placement and reunification	29	12%	25	15%
Case closed after placement and discharged to guardianship	6	2%	7	4%
Case closed after placement and adoption	4	2%	1	1%
Child at home at case assignment[1]	121	50%	65	39%
Child removed after case assignment[2]	18	15%	15	23%
Ever removed[3]	140	58%	115	69%
Ever placed with relative**	86	61%	53	46%
Ever placed in foster care**	65	46%	74	64%
Ever placed in residential	19	14%	3	3%
Ever placed with siblings	93	66%	59	51%

* p < .10, ** p < .05, *** p < .00
1. Note that a greater proportion of control cases were already in placement when the RCT began. This difference is not a result of the MDT.
2. This is an observational finding because the frequency of the event is low and the sample size is small. Descriptively the MDT group has a 38% lower rate of removals within this group.
3. Note that the differences in the proportion of cases ever removed is due in large part to the greater proportion of control cases that were already in placement with the RCT began.

These analyses point to the MDTs impact on preserving family connections in early experiences of court involvement and during placement. The absence of an impact on permanency after placement suggests that either the MDTs differential influence on more complex cases was limited or that the MDTs did not have enough time to demonstrate a differential impact: 43% of their cases were still open at the of the study.

12.6 Reasons for the MDT's Impact

12.6.1 Respect for Social Work Skillset

Throughout the study, it was clear that the social workers were driving the creative process. The social workers conducted independent case investigations, talked to collateral parties, met with the child in their homes or placements to assess their needs, monitored implementation of case service plans and court orders, and ensured timely and purposeful delivery of services.

For their treatment cases, the attorneys learned to recognize and accept the social workers' skillset and divided the casework along those lines. Prior to the study and to various degrees, the attorneys were making attempts to handle the needs assessment and case planning aspects of all their cases. They did their statutorily required visits and tried to stay involved in the decisions the agency made about their clients. But once some of their cases began to be assigned to the treatment group, they increasingly relied on the social workers to do the out of court work for those cases.

The attorneys understood that the social workers were contributing in ways that they could not have imagined and were doing things for which the attorneys neither had the training nor time. For example, one attorney shared that when one case was assigned as a MDT case she thought a social worker was not needed. But the social worker "worked magic" and the case closed quickly. The attorney's reaction was, "Oh, that's how that's supposed to work." The social workers thrived when they were trusted to creatively approach their cases and were given the flexibility to do what was needed, as they determined it.

12.6.2 Collaboration with the Child Welfare Agency

Prior to the beginning of case assignments, the study met with the county's Department of Health and Human Services leadership to garner their support for the project. The study also asked them to communicate to all of their employees that the children's attorneys now had social workers working on their behalf for some of their cases.

The agency workers were reticent at first with the social workers, but they came to rely on them. The MDT social workers were able to build a rapport and trust with the agency workers. This led to the MDT social workers being included in communications, which in turned enabled them to intervene if necessary. For example, the MDT social workers were routinely invited to and attended family team meetings where they often felt that they were critical facilitators, particularly when the relationship between the parent and the caseworker had broken down.

In fact, the social workers' effectiveness was sometimes due to them acting as a buffer between the parents and the agency. In cases where the relationship between the parents and the agency turned hostile, the MDT social workers' involvement mitigated the effect of the poor relationship. For example, the social workers would visit the families at the same time the agency caseworkers were there, which often helped facilitate effective services for the parents. And the agency caseworkers were grateful. A caseworker said to an MDT social worker, "I don't know what I would do if you were not on this case."

The MDT social workers contributed to the service plans that the caseworker produced and had a direct influence on placement decisions due to this open communication with the agency. When caseworkers changed on the cases, the social workers were able to remain for the duration. The continuity that the MDT social workers provided for the families and for each new caseworker helped avoid delays in the case.

Unlike many of the agency caseworkers, the MDT social workers were not overly burdened with paperwork and case management, and had the time for frequent visits. They were able to see and learn things that the caseworkers were not. In many cases, the MDT social workers gained a reputation for knowing the most about the families. Some parents reached out directly to the MDT social workers instead of their caseworkers for help. The social workers were mindful of client confidentiality issues and were careful to refer parents to their attorneys. But, the social workers would do what they could for the parents when they believed that it was in the child's best interest to be with her parents. Supporting the parents was part of and consistent with their role in supporting the child.

12.6.3 Early Intervention

For the cases where the petition was authorized with the children still in the home, the MDT operated much like traditional family preservation services.[45] The MDT social workers employed all the best practices of their trade—they focused on their clients' needs, identified strengths as well as deficits, provided concrete support, promoted competence, demonstrated respect for their clients, and engaged in a wide variety of problem-solving and advocacy activities.[46]

When the children were still in the home at the time the petition was authorized, the social workers began working with the parents right away. Again, they built rapport and that trust often led to the parents being able to resolve whatever situation they were facing. The social workers were able to identify barriers and helped remove them. They were providing concrete services such as access to food, furniture, transportation, childcare, or medical attention. The social workers would "get in there and do the social work."

The role the social workers played as buffer between the parents and the agency was particularly important for these cases. As one of the study's social workers explained, removals can be "personal" and the data collector for the study observed that the

---

45. Becky F. Antle, Dana N. Christensen, Michiel A. van Zyl, Anita P. Barbee, *The Impact of the Solution Based Casework (SBC) Practice Model on Federal Outcomes in Public Child Welfare*, Child Abuse and Neglect 36 (2012) 342-353.

46. *Id* at 36.

caseworker's anger towards a parent is "palpable" in court reports. The MDT social workers believed that their ability to defuse tensions and keep the parties focused on resolving the issues was key to their ability to positively impact cases.

12.7 Weaknesses within the MDT

12.7.1 Team Climate

While the findings from this study provide evidence that social work services provided through the child representative result in quicker resolution of some cases and the preservation of more family connections, another critical lesson is that the availability of those services for attorneys may be threatened when the social workers are not treated with respect and do not feel part of a team. Specifically for this study, the office climate and the different expectations of professional culture proved to be the most persistent challenge of the MDT. Even after two the attorneys withdrew, the remaining three attorneys continued to engage with the social workers infrequently and the social workers continued to feel isolated and unappreciated.

For the majority of the cases, the MDT did not function as a team and this was primarily due to the social workers' general lack of access to the attorneys. The social workers were grateful for the eventual freedom that the attorneys gave them on their cases, but for much of the project the social workers wished they could establish a more team-like approach. In fact, the social workers felt that they could have accomplished even more if a team approach would have taken root. By the end of the project, the social workers decided not to continue working with the attorneys and the project disbanded.

12.7.2 Inadequate Protection for Client Privileges

The MDT never established a clear process for protecting their clients' confidences and they practiced in a culture that tolerated blurred lines of privilege. Michigan's Rules of Professional Conduct required the MDT social workers to abide by attorney-client privilege for their clients and to have permission before talking with represented parties.[47]

The social workers were trained on confidentiality issues and reported being responsible in protecting the child's confidences. However, they were not routinely asking their clients their perspectives on sharing information and they were not explicitly asking permission to talk with the parents. The social workers routinely provided reports to the court and the other parties' attorneys were aware of the contact the social workers were having with the agency workers and parents.

---

47. MRPC 5.3 (responsibilities regarding nonlawyer assistants) and rule 4.2 (communications with persons represented by counsel).

The culture in these cases was such that the parents' attorneys did not object to the reports the social workers were giving in court, asked the social workers how their clients were doing, and sometimes complimented them on their achievements on the case, which created a sense of implicit permission.[48]

12.8 Conclusion

The lack of teamwork between social workers and attorneys did not prevent the MDT from resolving some cases more quickly and preserving more family connections. However, ongoing and inadequately addressed poor office climate conditions within the MDT damaged the attorneys' ability to retain the social workers. A study of MDT's in Australia concluded that, "The danger is that tensions will escalate to the point where each profession would prefer not to work with the other. . . If this were lost, it would be a loss to both the legal profession and clients."

To avoid this loss, the legal profession should provide greater exposure to opportunities to collaborate with social workers and work to break down the silos in which each profession tends to work. These opportunities should include trainings or workshops that focus on improving understanding of how each profession contributes to successful outcomes and encourage recognition and appreciation of those contributions. Only through increasing understanding, recognition and appreciation can mutual trust and respect grow. And, as this MDT experience has highlighted, a professionally respectful climate is key to ensuring that the two professions continue to collaborate.

The Flint MDT study demonstrated that having social work services delivered as part of the child's representation in child welfare proceedings resulted in quicker resolution of some cases and the preservation of more family connections. The MDT's social workers' only objective was to do what was in the best interest of the child and every decision was filtered through that lens.

The social workers were able to enter the child's world and better understand his needs and wishes. This meant to the social workers that sometimes to help the child, they needed to help the parent. This thinking is contradictory to the adversarial legal system in which they were operating, which assumes one party's rights are opposed to another's. Reconciling the process of providing quality representation to individuals while maintaining the ability to effectively advocate for the family, when that is what's best, should be key when employing MDTs.

---

48. Walsh, *supra* note 16 p 769.

CHAPTER 13

How to Improve Legal Representation of Children in America's Child Welfare System

Abstract
This final chapter provides a vision for the future of child representation based on the QIC experience, which includes:

- implementing the QIC consensus role of the child's lawyer in every state,
- organizing the delivery of legal services for children statewide,
- encouraging supportive communities of learning among the lawyers, and
- promoting the promise of multidisciplinary legal representation.

13.1 Introduction

The central argument of this book is that a consensus on the role of the child's legal representative, as reflected in the QIC Best Practice Model of Child Representation, is at hand. The QIC review of the academic literature, national standards, conference recommendations and stakeholder opinion documents the evolution of lawyer representation of children and reveals an emerging consensus on nearly all aspects of the role and duties of the child's legal representative. (See Chapter 4.) Our national needs assessment of 2010 revealed far more agreement on the role and duties of the child's legal representative than was commonly thought. Even the differences across the gulf of client-directed versus best interests are narrowed.

Our goal is to present a broad story that captures child representation as it is today and provides an empirical foundation of evidence based practice from which to pivot to the next stage of development. The Chapin Hall team provides some unique and insightful empirical data about our field and Robbin Pott's study of the lawyer-social worker team representation of children in Flint, Michigan confirm the anecdotal experiences of many across the country. More sound social science is needed to help us better understand how best to provide and organize legal representation of children.

This is the chapter that shifts from the foundational material in the previous chapters and turns our attention toward the future of child representation. Drawing upon our policy research and the QIC empirical findings, here are our recommendations.

13.2 Adopt a Public Health Model of Child Protection

This is a book about lawyer case-by-case advocacy. Yet our effectiveness is inextricably linked to the social and political milieu of our practice. We are not alone and factors external to our case advocacy and the family court system either enhance or compromise our efforts. The legal system cannot be the principal child welfare response in America. Certainly the court serves as the gatekeeper for the child welfare system, and only rarely does a child enter or leave foster care without a court order.

Many argue that too many children are lined up at that gate and that courts are asked to do too much. Enhanced public health policies for children and families hold the promise of protecting and nurturing children so that fewer of them end up at the courthouse steps. Our case-by-case effectiveness skyrockets if fewer children are petitioned to the court, leaving only the neediest requiring our attention.

Josh Gupta-Kagan writes: "A public health model would enable society to respond to the millions of children facing mild harms more effectively and would enable child protection authorities to respond to the more serious cases more effectively. . . . [F]ocus coercive interventions on the most severe cases."[1] Michael Wald points out that although reports of physical abuse and sexual abuse of children have declined dramatically over the past 25 years, reports of neglect continue unabated.[2] Cases recorded as neglect account for 75% of substantiations and 60% of all foster care placements.[3] The upstream preventive approach offered by a public health approach holds the promise of reducing the number of children maltreated and responding to those who are maltreated in a more effective fashion.

---

1. Josh Gupta-Kagan, Toward a Public Health Legal Structure for Child Welfare, 92 NEBRASKA L. REV. 897 (2014) at 965.

2. Michael Wald, Beyond CPS: Developing an Effective System for Helping Children in Neglectful Families, Research Paper No. 2554074; http://ssrn.com/abstract-2554074.

3. Id. at 1. Certainly all cases categorized as "neglect" are not mild and some place children at considerable risk. Children die from neglect and can be permanently harmed from neglect. Nonetheless a public health approach is more consistent with our constitutional values of family integrity and can safely reduce the numbers entering our legal system.

One of my mentors, the pediatrician Ray Helfer, spoke of preventing child maltreatment and taking positive action to enhance parenting, to avoid the negative of child abuse and neglect:

> With very few exceptions, if one wishes to prevent something bad from happening, the development of something good must come first. Eliminating cholera and dysentery from our society required the development of sewers and clean water systems. Preventing polio required building polio antibody levels in the bodies of our children through vaccination. Fire prevention necessitates cleaning up our closets and installing sprinkler systems. Likewise, to prevent child abuse and other adverse outcomes . . . within our families, we must enhance the interpersonal skills of those very folks who like each other the most and who will make up our future families, the mothers and fathers to be.[4]

The current child protection system relies too much on an adversarial investigative approach that infringes upon the fundamental liberty interests of millions of children and parents. A parental fault paradigm may be appropriate for a coercive intervention in the family, but there are other approaches to protecting and nourishing children. Clare Huntington writes:

> The child welfare system suffers from a fundamental misorientation. The prevailing response to families at risk of abuse and neglect is to wait for a crisis, then act. In many cases, the state intervenes only after abuse or neglect has occurred. At that point, the state often removes a child from her home and places her in foster care, which can be rife with its own dangers. Once the child is out of the home, the state takes largely ineffective steps to reunite the family. This post hoc approach to child welfare has devastating effects for children, parents, and the state. By the time intervention occurs, children have already been harmed. Parents have already succumbed to various ills such as substance abuse. And the state's interest in the stability of families has been compromised, despite the system's 22 billion dollar annual price tag.[5]

Professor Huntington argues for a family's robust and supportive and voluntary engagement with the state to meet the needs of the child but without a loss of family self-determination.

---

4. Ray Helfer, *An Overview of Prevention,* in The Battered Child, Fourth Edition (Helfer & Kempe Eds) 1987 at 425.
5. Clare Huntington, Mutual Dependency in Child Welfare, 82 NOTRE DAME L.REV.1485 (April 2007).

Wald, Gupta-Kagan, Huntington and others endorse a public health approach to support families—and consequently improve the welfare of children. Broader family friendly policies may do away with the need to petition so many of them into the court child protection system. Michael Wald would build on the existing Women, Infant and Children program and a network of home health visitors or pediatricians to assist parents with child rearing issues voluntarily and as needed, as a preventive and supportive service. "[G]iven the magnitude of the problem, child advocates should unite behind a set of programs and urge policy makers to adopt some version of the system I have outlined at scale and then work to improve it over time."[6]

"We will always have some need for a child welfare system" says Professor Huntington, "but rather than try so hard to fix the system, we should reduce the need for it."[7]

The QIC prescriptions include these macro issues since the broader social issues seriously affect the individual lawyer's ability to represent any child effectively.

13.3 Federal Leadership

CAPTA remains the Federal touchstone when it comes to advocacy for the allegedly abused or neglect child. It requires that states receiving CAPTA funds provide representation for children, either a lawyer or a lay volunteer or both, but does not specify the training or duties of that advocate other than that it be a person "who has received training appropriate to the role" who would "obtain first-hand a clear understanding of the situation and needs of the child and . . .make recommendations to the court concerning the best interests of the child."[8] The CAPTA reauthorization could reflect some of the findings of the QIC and the growing consensus as to what sort of advocacy a child requires in protection cases, including a more robust statement of the lawyer role. CAPTA should require that a child be represented by legal counsel in all child welfare proceedings. CAPTA should also direct the U.S. Children's Bureau to promulgate rules or guidelines governing child representation or provide direction in the form of recommended policies for recruitment and training of such lawyers. CAPTA could direct additional research dollars to identify and promote the optimum approaches to legal representation of children—and parents and the agency. The interface between the agency child protection response and the courts is far from optimum and improved lawyering for all parties can help.

The Federal government could enforce the existing CAPTA requirement that all children receive a guardian-ad-litem or lawyer in a child protection judicial proceeding. The QIC research found that many children in Georgia and Washington State did not receive *any* representation—not from a lay volunteer and not from a lawyer in any

---

6. *Supra* note 5 at 25.
7. Huntington, The Child Welfare System and the Limits of Determinacy, 77 Duke Jl of Law and Contemporary Problems, 221, 246 (2014).
8. 42 USC s5106a(b)(2)(A)(xiii).

role. This is consistent with research from other quarters that despite the CAPTA mandate, states are still not providing independent representation of all children in child welfare cases. First Star and the Children's Advocacy Institute call for Federal enforcement of the CAPTA requirement and report:

- In Florida, only 80% of abused and neglected children received a CAPTA-mandated GAL.
- In Ohio, 40% of the GALs never even met with the children they represented.
- In New Hampshire, hundreds of children go without the services of a CASA *guardian ad litem* every year.
- In one North Carolina county, 25% of the children who have been abused or neglected are going to court without advocates.[9]

Others have noted that Congress was wise in requiring an advocate for the child in these proceedings and the Children's Bureau should put the requirement into effect.[10] One step toward enforcement could be for the U.S. Children's Bureau to conduct an inquiry into states to determine whether children really are receiving the individual advocacy required by CAPTA. Children's Bureau could identify any shortfall and work with the states to make it up.

13.4 States Should Enact a Legal Structure to Support Child Representation

States should adopt the 2011 ABA Model Act as the statutory structure for legal representation of the child. Shortly after the QIC began its work, the ABA House of Delegates adopted the 2011 Model Act.[11] The Model Act is consistent with the findings and recommendations of the QIC (See discussion in Chapter Four.). The ABA 2011 Model Act, the 1996 ABA Standards and the QIC Best Practice Model are in essential harmony. This reflects an emerging consensus throughout the land on most of these questions. The 2011 Model Act provides the statutory structure, the 1996 ABA Standards and the QIC Best Practice Model provide the day to day standards, and the Six Core Skills provide the essential clinical skills required by a lawyer representing a child.

One of our QIC findings is that uncertainty as to the proper tasks and duties of the child's representative makes improvement much more difficult. In our baseline survey

---

9. *Shame on U.S.: Failings by All three Branches of Our Federal Government Leave Abused and Neglected Children Vulnerable to Further Harm*, (2015) at 59; available at http://www.caichildlaw.org/Misc/Shame%20on%20U.S._FINAL.pdf (last visited February 24, 2016).

10. Glynn, *The Child's Representation under CAPTA: It Is Time for Enforcement*, 6 Nev L.Rev. 1250 (Spring 2006).

11. ABA *Model Act Governing the Representation of Children in Abuse, Neglect, and Dependency Proceedings*.

we found areas of disagreement as to the proper elements of child representation. Many attorneys saw themselves as having only limited responsibility for certain tasks that the QIC Best Practice Model and other national recommendations see as important. (Chapter 8, §8.9, Table 7)

But the attorneys in our two states demonstrate a strength that is likely present elsewhere. Despite variances as to what tasks are properly child lawyer responsibilities, there was a consistency of opinion that favors thoughtful, active, representation that involves a relationship with the child. There also seems to be an appetite among lawyers for gaining more skills and improving their practice. They were receptive to learning new approaches and adopted new methods when trained and encouraged to do so.

13.5 Organization for Legal Services for Children

13.5.1 Advantages of Concentrated Practice

A general thrust of the QIC collective findings is that a specialized or concentrated lawyer caseload representing children is associated with a better practice in several respects. A homogeneous practice that is more focused on child representation allows the lawyer to specialize and invest more time and energy in continuing and improving their child welfare law professional skills. (§9.8.4) Where child representation constitutes only a small portion of an attorney's practice, he or she may be less likely to want to invest in developing these unique skills.

High attorney activity rates on individual cases is positively associated with the proportion of an attorney's practice devoted to child representation. (§9.7) In particular there is a higher level of contact with the child by staff attorneys and attorneys where child representation is a higher proportion of the caseload. (§9.7) Therefore an important influence on attorney behavior may be the organizational climate and culture with the advantage to a specialized law office. The analysis in Chapter 8, however, indicates that the potential benefits of specializing, 1) smaller caseloads, 2) higher relative concentrations of child representation cases and 3) a belief that the work is important and rewarding, may be achieved across the various organizational structures.

13.5.2 Child Welfare Law Offices

Staff attorney offices, in which lawyers are substantially involved in child representation, were found to offer a number of advantages. The staff had access to more resources than the solo practice and private law firm attorneys. Staff attorneys were more independent of the court because they were more likely to operate under contracts with the court while solo and private firm lawyers were more likely to receive appointments on a case by case basis and bill on a case-by-case basis. (§8.7) Not all findings support the superiority of staff attorney offices, however. For example, attorneys working for staff attorney offices are found to be less experienced and to report lower overall law incomes than attorneys working in other settings. (§8.12.6)

The empirical data provide support for dedicated staff attorney offices or otherwise concentrating the child representation within a modest number of lawyers in order to encourage the commitment, energy and skill development that seems to result. This is consistent with the recommendation of QIC-ChildRep Best Practice Model that each jurisdiction have an administrative structure, independent of the court that supports, trains, and holds accountable lawyers representing children.

Dedicated children's law offices seem to offer several advantages over alternative organizational settings. By pooling resources and expertise, child welfare legal offices provide their attorneys with greater opportunities for mentoring, training and professional consultation, and greater access to clinical and other support staff than alternative organizational settings.[12] A dedicated organization can provide lawyers a career path in the field. The organization can also hold lawyers accountable to high standards of practice. Contractual arrangements between child welfare legal offices and juvenile courts may promote independence of the child representatives and militate against attorneys restraining their advocacy to avoid alienating the individuals (e.g., judges, court clerks) responsible for making court appointments.

The NACC recommends a practice infrastructure to support the delivery of legal services to children. "[O]ne of the best mechanisms for delivery of high quality legal services to children is an institutional structure that allows multiple attorneys to focus their attention on the representation of children in general and the representation of children in child welfare law proceedings in particular—in other words, a dedicated child welfare law office."[13]

13.5.3 Where Case Volume Is Low; Statewide System

But our data show that some counties simply do not have the volume of cases to support a dedicated child welfare legal offices or a specialized children's lawyer. Dedicated child welfare legal offices might be preferable, but admonitions to establish such offices may be moot where the volume of dependency cases is insufficient to make such arrangements viable. The QIC found that staff attorneys were more likely to work in urban counties.

The QIC found that child representation usually constituted a fairly small proportion of a lawyer's practice. For most lawyers, child representation constituted less than 20% of their legal work. (§8.4) In the previous six months, one-third of the attorneys handled five or fewer cases. The national cognoscenti of child advocacy tend to focus on the specialty child welfare law office where children are represented by a dedicated

---

12. Leslie S. Heimov, Amanda G. Donnelly & Marvin Ventrell, *Rise of the Organizational Practice Of Child Welfare Law: The Child Welfare Law Office* 78 U. Colorado L. Rev. 1097-1117 (2007).
13. NACC, Child Welfare Law Office Guidebook (2006).

group of lawyers who develop considerable experience and expertise.[14] In the QIC sample, however, most children are not represented by such specialists, but rather by general practitioners handling a limited number of dependency cases. In many jurisdictions, especially those in rural counties, there may not be a sufficient number of dependency cases to support either a full-time or specialized dependency law practice.

A take-away for a local jurisdiction might be to select only a few lawyers to serve on the panel, rather than distributing the case assignments broadly. Even in a small-volume jurisdiction, the benefits of a more concentrated caseload could be realized.

A statewide response to this data would be to organize child representation using a statewide contracting model. This approach, which is currently implemented in a handful of states, appears to offer many of the same advantages attributed to child welfare legal offices, even when the lawyers are not necessarily housed together in the same office.[15] In general, these programs contract with individual attorneys to represent dependency cases within the jurisdiction. Participating attorneys are required to complete initial and ongoing training requirements and typically provide participating attorneys with ongoing support, including case consultation and professional mentoring. Caseloads are commonly limited. Programs set practice standards for contracted attorneys and, in some cases, promulgate minimum rates of compensation for attorney services.

Statewide networks, like a localized child welfare law office, also provide a valuable quality control and accountability function. Judges may appreciate the additional recourse when they are concerned about the quality of child representation practice. On the other hand, much like child welfare legal offices, these statewide network arrangements may lessen attorneys' dependence upon smooth relations with local courts and judges and reduce the judges' power to limit case assignments received by a particular attorney.

In short, the statewide network can create a financially predictable, supportive environment that encourages continued dedication to and specialization in child representation.

13.6 Recruit the Best and the Brightest and Most Committed

The QIC data has implications for efforts to hire, train, support and retain a cadre of high quality child representatives. One of the concerns often expressed is that selection of lawyers for children is somewhat random. Are these lawyers who were "accidentally

---

14. Guidebook; QIC see below.
15. See, for example, Arkansas, (Ark. Code. Ann. §9-27-401 established a state-wide system of employment or contracts for representing children). Colorado (Colorado Office of the Child's Representative; http://www.coloradochildrep.org/; Massachusetts, (Children and Family Law Division of the Massachusetts Committee for Public Counsel Services; and New York State of New York Office of Attorneys for Children.)

washed up on the shores of child welfare and decided to stay"? Truth is that some of these "accidental child lawyers" are quite good, but focused attention on developing a career path for the self-selected passionate and committed may pay dividends for the field.

Increasingly law schools are providing educational opportunities in child welfare law and students see child welfare as an inviting area of practice, not so much for the money, but for the satisfaction of the job. The ABA maintains a directory of children's law program around the country and a full list of all child law clinics associated with law schools.[16]

But the talent pool for child representation will not all come directly from law schools. Our QIC study found that the lawyers are hardly fresh out of school.[17] Most had practiced law for many years, with a mean of 13.5 years, and 56% had represented children for five or more years. The implications for recruitment and training may be that capable children's attorneys could be recruited at various stages of a legal career and that training opportunities should be available to prepare not only the beginning lawyer, but also the more experienced lawyer looking to add the personally rewarding child representation to an existing practice.[18]

It behooves the child welfare community to facilitate a match between the lawyer especially interested in the field and job opportunities. Where a jurisdiction delivers legal services to children and their parents through dedicated offices or concentrated caseloads, lawyers with a particularly strong interest in the field are more likely to find a foothold and pursue child welfare as career specialty.

A reason to facilitate a career path for the "passionate and committed" is the important observation from the attorney activity study that the attorney attitude about the importance of the role as a child representative and their perception of how impactful their work on cases is was positively associated with various activities. Sixty-four percent of our surveyed attorneys "strongly agreed" that their work as a children's lawyer was rewarding. Eighty-five percent agreed or strongly agreed that their work had a significant impact on the outcomes for the children they represent.[19] And it appears that a lawyer's beliefs about the importance of the work and their effectiveness is a

---

16. The ABA Section of Litigation, Children's Directory of Children's Law Programs at http://apps.americanbar.org/litigation/committees/childrights/directory.html. It is compilation of children's law programs across the country with a full list of all children's law centers, all children's legal clinics (associated with a law school) and all children's resource centers (that provide litigation support to children's lawyers). Program listings by state as well as a full pdf of the Directory is *available at* http://www.americanbar.org/content/dam/aba/publications/litigation_committees/childrights/directory.authcheckdam.pdf.

17. Orlebeke, Zinn, Duquette and Zhou, "Characteristics of Attorneys Representing Children,49 Fam. L. Q. 477 (Fall 2015). studied 126 lawyers in Washington and 143 in Georgia.

18. *Id.* at 505.

19. *Id.* at 500.

self-fulfilling prophecy and actually makes them more effective. That is, lawyers who believe in the importance of the work and their own effectiveness actually seem to be more effective. (§9.7)

One concern is that the financial compensation received by child representatives is low leading to a high level of attrition and diminution in practice quality.[20] The QIC data paint a somewhat more complicated picture, however. Although a majority of attorneys in both states report that the level of financial compensation is either somewhat or very inadequate, most report that their work as child representatives is both rewarding and impactful. And the level of attrition among these groups of child representatives appears low, especially as compared with agency caseworkers in child welfare. Paradoxically, attorneys who reported spending more time on their cases were more likely to say that their compensation was too low. Child representatives seem motivated by altruistic reasons that transcend financial concerns. The personal rewards these attorneys derive from child representation seems to reduce the drag of inadequate compensation.

13.7 Caseloads

The QIC data provides some insight into the question of what the proper caseload for attorneys should be. Our QIC assessment is that the *adjusted caseload* of our sample was 60 cases. That is, even when child representation occupied only a portion of a lawyer's practice, when the number of cases is adjusted for the percentage of effort required for child representation, the adjusted caseload was 60.

Caseload matters. The QIC lawyer activity data in Chapter 9 supports the common sense conclusion that caseload size limits what an attorney can do for any individual child. A one-standard-deviation increase (20 cases) in the size of dependency caseload is associated with a 22 percent decrease in the monthly rate of investigation and document review and a 9 percent decrease in the monthly rate of legal case preparation activities. (§9.7) The larger the caseload the less a lawyer can do for any individual child.

What is a reasonable caseload for lawyers representing children? Crushing caseloads in urban settings have been a troubling feature of child welfare law practice for many years and the QIC findings reinforce the importance of reasonable caseloads for attorneys doing this work. A 2006 survey for the NACC showed that 18 percent of respondents had more than 200 cases and an additional 25% had between 100 and 199.[21]

---

20. D'Andrea, Theresa (2012) "Money Talks": An Assessment of the Effects of Attorney Compensation on the Representation of Children in the Child Welfare System and How States Speak through Delivery Systems. *Children's Legal Rights Journal*, 32(3), 67-88.

21. Davidson & Pitchal, *Caseloads Must Be Controlled So All Child Clients May Receive Competent Lawyering,* http://papers.ssrn.com/sol3/papers.cfm?abstract_id=943059n.

The NACC recommends a standard of 100 active clients for a full-time attorney.[22] The NACC based this recommendation on a rough calculation that the average attorney has 2000 hours available per year and that the average child client would require about 20 hours of attention in the course of a year.[23] In *Kenny A* the court heard expert testimony from NACC along these lines. This evidence became a key consideration in the court's finding that foster children have a right to an effective lawyer in dependency cases who is not burdened by excessive caseloads.

A 2008 caseload study by the Judicial Council of California based on time and motion measures recommended a caseload of 77 clients per full-time dependency attorney to achieve an optimal best practice standard of performance.[24] The California Judicial Council set 141 as the maximum ceiling of cases a full-time attorney may carry. The Council also recognized the value of multidisciplinary representation when it proscribed a modified *maximum* caseload standard of 188 clients per attorney if there is a 0.5 FTE investigator/social worker complement for each full-time attorney position.

New York law sets the maximum caseload at 150[25]. The Massachusetts Committee for Public Counsel Services, which provides counsel for children and parents in dependency cases, enforces a caseload of 75 open cases.[26]

In a very detailed systematic study, a Pennsylvania workgroup carefully broke down the tasks and expected time required throughout the life of a case and matched that to attorney hours available in a year. They concluded that caseloads for children's lawyers should be set at 65 per full time lawyer.[27]

13.8 Multidisciplinary Law Practice

Multidisciplinary approaches to representing children are increasing popular and widely considered a good practice but up to now there are few studies of the challenges behind implementing such an office and little empirical evidence of the effect of lawyer-social worker collaboration on case process and outcomes. The QIC-ChildRep

---

22. National Association of Counsel for Children, *Child Welfare Law Guidebook*, 2006, at 54.

23. NACC, Pitchal, Freundlich, and Kendrick, *Evaluation of the Guardian ad Litem System in Nebraska*, (December 2009) at 42-43, available http://c.ymcdn.com/sites/www.naccchildlaw.org/resource/resmgr/nebraska/final_nebraska_gal_report_12.pdf?

24. Ca Dependency Counsel Caseload Standards A Report To The California Legislature April 2008 by the Judicial Council of California Administrative Office of the Courts Center for Families, Children & the Courts. This report is also available on the California Courts Web site: http://www.courtinfo.ca.gov/programs/cfcc/resources/publications/articles.htm.

25. 22 N.Y. Comp. Codes R. & Regs. Tit. 22, §127.5(a).

26. Massachusetts Policies and Procedures. https://www.publiccounsel.net/private_counsel_manual/CURRENT_MANUAL_2010/MANUALChap5links3.pdf.

27. 2014 Pennsylvania State Roundtable Report: Moving Children to Timely Permanency, available at 2014 Pennsylvania State Roundtable Report: Moving Children to Timely Permanency.

provides some of the first empirical assessment of the effectiveness of multidisciplinary representation of children. Using a random assignment experimental design children in Genesee County (Flint), Michigan, children represented by a team of a lawyer and social worker were compared with children represented by an attorney only. Despite the cultural challenges of lawyers and social workers collaborating together, multidisciplinary teams dramatically improved case outcomes and the experience of children facing foster care.

The MDT approach led to quicker case resolutions for some children and preserved family connections more often. Children served by the MDT had fewer removals after the intervention was assigned, fewer adjudications of jurisdiction, and fewer petitions to terminate the rights of parents. When children were removed, they were more likely to be placed with relatives and less likely to be placed in foster care. (§12.5.3) *Throughout the process observation, the study found that the attorneys' respect for the social work skillset, the social workers' ability to effectively collaborate with the child welfare agency and their intensive advocacy early in the case, as well as protections for client confidentiality, are keys to successfully employing multidisciplinary teams.*

Many of the leading child law offices collaborate with social service professionals and NACC endorses multidisciplinary practice.[28] Scott Hollander and Jonathon Budd of Pittsburgh's KidsVoice recommend: "A child welfare law office should apply a multidisciplinary approach to advocacy—inside and outside the courtroom—that integrates various professional perspectives and expertise." No single profession possesses the broad range of skills necessary to successfully identify and advocate for a child's needs. The QIC strongly recommends that communities adopt the practice of lawyers representing children in a collaborative team, working side-by-side with social workers or similarly trained professionals.

13.9 Training

Both the 1996 ABA Standards and our QIC Best Practice Model recommend that lawyers representing children have access to basic training and systematic continuing professional development. The administrative agency responsible for delivering legal services for children should assume the responsibility for on-going education and mentorship, including encouraging lawyers to become NACC Child Welfare Law Specialists (CWLS). Training has both a macro and micro aspect.

The QIC empirical data show that lawyers seemed receptive to training and improving their practice level. A major take-away from the QIC experiment is that when the attorneys in Georgia and Washington State were offered an approach to child representation that was touted as a model that could help them improve practice and get better

---

28. Hollander and Budd, *Multidisciplinary Practice*, in NACC Child Welfare Law Office Guidebook at 51. Guidebook available at: https://c.ymcdn.com/sites/naccchildlaw.site-ym.com/resource/resmgr/clop/clopguidebookfinal4-06.pdf.

results for their child clients, they lapped it up. Apart from whatever merits might be found in the Six Core Skills themselves, the lawyers were eager to learn and responded very well to the promise and prospect of improvement. To their credit, they learned and implemented the approach we offered them. It was as if they said, "Tell us what good practice is, and we will do it." The lawyers' earnest receptivity to training in the role bodes well for future efforts.

We also learned that lawyers learn well from one another, from peer to peer conversations, facilitated by a respected professional. An encouraging finding is the commitment to the importance of the work and willingness to assist others in doing it. Despite the fact that most attorneys were solo practitioners, more than 80% said that individuals were often or almost always available to discuss cases with them. (§8.9)

The concentration of child representation practice has significant implications for recruiting and training lawyers. A high volume of children's cases might allow a lawyer to specialize and possibly earn a reasonable income from child welfare law practice. But where the volume and concentration of cases is low, lawyers will be less willing to invest in the unique skills required for child representation.

This has implications for how training and other professional development is organized and delivered. In low volume less populated areas educators need to respect the limited time and resources attorneys can devote to this practice and identify trainings that are targeted to the most critical skills. The lack of specialization puts a premium on distance learning and on-line professional education courses that attorneys could take on their own schedules.[29]

The discussion of lawyer activities in Chapter 9 surfaces the effect of lawyer attitudes, beliefs and biases and opens up some lessons for training, supervision and mentorship. Lawyers could reflect on how they spend their time and consider whether that is the optimum distribution.

For example, does the lawyer spend more time with older girls than toddlers because the older girl has more issues to address or because the lawyer is more comfortable dealing with older girls who actually are glad to speak with them, compared with a sullen teen boy or wary toddler? This awareness may lead to reprioritization or even to providing clinical training in skills necessary to build trust and break through to the uncommunicative teen or read a toddler, and thus get information about them and their needs. (§9.6)

Building a general agreement as to what the tasks and duties of the child's lawyer are is salutary. The QIC empirical information shows that uncertainty—as to specific duties, how to best spend one's energy, and what the overall role of the child lawyer is—makes engagement more difficult. Merely clarifying these basic expectations may serve to improve the practice. Support for this inference comes from the fact that the

---

29. Id. at 506.

attorney's professed level of responsibility for various case-related tasks is positively associated with increased contacts with the child and family. (§9.7) That is, when an attorney believes it is his or her responsibility to do a task, they do it! Training that explicitly communicates a broad scope of responsibility and identifies desirable tasks may improve performance.

Likewise, the subjective view of whether the work is rewarding is positively related to higher rates of desirable activities. (§9.7) This is basic common sense; if a person finds an action rewarding, they work harder at it. The inference is that training that builds an *esprit de corps*, or that builds up enthusiasm for the child advocacy field itself, may itself have a direct impact on performance. This may be especially valuable where cynicism and futility are common.

We find good news in that we found no activity differences based on ethnicity or race. And no differences were found based on relative versus non-relative placements.

13.10 Certification

Specialty certification of lawyers can add to the quality and sophistication of a state's work force and improve the quality of representation that children (and parents and the agency) receive. In 2004 the ABA recognized a legal specialty in child welfare law and accredited the NACC to certify lawyers as specialists in the field. The specialization area is defined as "the practice of law representing children, parents or the government in all child protection proceedings including emergency, temporary custody, adjudication, disposition, foster care, permanency planning, termination, guardianship, and adoption. Child Welfare Law does not include representation in private custody and adoption disputes where the state is not a party."[30] There are now about 600 NACC Certified Child Welfare Law Specialists in 43 jurisdictions.[31]

Child Welfare Law Certification is modeled after physician board certification and requires that attorneys satisfy certain requirements to apply. The applicant must make a satisfactory showing of substantial involvement relevant to child welfare law, with at least thirty (30) percent of his or her time involved in child welfare law during the three (3) years preceding the filing of the application. The major requirements are:

- Three or more years practicing law
- 30% or more of the last three years involved in child welfare law
- 36 hours of continuing learning education within the last three years in courses relevant to child welfare law (45 hours in CA, and 36 hours + nine hours of ethics courses in AZ)

---

30. http://www.naccchildlaw.org/?page=Certification; last visited, 6-07-16.
31. *Id.*

- A writing sample drafted within the last three years that demonstrates legal analysis in the field of child welfare law

  For a complete list of requirements, please see the NACC Certification Standards[32]

13.11 Research Agenda

More analysis and reflection is required about these data, these findings and their meaning. We encourage researchers to review the full Evaluation Report by Chapin Hall available on their website at http://www.chapinhall.org. Our data are available at the National Data Archive on Child Abuse and Neglect.

Broadly speaking, there are at least two important research questions about child representation that merit attention. First, which types of activities yield the greatest impact, and do these impacts vary across case types, outcomes, and practice contexts? For example, is contact with children's families equally important for younger vs. older children, victims of sexual abuse vs. neglect, or for cases with permanency goals of reunification vs. guardianship? Collectively, these questions would begin to address the broader question of which practices, under which circumstances, constitute impactful child representation.

Second, does increased attorney activity actually lead to better outcomes for children in dependency cases? On its face, the answer would seem to be obvious, that is, more attorney activity is better. However, given the multiplicity of factors that influence case outcomes, and potentially mitigate the impact of attorneys' efforts, there may be a point of diminishing returns where more attorney action does not contribute significantly to improving the overall outcome. There are many other contextual factors that limit the ability of a single party (attorneys or anyone else) to influence outcomes. Thus, the question of whether more is better seems well-justified. Child representation takes place in a context with other parties, organizations and institutions. This may be a situation in which a rising tide is necessary to lift all boats.

13.12 Conclusion

The practice of law for children continues to evolve at a fairly rapid rate. It has evolved from a cottage industry of "kiddie law" to a sophisticated legal specialty. Increasingly there is a consensus on how lawyers should approach representing children. Whether the lawyer is charged with representing the child's wishes or the child's best interest, the lawyer's tasks and duties are essentially the same.

Empirical evidence is beginning to provide helpful guidance as to organization and delivery of legal services to the child. A national model of practice has emerged. Above all we want this book to be practically helpful to legislators, judges, policy makers, and especially to Court Improvement Project directors and to the U.S. Children's Bureau.

---

32. *Id.*

ACKNOWLEDGMENTS

One quiet late April morning in 2009 I was in my office minding my own business, wrapping up the semester's activities, when I got a call from Washington, DC. "Hi, I'm Karl Ensign, of Planning and Learning Technologies (PAL-Tech)," the new voice said. "There is a new RFP (Request for Proposal) out from the U.S. Children's Bureau. Have you seen it? Check it out. We want to apply for this and we want you to lead the effort as the P.I (Principal Investigator)" My life hasn't been the same since.

The RFP for the National Quality Improvement Center for the Representation of Children in the Child Welfare System was the U.S. Children's Bureau's (CB) most far-reaching initiative yet for improving legal representation of children. I learned later that CB's Emily Cooke had advocated for an ambitious research and consensus building project on child representation for many years and the stars finally aligned in the form of this RFP. Emily Cooke was my first Federal Project Officer (FPO). I still have my file labeled "Emily's List" of tasks and directions as we first set up the project. She had clear ideas for the foundation of the project and communicated them to me very clearly. Well begun is half-done, right? I felt this was her "baby" that was put temporarily in my foster care to nourish to the next step. Thank you Emily for your clear vision and direction.

Upon her retirement, after a long and illustrious career at CB, the FPO duties were assumed by David Kelly who has been an ideal FPO, and a terrifically nice guy to boot. Always supportive. Always available for direction when needed, but leaving the details to me and my team. What a great talent David is at CB; he understands the law and courts and how they fit in to the overall child welfare system. He is creative and committed—and I think he understands the urgency that drives recreating our child welfare system. He has already done great things for child welfare and I expect even more from him as time goes on. Thank you, David. You're the best. Aqui vamos!

In our first year Needs Assessment my partnership with Karl Ensign and PAL-Tech was very productive and very satisfying. With the support of Cynthia Samples, Robyn Ristau, and others at PAL-Tech, Karl and I identified the "state of play" as to child representation in the U.S. which was to be the foundation of the QIC project to come. Karl, I owe you so much, as do the people who will learn and benefit from this project. Thank you.

With Emily Cooke's guidance we developed a National Advisory Committee without peer. This carefully balanced group helped us explore options and eventually sharpen our focus.

- Maryellen Bearzi—Protective Services Division, New Mexico,
- Frank Cervone—Support Center for Child Advocates, Philadelphia, PA
- Kay Farley—National Center for State Courts
- Martin Guggenheim, New York University Law School, New York, NY
- BJ Jones—North Dakota Tribal Judicial Institute
- Mimi Laver—American Bar Association Center on Children and the Law, Washington, DC
- Hon. Patricia Martin –National Council for Juvenile and Family Court Judges, Chicago, IL
- Michael Piraino—National Court Appointed Special Advocates
- Carol Wilson Spigner, University of Pennsylvania School of Social Work, State College, PA
- Mark Testa—University of North Carolina School of Social Work,
- Nancy Thoennes, Center for Policy Research, Denver, CO
- Casey Trupin—Columbia Legal Services, Seattle, WA

Thank you all very much for your time and advice and for giving this project such a strong start.

Already in the first year we began thinking about appropriate empirical questions and a research design so we turned to Robert Nelson at the American Bar Foundation who convened a group of research scholars to consider our empirical questions and possible options. Thanks to Bob, to Beth Mertz who headed the effort, and to Gail Goodman, and Sarah Ramsey. Doing double duty were Nancy Thoennes, Martin Guggenheim, and Mark Testa who participated in these research design discussions and also served on the QIC Advisory Board.

Enter Chapin Hall at the University of Chicago. Led by Britany Orlebeke and including Andy Zinn, Ada Skyles, and Xiaomeng Zhou, Chapin Hall became the essential research partner in this effort. Fred Wulczyn made sure we started on the proper footing. Chapin Hall is well-known in the child welfare community as the premier empirical research team. They absorbed the findings of the QIC needs assessment, reviewed the advice of the American Bar Foundation advisory group, and then went through their own deliberations. The result is the ambitious and cogent research plan you see reported here. Talk about smart, rigorous, and methodical, these folks are awesome.

I wanted to answer ALL the pressing questions in this one effort; you taught me that sound research requires a disciplined focus. Thank you for the tutoring in the complexities of managing a complex research project and for putting up with my many naïve questions. Thanks especially for your hardheaded competence. I always knew we were in the hands of experts. There is more from the social science perspective to learn about lawyers and courts in child welfare, much more. These are the folks to do it. And thanks too for the friendships we have built over these six years of collaboration.

The QIC was administratively simple in the first year, but by year two things got pretty complicated. But all was smooth sailing thanks to the addition of Assistant Director Robbin Pott, executive extraordinaire and valued advisor. Everyone who has worked with her realizes her intelligence and gift for organization. I really appreciate her heart, her passion for social justice. Apart from keeping the QIC project running smoothly, Robbin took on the challenging multidisciplinary representation study in Flint. This is one of the major products of the QIC effort and will have a lasting impact on our field. Alicia Lixey provided reliable administrative support for the QIC as she has for the Child Advocacy Law Clinic for so many years. Her happy disposition is a pleasure. Mike Halerz, of Terapixel, Inc. in Ann Arbor, designed our website and our logo and was always available for consult when we needed him.

By the end of the first year we had developed the QIC Best Practice Model and were facing the challenge of how to train lawyers in the model in a way that would be straightforward, easy to grasp and retain, but also could be done in a relatively short period of time. In early 2011 Cecilia Fiermonte did the initial work on a two-day curriculum. We built upon Cecilia's framework for an initial pilot and modified it again for the final QIC training. Cecilia is a great talent, with a broad and deep understanding of the law, policy and practice related to child welfare and a good understanding of adult learning styles. Her initial materials really set us on the right foot. Thank you so much Cecilia.

Tim Jaasko-Fisher, then of the Court Improvement Training Academy at the University of Washington Law School, observed the first pilot of the two-day training in Ann Arbor in May 2011. He liked the content but thought it could be delivered more effectively. He was right. Tim opened my eyes to Liberating Structures and other fresh approaches to harnessing and channeling ideas from a group. Tim named the "pods" and his commitment to "communities of learning" guided our efforts for keeping the Six Core Skills learning alive. Tim was one of the major QIC trainers and has a special skill for engaging learners and making it fun. He ran the regular pod meetings in Washington, assisted by Rob Wyman. I miss working with you on a regular basis, Tim.

Tim also engaged the Mockingbird Society, an organization of former foster youth in Washington State. We all know that the voices of the children and youth are often overlooked, not heard. We developed a scenario and a video for the training with assistance from Mockingbird Society. A special thanks to Deonate Cruz who played Marco in our video and to Dominique as Margo. The conversation that Tim led with these two youth, about their experiences in foster care and with lawyers, was one of the high points of the QIC training. Janet Gwilym, then a 2d year law student at University of Washington, conducted the interviews with Marco. She was given little preparation time but she set up our training objectives just right. She is a gutsy and courageous lawyer by now and her clients are lucky to have her. Thanks to you all.

Melissa Carter, Director of the Barton Child Law Center at Emory Law School was also a key developer of the QIC training package and a major trainer for all the sessions in Washington State and Georgia. She is a respected presence in Georgia for her effective advocacy. Her confidence and competence and clear presentations really won our audiences. I love her positive and hard-working approach. Melissa ran the pod meetings in Georgia. Thank you, Melissa.

An essential element of the QIC training was child development, interviewing and the effects of trauma. My Michigan colleague, psychologist Dr. Kate Rosenblum, developed that package and did the training in Georgia to rave reviews. Dr. Fran Lexcen, a psychologist with similar training and experience as Kate's, did the child development and trauma training in Washington State. She was wonderful to work with and received similar raves from the lawyers. Thank you Kate and Fran.

My Michigan Law School colleague, Frank Vandervort, contributed to this effort in so many ways that a thank you hardly covers it. In the first year or so Frank was my consigliere. I discussed most major decisions with him and received excellent counsel. He was a major contributor to the QIC training package, especially around negotiation, conflict resolution and advocacy approaches. Frank was one of the trainers in the Michigan pilot and in Georgia with excellent results. You would think this would be enough to be thankful for, but Frank also reviewed this entire book in draft form and gave detailed insightful comments. (His unvarnished, candid comments were, well,...frank.) His comments brought the book to a new level.

Vivek Sankaran, another of my Michigan Law colleagues and now Director of the Child Advocacy Law Clinic, also reviewed the complete manuscript and provided direction and helpful critique. Vivek says we need a QIC-type opportunity for parent representation.

The leadership of each of our partner states was extraordinary. Michelle Barclay of Supreme Court of Georgia Committee on Justice for Children is a strong and clear-minded leader. Her commitment to this project and constantly innovative spirit is an inspiration to us all. She was assisted by Pat Buonodono of the Administrative Office of the Courts and Araceli Jacobs. Araceli earned the trust of the lawyers and local court clerks and worked tirelessly to get the data that we needed. She's amazing. Jane Okrasinski and Darice Good provided the coaching and, along with Melissa Carter, conducted the pod meetings for the Georgia lawyers, which kept the QIC Six Core Skills ideas alive throughout the project. Thank you all, very, very much.

In Washington State, Justice Bobbe Bridge (Ret.) is unequaled as an advocate for children and youth. Since leaving the Washington State Supreme Court she started the Center for Children and Youth Justice (CCYJ) in Seattle. Our formal partners in Washington were the CCYJ and the Washington Office of Civil Legal Aid (OCLA), on behalf

ACKNOWLEDGMENTS

of the Washington State Supreme Court Commission on Children in Foster Care. At CCYJ, Hathaway Burden, a young superstar, now in law school, handled the complex management issues inherent in this project. She was succeeded by a proud Michigan law & MSW graduates Hannah Gold and Gina Cumbo. The highest accolades go to Rob Wyman who contacted each and every Washington State lawyer who represented children and asked him or her to agree to participate in this study. Rob's credibility as a coach came from his extensive trial practice and experience as a supervising lawyer leavened by insight and sensitivity reflecting his MSW training. He was extraordinarily effective. He and Tim Jaasko-Fisher were terrific in the pod meeting. What a team in Washington State! Thank you.

Chapin Hall depended upon reliable and committed state collaboration to get the data in a reliable form. I share their appreciation of George Li, from the Georgia Administrative Office of the Courts, who was willing to share his expertise with the court's data system throughout the project. We also thank the staff of the Washington State Center for Court Research—Charlotte Jensen, Matt Orme, and Carl McCurley.

None of this work, and certainly not my involvement in it, would have been possible without the incredible support and nurturing environment of the Michigan Law School (UML). This extraordinary institution has encouraged and sustained our child welfare law work for over 40 years—when the place of "kiddie law" and clinical law was far from established as an appropriate part of a top tier law school. UML took a chance over these decades that not all law schools would have taken. Apropos of the QIC, my dean in 2009, Evan Caminker, was not only supportive but was willing to forgo considerable indirect costs in order to make our proposal to CB more competitive and free up more resources for the work - and thus less for institutional support. Not every dean would agree to that. That means that Michigan law, directly and indirectly, supported some of the work of the QIC. I thank Evan Caminker, our current Dean Mark West, but also the entire institution. It is an extraordinary place with extraordinary people.

Finally, and probably most importantly, we thank the attorneys in Georgia and Washington State who agreed to participate in the project and the evaluation, and who completed thousands of surveys over multiple years. Their cooperation and willingness to share the details of their work, helps us better understand the process and effect of their advocacy for children. The lawyers hoped that their involvement in this study would somehow help improve legal representation of children on a national level. May their hopes be fulfilled! They are the true heroes in this field and we dedicate this book to them and the many other lawyers who work day in and day out representing children, their parents, and the child welfare agency in America's still inadequate child protection system. Thank you! On we go!

APPENDIX A

QIC Best Practice Model of Child Representation

The QIC Best Practice Model sets out the *duties* of the individual child representative and the important *organizational and administrative supports* required in order for the child's representative to adequately perform those duties. Language that differs from the 1996 ABA Standards is highlighted.

PART ONE

Definitions:
Child's Representative means the individual or office charged with providing legal services for a child who is the subject of judicial child welfare proceedings. The *child's representative* (CR) is to ensure that the child's interests are identified and presented to the court. The duties of the CR are as presented below. Although the CR will be providing legal representation to the child, the CR functions may be fulfilled by a team of multidisciplinary professionals, including a lawyer plus social workers, paralegals and/or lay advocates.

I. General Duties of the Child's Legal Representative

1. *Appointment*: The child's representative should be appointed and begin service prior to the first judicial proceeding. The ideal arrangement would be for the CR to be appointed sufficiently in advance of the first hearing so as to provide time for some preliminary investigation and exploration of options to protect the child with

minimum disruption of the child's world. The CR should serve until the court's child welfare authority over the child ends, including through appeals.

2. *Child's Interests*: The CR shall serve as the independent representative for the child as determined by state law. Whether the lawyer takes his or her direction from the child or makes a best interest judgment as to what the goals of the litigation should be, once the goals are determined the lawyer is expected to aggressively fulfill the duties and obligations set forth here.

   Although the majority of state laws adopt a 'best interests" or dual role for their child representative, some states have moved to a client directed representation for older children and best interests or substituted judgment for younger children. The QIC-ChildRep is interested in studying what difference, if any, different ways of accommodating the child's wishes makes as to case processing or case outcomes.

3. *Basic Obligations*: The CR should:
   a) Obtain copies of all pleadings and relevant notices;
   b) Participate in depositions, negotiations, discovery, pretrial conferences, and hearings;
   c) Inform other parties and their representatives that he or she is representing the child and expects reasonable notification prior to case conferences, changes of placement, and other changes of circumstances affecting the child and the child's family;
   d) Participate fully in all placement decisions; seek to disrupt the child's world as little as possible; "remove the danger, not the child"; assure that all placement decisions are made with care and deliberation; when placement is necessary help identify placement alternatives;
   e) Attempt to reduce case delays and ensure that the court recognizes the need to speedily promote permanency for the child;
   f) Counsel the child concerning the subject matter of the litigation, the child's rights, the court system, the proceedings, the lawyer's role, and what to expect in the legal process;
   g) Develop a theory and strategy of the case to implement at hearings, including factual and legal issues; and
   h) Identify appropriate family and professional resources for the child

4. *Conflict Situations*: The court may appoint one lawyer to represent siblings so long as there is no conflict of interest.

5. *Determining Decision-making Capacity*: The CR should be vigilant and thoughtful about maximizing the child client's participation in determining the positions to be taken in the case. Even a lawyer acting in the role of a best interest attorney or guardian ad litem should encourage the child to participate in the decision-making process to the extent that the child is able to do so. The functional capacity to direct representation or contribute to positions taken exists on a continuum, even for

adults. ("...[T]he lawyer shall, as far as reasonably possible, maintain a normal client-lawyer relationship with the client." ABA Model Rules of Prof Resp, 1.14) The CR should consider whether the child client has sufficient capacity to make a decision or to have significant input with respect to a particular issue at a particular time.

6. *Client Preferences*: When it comes to accommodating a child's wishes and preferences, perhaps the best an attorney can do is to really listen to the child, understand what is important from the child's perspective and how decisions will impact on the child's experience of his or her life, and act with humility when considering taking a position which significantly differs from the child's expressed wishes. (See Duquette and Haralambie, "Representing Children and Youth," in CHILD WELFARE LAW AND PRACTICE, 2d Edition, (2010), Duquette and Haralambie, Editors.) The CR must understand "how this client speaks, how this client sees the world, what this client values, and what shows this client respect." (Jean Koh Peters, Representing Children in Child Protective Proceedings: Ethical and Practical Dimensions p. 258 (1997))

2. Out of Court: Actions to Be Taken

1. *Meet With Child*. Establishing and maintaining a relationship with a child is the foundation of representation. Therefore, irrespective of the child's age, the child's representative should visit with the child prior to court hearings and when apprised of emergencies or significant events impacting on the child. Building a trusting relationship with the child is essential to successful representation. The CR can establish an appropriate tone with questions like "How can I help you? How can I be of service to you?" The child is the client and the lawyer should aggressively seek to meet the needs and interests of the child, just as the lawyer would for an adult or corporate client.

2. *Investigate*. To support the client's position, the child's representative should conduct thorough, continuing, and independent investigations and discovery that may include, but should not be limited to:
   a) Reviewing the child's social services, psychiatric, psychological, drug and alcohol, medical, law enforcement, school, and other records relevant to the case;
   b) Reviewing the court files of the child and siblings, case-related records of the social service agency and other service providers;
   c) Contacting lawyers for other parties and non-lawyer guardians ad litem or court-appointed special advocates (CASA) for background information;
   d) Contacting and meeting with the parents/legal guardians/caretakers of the child, with permission of their lawyer;
   e) Assist in identifying relatives from maternal and paternal sides of the family who might provide emotional and other support to the child and family or become a caretaker for the child.

f) Obtaining necessary authorizations for the release of information
g) Interviewing individuals involved with the child, including school personnel, child welfare case workers, foster parents and other caretakers, neighbors, relatives, school personnel, coaches, clergy, mental health professionals, physicians, law enforcement officers, and other potential witnesses.
h) Reviewing relevant photographs, video or audio tapes and other evidence; and
i) Attending treatment, placement administrative hearings, and other proceedings involving legal issues, and school case conferences or staffing concerning the child as needed.

3. *Advice and Counseling:* The CR and child client should work together to set the goals of the representation. Representing children involves more than investigation and advocacy. All attorneys have the duty to help a client understand their legal rights and obligations and identify the practical options. This is no less true for a child client. State law and the child's age and maturity will govern to what extent the CR accommodates the child's wishes in setting the goals of the advocacy. But in any event and consistent with the child's level of maturity and understanding, the child's representative will discuss the total circumstances with the child, strive to understand the child's world and perspective, assist the child in understanding the situation and the options available to him/her, and counsel the child as to the positions to be taken. The CR should advise the client as to the jurisdiction's rules—and limitations, if any—governing attorney-client privilege and confidentiality.

4. *File Pleadings.* The child's representative should file petitions, motions, responses or objections as necessary to represent the child. Relief requested may include, but is not limited to:
   a) A mental or physical examination of a party or the child;
   b) A parenting, custody or visitation evaluation;
   c) An increase, decrease, or termination of contact or visitation;
   d) Restraining or enjoining a change of placement;
   e) Contempt for non-compliance with a court order;
   f) Termination of the parent-child relationship;
   g) Child support;
   h) A protective order concerning the child's privileged communications or tangible or intangible property;
   i) Requesting services for child or family; and
   j) Dismissal of petitions or motions.

5. *Request Services.* The child's representative should seek appropriate services (by court order if necessary) to access entitlements, to protect the child's interests and to implement a service plan. These services may include, but not be limited to:
   a) Family preservation-related prevention or reunification services;
   b) Sibling and family visitation;

c) Child support;
   d) Domestic violence prevention, intervention, and treatment;
   e) Medical and mental health care;
   f) Drug and alcohol treatment;
   g) Parenting education;
   h) Semi-independent and independent living services;
   i) Long-term foster care;
   j) Termination of parental rights action;
   k) Adoption services;
   l) Education;
   m) Recreation or social services;
   n) Housing;
   o) Appropriate discharge plan, including services to assist the youth aging out of foster care.
6. *Child With Special Needs.* Consistent with the child's wishes, the child's representative should assure that a child with special needs receives appropriate services to address the physical, mental, or developmental disabilities. These services may include, but should not be limited to:
   a) Special education and related services;
   b) Supplemental security income (SSI) to help support needed services;
   c) Therapeutic foster or group home care; and
   d) Residential in-patient and out-patient psychiatric treatment.
7. *Adopt a Problem-solving Approach.* The child's representative should continually search for appropriate non-adversarial resolution of the case that protects the child and meets the child's needs. The CR should adopt a problem-solving attitude and seek cooperative resolution of the case whenever possible. The CR should also initiate and participate in settlement negotiations to seek expeditious resolution of the case, keeping in mind the effect of continuances and delays on the child. The child's representative should use suitable mediation and family conferencing resources.

3. In-Court: Active Participation in Hearings

1. *Court Appearances.* The child's representative should attend all hearings and participate in all telephone or other conferences with the court unless a particular hearing involves issues completely unrelated to the child.
2. *Client Explanation.* The child's representative should explain to the client, in a developmentally appropriate manner, what is expected to happen before, during and after each hearing.
3. *Motions and Objections.* The child's representative should make appropriate motions, including motions *in limine* and evidentiary objections, to advance the child's position at trial or during other hearings. If necessary, the child's representative

should file briefs in support of evidentiary issues. Further, during all hearings, the child's representative should preserve legal issues for appeal, as appropriate.
4. *Presentation of Evidence.* The child's representative should present and cross examine witnesses, offer exhibits, and provide independent evidence as necessary.
5. *Child at Hearing.* In most circumstances, the child should be present at significant court hearings, regardless of whether the child will testify.
6. *Expanded Scope of Representation.* The child's representative may request authority from the court to pursue issues on behalf of the child, administratively or judicially, even if those issues do not specifically arise from the court appointment. For example:
   a) Child support;
   b) Delinquency or status offender matters;
   c) SSI and other public benefits;
   d) Custody;
   e) Guardianship;
   f) Paternity;
   g) Personal injury;
   h) School/education issues, especially for a child with disabilities;
   i) Mental health proceedings;
   j) Termination of parental rights; and
   k) Adoption.
7. *Obligations After Disposition:* The child's representative should seek to ensure continued representation of the child during the pendency of the court's jurisdiction over the child.

4. Post-Hearing

1. *Review of Court's Order.* The child's attorney should review all written orders to ensure that they conform with the court's verbal orders and statutorily required findings and notices.
2. *Communicate Order to Child.* The child's attorney should discuss the order and its consequences with the child.
3. *Implementation.* The child's attorney should monitor the implementation of the court's orders and communicate to the responsible agency and, if necessary, the court, any non-compliance.

5. Appellate Advocacy

1. *Decision to Appeal.* The child's attorney should consider and discuss with the child, as developmentally appropriate, the possibility of an appeal. If after such consultation, the child wishes to appeal the order, and the appeal has merit, the lawyer should take all steps necessary to perfect the appeal and seek appropriate

temporary orders or extraordinary writs necessary to protect the interests of the child while the appeal is pending.
2. *Withdrawal* If the child's attorney determines that an appeal would be frivolous or that he or she lacks the necessary experience or expertise to handle the appeal, the lawyer should notify the court and seek to be discharged or replaced.
3. *Participation in Appeal.* The child's attorney should participate in an appeal filed by another party unless discharged.
4. *Conclusion of Appeal.* When the decision is received, the child's attorney should explain the outcome of the case to the child.

6. Cessation of Representation
1. The child's attorney should represent the child to the end of the court's jurisdiction and then discuss the ending of the legal representation and determine what contacts, if any, the child's attorney and the child will continue to have.

PART TWO
ORGANIZATIONAL AND ADMINISTRATIVE SUPPORTS FOR THE CHILD REPRESENTATIVE

7. General Representation Rules
1. Administrative structure is clear for appointment, support and accountability of the CR.
2. The child's representative should be independent from the court, court services, the parties and the state. The CR should retain full authority for independent action.

8. Lawyer Training
1. The court or administrative agency providing child representation should assure that each CR, whether a private practitioner or a part of a child welfare law office, be qualified by training or experience to fulfill the duties of the role.
2. The court or administrative agency providing child representation should provide on-going training programs on the role of a child's representative. Training programs should prepare the lawyer just beginning work in child welfare, provide continuing training, and encourage certification of experienced lawyers as specialists in the child welfare field.
3. Training should include:
    a) Information about relevant federal and state laws and agency regulations;
    b) Information about relevant court decisions and court rules;
    c) Overview of the court process and key personnel in child-related litigation;
    d) Description of applicable guidelines and standards for representation;
    e) Focus on child development, needs, and abilities;

f) Information on the multidisciplinary input required in child-related cases, including information on local experts who can provide consultation and testimony on the reasonableness and appropriateness of efforts made to safely maintain the child in his or her home;

g) Information concerning family dynamics and dysfunction including substance abuse, and the use of kinship care;

h) Information on accessible child welfare, family preservation, medical, educational, and mental health resources for child clients and their families, including placement, evaluation/diagnostic, and treatment services; the structure of agencies providing such services as well as provisions and constraints related to agency payment for services; and

i) Provision of written material (e.g., representation manuals, checklists, sample forms), including listings of useful material available from other sources.

4. The court or administrative agency providing child representation, should provide individual court-appointed attorneys who are new to child representation the opportunity to practice under the guidance of a senior lawyer mentor.

9. Lawyer Compensation

1. The court or administrative agency providing child representation, should assure that child's representatives receive adequate and timely compensation throughout the term of the appointment that reflects the complexity of the case and includes both in court and out-of-court preparation, participation in case reviews and post-dispositional hearings, and appeals. The rate of payment for these legal services should be commensurate with the fees paid to equivalently experienced individual court-appointed lawyers who have similar qualifications and responsibilities.

2. The court or administrative agency providing child representation, should assure that the child's representative has access to or is provided with reimbursement for experts, investigative services, paralegals, research costs, and other services, such as copying of medical records, long distance phone calls, service of process, and transcripts of hearings as a fundamental part of providing competent representation.

10. Caseload Levels

1. The court or administrative agency providing child representation, should assure that caseloads of the child representatives are of manageable size so that the CR can adequately discharge the duties to the child client.

APPENDIX B
1996 American Bar Association Standards of Practice for Lawyers Who Represent Children in Abuse and Neglect Cases

AMERICAN BAR ASSOCIATION
STANDARDS OF PRACTICE FOR LAWYERS
WHO REPRESENT CHILDREN IN ABUSE AND NEGLECT CASES
Approved by the American Bar Association House of Delegates, February 5, 1996

PREFACE

All children subject to court proceedings involving allegations of child abuse and neglect should have legal representation as long as the court jurisdiction continues. These Abuse and Neglect Standards are meant to apply when a lawyer is appointed for a child in any legal action based on: (a) a petition filed for protection of the child; (b) a request to a court to change legal custody, visitation, or guardianship based on allegations of child abuse or neglect based on sufficient cause; or (c) an action to terminate parental rights.

These Standards apply only to lawyers and take the position that although a lawyer *may* accept appointment in the dual capacity of a "lawyer/guardian ad litem," the lawyer's primary duty must still be focused on the protection of the legal rights of the child client. The lawyer/guardian ad litem should therefore perform all the functions of a "child's attorney," except as otherwise noted.

These Standards build upon the ABA-approved JUVENILE JUSTICE STANDARDS RELATING TO COUNSEL FOR PRIVATE PARTIES (1979) which include important directions for lawyers representing children in juvenile court matters generally, but do not contain sufficient guidance to aid lawyers representing children in abuse and neglect cases. These Abuse and Neglect Standards are also intended to help implement a series of ABA-approved policy resolutions (in Appendix) on the importance of legal representation and the improvement of lawyer practice in child protection cases.

In support of having lawyers play an active role in child abuse and neglect cases, in August 1995 the ABA endorsed a set of RESOURCE GUIDELINES: IMPROVING COURT PRACTICE IN CHILD ABUSE & NEGLECT CASES produced by the National Council of Juvenile and Family Court Judges. The RESOURCE GUIDELINES stress the importance of quality representation provided by competent and diligent lawyers by supporting: 1) the approach of vigorous representation of child clients; and 2) the actions that courts should take to help assure such representation.

These Standards contain two parts. Part I addresses the specific roles and responsibilities of a lawyer appointed to represent a child in an abuse and neglect case. Part II provides a set of standards for judicial administrators and trial judges to assure high quality legal representation.

PART I– STANDARDS FOR THE CHILD'S ATTORNEY

A. DEFINITIONS

A-1. The Child's Attorney. The term "child's attorney" means a lawyer who provides legal services for a child and who owes the same duties of undivided loyalty, confidentiality, and competent representation to the child as is due an adult client.

Commentary
These Standards explicitly recognize that the child is a separate individual with potentially discrete and independent views. To ensure that the child's independent voice is heard, the child's attorney must advocate the child's articulated position. Consequently, the child's attorney owes traditional duties to the child as client consistent with ER 1.14(a) of the Model Rules of Professional Conduct. In all but the exceptional case, such as with a preverbal child, the child's attorney will maintain this traditional relationship with the child/client. As with any client, the child's attorney may counsel against the pursuit of a particular position sought by the child. The child's attorney should recognize that the child may be more susceptible to intimidation and manipulation than some adult clients. Therefore, the child's attorney should ensure that the decision the child ultimately makes reflects his or her actual position.

A-2. Lawyer Appointed as Guardian Ad Litem. A lawyer appointed as "guardian ad litem" for a child is an officer of the court appointed to protect the child's interests without being bound by the child's expressed preferences.

Commentary
In some jurisdictions the lawyer may be appointed as guardian ad litem. These Standards, however, express a clear preference for the appointment as the "child's attorney." These Standards address the lawyer's obligations to the child as client.

A lawyer appointed as guardian ad litem is almost inevitably expected to perform legal functions on behalf of the child. Where the local law permits, the lawyer is expected to act in the dual role of guardian ad litem and lawyer of record. The chief distinguishing factor between the roles is the manner and method to be followed in determining the legal position to be advocated. While a guardian ad litem should take the child's point of view into account, the child's preferences are not binding, irrespective of the child's age and the ability or willingness of the child to express preferences. Moreover, in many states, a guardian ad litem may be required by statute or custom to perform specific tasks, such as submitting a report or testifying as a fact or expert witness. These tasks are not part of functioning as a "lawyer."

These Standards do not apply to nonlawyers when such persons are appointed as guardians ad litem or as "court appointed special advocates" (CASA). The nonlawyer guardian ad litem cannot and should not be expected to perform any legal functions on behalf of a child.

A-3. Developmentally Appropriate. "Developmentally appropriate" means that the child's attorney should ensure the child's ability to provide client-based directions by structuring all communications to account for the individual child's age, level of education, cultural context, and degree of language acquisition.

Commentary
The lawyer has an obligation to explain clearly, precisely, and in terms the client can understand the meaning and consequences of action. See DAVID A. BINDER & SUSAN C. PRICE, LEGAL INTERVIEWING AND COUNSELING: A CLIENT-CENTERED APPROACH (1977). A child client may not understand the legal terminology and for a variety of reasons may choose a particular course of action without fully appreciating the implications. With a child the potential for not understanding may be even greater. Therefore, the child's attorney has additional obligations based on the child's age, level of education, and degree of language acquisition. There is also the possibility that because of a particular child's developmental limitations, the lawyer may not completely understand the child's responses. Therefore, the child's attorney must learn how to ask developmentally appropriate questions and how to interpret the child's responses. See ANNE GRAFFAM WALKER, HANDBOOK ON QUESTIONING CHILDREN: A LINGUISTIC PERSPECTIVE (ABA Center on Children and the Law 1994). The child's attorney may work with social workers or other professionals to assess a child's developmental abilities and to facilitate communication.

B. GENERAL AUTHORITY AND DUTIES

B-1. Basic Obligations. The child's attorney should:

(1) Obtain copies of all pleadings and relevant notices;
(2) Participate in depositions, negotiations, discovery, pretrial conferences, and hearings;
(3) Inform other parties and their representatives that he or she is representing the child and expects reasonable notification prior to case conferences, changes of placement, and other changes of circumstances affecting the child and the child's family;
(4) Attempt to reduce case delays and ensure that the court recognizes the need to speedily promote permanency for the child;
(5) Counsel the child concerning the subject matter of the litigation, the child's rights, the court system, the proceedings, the lawyer's role, and what to expect in the legal process;
(6) Develop a theory and strategy of the case to implement at hearings, including factual and legal issues; and
(7) Identify appropriate family and professional resources for the child.

Commentary
The child's attorney should not be merely a fact-finder, but rather, should zealously advocate a position on behalf of the child. (The same is true for the guardian ad litem, although the position to be advocated may be different). In furtherance of that advocacy, the child's attorney must be adequately prepared prior to hearings. The lawyer's presence at and active participation in all hearings is absolutely critical. See, RESOURCE GUIDELINES, *at 23.*

Although the child's position may overlap with the position of one or both parents, third-party caretakers, or a state agency, the child's attorney should be prepared to participate fully in any proceedings and not merely defer to the other parties. Any identity of position should be based on the merits of the position, and not a mere endorsement of another party's position.

While subsection (4) recognizes that delays are usually harmful, there may be some circumstances when delay may be beneficial. Section (7) contemplates that the child's attorney will identify counseling, educational and health services, substance abuse programs for the child and other family members, housing and other forms of material assistance for which the child may qualify under law. The lawyer can also identify family members, friends, neighbors, or teachers with whom the child feels it is important to maintain contact; mentoring programs, such as Big Brother/Big Sister; recreational opportunities that develop social skills and self-esteem; educational support programs; and volunteer opportunities which can enhance a child's self-esteem.

B-2. Conflict Situations. (1) If a lawyer appointed as guardian ad litem determines that there is a conflict caused by performing both roles of guardian ad litem and child's attorney, the lawyer should continue to perform as the child's attorney and withdraw as guardian ad litem. The lawyer should request appointment of a guardian ad litem without revealing the basis for the request.

(2) If a lawyer is appointed as a "child's attorney" for siblings, there may also be a conflict which could require that the lawyer decline representation or withdraw from representing all of the children.

Commentary
The primary conflict that arises between the two roles is when the child's expressed preferences differ from what the lawyer deems to be in the child's best interests. As a practical matter, when the lawyer has established a trusting relationship with the child, most conflicts can be avoided. While the lawyer should be careful not to apply undue pressure to a child, the lawyer's advice and guidance can often persuade the child to change an imprudent position or to identify alternative choices if the child's first choice is denied by the court.

The lawyer-client role involves a confidential relationship with privileged communications, while a guardian ad litem-client role may not be confidential. Compare Alaska Bar Assoc. Ethics Op. #854 (1985) (lawyer-client privilege does not apply when the lawyer is appointed to be child's guardian ad litem) with Bentley v. Bentley, 448 N.Y.S.2d 559 (App. Div. 1982) (communication between minor children and guardian ad litem in divorce custody case is entitled to lawyer-client privilege). Because the child has a right to confidentiality and advocacy of his or her position, the child's attorney can never abandon this role. Once a lawyer has a lawyer-client relationship with a minor, he or she cannot and should not assume any other role for the child, especially as guardian ad litem. When the roles cannot be reconciled, another person must assume the guardian ad litem role. See Arizona State Bar Committee on Rules of Professional Conduct, Opinion No. 86-13 (1986).

B-3. Client Under Disability. The child's attorney should determine whether the child is "under a disability" pursuant to the Model Rules of Professional Conduct or the Model Code of Professional Responsibility with respect to each issue in which the child is called upon to direct the representation.

Commentary
These Standards do not accept the idea that children of certain ages are "impaired," "disabled," "incompetent," or lack capacity to determine their position in litigation. Further, these Standards reject the concept that any disability must be globally determined.
Rather, disability is contextual, incremental, and may be intermittent. The child's ability to contribute to a determination of his or her position is functional, depending upon the particular position and the circumstances prevailing at the time the position must be determined. Therefore, a child may be able to determine some positions in the case but not others. Similarly, a child may be able to direct the lawyer with respect to a particular issue at one time but not at another. This Standard relies on empirical knowledge about competencies with respect to both adults and children. See, e.g., ALLEN E. BUCHANAN & DAN W. BROCK, DECIDING FOR OTHERS: THE ETHICS OF SURROGATE DECISION MAKING 217 (1989).

B-4. Client Preferences. The child's attorney should elicit the child's preferences in a developmentally appropriate manner, advise the child, and provide guidance. The child's attorney should represent the child's expressed preferences and follow the child's direction throughout the course of litigation.

Commentary
The lawyer has a duty to explain to the child in a developmentally appropriate way such information as will assist the child in having maximum input in determination of the particular position at issue. The lawyer should inform the child of the relevant facts and applicable laws and the ramifications of taking various positions, which may include the impact of such decisions on other family members or on future legal proceedings. The lawyer may express an opinion concerning the likelihood of the court or other parties accepting particular positions. The lawyer may inform the child of an expert's recommendations germane to the issue.

As in any other lawyer/client relationship, the lawyer may express his or her assessment of the case, the best position for the child to take, and the reasons underlying such recommendation. A child, however, may agree with the lawyer for inappropriate reasons. A lawyer must remain aware of the power dynamics inherent in adult/child relationships. Therefore, the lawyer needs to understand what the child knows and what factors are influencing the child's decision. The lawyer should attempt to determine from the child's opinion and reasoning what factors have been most influential or have been confusing or glided over by the child when deciding the best time to express his or her assessment of the case.

Consistent with the rules of confidentiality and with sensitivity to the child's privacy, the lawyer should consult with the child's therapist and other experts and obtain appropriate records. For example, a child's therapist may help the child to understand why an expressed position is dangerous, foolish, or not in the child's best interests. The therapist might also assist the lawyer in understanding the child's perspective, priorities, and individual needs. Similarly, significant persons in the child's life may educate the lawyer about the child's needs, priorities, and previous experiences.

The lawyer for the child has dual fiduciary duties to the child which must be balanced. On one hand, the lawyer has a duty to ensure that the child client is given the information necessary to make an informed decision, including advice and guidance. On the other hand, the lawyer has a duty not to overbear the will of the child. While the lawyer may attempt to persuade the child to accept a particular position, the lawyer may not advocate a position contrary to the child's expressed position except as provided by these Abuse and Neglect Standards or the Code of Professional Responsibility.

While the child is entitled to determine the overall objectives to be pursued, the child's attorney, as any adult's lawyer, may make certain decisions with respect to the manner of achieving those objectives, particularly with respect to procedural matters. These Abuse and Neglect Standards do not require the lawyer to consult with the child on matters which would not require consultation with an adult client. Further, the Standards do not require the child's attorney to discuss with the child issues for which it is not feasible to obtain the child's direction because of the child's developmental limitations, as with an infant or preverbal child.

(1) To the extent that a child cannot express a preference, the child's attorney shall make a good faith effort to determine the child's wishes and advocate accordingly or request appointment of a guardian ad litem.

Commentary

There are circumstances in which a child is unable to express a position, as in the case of a preverbal child, or may not be capable of understanding the legal or factual issues involved. Under such circumstances, the child's attorney should continue to represent the child's legal interests and request appointment of a guardian ad litem. This limitation distinguishes the scope of independent decision-making of the child's attorney and a person acting as guardian ad litem.

(2) To the extent that a child does not or will not express a preference about particular issues, the child's attorney should determine and advocate the child's legal interests.

Commentary

The child's failure to express a position is distinguishable from a directive that the lawyer not take a position with respect to certain issues. The child may have no opinion with respect to a particular issue, or may delegate the decision-making authority. For example, the child may not want to assume the responsibility of expressing a position because of loyalty conflicts or the desire not to hurt one of the other parties. The lawyer should clarify with the child whether the child wants the lawyer to take a position or remain silent with respect to that issue or wants the preference expressed only if the parent or other party is out of the courtroom. The lawyer is then bound by the child's directive. The position taken by the lawyer should not contradict or undermine other issues about which the child has expressed a preference.

(3) If the child's attorney determines that the child's expressed preference would be seriously injurious to the child (as opposed to merely being contrary to the lawyer's opinion of what would be in the child's interests), the lawyer may request appointment of a separate guardian ad litem and continue to represent the child's expressed preference, unless the child's position is prohibited by law or without any factual foundation. The child's attorney shall not reveal the basis of the request for appointment of a guardian ad litem which would compromise the child's position.

Commentary

One of the most difficult ethical issues for lawyers representing children occurs when the child is able to express a position and does so, but the lawyer believes that the position chosen is wholly inappropriate or could result in serious injury to the child. This is particularly likely to happen with respect to an abused child whose home is unsafe, but who desires to remain or return home. A child may desire to live in a dangerous situation because it is all he or she knows, because of a feeling of blame or of responsibility to take care of the parents, or because of threats. The child may choose to deal with a known situation rather than risk the unknown world of a foster home or other out-of-home placement.

In most cases the ethical conflict involved in asserting a position which would seriously endanger the child, especially by disclosure of privileged information, can be resolved through the lawyer's counseling function. If the lawyer has taken the time to establish rapport with the child and gain that child's trust, it is likely that the lawyer will be able to persuade the child to abandon a dangerous position or at least identify an alternate course.

If the child cannot be persuaded, the lawyer has a duty to safeguard the child's interests by requesting appointment of a guardian ad litem, who will be charged with advocating the child's best interests without being bound by the child's direction. As a practical matter, this may not adequately protect the child if the danger to the child was revealed only in a confidential disclosure to the lawyer, because the guardian ad litem may never learn of the disclosed danger.

Confidentiality is abrogated for various professionals by mandatory child abuse reporting laws. Some states abrogate lawyer-client privilege by mandating reports. States which do not abrogate the privilege may permit reports notwithstanding professional privileges. The policy considerations underlying abrogation apply to lawyers where there is a substantial danger of serious injury or death. Under such circumstances, the lawyer must take the minimum steps which would be necessary to ensure the child's safety, respecting and following the child's direction to the greatest extent possible consistent with the child's safety and ethical rules.

The lawyer may never counsel a client or assist a client in conduct the lawyer knows is criminal or fraudulent. See ER 1.2(d), Model Rules of Professional Conduct, DR 7-102(A)(7), Model Code of Professional Responsibility. Further, existing ethical rules requires the lawyer to disclose confidential information to the extent necessary to prevent the client from committing a criminal act likely to result in death or substantial bodily harm, see ER 1.6(b), Model Rules of Professional Conduct, and permits the lawyer to reveal the intention of the client to commit a crime. See ER 1.6(c), Model Rules of Professional Conduct, DR 4-101(C)(3), Model Code of Professional Responsibility. While child abuse, including sexual abuse, are crimes, the child is presumably the victim, rather than the perpetrator of those crimes. Therefore, disclosure of confidences is designed to protect the client, rather than to protect a third party from the client. Where the child is in grave danger of serious injury or death, the child's safety must be the paramount concern.

The lawyer is not bound to pursue the client's objectives through means not permitted by law and ethical rules. See DR-7-101(A)(1), Model Code of Professional Responsibility. Further, lawyers may be subject personally to sanctions for taking positions that are not well grounded in fact and warranted by existing law or a good faith argument for the extension, modification, or reversal of existing law.

B-5. Child's Interests. The determination of the child's legal interests should be based on objective criteria as set forth in the law that are related to the purposes of the proceedings. The criteria should address the child's specific needs and preferences, the goal of expeditious resolution of the case so the child can remain or return home or be placed in a safe, nurturing, and permanent environment, and the use of the least restrictive or detrimental alternatives available.

Commentary
A lawyer who is required to determine the child's interests is functioning in a nontraditional role by determining the position to be advocated independently of the client. The lawyer should base the position, however, on objective criteria concerning the child's needs and interests, and not merely on the lawyer's personal values, philosophies, and experiences. The child's various needs and interests may be in conflict and must be weighed against each other. Even nonverbal children can communicate their needs and interests through their behaviors and developmental levels. See generally JAMES GARBARINO & FRANCES M. STOTT, WHAT CHILDREN CAN TELL US: ELICITING, INTERPRETING, AND EVALUATING CRITICAL INFORMATION FROM CHILDREN (1992). The lawyer may seek the advice and consultation of experts and other knowledgeable people in both determining and weighing such needs and interests.

A child's legal interests may include basic physical and emotional needs, such as safety, shelter, food, and clothing. Such needs should be assessed in light of the child's vulnerability, dependence upon others, available external resources, and the degree of risk. A child needs family affiliation and stability of placement. The child's developmental level, including his or her sense of time, is relevant to an assessment of need. For example, a very young child may be less able to tolerate separation from a primary caretaker than an older child, and if separation is necessary, more frequent visitation than is ordinarily provided may be necessary.

In general, a child prefers to live with known people, to continue normal activities, and to avoid moving. To that end, the child's attorney should determine whether relatives, friends, neighbors, or other people known to the child are appropriate and available as placement resources. The lawyer must determine the child's feelings about the proposed caretaker, however, because familiarity does not automatically confer positive regard. Further, the lawyer may need to balance competing stability interests, such as living with a relative in another town versus living in a foster home in the same neighborhood. The individual child's needs will influence this balancing task.

In general, a child needs decisions about the custodial environment to be made quickly. Therefore, if the child must be removed from the home, it is generally in the child's best interests to have rehabilitative or reunification services offered to the family quickly. On the other hand, if it appears that reunification will be unlikely, it is generally in the child's best interests to move quickly toward an alternative permanent plan. Delay and indecision are rarely in a child's best interests.

In addition to the general needs and interests of children, individual children have particular needs, and the lawyer must determine the child client's individual needs. There are few rules which apply across the board to all children under all circumstances.

C. ACTIONS TO BE TAKEN

C-1. Meet With Child. Establishing and maintaining a relationship with a child is the foundation of representation. Therefore, irrespective of the child's age, the child's attorney should visit with the child prior to court hearings and when apprised of emergencies or significant events impacting on the child.

Commentary

Meeting with the child is important before court hearings and case reviews. In addition, changes in placement, school suspensions, in-patient hospitalizations, and other similar changes warrant meeting again with the child. Such in-person meetings allow the lawyer to explain to the child what is happening, what alternatives might be available, and what will happen next. This also allows the lawyer to assess the child's circumstances, often leading to a greater understanding of the case, which may lead to more creative solutions in the child's interest. A lawyer can learn a great deal from meeting with child clients, including a preverbal child. See, e.g., JAMES GARBARINO, ET AL, WHAT CHILDREN CAN TELL US: ELICITING, INTERPRETING, AND EVALUATING CRITICAL INFORMATION FROM CHILDREN (1992).

C-2. Investigate. To support the client's position, the child's attorney should conduct thorough, continuing, and independent investigations and discovery which may include, but should not be limited to:

(1) Reviewing the child's social services, psychiatric, psychological, drug and alcohol, medical, law enforcement, school, and other records relevant to the case;

Commentary

Thorough, independent investigation of cases, at every stage of the proceedings, is a key aspect of providing competent representation to children. See, RESOURCE GUIDELINES, AT 23. The lawyer may need to use subpoenas or other discovery or motion procedures to obtain the relevant records, especially those records which pertain to the other parties. In some jurisdictions the statute or the order appointing the lawyer for the child includes provision for obtaining certain records.

    (2)   Reviewing the court files of the child and siblings, case-related records of the social service agency and other service providers;

Commentary

Another key aspect of representing children is the review of all documents submitted to the court as well as relevant agency case files and law enforcement reports. See, RESOURCE GUIDELINES, at 23. Other relevant files that should be reviewed include those concerning child protective services, developmental disabilities, juvenile delinquency, mental health, and educational agencies. These records can provide a more complete context for the current problems of the child and family. Information in the files may suggest additional professionals and lay witnesses who should be contacted and may reveal alternate potential placements and services.

    (3)   Contacting lawyers for other parties and nonlawyer guardians ad litem or court-appointed special advocates (CASA) for background information;

Commentary

The other parties' lawyers may have information not included in any of the available records. Further, they can provide information on their respective clients' perspectives. The CASA is typically charged with performing an independent factual investigation, getting to know the child, and speaking up to the court on the child's "best interests." Volunteer CASAs may have more time to perform their functions than the child's attorney and can often provide a great deal of information to assist the child's attorney. Where there appears to be role conflict or confusion over the involvement of both a child's attorney and CASA in the same case, there should be joint efforts to clarify and define mutual responsibilities. See, RESOURCE GUIDELINES, at 24.

    (4)   Contacting and meeting with the parents/legal guardians/caretakers of the child, with permission of their lawyer;

Commentary

Such contact generally should include visiting the home, which will give the lawyer additional information about the child's custodial circumstances.

    (5)   Obtaining necessary authorizations for the release of information;

Commentary

If the relevant statute or order appointing the lawyer for the child does not provide explicit authorization for the lawyer's obtaining necessary records, the lawyer should attempt to obtain authorizations for release of information from the agency and from the parents, with their lawyer's consent. Even if it is not required, an older child should be asked to sign authorizations for release of his or her own records, because such a request demonstrates the lawyer's respect for the client's authority over information.

    (6)   Interviewing individuals involved with the child, including school personnel, child welfare case workers, foster parents and other caretakers, neighbors, relatives, school personnel, coaches, clergy, mental health professionals, physicians, law enforcement officers, and other potential witnesses;

Commentary

In some jurisdictions the child's attorney is permitted free access to agency case workers. In others, contact with the case worker must be arranged through the agency's lawyer.

    (7)   Reviewing relevant photographs, video or audio tapes and other evidence; and

Commentary

It is essential that the lawyer review the evidence personally, rather than relying on other parties' or counsel's descriptions and characterizations of the evidence.

(8) Attending treatment, placement, administrative hearings, other proceedings involving legal issues, and school case conferences or staffings concerning the child as needed.

Commentary

While some courts will not authorize compensation for the child's attorney to attend such collateral meetings, such attendance is often very important. The child's attorney can present the child's perspective at such meetings, as well as gather information necessary to proper representation. In some cases the child's attorney can be pivotal in achieving a negotiated settlement of all or some issues. The child's attorney may not need to attend collateral meetings if another person involved in the case, such as a social worker who works the lawyer, can get the information or present the child's perspective.

C-3. File Pleadings. The child's attorney should file petitions, motions, responses or objections as necessary to represent the child. Relief requested may include, but is not limited to:

(1) A mental or physical examination of a party or the child;
(2) A parenting, custody or visitation evaluation;
(3) An increase, decrease, or termination of contact or visitation;
(4) Restraining or enjoining a change of placement;
(5) Contempt for non-compliance with a court order;
(6) Termination of the parent-child relationship;
(7) Child support;
(8) A protective order concerning the child's privileged communications or tangible or intangible property;
(9) Request services for child or family; and
(10) Dismissal of petitions or motions.

Commentary

Filing and arguing necessary motions is an essential part of the role of a child's attorney. See, RESOURCE GUIDELINES, at 23. Unless the lawyer is serving in a role which explicitly precludes the filing of pleadings, the lawyer should file any appropriate pleadings on behalf of the child, including responses to the pleadings of the other parties. The filing of such pleadings can ensure that appropriate issues are properly before the court and can expedite the court's consideration of issues important to the child's interests. In some jurisdictions, guardians ad litem are not permitted to file pleadings, in which case it should be clear to the lawyer that he or she is not the "child's attorney" as defined in these Standards.

C-4. Request Services. Consistent with the child's wishes, the child's attorney should seek appropriate services (by court order if necessary) to access entitlements, to protect the child's interests and to implement a service plan. These services may include, but not be limited to:

(1) Family preservation-related prevention or reunification services;
(2) Sibling and family visitation;
(3) Child support;
(4) Domestic violence prevention, intervention, and treatment;
(5) Medical and mental health care;
(6) Drug and alcohol treatment;
(7) Parenting education;
(8) Semi-independent and independent living services;

(9) Long-term foster care;
(10) Termination of parental rights action;
(11) Adoption services;
(12) Education;
(13) Recreational or social services; and
(14) Housing.

Commentary

The lawyer should request appropriate services even if there is no hearing scheduled. Such requests may be made to the agency or treatment providers, or if such informal methods are unsuccessful, the lawyer should file a motion to bring the matter before the court. In some cases the child's attorney should file collateral actions, such as petitions for termination of parental rights, if such an action would advance the child's interest and is legally permitted and justified. Different resources are available in different localities.

C-5. Child With Special Needs. Consistent with the child's wishes, the child's attorney should assure that a child with special needs receives appropriate services to address the physical, mental, or developmental disabilities. These services may include, but should not be limited to:

(1) Special education and related services;
(2) Supplemental security income (SSI) to help support needed services;
(3) Therapeutic foster or group home care; and
(4) Residential/in-patient and out-patient psychiatric treatment.

Commentary

There are many services available from extra-judicial, as well as judicial, sources for children with special needs. The child's attorney should be familiar with these other services and how to assure their availability for the client. See generally, THOMAS A. JACOBS, CHILDREN & THE LAW: RIGHTS & OBLIGATIONS (1995); LEGAL RIGHTS OF CHILDREN (2d ed. Donald T. Kramer, ed., 1994).

C-6. Negotiate Settlements. The child's attorney should participate in settlement negotiations to seek expeditious resolution of the case, keeping in mind the effect of continuances and delays on the child. The child's attorney should use suitable mediation resources.

Commentary

Particularly in contentious cases, the child's attorney may effectively assist negotiations of the parties and their lawyers by focusing on the needs of the child. If a parent is legally represented, it is unethical for the child's attorney to negotiate with a parent directly without the consent of the parent's lawyer. Because the court is likely to resolve at least some parts of the dispute in question based on the best interests of the child, the child's attorney is in a pivotal position in negotiation.

Settlement frequently obtains at least short term relief for all parties involved and is often the best resolution of a case. The child's attorney, however, should not become merely a facilitator to the parties' reaching a negotiated settlement. As developmentally appropriate, the child's attorney should consult the child prior to any settlement becoming binding.

D. HEARINGS

D-1. Court Appearances. The child's attorney should attend all hearings and participate in all telephone or other conferences with the court unless a particular hearing involves issues completely unrelated to the child.

D-2. Client Explanation. The child's attorney should explain to the client, in a developmentally appropriate manner, what is expected to happen before, during and after each hearing.

D-3. Motions and Objections. The child's attorney should make appropriate motions, including motions *in limine* and evidentiary objections, to advance the child's position at trial or during other hearings. If necessary, the child's attorney should file briefs in support of evidentiary issues. Further, during all hearings, the child's attorney should preserve legal issues for appeal, as appropriate.

D-4. Presentation of Evidence. The child's attorney should present and cross examine witnesses, offer exhibits, and provide independent evidence as necessary.

Commentary
The child's position may overlap with the positions of one or both parents, third-party caretakers, or a child protection agency. Nevertheless, the child's attorney should be prepared to participate fully in every hearing and not merely defer to the other parties. Any identity of position should be based on the merits of the position (consistent with Standard B-6), and not a mere endorsement of another party's position.

D-5. Child at Hearing. In most circumstances, the child should be present at significant court hearings, regardless of whether the child will testify.

Commentary
A child has the right to meaningful participation in the case, which generally includes the child's presence at significant court hearings. Further, the child's presence underscores for the judge that the child is a real party in interest in the case. It may be necessary to obtain a court order or writ of habeas corpus ad testificandum to secure the child's attendance at the hearing.

A decision to exclude the child from the hearing should be made based on a particularized determination that the child does not want to attend, is too young to sit through the hearing, would be severely traumatized by such attendance, or for other good reason would be better served by nonattendance. There may be other extraordinary reasons for the child's non-attendance. The lawyer should consult the child, therapist, caretaker, or any other knowledgeable person in determining the effect on the child of being present at the hearing. In some jurisdictions the court requires an affirmative waiver of the child's presence if the child will not attend. Even a child who is too young to sit through the hearing may benefit from seeing the courtroom and meeting, or at least seeing, the judge who will be making the decisions. The lawyer should provide the court with any required notice that the child will be present. Concerns about the child being exposed to certain parts of the evidence may be addressed by the child's temporary exclusion from the court room during the taking of that evidence, rather than by excluding the child from the entire hearing.

The lawyer should ensure that the state/custodian meets its obligation to transport the child to and from the hearing. Similarly, the lawyer should ensure the presence of someone to accompany the child any time the child is temporarily absent from the hearing.

D-6. Whether Child Should Testify. The child's attorney should decide whether to call the child as a witness. The decision should include consideration of the child's need or desire to testify, any repercussions of testifying, the necessity of the child's direct testimony, the availability of other evidence or hearsay exceptions which may substitute for direct testimony by the child, and the child's developmental ability to provide direct testimony and withstand possible cross-examination. Ultimately, the child's attorney is bound by the child's direction concerning testifying.

Commentary

There are no blanket rules regarding a child's testimony. While testifying is undoubtedly traumatic for many children, it is therapeutic and empowering for others. Therefore, the decision about the child's testifying should be made individually, based on the circumstances of the individual child and the individual case. The child's therapist, if any, should be consulted both with respect to the decision itself and assistance with preparation. In the absence of compelling reasons, a child who has a strong desire to testify should be called to do so. See ANN M. HARALAMBIE, THE CHILD'S LAWYER: A GUIDE TO REPRESENTING CHILDREN IN CUSTODY, ADOPTION, AND PROTECTION CASES ch. 4 (1993). If the child should not wish to testify or would be harmed by being forced to testify, the lawyer should seek a stipulation of the parties not to call the child as a witness or seek a protective order from the court. If the child is compelled to testify, the lawyer should seek to minimize the adverse consequences by seeking any appropriate accommodations permitted by local law, such as having the testimony taken informally, in chambers, without presence of the parents. See JOHN E.B. MYERS, 2 EVIDENCE IN CHILD ABUSE AND NEGLECT CASES ch. 8 (1992). The child should know whether the in-chambers testimony will be shared with others, such as parents who might be excluded from chambers, before agreeing to this forum. The lawyer should also prepare the child for the possibility that the judge may render a decision against the child's wishes which will not be the child's fault.

D-7. Child Witness. The child's attorney should prepare the child to testify. This should include familiarizing the child with the courtroom, court procedures, and what to expect during direct and cross-examination and ensuring that testifying will cause minimum harm to the child.

Commentary

The lawyer's preparation of the child to testify should include attention to the child's developmental needs and abilities as well as to accommodations which should be made by the court and other lawyers. The lawyer should seek any necessary assistance from the court, including location of the testimony (in chambers, at a small table etc.), determination of who will be present, and restrictions on the manner and phrasing of questions posed to the child.

The accuracy of children's testimony is enhanced when they feel comfortable. See, generally, Karen Saywitz, Children in Court: Principles of Child Development for Judicial Application, in A JUDICIAL PRIMER ON CHILD SEXUAL ABUSE 15 (Josephine Bulkley & Claire Sandt, eds., 1994). Courts have permitted support persons to be present in the courtroom, sometimes even with the child sitting on the person's lap to testify. Because child abuse and neglect cases are often closed to the public, special permission may be necessary to enable such persons to be present during hearings. Further, where the rule sequestering witnesses has been invoked, the order of witnesses may need to be changed or an exemption granted where the support person also will be a witness. The child should be asked whether he or she would like someone to be present, and if so, whom the child prefers. Typical support persons include parents, relatives, therapists, Court Appointed Special Advocates (CASA), social workers, victim-witness advocates, and members of the clergy. For some, presence of the child's attorney provides sufficient support.

D-8. Questioning the Child. The child's attorney should seek to ensure that questions to the child are phrased in a syntactically and linguistically appropriate manner.

Commentary

The phrasing of questions should take into consideration the law and research regarding children's testimony, memory, and suggestibility. See generally, Karen Saywitz, supra D -7; CHILD VICTIMS, CHILD WITNESSES: UNDERSTANDING AND IMPROVING TESTIMONY (Gail S. Goodman & Bette L. Bottoms, eds. 1993); ANN HARALAMBIE, 2 HANDLING CHILD CUSTODY, ABUSE, AND ADOPTION CASES 24.09 v24.22 (2nd ed. 1993); MYERS, *supra* D-6, at Vol. 1, ch 2; Ellen Matthews & Karen Saywitz, *Child Victim Witness Manual*, 12/1 C.J.E.R.J. 40 (1992).

> The information a child gives in interviews and during testimony is often misleading because the adults have not understood how to ask children developmentally appropriate questions and how to interpret their answers properly. See WALKER, SUPRA, A-3 Commentary. The child's attorney must become skilled at recognizing the child's developmental limitations. It may be appropriate to present expert testimony on the issue and even to have an expert present during a young child's testimony to point out any developmentally inappropriate phrasing.

D-9. Challenges to Child's Testimony/Statements. The child's competency to testify, or the reliability of the child's testimony or out-of-court statements, may be called into question. The child's attorney should be familiar with the current law and empirical knowledge about children's competency, memory, and suggestibility and, where appropriate, attempt to establish the competency and reliability of the child.

Commentary

> Many jurisdictions have abolished presumptive ages of competency. See HARALAMBIE, SUPRA D-8 AT 24.17. The jurisdictions which have rejected presumptive ages for testimonial competency have applied more flexible, case-by-case analyses. See Louis I. Parley, Representing Children in Custody Litigation, 11 J. AM. ACAD. MATRIM. LAW. 45, 48 (Winter 1993). Competency to testify involves the abilities to perceive and relate.
>
> If necessary, the child's attorney should present expert testimony to establish competency or reliability or to rehabilitate any impeachment of the child on those bases. See generally, Karen Saywitz, supra D-8 at 15; CHILD VICTIMS, SUPRA D-8; Haralambie, supra D-8; J. MYERS, SUPRA D-8; Matthews & Saywitz, supra D-8.

D-10. Jury Selection. In those states in which a jury trial is possible, the child's attorney should participate in jury selection and drafting jury instructions.

D-11. Conclusion of Hearing. If appropriate, the child's attorney should make a closing argument, and provide proposed findings of fact and conclusions of law. The child's attorney should ensure that a written order is entered.

Commentary

> One of the values of having a trained child's attorney is such a lawyer can often present creative alternative solutions to the court. Further, the child's attorney is able to argue the child's interests from the child's perspective, keeping the case focused on the child's needs and the effect of various dispositions on the child.

D-12. Expanded Scope of Representation. The child's attorney may request authority from the court to pursue issues on behalf of the child, administratively or judicially, even if those issues do not specifically arise from the court appointment. For example:

   (1)   Child support;
   (2)   Delinquency or status offender matters;
   (3)   SSI and other public benefits;
   (4)   Custody;
   (5)   Guardianship;
   (6)   Paternity;
   (7)   Personal injury;
   (8)   School/education issues, especially for a child with disabilities;
   (9)   Mental health proceedings;
   (10) Termination of parental rights; and

(11) Adoption.

Commentary
The child's interests may be served through proceedings not connected with the case in which the child's attorney is participating. In such cases the lawyer may be able to secure assistance for the child by filing or participating in other actions. See, e.g., In re Appeal in Pima County Juvenile Action No. S-113432, 872 P.2d 1240 (Ariz. Ct. App. 1994). With an older child or a child with involved parents, the child's attorney may not need court authority to pursue other services. For instance, federal law allows the parent to control special education. A Unified Child and Family Court Model would allow for consistency of representation between related court proceedings, such as mental health or juvenile justice.

D-13. Obligations after Disposition. The child's attorney should seek to ensure continued representation of the child at all further hearings, including at administrative or judicial actions that result in changes to the child's placement or services, so long as the court maintains its jurisdiction.

Commentary
Representing a child should reflect the passage of time and the changing needs of the child. The bulk of the child's attorney's work often comes after the initial hearing, including ongoing permanency planning issues, six month reviews, case plan reviews, issues of termination, and so forth. The average length of stay in foster care is over five years in some jurisdictions. Often a child's case workers, therapists, other service providers or even placements change while the case is still pending. Different judges may hear various phases of the case. The child's attorney may be the only source of continuity for the child. Such continuity not only provides the child with a stable point of contact, but also may represent the institutional memory of case facts and procedural history for the agency and court. The child's attorney should stay in touch with the child, third party caretakers, case workers, and service providers throughout the term of appointment to ensure that the child's needs are met and that the case moves quickly to an appropriate resolution.

Generally it is preferable for the lawyer to remain involved so long as the case is pending to enable the child's interest to be addressed from the child's perspective at all stages. Like the JUVENILE JUSTICE STANDARDS, these ABUSE AND NEGLECT STANDARDS require ongoing appointment and active representation as long as the court retains jurisdiction over the child. To the extent that these are separate proceedings in some jurisdictions, the child's attorney should seek reappointment. Where reappointment is not feasible, the child's attorney should provide records and information about the case and cooperate with the successor to ensure continuity of representation.

E. POST-HEARING

E-1. Review of Court's Order. The child's attorney should review all written orders to ensure that they conform with the court's verbal orders and statutorily required findings and notices.

E-2. Communicate Order to Child. The child's attorney should discuss the order and its consequences with the child.

Commentary
The child is entitled to understand what the court has done and what that means to the child, at least with respect to those portions of the order that directly affect the child. Children may assume that orders are final and not subject to change. Therefore, the lawyer should explain whether the order may be modified at another hearing, or whether the actions of the parties may affect how the order is carried out. For example, an order may permit the agency to return the child to the parent if certain goals are accomplished.

E-3. Implementation. The child's attorney should monitor the implementation of the court's orders and communicate to the responsible agency and, if necessary, the court, any non-compliance.

Commentary
The lawyer should ensure that services are provided and that the court's orders are implemented in a complete and timely fashion. In order to address problems with implementation, the lawyer should stay in touch with the child, case worker, third party caretakers, and service providers between review hearings. The lawyer should consider filing any necessary motions, including those for civil or criminal contempt, to compel implementation. See, RESOURCE GUIDELINES, at 23.

F. APPEAL

F-1. Decision to Appeal. The child's attorney should consider and discuss with the child, as developmentally appropriate, the possibility of an appeal. If after such consultation, the child wishes to appeal the order, and the appeal has merit, the lawyer should take all steps necessary to perfect the appeal and seek appropriate temporary orders or extraordinary writs necessary to protect the interests of the child during the pendency of the appeal.

Commentary
The lawyer should explain to the child not only the legal possibility of an appeal, but also the ramifications of filing an appeal, including the potential for delaying implementation of services or placement options. The lawyer should also explain whether the trial court's orders will be stayed pending appeal and what the agency and trial court may do pending a final decision.

F-2. Withdrawal. If the child's attorney determines that an appeal would be frivolous or that he or she lacks the necessary experience or expertise to handle the appeal, the lawyer should notify the court and seek to be discharged or replaced.

F-3. Participation in Appeal. The child's attorney should participate in an appeal filed by another party unless discharged.

Commentary
The child's attorney should take a position in any appeal filed by the parent, agency, or other party. In some jurisdictions, the lawyer's appointment does not include representation on appeal. If the child's interests are affected by the issues raised in the appeal, the lawyer should seek an appointment on appeal or seek appointment of appellate counsel to represent the child's position in the appeal.

F-4. Conclusion of Appeal. When the decision is received, the child's attorney should explain the outcome of the case to the child.

Commentary
As with other court decisions, the lawyer should explain in terms the child can understand the nature and consequences of the appellate decision. In addition, the lawyer should explain whether there are further appellate remedies and what more, if anything, will be done in the trial court following the decision.

F-5. Cessation of Representation. The child's attorney should discuss the end of the legal representation and determine what contacts, if any, the child's attorney and the child will continue to have.

Commentary
When the representation ends, the child's lawyer should explain in a developmentally appropriate manner why the representation is ending and how the child can obtain assistance in the future should it become necessary. It is important for there to be closure between the child and the lawyer.

QIC BEST PRACTICE MODEL OF CHILD REPRESENTATION

PART II– ENHANCING THE JUDICIAL ROLE IN CHILD REPRESENTATION

PREFACE

Enhancing the legal representation provided by court-appointed lawyers for children has long been a special concern of the American Bar Association [*see, e.g.,* JUVENILE JUSTICE STANDARDS RELATING TO *COUNSEL FOR PRIVATE PARTIES* (1979); ABA Policy Resolutions on Representation of Children (Appendix). Yet, no matter how carefully a bar association, legislature, or court defines the duties of lawyers representing children, practice will only improve if judicial administrators and trial judges play a stronger role in the selection, training, oversight, and prompt payment of court-appointed lawyers in child abuse/neglect and child custody/visitation cases.

The importance of the court's role in helping assure competent representation of children is noted in the JUVENILE JUSTICE STANDARDS RELATING TO COURT ORGANIZATION AND ADMINISTRATION (1980) which state in the Commentary to 3.4D that effective representation of parties is "essential" and that the presiding judge of a court "might need to use his or her position to achieve" it. In its RESOURCE GUIDELINES: IMPROVING COURT PRACTICE IN CHILD ABUSE & NEGLECT CASES (1995), the National Council of Juvenile and Family Court Judges stated, "Juvenile and family courts should take active steps to ensure that the parties in child abuse and neglect cases have access to competent representation. . . ." In jurisdictions which engage nonlawyers to represent a child's interests, the court should ensure they have access to legal representation.

These Abuse and Neglect Standards, like the RESOURCE GUIDELINES, recognize that the courts have a great ability to influence positively the quality of counsel through setting judicial prerequisites for lawyer appointments including requirements for experience and training, imposing sanctions for violation of standards (such as terminating a lawyer's appointment to represent a specific child, denying further appointments, or even fines or referrals to the state bar committee for professional responsibility). The following Standards are intended to assist the judiciary in using its authority to accomplish the goal of quality representation for all children before the court in abuse/neglect related proceedings.

G. THE COURT'S ROLE IN STRUCTURING CHILD REPRESENTATION

G-1. Assuring Independence of the Child's Attorney. The child's attorney should be independent from the court, court services, the parties, and the state.

Commentary

To help assure that the child's attorney is not compromised in his or her independent action, these Standards propose that the child's lawyer be independent from other participants in the litigation. "Independence" does not mean that a lawyer may not receive payment from a court, a government entity (e.g., program funding from social services or justice agencies), or even from a parent, relative, or other adult so long as the lawyer retains the full authority for independent action. For ethical conflict reasons, however, lawyers should never accept compensation as retained counsel for the child from a parent accused of abusing or neglecting the child. The child's attorney should not prejudge the case. The concept of independence includes being free from prejudice and other limitations to uncompromised representation.

JUVENILE JUSTICE STANDARD 2.1(d) states that plans for providing counsel for children "must be designed to guarantee the professional independence of counsel and the integrity of the lawyer-client relationship." The Commentary strongly asserts there is "no justification for . . . judicial preference" to compromise a lawyer's relationship with the child client and notes the "willingness of some judges to direct lawyers' performance and thereby compromise their independence."

G-2. Establishing Uniform Representation Rules. The administrative office for the state trial, family, or juvenile court system should cause to be published and disseminated to all relevant courts a set of uniform, written rules and procedures for court-appointed lawyers for minor children.

Commentary

Although uniform rules of court to govern the processing of various types of child-related judicial proceedings have become common, it is still rare for those rules to address comprehensively the manner and scope of representation for children. Many lawyers representing children are unclear as to the court's expectations. Courts in different communities, or even judges within the same court, may have differing views regarding the manner of child representation. These Standards promote statewide uniformity by calling for written publication and distribution of state rules and procedures for the child's attorney.

G-3. Enhancing Lawyer Relationships with Other Court Connected Personnel. Courts that operate or utilize Court Appointed Special Advocate (CASA) and other nonlawyer guardians ad litem, and courts that administer nonjudicial foster care review bodies, should assure that these programs and the individuals performing those roles are trained to understand the role of the child's attorney. There needs to be effective coordination of their efforts with the activities of the child's attorney, and they need to involve the child's attorney in their work. The court should require that reports from agencies be prepared and presented to the parties in a timely fashion.

Commentary

Many courts now regularly involve nonlawyer advocates for children in various capacities. Some courts also operate programs that, outside of the courtroom, review the status of children in foster care or other out-of-home placements. It is critical that these activities are appropriately linked to the work of the child's attorney, and that the cour through training, policies, and protocols helps assure that those performing the nonlegal tasks (1) understand the importance and elements of the role of the child's attorney, and (2) work cooperatively with such lawyers. The court should keep abreast of all the different representatives involved with the child, the attorney, social worker for government or private agency, CASA volunteer, guardian ad litem, school mediator, counselors, etc.

H. THE COURT'S ROLE IN APPOINTING THE CHILD'S ATTORNEY

H-1. Timing of Appointments. The child's attorney should be appointed immediately after the earliest of:

(1) The involuntary removal of the child for placement due to allegations of neglect, abuse or abandonment;
(2) The filing of a petition alleging child abuse and neglect, for review of foster care placement, or for termination of parental rights; or
(3) Allegations of child maltreatment, based upon sufficient cause, are made by a party in the context of proceedings that were not originally initiated by a petition alleging child maltreatment.

Commentary

These *ABUSE AND NEGLECT STANDARDS* take the position that courts must assure the appointment of a lawyer for a child as soon as practical (ideally, on the day the court first has jurisdiction over the case, and hopefully, no later than the next business day). The three situations are described separately because:

(1) A court may authorize, or otherwise learn of, a child's removal from home prior to the time a formal petition is instituted. Lawyer representation of (and, ideally, contact with) the child prior to the initial court hearing following removal (which in some cases may be several days) is important to protect the child's interests;

(2) Once a petition has been filed by a government agency (or, where authorized, by a hospital or other agency with child protection responsibilities), for any reason related to a child's need for protection, the child should have prompt access to a lawyer; and

(3) There are cases (such as custody, visitation, and guardianship disputes and family-related abductions of children) where allegations, with sufficient cause, of serious physical abuse, sexual molestation, or severe neglect of a child are presented to the court not by a government agency (i.e., child protective services) but by a parent, guardian, or other relative. The need of a child for competent, independent representation by a lawyer is just as great in situation (3) as with cases in areas (1) and (2).

H-2. Entry of Compensation Orders. At the time the court appoints a child's attorney, it should enter a written order addressing compensation and expense costs for that lawyer, unless these are otherwise formally provided for by agreement or contract with the court, or through another government agency.

Commentary

Compensation and expense reimbursement of individual lawyers should be addressed in a specific written court order is based on a need for all lawyers representing maltreated children to have a uniform understanding of how they will be paid. Commentary to Section 2.1(b) of the JUVENILE JUSTICE STANDARDS observes that it is common for court-appointed lawyers to be confused about the availability of reimbursement of expenses for case-related work.

H-3. Immediate Provision of Access. Unless otherwise provided for, the court should upon appointment of a child's attorney, enter an order authorizing that lawyer access between the child and the lawyer and to all privileged information regarding the child, without the necessity of a further release. The authorization should include, but not be limited to: social services, psychiatric, psychological treatment, drug and alcohol treatment, medical, evaluation, law enforcement, and school records.

Commentary

Because many service providers do not understand or recognize the nature of the role of the lawyer for the child or that person's importance in the court proceeding, these Standards call for the routine use of a written court order that clarifies the lawyers right to contact with their child client and perusal of child-related records. Parents, other caretakers, or government social service agencies should not unreasonably interfere with a lawyer's ability to have face-to-face contact with the child client nor to obtain relevant information about the child's social services, education, mental health, etc. Such interference disrupts the lawyer's ability to control the representation and undermines his or her independence as the child's legal representative.

H-4. Lawyer Eligibility for and Method of Appointment. Where the court makes individual appointment of counsel, unless impractical, before making the appointment, the court should determine that the lawyer has been trained in representation of children and skilled in litigation (or is working under the supervision of an lawyer who is skilled in litigation). Whenever possible, the trial judge should ensure that the child's attorney has had sufficient training in child advocacy and is familiar with these Standards. The trial judge should also ensure that (unless there is specific reason to appoint a specific lawyer because of their special qualifications related to the case, or where a lawyer's current caseload would prevent them from adequately handling the case) individual lawyers are appointed from the ranks of eligible members of the bar under a fair, systematic, and sequential appointment plan.

Commentary

The JUVENILE JUSTICE STANDARDS 2.2(c) provides that where counsel is assigned by the court, this lawyer should be drawn from "an adequate pool of competent attorneys." In general, such competency can only be gained through relevant continuing legal education and practice-related experience. Those Standards also promote the use of a rational court appointment process drawing from the ranks of qualified lawyers. The Abuse and Neglect Standards reject the concept of ad hoc appointments of counsel that are made without regard to prior training or practice.

H-5. Permitting Child to Retain a Lawyer. The court should permit the child to be represented by a retained private lawyer if it determines that this lawyer is the child's independent choice, and such counsel should be substituted for the appointed lawyer. A person with a legitimate interest in the child's welfare may retain private counsel for the child and/or pay for such representation, and that person should be permitted to serve as the child's attorney, subject to approval of the court. Such approval should not be given if the child opposes the lawyer's representation or if the court determines that there will be a conflict of interest. The court should make it clear that the person paying for the retained lawyer does not have the right to direct the representation of the child or to receive privileged information about the case from the lawyer.

Commentary

Although such representation is rare, there are situations where a child, or someone acting on a child's behalf, seeks out legal representation and wishes that this lawyer, rather than one appointed by the court under the normal appointment process, be recognized as the sole legal representative of the child. Sometimes, judges have refused to accept the formal appearances filed by such retained lawyers. These Standards propose to permit, under carefully scrutinized conditions, the substitution of a court-appointed lawyer with the retained counsel for a child.

I. THE COURT'S ROLE IN LAWYER TRAINING

I-1. Judicial Involvement in Lawyer Training. Trial judges who are regularly involved in child-related matters should participate in training for the child's attorney conducted by the courts, the bar, or any other group.

Commentary

JUVENILE JUSTICE STANDARDS 2.1 indicates that it is the responsibility of the courts (among others) to ensure that competent counsel are available to represent children before the courts. That Standard further suggests that lawyers should "be encouraged" to qualify themselves for participation in child-related cases "through formal training." The Abuse and Neglect Standards go further by suggesting that judges should personally take part in educational programs, whether or not the court conducts them. The National Council of Juvenile and Family Court Judges has suggested that courts can play in important role in training lawyers in child abuse and neglect cases, and that judges and judicial officers can volunteer to provide training and publications for continuing legal education seminars. See, RESOURCE GUIDELINES, at 22.

I-2. Content of Lawyer Training. The appropriate state administrative office of the trial, family, or juvenile courts should provide educational programs, live or on tape, on the role of a child's attorney. At a minimum, the requisite training should include:

(1) Information about relevant federal and state laws and agency regulations;
(2) Information about relevant court decisions and court rules;
(3) Overview of the court process and key personnel in child-related litigation;
(4) Description of applicable guidelines and standards for representation;
(5) Focus on child development, needs, and abilities;
(6) Information on the multidisciplinary input required in child-related cases, including information on local experts who can provide consultation and testimony on the reasonableness and appropriateness of efforts made to safely maintain the child in his or her home;
(7) Information concerning family dynamics and dysfunction including substance abuse, and the use of kinship care;
(8) Information on accessible child welfare, family preservation, medical, educational, and mental health resources for child clients and their families, including placement, evaluation/diagnostic, and treatment services; the structure of agencies providing such services as well as provisions and constraints related to agency payment for services; and
(9) Provision of written material (e.g., representation manuals, checklists, sample forms), including

listings of useful material available from other sources.

Commentary
The ABUSE AND NEGLECT STANDARDS take the position that it is not enough that judges mandate the training of lawyers, or that judges participate in such training. Rather, they call upon the courts to play a key role in training by actually sponsoring (e.g., funding) training opportunities. The pivotal nature of the judiciary's role in educating lawyers means that courts may, on appropriate occasions, stop the hearing of cases on days when training is held so that both lawyers and judges may freely attend without docket conflicts. The required elements of training are based on a review of well-regarded lawyer training offered throughout the country, RESOURCE GUIDELINES, and many existing manuals that help guide lawyers in representing children.

I-3. Continuing Training for Lawyers. The court system should also assure that there are periodic opportunities for lawyers who have taken the "basic" training to receive continuing and "new developments" training.

Commentary
Many courts and judicial organizations recognize that rapid changes occur because of new federal and state legislation, appellate court decisions, systemic reforms, and responses to professional literature. Continuing education opportunities are critical to maintain a high level of performance. These Standards call for courts to afford these "advanced" or "periodic" training to lawyers who represent children in abuse and neglect related cases.

I-4. Provision of Mentorship Opportunities. Courts should provide individual court-appointed lawyers who are new to child representation the opportunity to practice under the guidance of a senior lawyer mentor.

Commentary
In addition to training, particularly for lawyers who work as sole practitioners or in firms that do not specialize in child representation, courts can provide a useful mechanism to help educate new lawyers for children by pairing them with more experienced advocates. One specific thing courts can do is to provide lawyers new to representing children with the opportunity to be assisted by more experienced lawyers in their jurisdiction. Some courts actually require lawyers to "second chair" cases before taking an appointment to a child abuse or neglect case. See, RESOURCE GUIDELINES, at 22.

J. THE COURT'S ROLE IN LAWYER COMPENSATION

J-1. Assuring Adequate Compensation. A child's attorney should receive adequate and timely compensation throughout the term of appointment that reflects the complexity of the case and includes both in court and out-of-court preparation, participation in case reviews and post-dispositional hearings, and involvement in appeals. To the extent that the court arranges for child representation through contract or agreement with a program in which lawyers represent children, the court should assure that the rate of payment for these legal services is commensurate with the fees paid to equivalently experienced individual court-appointed lawyers who have similar qualifications and responsibilities.

Commentary
JUVENILE JUSTICE STANDARDS 2.1(b) recognize that lawyers for children should be entitled to reasonable compensation for both time and services performed "according to prevailing professional standards," which takes into account the "skill required to perform...properly," and which considers the need for the lawyer to perform both counseling and resource identification/evaluation activities. The RESOURCE GUIDELINES, at 22, state that it is "necessary to provide reasonable compensation" for improved lawyer representation of children and that where necessary judges should "urge state legislatures and local governing bodies to provide sufficient funding" for quality legal representation.

Because some courts currently compensate lawyers only for time spent in court at the adjudicative or initial disposition stage of cases, these Standards clarify that compensation is to be provided for out-of-court preparation time, as well as for the lawyer's involvement in case reviews and appeals. "Out-of-court preparation" may include, for example, a lawyer's participation in social services or school case conferences relating to the client.

These Standards also call for the level of compensation where lawyers are working under contract with the court to provide child representation to be comparable with what experienced individual counsel would receive from the court. Although courts may, and are encouraged to, seek high quality child representation through enlistment of special children's law offices, law firms, and other programs, the motive should not be a significantly different (i.e., lower) level of financial compensation for the lawyers who provide the representation.

J-2. Supporting Associated Costs. The child's attorney should have access to (or be provided with reimbursement for experts, investigative services, paralegals, research costs, and other services, such as copying medical records, long distance phone calls, service of process, and transcripts of hearings as requested.

Commentary

The ABUSE AND NEGLECT STANDARDS expand upon JUVENILE JUSTICE STANDARDS 2.1(c) which recognizes that a child's attorney should have access to "investigatory, expert and other nonlegal services" as a fundamental part of providing competent representation.

J-3. Reviewing Payment Requests. The trial judge should review requests for compensation for reasonableness based upon the complexity of the case and the hours expended.

Commentary

These Standards implicitly reject the practice of judges arbitrarily "cutting down" the size of lawyer requests for compensation and would limit a judge's ability to reduce the amount of a per/case payment request from a child's attorney unless the request is deemed unreasonable based upon two factors: case complexity and time spent.

J-4. Keeping Compensation Levels Uniform. Each state should set a uniform level of compensation for lawyers appointed by the courts to represent children. Any per/hour level of compensation should be the same for all representation of children in all types of child abuse and neglect-related proceedings.

Commentary

These Standards implicitly reject the concept (and practice) of different courts within a state paying different levels of compensation for lawyers representing children. They call for a uniform approach, established on a statewide basis, towards the setting of payment guidelines.

K. THE COURT'S ROLE IN RECORD ACCESS BY LAWYERS

K-1. Authorizing Lawyer Access. The court should enter an order in child abuse and neglect cases authorizing the child's attorney access to all privileged information regarding the child, without the necessity for a further release.

Commentary

This Standard requires uniform judicial assistance to remove a common barrier to effective representation, i.e., administrative denial of access to significant records concerning the child. The language supports the universal issuance of broadly-worded court orders that grant a child's attorney full access to information (from individuals) or records (from agencies) concerning the child.

K-2. Providing Broad Scope Orders. The authorization order granting the child's attorney access to records should include social services, psychiatric, psychological treatment, drug and alcohol treatment, medical, evaluation, law enforcement, school, and other records relevant to the case.

Commentary
This Standard further elaborates upon the universal application that the court's access order should be given, by listing examples of the most common agency records that should be covered by the court order.

L. THE COURT'S ROLE IN ASSURING REASONABLE LAWYER CASELOADS

L-1. Controlling Lawyer Caseloads. Trial court judges should control the size of court-appointed caseloads of individual lawyers representing children, the caseloads of government agency-funded lawyers for children, or court contracts/agreements with lawyers for such representation. Courts should take steps to assure that lawyers appointed to represent children, or lawyers otherwise providing such representation, do not have such a large open number of cases that they are unable to abide by Part I of these Standards.

Commentary
THE ABUSE AND NEGLECT STANDARDS go further than JUVENILE JUSTICE STANDARD 2.2(b) which recognize the "responsibility of every defender office to ensure that its personnel can offer prompt, full, and effective counseling and representation to each (child) client" and that it "should not accept more assignments than its staff can adequately discharge" by specifically calling upon the courts to help keep lawyer caseloads from getting out of control. The Commentary to 2.2.(b) indicates that: Caseloads must not be exceeded where to do so would "compel lawyers to forego the extensive fact investigation required in both contested and uncontested cases, or to be less than scrupulously careful in preparation for trial, or to forego legal research necessary to develop a theory of representation." We would add: "...or to monitor the implementation of court orders and agency case plans in order to help assure permanency for the child."

L-2. Taking Supportive Caseload Actions. If judges or court administrators become aware that individual lawyers are close to, or exceeding, the levels suggested in these Standards, they should take one or more of the following steps:

(1) Expand, with the aid of the bar and children's advocacy groups, the size of the list from which appointments are made;
(2) Alert relevant government or private agency administrators that their lawyers have an excessive caseload problem;
(3) Recruit law firms or special child advocacy law programs to engage in child representation;
(4) Review any court contracts/agreements for child representation and amend them accordingly, so that additional lawyers can be compensated for case representation time; and
(5) Alert state judicial, executive, and legislative branch leaders that excessive caseloads jeopardize the ability of lawyers to competently represent children pursuant to state-approved guidelines, and seek funds for increasing the number of lawyers available to represent children.

Commentary
This Standard provides courts with a range of possible actions when individual lawyer caseloads appear to be inappropriately high.

APPENDIX

Previous American Bar Association Policies Related to Legal Representation of Abused and Neglected Children

GUARDIANS AD LITEM
FEBRUARY 1992

BE IT RESOLVED, that the American Bar Association urges:

(1) Every state and territory to meet the full intent of the Federal Child Abuse Prevention and Treatment Act, whereby every child in the United States who is the subject of a civil child protection related judicial proceedings will be represented at all stages of these proceedings by a fully-trained, monitored, and evaluated guardian ad litem in addition to appointed legal counsel.

(2) That state, territory and local bar associations and law schools become involved in setting standards of practice for such guardians ad litem, clarify the ethical responsibilities of these individuals and establish minimum ethical performance requirements for their work, and provide comprehensive multidisciplinary training for all who serve as such guardians ad litem.

(3) That in every state and territory, where judges are given discretion to appoint a guardian ad litem in private child custody and visitation related proceedings, the bench and bar jointly develop guidelines to aid judges in determining when such an appointment is necessary to protect the best interests of the child.

COURT-APPOINTED SPECIAL ADVOCATES
AUGUST 1989

BE IT RESOLVED, that the American Bar Association endorses the concept of utilizing carefully selected, well trained lay volunteers, Court Appointed Special Advocates, in addition to providing attorney representation, in dependency proceedings to assist the court in determining what is in the best interests of abused and neglected children.
BE IT FURTHER RESOLVED, that the American Bar Association encourages its members to support the development of CASA programs in their communities.

COUNSEL FOR CHILDREN ENHANCEMENT
FEBRUARY 1987

BE IT RESOLVED, that the American Bar Association requests State and local bar associations to determine the extent to which statutory law and court rules in their States guarantee the right to counsel for children in juvenile court proceedings; and
BE IT FURTHER RESOLVED, that State and local bar associations are urged to actively participate and support amendments to the statutory law and court rules in their State to bring them in to compliance with the Institute of Judicial Administration/American Bar Association Standards Relating to Counsel for Private Parties; and
BE IT FURTHER RESOLVED, that State and local bar associations are requested to ascertain the extent to which, irrespective of the language in their State statutory laws and court rules, counsel is in fact provided for children in juvenile court proceedings and the extent to which the quality of representation is consistent with the standards and policies of the American Bar Association; and
BE IT FURTHER RESOLVED, that State and local bar associations are urged to actively support programs of training and education to ensure that lawyers practicing in juvenile court are aware of the American Bar Association's standards relating to representation of children and provide advocacy which meets those standards.

BAR ASSOCIATION AND ATTORNEY ACTION
FEBRUARY 1984

BE IT RESOLVED, that the American Bar Association urges the members of the legal profession, as well as state and local bar associations, to respond to the needs of children by directing attention to issues affecting children including, but not limited to: ... (7) establishment of guardian ad litem programs.

BAR AND ATTORNEY INVOLVEMENT IN CHILD PROTECTION CASES
AUGUST 1981

BE IT RESOLVED, that the American Bar Association encourages individual attorneys and state and local bar organizations to work more actively to improve the handling of cases involving abused and neglected children as well as children in foster care. Specifically, attorneys should form appropriate committees and groups within the bar to ... work to assure quality legal representation for children....

JUVENILE JUSTICE STANDARDS
FEBRUARY 1979

BE IT RESOLVED, that the American Bar Association adopt (the volume of the) Standards for Juvenile Justice (entitled) Counsel for Private Parties...

APPENDIX C

2011 ABA Model Act Governing Representation of Children in Abuse, Neglect, and Dependency Proceedings

AMERICAN BAR ASSOCIATION
SECTION OF LITIGATION

SECTION OF FAMILY LAW
CRIMINAL JUSTICE SECTION
COMMISSION ON HOMELESSNESS AND POVERTY
COMMISSION ON YOUTH AT RISK
GENERAL PRACTICE, SOLO AND SMALL FIRM DIVISION
STEERING COMMITTEE ON LEGAL AID AND INDIGENT DEFENSE
JUDICIAL DIVISION
PHILADELPHIA BAR ASSOCIATION
LOS ANGELES COUNTY BAR ASSOCIATION
LOUISIANA STATE BAR ASSOCIATION
YOUNG LAWYERS DIVISION
INDIVIDUAL RIGHTS AND RESPONSIBILITIES
GOVERNMENT AND PUBLIC SECTOR LAWYERS

REPORT TO THE HOUSE OF DELEGATES

RESOLUTION

RESOLVED, That the American Bar Association adopts the *Model Act Governing the Representation of Children in Abuse, Neglect, and Dependency Proceedings*, dated August, 2011.

101A

ABA Model Act Governing the Representation of Children in Abuse, Neglect, and Dependency Proceedings [1]

SECTION 1. DEFINITIONS. In this [act]:

(a) "Abuse and neglect proceeding" means a court proceeding under [cite state statute] for protection of a child from abuse or neglect or a court proceeding under [cite state statute] in which termination of parental rights is at issue.[2] These proceedings include:

    (1) abuse;

    (2) neglect;

    (3) dependency;

    (4) child in voluntary placement in state care;

    (5) termination of parental rights;

    (6) permanency hearings; and

    (7) post termination of parental rights through adoption or other permanency proceeding.

(b) A child is:

    (1) an individual under the age of 18; or

    (2) an individual under the age of 22 who remains under the jurisdiction of the juvenile court.

(c) "Child's lawyer" (or "lawyer for children") means a lawyer who provides legal services for a child and who owes the same duties, including undivided loyalty, confidentiality and competent representation, to the child as is due an adult client, subject to Section 7 of this Act.[3]

(d) "Best interest advocate" means an individual, not functioning or intended to function as the child's lawyer, appointed by the court to assist the court in determining the best interests of the child.

---

[1] This Model Act was drafted under the auspices of the ABA Section of Litigation Children's Rights Litigation Committee with the assistance of the Bar-Youth Empowerment Program of the ABA Center on Children and the Law and First Star. The Act incorporates some language from the provisions of the NCCUSL Representation of Children in Abuse, Neglect, and Custody Proceedings Act.

[2] NCCUSL, 2006 *Uniform Representation of Children in Abuse, Neglect, and Custody Proceedings*, Sec. 2(2) [Hereinafter NCCUSL Act]

[3] *Id.*, Sec. 2(6); American Bar Association, *Standards of Practice for Lawyers who Represent Children in Abuse and Neglect Cases*, Part I, Sec A-1, 29 Fam. L. Q. 375 (1995). The standards were formally adopted by the ABA House of Delegates in 1996. [Hereinafter ABA Standards].

101A

(e) **"Developmental level" is a measure of the ability to communicate and understand others, taking into account such factors as age, mental capacity, level of education, cultural background, and degree of language acquisition.**[4]

Legislative Note: States should implement a mechanism to bring children into court when they have been voluntarily placed into state care, if such procedures do not already exist. Court action should be triggered after a specific number of days in voluntary care (not fewer than 30 days, but not more than 90 days).

Commentary:

Under the Act, a "child's lawyer" is a client-directed lawyer in a traditional attorney-client relationship with the child. A "best interests advocate" does not function as the child's lawyer and is not bound by the child's expressed wishes in determining what to advocate, although the best interests advocate should consider those wishes.

The best interest advocate may be a lawyer or a lay person, such as a court-appointed special advocate, or CASA. The best interests advocate assists the court in determining the best interests of a child and will therefore perform many of the functions formerly attributable to guardians *ad litem*, but best interests advocates are not to function as the child's lawyer. A lawyer appointed as a best interest advocate shall function as otherwise set forth in state law.

SECTION 2. APPLICABILITY AND RELATIONSHIP TO OTHER LAW.

(a) This [act] applies to an abuse and neglect proceeding pending or commenced on or after [the effective date of this act].

(b) The child in these proceedings is a party.

SECTION 3. APPOINTMENT IN ABUSE OR NEGLECT PROCEEDING.

(a) The court shall appoint a child's lawyer for each child who is the subject of a petition in an abuse and neglect proceeding. The appointment of a child's lawyer must be made as soon as practicable to ensure effective representation of the child and, in any event, before the first court hearing.

(b) In addition to the appointment of a child's lawyer, the court may appoint a best interest advocate to assist the court in determining the child's best interests.

(c) The court may appoint one child's lawyer to represent siblings if there is no conflict of interest as defined under the applicable rules of professional conduct.[5] **The**

---
[4] ABA Standards, Part I, Sec A-3.
[5] NCCUSL Act, Sec. 4(c); *see also* ABA Standards, Part I, Sec B-1

court may appoint additional counsel to represent individual siblings at a child's lawyer's request due to a conflict of interest between or among the siblings.

(d) The applicable rules of professional conduct and any law governing the obligations of lawyers to their clients shall apply to such appointed lawyers for children.

(e) The appointed child's lawyer shall represent the child at all stages of the proceedings, unless otherwise discharged by order of court.[6]

(f) A child's right to counsel may not be waived at any court proceeding.

Commentary:

This act recognizes the right of every child to have quality legal representation and a voice in any abuse, neglect, dependency, or termination of parental rights proceeding, regardless of developmental level. Nothing in this Act precludes a child from retaining a lawyer. States should provide a lawyer to a child who has been placed into state custody through a voluntary placement arrangement. The fact that the child is in the state's custody through the parent's voluntary decision should not diminish the child's entitlement to a lawyer.

A best interest advocate does not replace the appointment of a lawyer for the child. A best interest advocate serves to provide guidance to the court with respect to the child's best interest and does not establish a lawyer-client relationship with the child. Nothing in this Act restricts a court's ability to appoint a best interest advocate in any proceeding. Because this Act deals specifically with lawyers for children, it will not further address the role of the best interest advocate.

The child is entitled to conflict-free representation and the applicable rules of professional conduct must be applied in the same manner as they would be applied for lawyers for adults. A lawyer representing siblings should maintain the same lawyer-client relationship with respect to each child.

SECTION 4. QUALIFICATIONS OF THE CHILD'S LAWYER.

(a) The court shall appoint as the child's lawyer an individual who is qualified through training and experience, according to standards established by [insert reference to source of standards].

(b) Lawyers for children shall receive initial training and annual continuing legal education that is specific to child welfare law. Lawyers for children shall be familiar with all relevant federal, state, and local applicable laws.

(c) Lawyers for children shall not be appointed to new cases when their present

---

[6] ABA Standards, Sec D-13; F-1-5; *see generally* La. Sup. Ct. R. XXXIII, Standard 1; *see generally* Ariz. R. Proc. Juv. Ct. R. 39(b).

101A

caseload exceeds more than a reasonable number given the jurisdiction, the percent of the lawyer's practice spent on abuse and neglect cases, the complexity of the case, and other relevant factors.

Legislative Note: States that adopt training standards and standards of practice for children's lawyers should include the bracketed portion of this section and insert a reference to the state laws, court rules, or administrative guidelines containing those standards.[7]
Jurisdictions are urged to specify a case limit at the time of passage of this Act.

Commentary:

States should establish minimum training requirements for lawyers who represent children. Such training should focus on applicable law, skills needed to develop a meaningful lawyer-client relationship with child-clients, techniques to assess capacity in children, as well as the many interdisciplinary issues that arise in child welfare cases.

The lawyer needs to spend enough time on each abuse and neglect case to establish a lawyer-client relationship and zealously advocate for the client. A lawyer's caseload must allow realistic performance of functions assigned to the lawyer under the [Act]. The amount of time and the number of children a lawyer can represent effectively will differ based on a number of factors, including type of case, the demands of the jurisdiction, whether the lawyer is affiliated with a children's law office, whether the lawyer is assisted by investigators or other child welfare professionals, and the percent of the lawyer's practice spent on abuse and neglect cases. States are encouraged to conduct caseload analyses to determine guidelines for lawyers representing children in abuse and neglect cases.

SECTION 5. ORDER OF APPOINTMENT.

(a) Subject to subsection (b), an order of appointment of a child's lawyer shall be in writing and on the record, identify the lawyer who will act in that capacity, and clearly set forth the terms of the appointment, including the reasons for the appointment, rights of access as provided under Section 8, and applicable terms of compensation as provided under Section 12.

(b) In an order of appointment issued under subsection (a), the court may identify a private organization, law school clinical program or governmental program through which a child's lawyer will be provided. The organization or program shall designate the lawyer who will act in that capacity and notify the parties and the court of the name of the assigned lawyer as soon as practicable.[8] **Additionally, the organization or program shall notify the parties and the court of any changes in the individual assignment.**

---

[7] ABA Standards, Part II, Sec L-1-2.
[8] NCCUSL Act, Sec. 9

SECTION 6. DURATION OF APPOINTMENT.

Unless otherwise provided by a court order, an appointment of a child's lawyer in an abuse and neglect proceeding continues in effect until the lawyer is discharged by court order or the case is dismissed.[9] The appointment includes all stages thereof, from removal from the home or initial appointment through all available appellate proceedings. With the permission of the court, the lawyer may arrange for supplemental or separate counsel to handle proceedings at an appellate stage.[10]

Commentary:

As long as the child remains in state custody, even if the state custody is long-term or permanent, the child should retain the right to counsel so that the child's lawyer can deal with the issues that may arise while the child is in custody but the case is not before the court.

SECTION 7. DUTIES OF CHILD'S LAWYER AND SCOPE OF REPRESENTATION.

(a) A child's lawyer shall participate in any proceeding concerning the child with the same rights and obligations as any other lawyer for a party to the proceeding.

(b) The duties of a child's lawyer include, but are not limited to:

(1) taking all steps reasonably necessary to represent the client in the proceeding, including but not limited to: interviewing and counseling the client, preparing a case theory and strategy, preparing for and participating in negotiations and hearings, drafting and submitting motions, memoranda and orders, and such other steps as established by the applicable standards of practice for lawyers acting on behalf of children in this jurisdiction;

(2) reviewing and accepting or declining, after consultation with the client, any proposed stipulation for an order affecting the child and explaining to the court the basis for any opposition;

(3) taking action the lawyer considers appropriate to expedite the proceeding and the resolution of contested issues;

(4) where appropriate, after consultation with the client, discussing the possibility of settlement or the use of alternative forms of dispute resolution and participating in such processes to the extent permitted under the law of this state;[11]

(5) meeting with the child prior to each hearing and for at least one in-person meeting every quarter;

---

[9] *Id.*, Sec. 10(a)
[10] ABA Standards, Part I, Sec D-13; F-1-5; *see generally* La. Sup. Ct. R. XXXIII, Standard 1.; *see generally* Ariz. R. Proc. Juv. Ct. R. 39(b).
[11] NCCUSL Act, Sec. 11 Alternative A..

101A

(6) where appropriate and consistent with both confidentiality and the child's legal interests, consulting with the best interests advocate;

(7) prior to every hearing, investigating and taking necessary legal action regarding the child's medical, mental health, social, education, and overall well-being;

(8) visiting the home, residence, or any prospective residence of the child, including each time the placement is changed;

(9) seeking court orders or taking any other necessary steps in accordance with the child's direction to ensure that the child's health, mental health, educational, developmental, cultural and placement needs are met; and

(10) representing the child in all proceedings affecting the issues before the court, including hearings on appeal or referring the child's case to the appropriate appellate counsel as provided for by/mandated by [insert local rule/law etc.].

Commentary:

The national standards mentioned in (b)(1) include the *ABA Standards of Practice for Lawyers who Represent Children in Abuse and Neglect Cases.*

In order to comply with the duties outlined in this section, lawyers must have caseloads that allow realistic performance of these functions.

The child's lawyer may request authority from the court to pursue issues on behalf of the child, administratively or judicially, even if those issues do not specifically arise from the court appointment.[12] Such ancillary matters include special education, school discipline hearings, mental health treatment, delinquency or criminal issues, status offender matters, guardianship, adoption, paternity, probate, immigration matters, medical care coverage, SSI eligibility, youth transitioning out of care issues, postsecondary education opportunity qualification, and tort actions for injury, as appropriate.[13] The lawyer should make every effort to ensure that the child is represented by legal counsel in all ancillary legal proceedings, either personally, when the lawyer is competent to do so, or through referral or collaboration. Having one lawyer represent the child across multiple proceedings is valuable because the lawyer is better able to understand and fully appreciate the various issues as they arise and how those issues may affect other proceedings.

(c) When the child is capable of directing the representation by expressing his or her objectives, the child's lawyer shall maintain a normal client-lawyer relationship with the child in accordance with the rules of professional conduct. In a developmentally appropriate manner, the lawyer shall elicit the child's wishes and advise the child as to

---

[12] ABA Standards, Part I, Section D-12.
[13] *Id.*

options.

Commentary:

The lawyer-client relationship for the child's lawyer is fundamentally indistinguishable from the lawyer-client relationship in any other situation and includes duties of client direction,[14] confidentiality,[15] diligence,[16] competence,[17] loyalty,[18] communication,[19] and the duty to provide independent advice.[20] Client direction requires the lawyer to abide by the client's decision about the objectives of the representation. In order for the child to have an independent voice in abuse and neglect proceedings, the lawyer shall advocate for the child's counseled and expressed wishes.[21] Moreover, providing the child with an independent and client-directed lawyer ensures that the child's legal rights and interests are adequately protected.

The child's lawyer needs to explain his or her role to the client and, if applicable, explain in what strictly limited circumstances the lawyer cannot advocate for the client's expressed wishes and in what circumstances the lawyer may be required to reveal confidential information. This explanation should occur during the first meeting so the client understands the terms of the relationship.

In addition to explaining the role of the child's lawyer, the lawyer should explain the legal process to the child in a developmentally appropriate manner as required by Rule 1.4 of the ABA Model Rules of Professional Conduct or its equivalent.[22] This explanation can and will change based on age, cognitive ability, and emotional maturity of the child. The lawyer needs to take the time to explain thoroughly and in a way that allows and encourages the child to ask questions and that ensures the child's understanding. The lawyer should also facilitate the child's participation in the proceeding (See Section 9).

In order to determine the objectives of the representation of the child, the child's lawyer should develop a relationship with the client. The lawyer should achieve a thorough knowledge of the child's circumstances and needs. The lawyer should visit the child in the child's home, school, or other appropriate place where the child is comfortable. The lawyer should observe the child's interactions with parents, foster parents, and other caregivers. The lawyer should maintain regular and ongoing contact with the child throughout the case.

The child's lawyer helps to make the child's wishes and voice heard but is not merely the child's

---

[14] ABA Model Rules of Professional Responsibility (hereinafter M.R.) 1.2
[15] M.R. 1.6
[16] M.R. 1.3
[17] M.R. 1.1
[18] M.R. 1.7
[19] M.R. 1.4
[20] M.R. 2.1
[21] ABA Standards, commentary A-1
[22] M.R. 1.4

mouthpiece. As with any lawyer, a child's lawyer is both an advocate and a counselor for the client. Without unduly influencing the child, the lawyer should advise the child by providing options and information to assist the child in making decisions. The lawyer should explain the practical effects of taking various positions, the likelihood that a court will accept particular arguments, and the impact of such decisions on the child, other family members, and future legal proceedings.[23] The lawyer should investigate the relevant facts, interview persons with significant knowledge of the child's history, review relevant records, and work with others in the case.

(d) The child's lawyer shall determine whether the child has diminished capacity pursuant to the Model Rules of Professional Conduct. {STATES MAY CONSIDER INSERTING THE FOLLOWING TWO SENTENCES:} [Under this subsection a child shall be presumed to be capable of directing representation at the age of ___. The presumption of diminished capacity is rebutted if, in the sole discretion of the lawyer, the child is deemed capable of directing representation.] In making the determination, the lawyer should consult the child and may consult other individuals or entities that can provide the child's lawyer with the information and assistance necessary to determine the child's ability to direct the representation.

When a child client has diminished capacity, the child's lawyer shall make a good faith effort to determine the child's needs and wishes. The lawyer shall, as far as reasonably possible, maintain a normal client-lawyer relationship with the client and fulfill the duties as outlined in Section 7(b) of this Act. During a temporary period or on a particular issue where a normal client-lawyer relationship is not reasonably possible to maintain, the child's lawyer shall make a substituted judgment determination. A substituted judgment determination includes determining what the child would decide if he or she were capable of making an adequately considered decision, and representing the child in accordance with that determination. The lawyer should take direction from the child as the child develops the capacity to direct the lawyer. The lawyer shall advise the court of the determination of capacity and any subsequent change in that determination.

Commentary:

A determination of incapacity may be incremental and issue-specific, thus enabling the child's lawyer to continue to function as a client-directed lawyer as to major questions in the proceeding. Determination of diminished capacity requires ongoing re-assessment. A child may be able to direct the lawyer with respect to a particular issue at one time but not another. Similarly, a child may be able to determine some positions in the case, but not others. For guidance in assessing diminished capacity, see the commentary to Section (e). The lawyer shall advise the court of the determination of capacity and any subsequent change in that

---

[23] M.R. 2.1

determination.

In making a substituted judgment determination, the child's lawyer may wish to seek guidance from appropriate professionals and others with knowledge of the child, including the advice of an expert. A substituted judgment determination is not the same as determining the child's best interests; determination of a child's best interests remains solely the province of the court. Rather, it involves determining what the child would decide if he or she were able to make an adequately considered decision.[24] A lawyer should determine the child's position based on objective facts and information, not personal beliefs. To assess the needs and interests of *this* child, the lawyer should observe the child in his or her environment, and consult with experts.[25]

In formulating a substituted judgment position, the child's lawyer's advocacy should be child-centered, research-informed, permanency-driven, and holistic.[26] The child's needs and interests, not the adults' or professionals' interests, must be the center of all advocacy. For example, lawyers representing very young children must truly *see* the world through the child's eyes and formulate their approach from that perspective, gathering information and gaining insight into the child's experiences to inform advocacy related to placement, services, treatment and permanency.[27] The child's lawyer should be proactive and seek out opportunities to observe and interact with the very young child client. It is also essential that lawyers for very young children have a firm working knowledge of child development and special entitlements for children under age five.[28]

When determining a substituted judgment position, the lawyer shall take into consideration the child's legal interests based on objective criteria as set forth in the laws applicable to the proceeding, the goal of expeditious resolution of the case and the use of the least restrictive or detrimental alternatives available. The child's lawyer should seek to speed the legal process, while also maintaining the child's critical relationships.

The child's lawyer should not confuse inability to express a preference with unwillingness to express a preference. If an otherwise competent child chooses not to express a preference on a particular matter, the child's lawyer should determine if the child wishes the lawyer to take no position in the proceeding, or if the child wishes the lawyer or someone else to make the decision for him or her. In either case, the lawyer is bound to follow the client's direction. A child may be able to direct the lawyer with respect to a particular issue at one time but not at another. A child may be able to determine some positions in the case but not others.

---

[24] Massachusetts Committee For Public Counsel Services, *Performance Standards Governing The Representation Of Children And Parents in Child Welfare Cases*, Chapter Four: Performance Standards and Complaint Procedures 4-1, Section 1.6(c) (2004).

[25] Candice L. Maze, JD, *Advocating for Very Young Children in Dependency Proceedings: The Hallmarks of Effective, Ethical Representation*, ABA Center on Children and the Law, October, 2010.

[26] *Id.*

[27] *Id.*

[28] *Id.*

(e) When the child's lawyer reasonably believes that the client has diminished capacity, is at risk of substantial physical, financial or other harm unless action is taken, and cannot adequately act in the client's own interest, the lawyer may take reasonably necessary protective action, including consulting with individuals or entities that have the ability to take action to protect the client and, in appropriate cases, seeking the appointment of a best interest advocate or investigator to make an independent recommendation to the court with respect to the best interests of the child.

When taking protective action, the lawyer is impliedly authorized under Model Rule 1.6(a) to reveal information about the child, but only to the extent reasonably necessary to protect the child's interests.[29] Information relating to the representation of a child with diminished capacity is protected by Rule 1.6 and Rule 1.14 of the ABA Model Rules of Professional Conduct. [OR ENTER STATE RULE CITATION]

Commentary:

Consistent with Rule 1.14, ABA Model Rules of Professional Conduct (2004), the child's lawyer should determine whether the child has sufficient maturity to understand and form an attorney-client relationship and whether the child is capable of making reasoned judgments and engaging in meaningful communication. It is the responsibility of the child's lawyer to determine whether the child suffers from diminished capacity. This decision shall be made after sufficient contact and regular communication with the client. Determination about capacity should be grounded in insights from child development science and should focus on the child's decision-making process rather than the child's choices themselves. Lawyers should be careful not to conclude that the child suffers diminished capacity from a client's insistence upon a course of action that the lawyer considers unwise or at variance with lawyer's view.[30]

When determining the child's capacity the lawyer should elicit the child's expressed wishes in a developmentally appropriate manner. The lawyer should not expect the child to convey information in the same way as an adult client. A child's age is not determinative of diminished capacity. For example, even very young children are regarded as having opinions that are entitled to weight in legal proceedings concerning their custody.[31]

Criteria for determining diminished capacity include the child's developmental stage, cognitive ability, emotional and mental development, ability to communicate, ability to understand consequences, consistency of the child's decisions, strength of wishes and the opinions of others, including social workers, therapists, teachers, family members or a hired expert.[32] To assist in

---

[29] M.R. 1.14(c)
[30] Restatement (Third) of the Law Governing Lawyers Sec. 24 c. c (2000).
[31] M.R. 1.14 cmt. 1
[32] M.R. 1.14, cmt. 1

the assessment, the lawyer should ask questions in developmentally appropriate language to determine whether the child understands the nature and purpose of the proceeding and the risks and benefits of a desired position.[33] A child may have the ability to make certain decisions, but not others. A child with diminished capacity often has the ability to understand, deliberate upon, and reach conclusions about matters affecting the child's own well-being such as sibling visits, kinship visits and school choice and should continue to direct counsel in those areas in which he or she does have capacity. The lawyer should continue to assess the child's capacity as it may change over time.

When the lawyer determines that the child has diminished capacity, the child is at risk of substantial harm, the child cannot adequately act in his or her own interest, and the use of the lawyer's counseling role is unsuccessful, the lawyer may take protective action. Substantial harm includes physical, sexual and psychological harm. Protective action includes consultation with family members, or professionals who work with the child. Lawyers may also utilize a period of reconsideration to allow for an improvement or clarification of circumstances or to allow for an improvement in the child's capacity.[34] This rule reminds lawyers that, among other things, they should ultimately be guided by the wishes and values of the child to the extent they can be determined.[35]

"Information relating to the representation is protected by Model Rule 1.6. Therefore, unless authorized to do so, the lawyer may not disclose such information. When taking protective action pursuant to this section, the lawyer is impliedly authorized to make necessary disclosures, even when the client directs the lawyer to the contrary."[36] However the lawyer should make every effort to avoid disclosures if at all possible. Where disclosures are unavoidable, the lawyer must limit the disclosures as much as possible. Prior to any consultation, the lawyer should consider the impact on the client's position, and whether the individual is a party who might use the information to further his or her own interests. "At the very least, the lawyer should determine whether it is likely that the person or entity consulted with will act adversely to the client's interests before discussing matters related to the client."[37] If any disclosure by the lawyer will have a negative impact on the client's case or the lawyer-client relationship, the lawyer must consider whether representation can continue and whether the lawyer-client relationship can be re-established. "The lawyer's position in such cases is an unavoidably difficult one."[38]

A request made for the appointment of a best interest advocate to make an independent recommendation to the court with respect to the best interests of the child should be reserved for

---

[33] Anne Graffam Walker, Ph.D. *Handbook on Questioning Children: A Linguistic Perspective* 2nd Edition ABA Center on Children and the Law Copyright 1999 by ABA.
[34] M.R. 1.14 cmt. 5
[35] M.R. 1.14 cmt. 5
[36] M.R. 1.14, cmt. 8
[37] M.R. 1.14, cmt. 8
[38] M.R. 1.14, cmt 8

101A

extreme cases, i.e. where the child is at risk of substantial physical harm, cannot act in his or her own interest and all protective action remedies have been exhausted. Requesting the judge to appoint a best interest advocate may undermine the relationship the lawyer has established with the child. It also potentially compromises confidential information the child may have revealed to the lawyer. The lawyer cannot ever become the best interest advocate, in part due to confidential information that the lawyer receives in the course of representation. Nothing in this section restricts a court from independently appointing a best interest advocate when it deems the appointment appropriate.

SECTION 8. ACCESS TO CHILD AND INFORMATION RELATING TO THE CHILD.

(a) Subject to subsections (b) and (c), when the court appoints the child's lawyer, it shall issue an order, with notice to all parties, authorizing the child's lawyer to have access to:

(1) the child; and

(2) confidential information regarding the child, including the child's educational, medical, and mental health records, social services agency files, court records including court files involving allegations of abuse or neglect of the child, any delinquency records involving the child, and other information relevant to the issues in the proceeding, and reports that form the basis of any recommendation made to the court.

(b) A child's record that is privileged or confidential under law other than this [act] may be released to a child's lawyer appointed under this [act] only in accordance with that law, including any requirements in that law for notice and opportunity to object to release of records. Nothing in this act shall diminish or otherwise change the attorney-client privilege of the child, nor shall the child have any lesser rights than any other party in regard to this or any other evidentiary privilege. Information that is privileged under the lawyer-client relationship may not be disclosed except as otherwise permitted by law of this state other than this [act].

(c) An order issued pursuant to subsection (a) shall require that a child's lawyer maintain the confidentiality of information released pursuant to Model Rule 1.6. The court may impose any other condition or limitation on an order of access which is required by law, rules of professional conduct, the child's needs, or the circumstances of the proceeding.

(d) The custodian of any record regarding the child shall provide access to the record to an individual authorized access by order issued pursuant to subsection (a).

(e) Subject to subsection (b), an order issued pursuant to subsection (a) takes effect upon issuance.[39]

---

[39] NCCUSL Act, Sec. 15

101A

SECTION 9. PARTICIPATION IN PROCEEDINGS.

(a) Each child who is the subject of an abuse and neglect proceeding has the right to attend and fully participate in all hearings related to his or her case.

(b) Each child shall receive notice from the child welfare agency worker and the child's lawyer of his or her right to attend the court hearings.

(c) If the child is not present at the hearing, the court shall determine whether the child was properly notified of his or her right to attend the hearing, whether the child wished to attend the hearing, whether the child had the means (transportation) to attend, and the reasons for the non-appearance.

(d) If the child wished to attend and was not transported to court the matter shall be continued.

(e) The child's presence shall only be excused after the lawyer for the child has consulted with the child and, with informed consent, the child has waived his or her right to attend.

(f) A child's lawyer appointed under this [act] is entitled to:

(1) receive a copy of each pleading or other record filed with the court in the proceeding;

(2) receive notice of and attend each hearing in the proceeding [and participate and receive copies of all records in any appeal that may be filed in the proceeding];

(3) receive notice of and participate in any case staffing or case management conference regarding the child in an abuse and neglect proceeding; and

(4) receive notice of any intent to change the child's placement. In the case of an emergency change, the lawyer shall receive notice as soon as possible but no later than 48 hours following the change of placement.

(g) A child's lawyer appointed under this [act] may not engage in ex parte contact with the court except as authorized by the applicable rules of professional conduct, court order, or other law.

(h) Subject to court approval, a party may call any best interest advocate as a witness for the purpose of cross-examination regarding the advocate's report, even if the advocate is not listed as a witness by a party.

[(i) In a jury trial, disclosure to the jury of the contents of a best interest advocate's report is subject to this state's rules of evidence.][40]

---

[40] NCCUSL Act, Sec. 16

Commentary:

Courts need to provide the child with notification of each hearing. The Court should enforce the child's right to attend and fully participate in all hearings related to his or her abuse and neglect proceeding.[41] Having the child in court emphasizes for the judge and all parties that this hearing is about the child. Factors to consider regarding the child's presence at court and participation in the proceedings include: whether the child wants to attend, the child's age, the child's developmental ability, the child's emotional maturity, the purpose of the hearing and whether the child would be severely traumatized by such attendance.

Lawyers should consider the following options in determining how to provide the most meaningful experience for the child to participate: allowing the child to be present throughout the entire hearing, presenting the child's testimony in chambers adhering to all applicable rules of evidence, arranging for the child to visit the courtroom in advance, video or teleconferencing the child into the hearing, allowing the child to be present only when the child's input is required, excluding the child during harmful testimony, and presenting the child's statements in court adhering to all applicable rules of evidence.

Courts should reasonably accommodate the child to ensure the hearing is a meaningful experience for the child. The court should consider: scheduling hearing dates and times when the child is available and least likely to disrupt the child's routine, setting specific hearing times to prevent the child from having to wait, making courtroom waiting areas child friendly, and ensuring the child will be transported to and from each hearing.

The lawyer for the child plays an important role in the child's court participation. The lawyer shall ensure that the child is properly prepared for the hearing. The lawyer should meet the child in advance to let the child know what to expect at the hearing, who will be present, what their roles are, what will be discussed, and what decisions will be made. If the child would like to address the court, the lawyer should counsel with the child on what to say and how to say it. After the hearing, the lawyer should explain the judge's ruling and allow the child to ask questions about the proceeding.

Because of the wide range of roles assumed by best interest advocates in different jurisdictions, the question of whether a best interest advocate may be called as a witness should be left to the discretion of the court.

SECTION 10. LAWYER WORK PRODUCT AND TESTIMONY.

(a) Except as authorized by [insert reference to this state's rules of professional conduct] or court rule, a child's lawyer may not:

---

[41] American Bar Association Youth Transitioning from Foster Care August 2007; American Bar Association Foster Care Reform Act August 2005

(1) be compelled to produce work product developed during the appointment;

(2) be required to disclose the source of information obtained as a result of the appointment;

(3) introduce into evidence any report or analysis prepared by the child's lawyer; or

(4) provide any testimony that is subject to the attorney-client privilege or any other testimony unless ordered by the court.

Commentary:

Nothing in this act shall diminish or otherwise change the lawyer-work product or attorney-client privilege protection for the child, nor shall the child have any lesser rights than any other party with respect to these protections.

If a state requires lawyers to report abuse or neglect under a mandated reporting statute, the state should list that statute under this section.

SECTION 11. CHILD'S RIGHT OF ACTION.

(a) The child's lawyer may be liable for malpractice to the same extent as a lawyer for any other client.

(b) Only the child has a right of action for money damages against the child's lawyer for inaction or action taken in the capacity of child's lawyer.

SECTION 12. FEES AND EXPENSES IN ABUSE OR NEGLECT PROCEEDINGS.

(a) In an abuse or neglect proceeding, a child's lawyer appointed pursuant to this [act] is entitled to reasonable and timely fees and expenses in an amount set by [court or state agency to be paid from (authorized public funds)].[42]

(b) To receive payment under this section, the payee shall complete and submit a written claim for payment, whether interim or final, justifying the fees and expenses charged.

(c) If after a hearing the court determines that a party whose conduct gave rise to a finding of abuse or neglect is able to defray all or part of the fees and expenses set pursuant to subsection (a), the court shall enter a judgment in favor of [the state, state agency, or

---

[42] N.C. Gen. Stat. Ann. § 7B-603.

101A

540 political subdivision] against the party in an amount the court determines is reasonable.[43]
541
542 **SECTION 13. EFFECTIVE DATE.** This [act] takes effect on _____.

---

[43] NCCUSL Act, Sec. 19.

101A

Report

> "The participation of counsel on behalf of **all** parties subject to juvenile and family court proceedings is essential to the administration of justice and to the fair and accurate resolution of issues at all stages of those proceedings." IJA/ABA, Juvenile Justice Standards, Standards Relating to Counsel for Private Parties, Std. 1.1, at 11 (1980)(emphasis added).

Courts in abuse and neglect cases dramatically shape a child's entire future in that the court decides where a child lives, with whom the child will live and whether the child's parental rights will be terminated. No other legal proceeding that pertains to children has such a major effect on their lives. While the outcome of an abuse and neglect case has drastic implications for both the parents and the children involved, only children's physical liberty is threatened. An abuse and neglect case that results in removal of the child from the home may immediately or ultimately result in the child being thrust into an array of confusing and frightening situations wherein the State moves the child from placement to placement with total strangers, puts the child in a group home, commits the child to an institution, or even locks the child up in detention for running away or otherwise violating a court order. Our notion of basic civil rights, and ABA Policy and Standards, demand that children and youth have a trained legal advocate to speak on their behalf and to protect their legal rights. There would be no question about legal representation for a child who was facing a month in juvenile detention, so why is there an issue for a child in an abuse and neglect case, where State intervention may last up to 18 years? The trauma faced by children in these proceedings has been recognized by at least one federal court which held that foster children have a constitutional right to adequate legal representation.[1]

Despite the gravity of these cases, the extent to which a child is entitled to legal representation varies not only from state to state, but from case to case, and all too often, from hearing to hearing. The root of these inconsistencies lies in the lack of a mandate for legal representation for children in abuse and neglect cases, and the lack of uniform standards for the legal representation of children, coupled with the lack of sufficient training necessary for attorneys to provide adequate representation to their child clients.

In 1996 the ABA adopted the ABA Standards of Practice for Lawyers Who Represent Children in Abuse and Neglect Cases (hereinafter "ABA Abuse and Neglect Standards") calling for a lawyer for every child subject to abuse and neglect proceedings.[2] The ABA Abuse and Neglect standards state that "All children subject to court proceedings involving allegations of child abuse and neglect should have legal representation as long as the court jurisdiction continue." In 2005, the ABA unanimously passed policy that calls upon Congress, the States, and territories to ensure that "all dependent youth . . . be

---

[1] Kenny A. v. Perdue, 356 F. Supp. 2d 1353 (2005).

[2] American Bar Association, *ABA Standards of Practice for Lawyers Who Represent Children in Abuse and Neglect Cases* (1996) at preface.

101A

on equal footing with other parties in the dependency proceeding and have the right to quality legal representation, not simply an appointed lay guardian *ad litem* or lay volunteer advocate with no legal training, acting on their behalf in this court process."

The proposed *Model Act Governing the Representation of Children in Abuse, Neglect, and Dependency Proceedings* (hereinafter "Model Act") focuses on the representation of children in abuse and neglect cases to ensure that states have a model of ethical representation for children that is consistent with the ABA Abuse and Neglect Standards,[3] ABA Policy, and the ABA Model Rules of Professional Conduct (hereinafter "ABA Model Rules").

Although many states require that a lawyer be appointed for a child in an abuse and neglect proceeding, some require that the child's lawyer be "client directed" and others require the lawyer to act as a guardian *ad litem* whereby the attorney is charged with the duty of protecting and serving the "best interests" of the child. Often there is not "careful delineation of the distinctions between the ethical responsibilities of a lawyer to the client and the professional obligations of the lay guardian *ad litem* as a best interests witness for the court."[4] The states' use of different statutory language and mandated roles for child representation has led to much confusion within the field.

The proposed Model Act conforms to the clearly stated preference in the ABA Abuse and Neglect Standards for a client-directed lawyer for each child. Similarly, the proposed Model Act is consistent with the ABA Model Rules. The Model Act states that the child's lawyer should form an attorney-client relationship which is "fundamentally indistinguishable from the attorney-client relationship in any other situation and which includes duties of client direction, confidentiality, diligence, competence, loyalty, communication, and the duty to advise."[5]

Consonant with the ABA Model Rules, the drafters of the Model Act started from the premise that all child clients have the capacity to form an attorney-client relationship. An attorney must enter into representation of a child treating the child client as he or she would any other client to every extent possible. The attorney should give the child frank advice on what he or she thinks is the best legal remedy to achieve the child's expressed wishes. This decision should not be based on the attorney's mores or personal opinions; rather it should focus on the attorney's knowledge of the situation, the law, options

---

[3] American Bar Association, *ABA Standards of Practice for Lawyers Who Represent Children in Abuse and Neglect Cases* (1996) The Standards can be found at http://www.abanet.org/leadership/2006/annual/onehundredfourteen.doc

[4] *Uniform Representation of Children in Abuse and Neglect, and Custody Proceedings Act* (hereinafter "NCCUSL Act"), National Conference of Commissioners of Uniform State Law. Prefatory Note (2007); the text of the final act can be found at http://www.law.upenn.edu/bll/archives/ulc/rarccda/2007_final.htm. *See* Atwood, *supra* note 1, at 188-91; Howard A. Davidson, *Child Protection Policy and Practice at Century's End*, 33 FAM. L. Q. 765, 768-69 (1999). For information about different state practices *see* Representing Children Worldwide 2005 (www.law.yale.edu/rcw) or *A Child's Right to Counsel. First Star's National Report Card on Legal Representation for Children* 2007.

[5] ABA Model Act, Commentary to Section 7(c) which refers to ABA Model Rules 1.2, 1.6, 1.3, 1.1, 1.7, 1.4 and 2.1.

available and the child's wishes. The proposed Model Act also provides specific guidance for lawyers charged with representing those child clients with diminished capacity. Some children (including infants, pre-verbal children, and children who are mentally or developmentally challenged) do not have the capacity to form a lawyer-client relationship. These child clients should be considered the exception, not the rule, and the structure of representation for children as a whole should be based upon a theory of competence and capacity.

Providing children in abuse and neglect cases with a client-directed 'traditional' lawyer is consistent with the thinking of national children's law experts. A conference on the representation of children was held at Fordham Law School in 1995 entitled *Ethical Issues in the Legal Representation of Children*. The conference examined the principles set out in the then-proposed (later adopted) ABA Abuse and Neglect Standards and conferees clearly recommended that lawyers for children should act as lawyers, not as guardians *ad litem*.[6] The co-sponsors and participants at the Fordham conference included national children's law organizations and many ABA entities.[7]

Ten years later in 2006, children's law experts gathered again at a conference at the University of Nevada, Las Vegas (UNLV), to review the state of legal representation of children. Like the Fordham Conference, the UNLV participants produced a set of recommendations.[8] The UNLV Recommendations encourage lawyers to seek to empower children by helping them develop decision-making capacity. Regarding the role of the lawyer, the UNLV Recommendations strongly support client-directed representation for children capable of making considered decisions.[9] Again, the list of co-sponsors and participants included nationally respected children's law organizations and many ABA entities.[10]

---

[6] *Recommendations of the Conference on Ethical Issues in the Legal Representation of Children*, 64 FORDHAM L. REV. 1301 (1996) (Fordham Recommendations) (attorney must follow child's expressed preferences and attempt to discern wishes in context in developmentally appropriate way if child is incapable of expressing viewpoint).

[7] Co-sponsors included the Administration for Children, Youth and Families, U.S. Department of Health and Human Services; ABA Center on Children and the Law, Young Lawyers Division; ABA Center for Professional Responsibility, ABA Section of Criminal Justice, Juvenile Justice Committee; ABA Section of Family Law; ABA Section of Individual Rights and Responsibilities; ABA Section of Litigation Task Force on Children; ABA Steering Committee on the Unmet Legal Needs of Children; Juvenile Law Center; National Association of Counsel for Children; National Center for Youth Law; National Counsel of Juvenile and Family Court Judges; Stein Center for Ethics and Public Interest Law, Fordham University School of Law.

[8] *See Recommendations of the UNLV Conference on Representing Children in Families: Children's Advocacy and Justice Ten Years after Fordham*, 6 NEV. L. J. 592-687 (2006) (UNLV Recommendations).

[9] As stated in the Recommendations, "[c]hildren's attorneys should take their direction from the client and should not substitute for the child's wishes the attorney's own judgment of what is best for children or for that child." *Id.* at 609.

[10] Co-sponsors of UNLV included the ABA Center on Children and the Law, Young Lawyers Division; ABA Center for Professional Responsibility; ABA Child Custody and Adoption Pro Bono Project; ABA Section of Family Law; ABA Section of Litigation; Home at Last, Children's Law Center of Los Angeles; Juvenile Law Center; National Association of Counsel for Children; National Center for Youth Law; National Council of Juvenile and Family Court Judges; National Juvenile Defender Center; Stein Center

101A

Consistent with the ABA Abuse and Neglect Standards, ABA policy, and the recommendations of national children's law experts, Section 3 of this Model Act mandates that an attorney, acting in a traditional role, should be appointed for every child who is the subject of an abuse or neglect proceeding.[11] Attorneys can identify legal issues regarding their child clients, use their legal skills to ensure the protection of their clients' rights and needs, and advocate for their clients. The Model Act requires lawyers to complete a thorough and independent investigation and participate fully in all stages of the litigation. Lawyers for children, as lawyers for any client, have a role as a counselor to their clients and should assist their clients in exploring the practical effects of taking various positions, the likelihood that a court will accept particular arguments, and the impact of such decisions on the child, other family members, and future legal proceedings.[12]

Lawyers for children allow children to be participants in the proceedings that affect their lives and safety. Children who are represented by a lawyer often feel the process is fairer because they had a chance to participate and to be heard. Consequently, children are more likely to accept the court's decision because of their own involvement in the process.

Requiring lawyers to represent children in abuse and neglect cases is also consistent with federal law. The Child Abuse Prevention and Treatment Act (CAPTA) requires the appointment of a "guardian *ad litem*" for a child as a condition of receiving federal funds for child abuse prevention and treatment programs. Providing a child with a lawyer is consistent with the requirements of CAPTA. No state with a lawyer model has been held out of compliance with CAPTA and Health and Human Services (HHS) has issued guidance suggesting that appointing counsel for a child promotes the child's "best interest" consistent with CAPTA.[13]

The Model Act also provides lawyers guidance when representing children with diminished capacity, which includes young children. Like all children in these proceedings, young children are entitled to proceedings that fully examine and address their needs, including *inter alia* their physical, behavioral, and developmental health and well-being, their education and early-learning needs, their need for family permanency and stability, and their need to be safe from harm. The Model Act also allows states to set an age of capacity if they so choose.

The Model Act allows and welcomes "best interest advocates" in child welfare cases. A best interest advocate is defined as "an individual, not functioning or intended to function

---

for Law and Ethics, Fordham University School of Law; Support Center for Child Advocates; and Youth Law Center.

[11] Federal law has long authorized the discretionary appointment of counsel for Indian children subject to the Indian Child Welfare Act. *See* 25 U.S.C. § 1912(b) (2000).

[12] Model Act, Commentary for Section (7)(c)(1).

[13] U.S. Department of HHS Children's Bureau, *Adoption 2002: The President's Initiative on Adoption and Permanence for Children*, Commentary to Guideline 15A

as the child's lawyer, appointed by the court to assist in determining the best interests of the child."[14] The advisor may be a court-appointed special advocate (CASA), a guardian *ad litem* or other person who has received training specific to the best interest of the child. The Act endorses and in no way restricts the widespread use of CASAs to fulfill the role of court appointed advisor.[15]

A state's law regarding abuse and neglect proceedings should be designed to provide children involved in an abuse and neglect case with a well-trained, high quality lawyer who is well-compensated and whose caseload allows for effective representation. Lawyers for children are essential for ensuring that the child's legal rights are protected. "Unless children are allowed by lawyers to set the objectives of their cases, they would not only be effectively deprived of a number of constitutional rights, they would be denied procedures that are fundamental to the rule of law."[16]

Children in dependency court proceedings are often taken from their parents, their siblings and extended families, their schools, and everything that is familiar to them. Children and youth deserve a voice when important and life-altering decisions are being made about them. They deserve to have their opinions heard, valued and considered. They have interests that are often distinct or are opposed to those of the state and their parents in dependency proceedings and, as the ABA has recognized many times, they deserve ethical legal representation.

In preparing this Model Act, the drafters have taken into consideration the enormous contributions of various organizations and advocates in defining standards of representation, most notably that of the American Bar Association (ABA), the National Association of Counsel for Children (NACC), the Uniform Law Commission (ULC), participants in the Representing Children in Families UNLV Conference, and the states themselves. In addition, drafters have sought input from the ABA Standing Committee on Ethics, various sections within the ABA, and more than 30 children's law centers around the country who represent children every day.

---

[14] Model Act, Section 1.
[15] The Court Appointed Special Advocate is a lay volunteer who advocates as a non-lawyer on behalf of a child in child abuse and neglect proceedings. Volunteers are screened and trained at the local level, but all CASA programs that are affiliated with the National Court Appointed Special Advocate Association must comply with the standards issued by that organization. *See* www.nationalcasa.org. In addition, many states have established their own standards to ensure that the volunteers representing children are competent and possess relevant training and experience. *See generally* Michael S. Piraino, *Lay Representation of Abused and Neglected Children: Variations on Court Appointed Special Advocate Programs and Their Relationship to Quality Advocacy*, 1 JOURNAL OF CENTER FOR CHILDREN AND THE COURTS 63 (1999). The Office of Juvenile Justice and Delinquency Prevention of the United States Department of Justice is authorized to enter into cooperative agreements with the National CASA Association to expand CASA programs nationally. *See* 42 U.S.C.A. § 13013 (2005 & Supp. 2006). One of the key strengths of the CASA program is that a CASA volunteer generally represents only one child at a time. Moreover, an attorney for the child working in tandem with a CASA volunteer can provide a powerful "team" approach in juvenile court. In addition, CASA volunteers may have access to the CASA program's own legal representative for legal advice.
[16] Martin Guggenheim, *A Paradigm for Determining the Role of Counsel for Children*, 64 Fordham L.Rev. 1399, 1423-24 (1996).

101A

Respectfully Submitted,
Hilarie Bass, Chair
Section of Litigation
August, 2011

INDEX

Abramson, S., 43
Abuse and neglect proceedings, 271–273, 285–286
Access
  to attorneys, 199, 200, 202, 210
  authorization of, 264
  to child and information relating to child, 282
  provision of, 261
  to records, 264–265
Accommodation of child's wishes, 38, 62–63
ACF (Administration for Children and Families), 37
Actively Evaluate Needs (skill)
  described, 67
  implementation of, 102, 165–166
  in Six Core Skills Training, 79–81
Adams, Lauren, 27, 54
Adequacy of compensation, 131, 157, 158, 162, 263–264
Adjudication, 206, 207
Adjusted caseload, 222
Administration, in Best Practice Model, 53
Administration for Children and Families (ACF), 37
Administrative data, 119–120, 164, 180
Administrative support, 132
Adoption 2002 program, 11
Adoptive homes, identifying, 134
Advance Case Planning (skill)
  described, 67
  implementation of, 102–103, 166
  in Six Core Skills Training, 86–89
Advice, 238
Advocacy. *See also* Child advocates
  appellate, 240–241
  attendance of outside meetings for, 52
  for child's wishes, 182–183
  dimensions of, 67, 68
  in multidisciplinary teams, 190
  needs and corollaries of, 83–84
  on other legal matters, 134–135, 141
  service, 134–136, 141, 183
Advocate Effectively (skill)
  described, 68
  implementation of, 104–105, 166
  in Six Core Skills Training, 83–84
Advocating for the Child in Protection Proceedings (Don Duquette), 9

Age
  of attorney, 125
  of child client, 116–118, 154, 155, 160, 177
Agenda, Six Core Skills Training, 69–70
Aging out, 89–90
Alternative theories of case, 82–83
Alving, M., 43
American Bar Association (ABA), 291. *See also Model Act Governing the Representation of Children in Abuse, Neglect, and Dependency Proceedings* (ABA) (2011 Model Act); Standards of Practice for Lawyers Who Represent Children in Abuse and Neglect Cases (ABA) (1996 ABA Standards)
  in child protection cases, 267
  child welfare law specialty in, 5
  guidance on child representation from, 9
  Juvenile Justice Standards Relating to Counsel for Private Parties, 9, 244, 259, 267
  Lund & Renne risk assessment model, 75–77
  Model Act of 2009, 19
  Model Rules of Ethics, 19
  Model Rules of Professional Conduct, 19–20, 22–25, 75, 192, 288
  policies related to representation of abused and neglected children from, 266–267
  Resolutions on Foster Care and Adoption, 31
  on role of children in dependency proceedings, 28
  Section on Litigation, 13, 221n.16
  on training programs for attorneys, 33
American Humane Association Conference, 40–41
Appeals, 241, 258
Appell, Annette, 16, 21n.70
Appellate advocacy, 240–241
Appointment
  2011 Model Act on, 272–275
  ABA Standards of 1996 on, 260–262
  age of child at, 116–118
  duration of, 275
  eligibility for, 261

order of, 274
  in QIC Best Practice Model, 52, 235–236
  state laws on, 112
  timing of, 115–117, 175–177, 260–261
Arkansas, 220n.15
Assertiveness, of child representative, 52
Assess Child Safety (skill)
  described, 67
  implementation of, 100–102, 166
  in Six Core Skills Training, 75–77
Assignment, timing of, 176–177
Associated costs, 264
Assumed-responsibility scale, 157, 158, 161
Attitudes, of attorneys, 225–226
Attorney engagement, 186–188
Attorney-level characteristics, activities and, 156–158, 161–162
Attorney samples, QIC-ChildRep research, 113–114
Attorney surveys, 120–121
  baseline, 120, 123, 133
  child-specific, 120–121, 146, 164, 166–167
  milestone, 120–121, 147, 166–167
Attorneys. *See also* Behaviors of attorneys
  access to, 199, 200, 202, 210
  collaboration of social workers and, 192–193, 198–199, 211, 224
  in multidisciplinary team study, 190
Attorneys representing children
  ABA standards for, 244–258
  activities of (*See* Child representation activities)
  caseloads for, 31–32, 222–223
  certification for, 226–227
  child representation experience of, 126–128, 139–140
  CLE courses taken by, 128, 129
  compensation for, 130–132, 140
  critiques of, 15–17
  demographics of, 124–125, 156
  duties and characteristics of, 26
  employment settings for, 124, 142–143
  on implementation of Six Core Skills (*See* Six Core Skills implementation)

Attorneys representing children (*cont.*)
  job satisfaction and impact ratings by, 138–139, 140
  in Michigan law, 62
  models for, 17–25
  organizational supports for, 132–133, 140
  other types of law practiced by, 128–130
  recruitment of, 220–222
  responsibilities of, 133–136, 140–141
  on *Six Core Skills,* 95–108
  task importance for, 136–138, 141
  training programs for, 33–34, 224–226
Attorneys representing children study, 123–142
  child representation experience in, 126–128, 139–140
  compensation in, 130–132, 140
  continuing legal education courses in, 128, 129
  demographics in, 124–125
  employment settings in, 124, 142–143
  job satisfaction and impact ratings in, 138–139, 140
  organizational supports in, 132–133, 140
  other types of law practiced in, 128–130
  task importance in, 136–138, 141
  view of responsibilities in, 133–136, 140–141
Atwood, Barbara, 19, 19n.63, 21n.70
Australia, 211
Authorization, of lawyer access, 264
Availability, of representation, 39
Average monthly rates of activities, 148
Average treatment effect on permanency, 176

Baby Court, 200
Baseline attorney surveys, 120, 123, 133
Batson, A., 44
Behaviors of attorneys
  after Six Core Skills Training, 68, 169–173
  change logic model for, 66–67
  in concentrated practices, 218
  measuring, 166–169, 179–180
  quality of, 180
Belonging, need for, 80
Berliner, L., 43
Best interest advocates, 18–19, 271
Best interests approach
  child's wishes in, 60–62
  client-directed vs., 10, 11, 17, 46, 56–63
  determining capacity to direct counsel in, 58, 59
  in Georgia, 113
  Needs Assessment data on, 46

problems with, 19–20
  in QIC Best Practice Model, 56–63
  responsibilities of attorney in, 141
  role of attorney in, 17–20
  Six Core Skills Training in jurisdictions with, 75
  stated interests of child vs., 10
Biological fathers, 152, 154, 159
Bright-line age limits, 13, 22, 59–60
Broad scope orders, 265
Budd, Jonathon, 224
Buss, Emily, 17, 17n.49, 25n.87, 27, 29

CACs (Child Advocacy Centers), 191–192
CAI. *See* Children's Advocacy Institute
Caliber Associates, 44
Calkins, C., 44
Capacity
  decision-making, 236–237
  determinations of, 57–60, 75, 183
  diminished, 23–25, 54, 59–62
  "dimmer switch" of, 61
Capacity to direct counsel, 57–60, 75
CAPTA. *See* Child Abuse Prevention and Treatment Act
Caregivers, 134–136, 169. *See also specific types*
Carry-over effects, 195
CASA. *See* Court Appointed Special Advocate Association
CASAs. *See* Court Appointed Special Advocates
Case planning. *See* Advance Case Planning (skill)
Case planning meetings, 134
Case plans
  reviews of, 169, 170
  safety plans vs., 76
  SMART criteria for, 86, 87
Case resolution
  in multidisciplinary teams, 201, 203–207, 224
  non-adversarial, 84–86, 173, 185
  in QIC-ChildRep research studies, 185
Case theory. *See also* Develop Case Theory (skill)
  activities to develop, 169, 170
  preliminary, 82
  in trial law, 81
Case time, activity level and, 159–160
Caseloads
  ABA Standards of 1996 on, 265
  attorney activity level and, 156, 157, 161, 162
  for attorneys representing children, 31–32, 222–223
  for child representatives, 29
  empirical research on, 44
  Needs Assessment data on, 38, 46
  in QIC Best Practice Model, 242
Caseworkers, 85–86, 154, 159. *See also* Child welfare agency workers

Center for Children & Youth Justice (CCYJ), 114
Center on Children and the Law, 13, 70
Certification, 226–227
Cessation, of representation, 241, 258
CFSRs (Child and Family Service Reviews), 4, 39
A challenge for change (G.A. Lukowski and H.J. Davies), 44
Challenges to testimony, 256
Change logic model, 66–67
Chapin Hall, 122n.13. *See also specific studies*
  QIC Best Practice Model evaluation by, viii–ix
  QIC-ChildRep research studies by, 109, 119–120, 214, 227
  Six Core Skills implementation evaluation by, 96
Child. *See also* Wishes of child
  attorney characteristics and contact with, 156–158
  child characteristics and contact with, 154–156
  defined, 271
  equal dignity for, 14–15
  Needs Assessment data on contact with, 38–41
  questioning of, 255–256
  rate of contact with, 149–150, 159
  right to council for, 8, 14
  role of, in dependency proceedings, 28–29
  service advocacy for, 134, 141
  Six Core Skills and contact with, 182
  with special needs, 239, 253
  timing of contact with, 152, 153
  understanding, 26–28
  wellbeing of, 201
Child abuse cases, 191–192, 214
Child Abuse Prevention and Treatment Act (CAPTA)
  and 2011 Model Act, 290
  and current state of child representation, 2, 3
  enforcement of, 36
  federal leadership from, 216–217
  in history of child representation, 8–9, 12
  and successful child representation, 28
The Child Abuse Prevention and Treatment Act—Promoting the Unauthorized Practice of Law (Gerald F. Glynn), 21n.70, 26n.87
Child Advocacy Centers (CACs), 191–192
Child Advocacy Law Clinic, vii
Child advocates. *See also* Attorneys representing children; Court Appointed Special Advocates (CASAs)
  best interest, 18–19, 271
  in Children's Bureau *Guidelines,* 11–12
  consensus on need for, 50

INDEX

duties of, ix, 8–9
importance of, 2–3
rates of children in court without, 217
role of, vii, 6
systemic pressures on, 30
Child and Family Service Reviews (CFSRs), 4, 39
Child development
attorney's competence in, 27–28
in QIC Best Practice Model, 54–55
as topic in Six Core Skills Training, 72–73
Child engagement, 182
Child-level characteristics, attorney activities and, 154–156, 160–161
Child-level outcomes
measures of, 164–165
in research studies by QIC-ChildRep, 185–186
and Six Core Skills Training, 173–177
Child protection
ABA policies on cases of, 267
public health model of, 214–216
Child representation
academic and policy discussions on, 7–34
benefits of good, 181
caseloads in, 222–223
certification in, 226–227
and constitutional arguments for child's right to council, 14
and critiques of attorneys for children, 15–17
current state of, 1–6
early models of, 7–9
empirical research on type of, 44
enhancing judicial role in, 259–265
and equal dignity for children in judicial process, 14–15
federal leadership on, 216–217
future improvements for, ix–x, 213–227
holistic approach to, 31
launching of QIC-ChildRep project, 5–6
legal role in, 5–6
literature on, 34
milestones in development of, 9–13
models for role of attorney in, 17–25
multidisciplinary approaches to, 223–224
organization of, 218–220
practices in successful, 25–31
with public health model of child protection, 214–216
reasonable caseloads in, 31–32
recruitment of attorneys for, 220–222
research agenda for, 227
state legal structures for, 217–218
training programs in, 33–34, 224–226
and U.S. Children's Bureau, 1–5

Child representation activities, ix
and attorney characteristics, 156–158, 161–162
and child characteristics, 154–156, 160–161
in concentrated practices, 218
effect of attitudes on, 225–226
frequency and rates of, 149–152
future research on, 227
in QIC Best Practice Model, 56
successful, 25–31
time spent on, 184
timing of, 152–154, 159–160
variability in, 158–159
Child representation activities study, 145–162
analysis approach in, 148–149
attorney-level characteristics in, 156–158, 161–162
child-level characteristics in, 154–156, 160–161
frequency and rates of activities in, 149–152
importance of, 145–147
milestone surveys in, 121
sampling for, 147–148
timing of activities in, 152–154, 159–160
variability in activities in, 158–159
Child representatives. See also Attorneys representing children
as best interest advocates, 18–19
non-lawyer, 8
roles of, 5–6, 9–13, 30
systemic pressures on, 29–31
U.S. Children's Bureau on, vii
Child samples
for Flint multidisciplinary team study, 204
for QIC-ChildRep research studies, 114–118
Child-specific attorney surveys. See also Milestone surveys
in child representation activities survey, 146
in QIC-ChildRep research studies, 120–121
in Six Core Skills Training evaluation, 164, 166–167
Child welfare agency workers, 202, 208–210. See also Caseworkers
Child welfare cases
legal representation of children in (See Child representation)
in legal system, 5–6
Child Welfare Law and Practice, Second Edition (Donald N. Duquette and Ann M. Haralambie) (Red Book), 69, 101
Child welfare law offices
advantages of practice in, 218–219
attorneys representing children in, 142
caseloads in, 222
Needs Assessment data from, 41–42

Child Welfare Law Specialists (CWLSs), 5n.18, 33, 224, 226–227
Child witnesses, 255
Children at home at case assignment, 206, 207, 209
Children's Advocacy Institute (CAI), 36–37, 51, 217
The Children's Law Center, 41–42
Children's Rights Litigation Committee, 13
Child's attorney. See also Attorneys representing children
appointment of, 260–262
defined, 11, 244–245
independence of, 259
Child's interests. See also Best interests approach
ABA Standards of 1996 on, 249–250
in QIC Best Practice Model, 236
stated, 10
Child's lawyer. See also Attorneys representing children
defined, 13, 271
duties of, 275–282
qualifications of, 273–274
Child's representative, defined, 51–52, 235. See also Child representatives
CIP. See Court Improvement Program
CIP (Court Improvement Program) Annual Program Assessments, 39
CLE. See Continuing legal education
Client-directed approach
best interests approach vs., 10, 11, 17, 46, 56–63
child engagement and, 182
child's wishes in, 55, 60–62
in Convention on Rights of the Child, 12–13
determining capacity to direct counsel in, 58–59
Needs Assessment data on, 46
problems with, 22
in QIC Best Practice Model, 56–63
responsibilities of attorney using, 141
role of attorney in, 17, 21–22
Six Core Skills Training in jurisdictions with, 75
task importance for attorneys using, 141
in Washington State, 113
Client explanation, 239, 254
Client preferences, 237, 247–249
Climate, for multidisciplinary teams, 200, 202–203, 210, 211
Clinton, Bill, 11
Cluster randomized control design, 121
Coaching contact reports, 93, 96
Coaching sessions
engagement in, 186–188
participation in, 165, 186–188
Six Core Skills in, 92–93, 95–96

Collaboration
  of attorneys and social workers, 192–193, 198–199, 211, 224
  with child welfare agency, 208–209
  in multidisciplinary legal offices, 192–193
  on multidisciplinary teams, 190–191
  Needs Assessment data on, 41
  in Non-Adversarial Case Resolution, 84–86
Colorado, 193
Communication
  ABA Standards of 1996 on, 257
  as child representation activity, 169, 173, 184
  on multidisciplinary teams, 200, 203
Community connections, 27–28, 40
Community of practice, 186–188
A comparison of types of attorney representation for children in California juvenile court dependency cases (Goodman, et al.), 44
Compensation
  ABA Standards of 1996 on, 263–264
  adequacy of, 131, 157, 158, 162, 263–264
  attorney activity levels and, 157, 158, 162
  for attorneys representing children, 130–132, 140, 222
  for child representatives, 29
  for participation in research studies, 114
  in QIC Best Practice Model, 242
  uniformity in, 264
Compensation arrangements, 131–132
Compensation orders, 261
Composite monthly rates, 149
Concentrated practice, 218–220
Conclusion of appeal, 241, 258
Conclusion of hearings, 256
Conferences, pretrial, 172, 185
Confidentiality
  in Michigan rules of professional conduct, 194–195
  in multidisciplinary teams, 191, 198, 209, 210–211
  for social workers vs. attorneys, 192
Conflict situations
  ABA Standards of 1996 on, 246–247
  in QIC Best Practice Model, 53, 236
Congregate care, 118, 156
The Connecticut Center for Child Advocacy, 41–42
Consulting activities, 169, 170
Contact
  attorney characteristics and, 156–158
  child characteristics and, 154–156, 160
  frequency of, 149–152, 168

  rates of, 149–150, 168
  timing of, 152–154
Continuing legal education (CLE), 33, 128, 129, 263
Control, on multidisciplinary teams, 199, 200
Counsel for children enhancement, ABA policies on, 266
Counseling, 75, 238
Court appearances, 239, 254
Court Appointed Special Advocate Association (CASA), 8, 14, 16, 112
Court Appointed Special Advocates (CASAs), 9
  in 2011 Model Act, 291
  ABA policies on, 266
  empirical research on, 43–44
  and implementation of Six Core Skills, 99, 101, 105
  in Needs Assessment, 37–40
  Six Core Skills Training and contact with, 169
Court-appointed special advocates for children in Washington State (Berliner, Fitzgerald and Alving), 43
Court Improvement Program (CIP), 3–4, 37, 227
Court Improvement Program (CIP) Annual Program Assessments, 39
Court orders, 171, 241, 257–258
Court(s)
  appointment of child's attorney by, 260–262
  and lawyer caseloads, 264–265
  and lawyer compensation, 263–264
  and lawyer training, 262–263
  problem-solving, 31, 41
  and record access, 264–265
  state, 3–4, 9
  structuring of child representation by, 259–260
  as supervisor of social services, 5–6
  tribal, 40
CSR, Inc., 9–10, 44
CWLSs. *See* Child Welfare Law Specialists

"Danny's Case" exercise, 83–84
Data collection, in Flint MDF study, 196–197
Data sources, for QIC-ChildRep research studies, 118–121, 147
Davidson, Howard, 30
Davies, H.J., 44
Decision-making capacity, 236–237
Decision to appeal, 241, 258
DeKalb County, 32
Delinquency law, counsel in, 8
Dependency cases, attorney responsibilities in, 133–136
Dependency counsel caseload study and service delivery model analysis (Judicial Council of California), 44

Dependency proceedings
  applications of Six Core Skills beyond, 97
  child's wishes in, 55
  role of child client in, 28–29
Develop Case Theory (skill)
  described, 68
  implementation of, 103–104, 166
  in Six Core Skills Training, 79–81, 171–172
Development, child. *See* Child development
Developmental level, defined, 272
Developmentally appropriate, defined, 245
Differential diagnosis, 82
Dignity, for child, 14–15
Diminished capacity
  determinations of, 23–25, 54, 59
  legal representation for clients with, 24–25
  weighting wishes of child with, 60–62
"Dimmer switch" of capacity, 61
Directory of Children's Law Programs, 221n.16
Disabilities, clients under, 247
Discrete time hazard model, 175n.3
Discussion Guide for Six Core Skills Training, 78
Disposition, obligations after, 240, 257
Dispositional hearings, 88–89
Distal collaterals
  child characteristics and contact with, 154–156, 160
  rates of contact with, 149–150
  timing of contact with, 153
Document review activities
  attorney characteristics and, 156–158
  rate of, 151, 152
  timing of, 153, 154, 160
Driving the bus, 68, 78, 103–105
Due process, for child clients, 180–181
Duquette, D.N., 9, 17, 22, 26n.87, 44, 69, 101

Early interventions, by multidisciplinary teams, 209–210
Early permanency, 176–177
Edelstein, R.S., 44
Education level, of attorneys representing children, 124, 125
The effectiveness of CASAs in achieving positive outcomes for children (P. Litzelfelner), 44
The effectiveness of court appointed special advocates to assist in permanency planning (C. Calkins and M. Millar), 44
Emergency placement and removal, 77–79
Empirical research, in QIC Needs Assessment, 42–45

INDEX

Employment setting(s)
 and attorney activity level, 156–158, 161–162
 of attorneys representing children, 124, 142–143
Engagement
 attorney, 186–188
 child, 182
 with family, 27–28
Enter the Child's World (skill)
 described, 67
 and determining capacity to direct counsel, 58
 implementation of, 98–100, 165–166, 181–183
 in Six Core Skills Training, 70–71, 73
 and understanding child development, 55
Equal dignity, for children, 14–15
Esteem needs, 80
Ethical Issues in the Legal Representation of Children Conference, 10, 289
Ethnicity. *See* Race and ethnicity
Evaluation of CASA representation (Caliber Associates), 44
Evaluation of the guardian ad litem system (Pitchal, Freundlich and Kendrick), 44
An evaluation of the North Dakota guardian ad litem project (Hess, Swanke and Batson), 44
Evidence, presentation of, 240, 254
Exit status, 175–178
Expediting Permanency (A.E. Zinn and J. Slowriver), 45
Expenses, 285
Experience
 and attorney activity level, 156, 157, 161
 of attorneys representing children, 126–128, 139–140
Explanation, client, 239, 254
Expressed wishes model. *See* Client-directed approach
External validity, 113

Families, of attorneys representing children, 125
Families of clients. *See also* Parents
 attorney characteristics and contact with, 157, 158
 child characteristics and contact with, 154–156
 engagement with, 27–28
 rates of contact with, 149–150
 service advocacy for, 183
 timing of contact with, 152, 153
Family-based care, 118
Family connections, 203–207, 224
Family Educational Rights and Privacy Act (FERPA), 80
Family unification, 30
FAMLINK data system, 120

Fathers, 152, 154, 159, 169
Federal government
 leadership on child representation from, 216–217
 state reports to, 39
Federle, Katherine Hunt, 14
Feedback, from child clients, 28
Fees, 285. *See also* Compensation
Fegert, J.M., 45
FERPA (Family Educational Rights and Privacy Act), 80
Final report on the validation and effectiveness study of legal representation through guardian ad litem (CSR, Inc.), 44
Financial support, 92
First Star, 33, 36–37, 51, 217
Fitzgerald, M., 43
Flint multidisciplinary team (MDT) study, ix, 189–211, 224
 and creation of MDT approach, 197–203
 and current understanding of MDTs, 191–193
 factors in MDT impact from, 208–210
 goals of, 189–190
 limitations of, 205–206
 methodology of, 193–197
 primary findings from, 203–207
 weaknesses of MDTs from, 210–211
Florida, 217
Focus groups, 39–41
Fordham II Conference, 12
Foster care, clients in, 89–91, 156
Foster care alumni, 41
Foster care cases, number of, 1–2
Fostering Connections to Success and Increasing Adoptions Act (2008), 33, 90, 103
Frequency, of contact, 149–152, 168
Freundlich, M.D., 44

GALs. *See* Guardians ad litem
Gender of client, attorney activity level and, 155, 156, 160
Genesee County Court, 194. *See also* Flint multidisciplinary team (MDT) study
Genesee County Department of Health and Human Services, 208
Georgia. *See also specific studies*
 attorney samples from, 113–114
 child samples from, 114–118
 data sources for research from, 119–121
 evaluation of Best Practice Model in, ix
 lack of representation in, 216
 local jurisdictional samples from, 110, 111
 pod meetings and coaching sessions in, 93
 research findings from, 179–188

research samples from, 110–118
Six Core Skills Training in, 69, 75
Georgia Department of Human Services, 120
Georgia Supreme Court Committee on Justice for Children Court Improvement Program (J4C), 114
Glynn, Gerald F., 21n.70, 26n.87
Goals
 of case, 83
 case planning to meet, 87
 of child clients, 182–183
 of Flint MDT study, 189–190
 intermediate, 83–84
 for parents, 135
Goodman, G.S., 44
Group reflection, 77
Guardians ad litem (GALs)
 ABA Standards of 1996 on, 11
 in CAPTA, 2, 3, 8
 as child representatives, 217
 in early child welfare cases, 7
 effectiveness of, 9–10
 empirical research on, 44–45
 in Georgia, 112, 113, 141
 NCJFCJ report on, 12
 previous ABA policies on, 266
Guggenheim, Martin, 15–16, 21n.70, 30
Guidelines for Public Policy and State Legislation Governing Permanence for Children (U.S. Children's Bureau), 11–12, 56
Gupta-Kagan, Josh, 214, 216

Haralambie, Ann, 21n.70, 27, 54, 69, 101
Health Insurance Portability and Accountability Act (HIPAA), 80
Hearings
 ABA Standards of 1996 on, 254–257
 dispositional, 88–89
 with multidisciplinary teams, 199, 201
 in QIC Best Practice Model, 240
Helfer, Ray, 215
Helping professionals, 132, 133
Hess, C., 44
HIPAA (Health Insurance Portability and Accountability Act), 80
Holistic approach to child representation, 31
Hollander, Scott, 224
Humility and Child Autonomy in Child Welfare and Custody Representation of Children (Ann Haralambie), 21n.70
Huntington, Clare, 215, 216

Identity Circle Exercise, 71
Impact ratings
 attorney activity level and, 158, 161
 for attorneys representing children, 138–139

Impact ratings (*cont.*)
    and effectiveness of attorneys, 221–222
Impaired clients, 23n.84
In-court actions, in QIC Best Practice Model, 53, 239–240
In re Gault, 8, 14
Independence, of child's attorney, 259
Independent living, preparedness for, 165
Indian Child Welfare Act, 128, 290n.11
Individuals to discuss cases with, availability of, 132, 133, 140
Informality, of child welfare proceedings, 31
Initial surveys, 147
Intelligent consumer model, 88
Interests, of child. *See* Child's interests
Intermediate goals, 83–84
Interview outcomes, 73
Interview techniques, 74
Interviewing, 73–74, 169, 170
Investigation activities
    ABA Standards of 1996 on, 250–252
    attorney characteristics and, 156–158
    in child protection system, 215
    in multidisciplinary teams, 191
    need for, 45
    at outside meetings, 52
    in QIC Best Practice Model, 237
    rate of, 151, 152
    timing of, 153, 154
Investigative staff, 132, 133, 140

J4C (Georgia Supreme Court Committee on Justice for Children Court Improvement Program), 114
Job satisfaction, 138–140, 201
"Journey to New Earth" exercise, 81
Judges
    Needs Assessment data from, 39–40
    role of, in child representation, 259–265
Judicial Council of California, 32, 44, 223
Jurisdiction, attorney activities and, 158–159
Jurisdictional samples, for research studies, 110–113
Jury selection, 256
Justice, procedural, 180–181
Juvenile Justice Standards Relating to Counsel for Private Parties (ABA), 9, 244, 259, 267

Kendrick, C., 44
Kenny A. ex rel. v. Perdue, 31–32, 223
Kid's Voice, 41–42
Kinship placement rates, 174–175
Kothekar, Aditi, 21n.70

L-GALs. *See* Lawyers-guardians ad litem
Language acquisition, 72
Lassiter (case), 14
Late permanency, 176–177
Law
    applicability and relationship to other, 272
    practiced by attorneys representing children, 128–130
Law in practice, in QIC Needs Assessment, 36, 37–42
Law schools, child welfare law in, 221
Lawyer training, 241–242, 262–263
Lawyers. *See also* Attorneys representing children; Child's lawyer
    basic obligations of, 52, 236, 246
    collaboration of caseworkers and, 85–86
    eligibility for appointment of, 261
    and other court connected personnel, 260
    permission to retain, 262
    "Two Distinct Lawyer Roles" model, 22
    vigorous and active participation of, 56
    work product of, 284–285
Lawyers for Children (organization), 41–42, 197n.36
Lawyers-guardians ad litem (L-GALs)
    ABA Standards of 1996 on, 245
    in Michigan, 61–62, 194
Learning communities, 186
Legal Aid Society's Juvenile Rights Practice, 41–42, 197n.36
Legal Aid's Foster Children's Project, 45
Legal case preparation activities
    and attorney characteristics, 156–158
    and child characteristics, 156
    rate of, 151, 152
    timing of, 153
Legal matters, advocating on other, 134–135, 141
Legal professionals, communication with other, 154, 169
Legal representation of children in child welfare cases. *See* Child representation
Legal representatives. *See also* Child representatives
    for clients with diminished capacity, 24–25
    duties of, 235–236
Legal research databases, 132, 133, 140
Lehrman, Debra, 19
Liberty, protecting child's, 180, 181
Litzelfelner, P., 44
Local judicial jurisdiction samples, for research studies, 110–113
Longer cases, child outcomes in, 185–186

Love, need for, 80
Lukowski, G.A., 44
Lund & Renne risk assessment model, 75–77

Marco's Case Exercise, 74, 75, 77–79, 88–89, 91–92
"Marco's Choice" video, 75
Maslow's hierarchy of needs, 79–80
Massachusetts Committee for Public Counsel Services, 32, 223
MDLOs (multidisciplinary legal offices), 193
MDTs. *See* Multidisciplinary teams
Meetings
    case planning, 134
    with the child, 52, 237, 250
    outside, 52
    pod, 92–94, 165, 186–188
    team, 172, 173, 185
Mentorship, 263
Michigan. *See also* Flint multidisciplinary team (MDT) study
    lawyer-guardian ad litem in, 194
    weighting of child's wishes in, 61–62
Midwest Child Welfare Tribal Gathering, 40
Milestone surveys. *See also* Child-specific attorney surveys
    for child representation activities study, 147
    in QIC-ChildRep research studies, 120–121
    in Six Core Skills Training evaluation, 166–167
Millar, M., 44
Mitchell, E.B., 44
Model Act Governing the Representation of Children in Abuse, Neglect, and Dependency Proceedings (ABA) (2011 Model Act), 9, 270–292
    access to child and information relating to child in, 282
    applicability and relationship to other law in, 272
    appointment in abuse or neglect proceeding in, 272–273
    on child development, 27
    child's right of action in, 285
    on clients with diminished capacity, 60–61
    definitions in, 271–272
    determinations of capacity in, 58–59
    development of, 13
    duration of appointment in, 275
    duties of child's lawyer and scope of representation in, 275–282
    effective date of, 286
    fees and expenses in abuse or neglect proceedings in, 285
    lawyer work product and testimony in, 284–285
    order of appointment in, 274

INDEX

participation in proceedings in, 283–284
and QIC Best Practice Model, 50–56
qualifications of child's lawyer in, 273–274
report on, 287–291
state adoption of, 217
Model Act of 2009 (ABA), 19
Model Rules of Ethics (ABA), 19
Model Rules of Professional Conduct (ABA), 19–20, 22–25, 75, 192, 288
Monitoring
 of attorneys, 39
 of child well-being, 89–91
Monthly rates of activities, 148–149
Mothers, 169
Motions
 ABA Standards of 1996 on, 254
 in QIC Best Practice Model, 239–240
 and Six Core Skills Training, 171
Multidisciplinary legal offices (MDLOs), 193
Multidisciplinary teams (MDTs), 51. *See also* Flint multidisciplinary team (MDT) study
 benefits of, 189–190
 case outcomes for, ix
 caseloads in, 32
 creation of, 197–203
 current understanding of, 191–193
 in future of child representation, 223–224
 impact-related factors in, 208–210
 weaknesses of, 210–211
Multistate Foster Care Data Archive, 119–120
Myers, J.E.B., 44

NACR. *See* Non-Adversarial Case Resolution
National Association of Counsel for Children (NACC)
 and 2011 Model Act, 291
 caseload recommendations by, 32, 222–223
 certification by, 5, 33, 226–227
 goal of, vii
 on multidisciplinary practices, 224
 practice infrastructure recommendations by, 219
National Association of Social Workers Code of Ethics, 195
National Council of Juvenile and Family Court Judges (NCJFCJ)
 appointment survey from, 12
 Needs Assessment data from, 39–40
 Resource Guidelines of, 10, 244, 259
National Data Archive on Child Abuse and Neglect, 110n.2, 227
National Quality Improvement Center on the Representation of Children in the Child Welfare System Best Practice Model of Child Representation (QIC Best Practice Model), 49–63. *See also Six Core Skills*
 and ABA Model Act of 2011, 50–53
 and ABA Standards of 1996, 10, 51–53
 accommodation of child's wishes in, 62–63
 and child welfare law offices, 219
 client-directed vs. best-interests representation in, 56–63
 development of, vii–viii
 as developmentally sophisticated approach, 54–55
 effectiveness of, viii–ix
 organizational and administrative supports in, 241–242
 overall value of, 96–98
 QIC Needs Assessment as basis for, 49–50
 relevance of child's wishes in, 55
 state adoption of, 217, 218
 text of, 235–242
 on training, 224
 vigorous and active participation of lawyer in, 56
National Quality Improvement Center on the Representation of Children in the Child Welfare System (QIC-ChildRep)
 assessment of multidisciplinary representation by, 223–224
 creation of, vii–viii, 5
 empirical research for, 42
 launching of, 5–6
 national needs assessment by (*See* QIC Needs Assessment)
 research studies by (*See* Research studies by QIC-ChildRep)
 website, 70
NCJFCJ. *See* National Council of Juvenile and Family Court Judges
Needs of child. *See also* Actively Evaluate Needs (skill); QIC Needs Assessment
 and activities of attorneys, 160
 and advocacy corollaries, 83–84
 consensus about, 45–46
 developmentally sophisticated approach to, 54–55
Neglect cases, number of, 214
Negotiating activities, 169, 170, 253
Nevada Law Journal, 12
New Hampshire, 217
New York State, 32, 223
1996 ABA Standards. *See* Standards of Practice for Lawyers Who Represent Children in Abuse and Neglect Cases (ABA)
Non-Adversarial Case Resolution (NACR), 84–86, 173, 185
Nonprofit agencies, 142, 156, 157, 161–162
North Carolina, 217

Objections, 239–240, 254
OCLA (Washington Office of Civil and Legal Aid), 114
Office of Juvenile Justice and Delinquency Prevention, 291n.22
Office of Public Defender, 131
Ohio, 217
Orders of appointment, 274
Organizational settings. *See* Employment settings
Organizational supports, for attorneys, 132–133, 140
Out of court actions, 52, 237–239
Out-of-home care placements, 114–115
Outside meetings, 52
Oversight, for attorneys, 39, 41

Paralegals, availability of, 132
Parental fault paradigm, 215
Parental rights, termination of, 206, 207
Parenting, enhancing, 215
Parents
 communication with, 169
 contact between attorneys and, 152, 154, 159
 establishing goals for, 135
 services advocacy for, 135, 136
 social workers, agency workers and, 208–210
Participation in appeal, 241, 258
Payment requests, 264
Pennsylvania, 32, 223
Performance, attorney, 38, 226
Permanency outcomes
 for multidisciplinary teams, 206, 207
 in QIC-ChildRep research studies, 185–186
 and Six Core Skills Training, 175–178
Permanency plans, 55, 91–92
Permission to retain lawyer, 262
Persuasion, at outside meetings, 52
Peters, Jean Koh, 12, 17, 21n.70, 26–27, 54, 61, 72
Pew Commission on Children in Foster Care, 3, 31, 33
Physiological needs, 80
PIPs (Program Improvement Plans), 4n.15
Pitchal, E.S., 14n.29, 44
Placement(s)
 changes in, 174–175, 199
 emergency, 77–79
 types of, 155, 156, 206, 207
Pleadings
 ABA Standards of 1996 on, 252
 in QIC Best Practice Model, 238
 and Six Core Skills Training, 169, 171
Pod meetings
 engagement in, 186–188
 participation in, 165, 186–188
 on Six Core Skills, 92–94

Post-hearing activities
  ABA Standards of 1996 on, 257–258
  in QIC Best Practice Model, 240
Pott, Robbin, 214
Power estimates, 122
The Practice of Law for Children (Marvin Ventrell), 16n.41
Preferences, client, 237, 247–249
Preliminary theory of case, 82
Presentation of evidence, 240, 254
Pretrial conferences, 172, 185
Prevalence of activities, calculating, 148–149
Private practice
  activity levels of attorneys in, 156–158, 161–162
  profile of attorneys representing children in, 124, 132, 133, 142–143
Privileges, protection for, 210–211. *See also* Confidentiality
Problem solving. *See also* Non-Adversarial Case Resolution (NACR)
  Needs Assessment data on, 38, 45
  in QIC Best Practice Model, 240
Problem-solving courts, 31, 41
Procedural justice, 180–181
Proceedings
  abuse and neglect, 271–273, 285–286
  dependency, 28–29, 55, 97
  participation in, 283–284
Process observation, 193–195
Professional development, 225
Professional evaluations, of clients, 80
Program Improvement Plans (PIPs), 4n.15
Progressive Era reform movement, 7
Protective actions, 24
Protective capacities (Lund & Renne model), 76
Provision of access, 261
Proximate collaterals
  attorney characteristics and contact with, 156–158
  child characteristics and contact with, 154–156
  rates of contact with, 149–150
  Six Core Skills Training and communication with, 169
  timing of contact with, 153, 154
Psychiatrists, consulting, 132, 133
Psychologists, consulting, 132, 133
Public health model of child protection, 214–216

QIC Best Practice Model. *See* National Quality Improvement Center on the Representation of Children in the Child Welfare System Best Practice Model of Child Representation
QIC-ChildRep. *See* National Quality Improvement Center on the Representation of Children in the Child Welfare System
QIC Needs Assessment, viii, 35–47
  as basis for QIC Best Practice Model, 49–50
  consensus in, 45–47
  existing empirical research in, 42–45
  of law in practice, 37–42
  state law in, 35–47
  and weighting of child's wishes, 60
Qualification standards, for attorneys, 46
Questioning of child, 255–256

Race and ethnicity
  of attorneys representing children, 124
  of clients, and activity rates of attorneys, 155, 156, 160–161
Ramsey, S.H., 31, 44
Randomized control trials, 194–196
Rapport, 27, 85
Recall bias, 146
Recommendations of the UNLV Conference on Representing Children in Families (UNLV Recommendations), 20n.65, 20n.66
  and 2011 Model Act, 289
  and developmentally sophisticated approach to child representation, 55
  on holistic representation of children, 31
  on implementation of training programs, 33
  on role of child in dependency proceedings, 28
  on understanding child client, 27
Reconsidering the Need for Counsel for Children in Custody, Visitation and Child Protection Proceedings (Martin Guggenheim), 21n.70
Record access, 264–265
Recruitment, of attorneys, 220–222
Red Book. *See Child Welfare Law and Practice,* Second Edition (Donald N. Duquette and Ann M. Haralambie)
Refocusing the Lens of Child Advocacy Reform on the Child (Aditi Kothekar), 21n.70
Relationship building, with child clients, 27, 45
Relationships, of lawyers and other court-connected personnel, 260
Relatives, identifying, 52
Removal, emergency, 77–79
Rephrasing Exercise, 72
Report and Working Draft of a Model Act Governing the Representation of Children in Abuse, Neglect, and Dependency Proceedings, 20n.66
Report Cards, by CAI and First Star, 36–37, 51
Representation of children in child abuse and neglect cases (D.N. Duquette and S.H Ramsay), 44
The representation of the legal interests of children and adolescents in Germany (M. Stotzel and J.M. Ferget), 45
Representation rules, 241
Representing Children (Barbara Atwood), 19n.63
Representing Children In Child Protective Proceedings (Jean Koh Peters), 12, 21n.70
Representing Children Representing What? (Annette Appell), 21n.70
Research studies by QIC-ChildRep, 109–122
  attorney compensation in, 222
  attorney samples, 113–114
  attorneys' receptivity to training in, 224–225
  on attorneys representing children, 123–143
  caseload in, 222
  child client samples, 114–118
  child outcomes in, 185–186
  on child representation activities, 145–162
  community of practice as factor in, 186–188
  data sources for, 118–121
  implementation of Six Core Skills in, 181–185
  limitations on, 179–180
  local judicial jurisdiction samples, 110–113
  methodology of, 121–122
  on multidisciplinary team approach, 189–211
  practice and policy implications of, 188
  procedural justice as outcome in, 180–181
  reflections on findings of, 179–188
  samples used in, 110–118
  on Six Core Skills Training, 163–178
  and statewide systems for child representations, 219–220
  subjects of, 109–110
Residential placements, 156, 160
Resolutions on Foster Care and Adoption (ABA), 31
Resource Guidelines (National Council of Juvenile and Family Court Judges), 10, 244, 259
Respect, in multidisciplinary teams, 208
Responsibilities
  attorney activities and assumed-responsibility scale, 157, 158, 161
  identified by attorneys representing children, 133–136, 140–141
Review surveys, 147
Reviews, of court orders, 240, 257
Right of action, 285

INDEX

Right to council, 8, 14
Roper v. Simmons, 60
Ross, Nicola M., 141
Rotational lists, 121–122
Rubber stamping, by judiciary, 30
Rule 1.14 (ABA Model Rules of Professional Conduct), 22–25, 75

"Safe runs," with coaches, 99
Safety assessment activities, 169–171
Safety needs, 80
Safety plan, 76–77
Samples
  for child representation activities study, 147–148
  for research studies by QIC-ChildRep, 110–118
Satisfaction, job, 138–140, 201
SCOMIS database, 119
Scope of representation
  2011 Model Act on, 275–282
  ABA Standards of 1996 on, 256–257
  in QIC Best Practice Model, 240
Section on Litigation (ABA), 13, 221n.16
Self-actualization, need for, 80
Service advocacy
  for children, 134, 141
  for parents/family members, 135, 136, 183
Service requests
  ABA Standards of 1996 on, 252–253
  in QIC Best Practice Model, 238–239
Services
  in case planning, 87–88
  in QIC Best Practice Model, 52–53
Settlements, negotiating, 253
Sexual behavior, 28
SHINES data system, 120
Sibling groups, of child clients, 118
Sibling placements, 164–165
Six Core Skills
  described, 65–68, 67–68
  measuring implementation of, 165–166
  pod meetings and coaching on, 92–94
  in QIC Best Practice Model, 55
  QIC Best Practice Model as basis for, 65–67
  state adoption of, 217
Six Core Skills implementation, 95–108
  actively evaluating needs, 102
  advance case planning, 102–103
  advocating effectively, 104–105
  assessing child safety, 100–102
  developing case theory, 103–104
  entering the child's world, 98–100
  local systemic challenges in, 105–107
  method of evaluating, 96
  and overall value of QIC approach, 96–98
  in QIC-ChildRep research studies, 181–185

research on (*See* Research studies by QIC-ChildRep)
  as topic in coaching sessions, 95–96
Six Core Skills Training, ix, 69–94
  on actively evaluating needs, 79–81
  on advance case planning, 86–89
  on advocating effectively, 83–84
  agenda and materials for, 69–70
  on assessing child safety, 75–77
  attorney behavioral changes after, 169–173
  and child-level outcomes, 173–177
  child's development and effects of trauma in, 72–73
  constraints on, 66
  on developing case theory, 79–81
  emergency placement and removal in, 77–79
  evaluation of, 92
  group reflection in, 77
  Identity Circle Exercise in, 71
  interviewing and counseling child clients in, 73–75
  introduction in, 70–71
  Marco's Case Exercise in, 77–79, 88–89, 91–92
  monitoring well-being in, 89–91
  Non-Adversarial Case Resolution in, 84–86
  and permanency outcomes, 177–178
  permanency planning in, 91–92
  pod meetings and coaching to reinforce, 92–94
  wrap-up of, 92
Six Core Skills Training evaluation study, 163–178
  attorney behavioral changes in, 169–173
  child-level outcomes in, 173–177
  implementation of intervention in, 165–166
  measuring attorney behavior for, 166–169
  milestone surveys in, 121
  permanency outcomes in, 177–178
  scope and methods used in, 164–165
Slowriver, J., 45
SMART criteria, for case plans, 86, 87
Social desirability bias, 146
Social services, court as supervisor of, 5–6
Social work, in QIC Best Practice Model, 107–108
Social workers
  agency workers, parents and, 208–210
  availability of, 132, 133, 140
  collaboration of attorneys and, 192–193, 198–199, 211, 224
  contributions of, to MDT teams, 199–200, 201–202, 208
  in multidisciplinary team study, 190, 197
  respect for skillset of, 208

Solo practitioners
  activity levels of, 156, 157
  profile of attorneys representing children as, 124, 132, 133, 136, 142–143
Special needs, children with, 239, 253
Special Populations, 20n.69
Speculative risks, 77
Staff attorney offices
  advantages of, 218–219
  profile of attorneys representing children at, 124, 132, 133
  profile of attorneys representing children in, 142
Stakeholders, Needs Assessment data from, 37–38
Standards of Practice for Lawyers Who Represent Children in Abuse and Neglect Cases (ABA) (1996 ABA Standards), 3, 9, 244–267
  and 2011 Model Act, 287–290
  adoption of, 10–11
  on best interests vs. client-centered approach, 46
  child law offices' use of, 42
  duties and characteristics of attorneys in, 26
  for enhancing the judicial role in child representation, 259–265
  policy statement of, 50
  previous ABA policies related to representation of abused and neglected children, 266–267
  and QIC Best Practice Model, viii, 51–56
  standards for child's attorney, 244–258
  state adoption of, 217
  on training, 224
  training programs in, 33
State courts, 3–4, 9
State law
  on attorney appointment in child welfare cases, 112
  on child representation, 217–218
  in QIC Needs Assessment, 35–47
State reports, to federal government, 39
State-wide systems of child representation, 219–220
Stated interests, 10
Statewide contracting model, 220
"Still face" video, 72–73
Stotzel, M., 45
Support personnel, 30
Supportive caseload actions, 265
Support(s)
  administrative, 132
  financial, 92
  on multidisciplinary teams, 200
  Needs Assessment data on, 38, 40, 46
  organizational, 132–133, 140
Susbstitute-judgment role, 113
Swanke, S., 44

Task importance, 136–138, 141
Team meetings, 172, 173, 185
Termination of parental rights, 206, 207
Testifying, by child, 254–255
Testimony
   in 2011 Model Act, 284–285
   challenges to, 256
Theory of case. *See* Case theory
Threats (Lund & Renne model), 76–77
Time spent, calculating, 184
Timing
   of appointment, 115–117, 175–177, 260–261
   of assignment, 176–177
   of child representation activities, 152–154, 159–160
   of contact, 152–154
Training. *See also* Six Core Skills Training
   ABA Standards of 1996 on, 241–242
   for attorneys representing children, 33–34, 224–226
   empirical research on, 44
   in multidisciplinary teams, 197–198
   Needs Assessment data on, 38–40, 46
   in QIC Best Practice Model, 241–242
Trauma, effects of, 72–73
Tribal court system, 40
Trust, building, 27, 85
"Two Distinct Lawyer Roles" model, 22
Two Distinct Roles/Bright Line Test (Donald N. Duquette), 26n.87

Uniform Law Commission (ULC), 291
Uniform Representation of Children in Abuse, Neglect, and Custody Proceedings Act (Barbara Atwood), 21n.70
Uniform representation rules, 259–260
United Nations Convention on the Rights of the Child (CRC), 12, 28
University of Michigan, 196n.34
University of Michigan Law School, vii, 5
University of Nevada Las Vegas (UNLV) Conference on child welfare, 12–13, 26, 289, 291.

See also Recommendations of the UNLV Conference on Representing Children in Families (UNLV Recommendations)
U.S. Children's Bureau, 56, 63, 227
   on child representation, 1–5
   on child representatives, vii
   Child Welfare Information Gateway of, 42
   creation of *QIC-ChildRep* by, vii–viii, 6
   and federal leadership on child representation, 216, 217
   testing of QIC Best Practice Model in, viii–ix
U.S. Department of Health and Human Services, 290
U.S. Department of Justice, 291n.22
U.S. Health and Human Services, 37
U.S. Supreme Court, bright-line age limits drawn by, 60
Use of court-appointed advocates to assist in permanency planning for minority children (S. Abramson), 43

Validity, external, 113
Ventrell, Marvin, 16n.41
Vigorous and active participation of lawyer, 56
Vulnerabilities (Lund & Renne model), 76

Wald, Michael, 214, 216
Walsh, Tamara, 193
Washington Office of Civil and Legal Aid (OCLA), 114
Washington State. *See also specific studies*
   attorney samples from, 113–114
   child client samples from, 114–118
   child representation experience of attorneys in, 127–128
   CLE courses of attorneys representing children in, 128
   compensation for attorneys in, 131–132
   data sources for QIC-ChildRep research from, 119–121
   demographics of attorneys in, 125
   evaluation of QIC Best Practice Model in, ix
   job satisfaction and impact ratings by attorneys in, 138
   lack of representation in, 216
   local jurisdictional samples from, 110, 111
   organizational supports for attorneys in, 133
   other types of law practiced by attorneys in, 130
   pod meetings and coaching sessions in, 93
   research findings from, 179–188
   research samples from, 110–118
   responsibilities of attorneys in, 136
   Six Core Skills Training in, 69, 75
   task importance for attorneys in, 136, 138
Washington State Department of Social and Health Services Children's Administration, 120
Weighting, of child's wishes, 60–62
Wellbeing, of child, 201
Wishes of child
   accommodation of, 38, 62–63
   advocacy for, 182–183
   in QIC Best Practice Model, 55
   weighting of, for child with diminished capacity, 60–62
Withdrawal, of appeal, 241, 258
Within-subject study design, 195, 196
Witnesses, child, 255
Women, Infant and Children program, 216
Work product, lawyer, 284–285
Working Group on the Best Interests of the Child and the Role of the Attorney, 12
Working relationships, strong, 85

"You're My What?": The Problem of Children's Misperceptions of Their Lawyer's Roles (Emily Buss), 17n.49, 25n.87
Youth Council Meeting, 41

Zealous attorney representation for children, 11
Zinn, A.E., 45